TRANSFORMING
YOUR

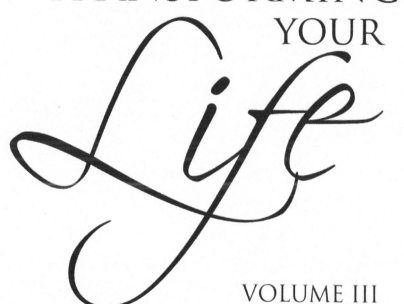

Life

VOLUME III

Transforming Your Life III

Sai Blackbyrn

with

Co-Authors from around the World

Transforming Your Life III

All Rights Reserved

Copyright 2020

Transforming Your Life III

sai@sai.coach

Sai Blackbyrn

Transforming Your Life III

ISBN 978-1-5272-6433-5

AUTHORS

Andrew Miller
Author, Speaker, Business Enjoyment Coach

Ann Moir-Bussy
Psychotherapist, Life Coach, Author, Consultant, Educator

Anna Jiang
Professor, Author, Speaker, Productivity Neurocoach

David & Deirdre Radosevich
Psychologists, Coaches, Entrepreneurs

Deb Canja
CEO, Parent Success Coach, Author, Speaker

Ekaterina Koretskaia
Transformational Coach, Author, Mother

Erneste Carla Zimmermann
Certified Life & Business Coach, Speaker, Author, Podcast &
Summit Host

Hugh Todd
Global Citizen, Educator, Father, Veteran Champion of Coaching

Jacqui Carrel
Rapid Transformational Therapist. Coach. Speaker. Author

Lis Manson
Speaking and Presentation Expert

Mike Jasper
Multi-millionaire, Business Coach

Peter Abrahamsen
Author, Speaker, Psychologist, Coach, Emotional Weightlifter

Russell Frazier
Personal Development Coach, Author, Entrepreneur, Veteran

Shemsheer A. Lallani
Holistic Health and Life Coach, Mentor and CEO

Sonia Saïdi
Leadership Coach, Entrepreneur, Mentor, Philanthropist

Tanya Focus
Thought Leader, Life Guide and Fulfilment Artist

Tim Wolford
Coach, Mentor, Teacher, Adventurer

Todd Kramer
Actor, Writer, Educator, Connection Facilitator, Kabbalist

Vijaya Nair
Physician, Entrepreneur, Transformational Coach, Author, Speaker

Wail Al Hunaidi
Entrepreneur, Consultant, Positive Psychologist, Speaker

FOREWORD

by Sai Blackbyrn

Transforming Your Life: Volume III follows an esteemed lineage of books, each of which has reached the bestseller status in multiple countries. The concept of our very first book was to find people who had not only faced unbelievable hardship and tragedy in their lives but had come out of it transformed—and molded by it to a point that their experiences took them to the top of their fields and their lives. These are successful people who now wanted to help other people follow their paths to come out of their personal traumas and tragedies, with flying colors. As we started to explore this world, we realized that there is more truth to this concept than even we realized. So, what we looked for were people at the very top of their game—people who have transformed the narrative of their past trauma or pain into one of power, success, and personal triumph. We realized that those were the people who had the most to teach other struggling people. We looked at the biggest success stories around us; we saw how they are only able to sustain that and sustain their own growth because they took the time to learn from their life's hurdles. The most highly-rated people were also the ones who were emotionally successful.

We looked at the most successful people at the very top of their game, we saw the monsters they had slain on the way, and we wanted to be ones to help them tell those stories. It takes us more than a year to scour the world for the most highly-qualified people to include in the *Transforming Your Life* series, and we do it very patiently—for it is our fervent belief that true transformation results in a stable and sustainable success. We looked for the very best of people, coaches, CEOs, and mentors who had a firm grasp of their own life and who had much to teach our audience beyond just their success story, if they wanted to reach out. Each author is a titan in their field, and they have the capacity to tell so many more stories like these and to help thousands. If you love a story, any story in the book, my personal recommendation would be to reach out to the author and see what else they might be able to teach you.

So, now that we knew what we were looking for, we realized that more and more people were ready and wanted to share their personal stories of loss, tragedy, and triumph; they overcame their personal trauma, and now they wanted to tell these stories far and wide. They wanted to tell everyone about the demons they had to fight on the way up the hill, and we absolutely agree! These stories shouldn't just be told to a few family members and friends; rather, these are universal stories that bind us all and can help us find our own unique path to stability and a happy life.

We realized that the people who had these stories were very heavily influenced by the events in their lives, to a point where their entire lives and businesses reflected the lessons from these stories; as we understood that, we saw it all around us. We saw how these coaches and mentors were using life lessons they have learned through their own hardship to transform the lives of those around them and those who take the time to learn from them.

In the *Transforming Your Life* series, our goal is to bring the best inspirations from around the world together—with those that have the most compelling and unique stories. These people have achieved amazing feats; we have brought together unique personalities: business titans, industry leaders, Olympic athletes, mothers, body builders, international speakers, corporate elites. These people share their journey of transformation and how they got where they are today, in the most honest way that they can.

Be prepared, these are stories of human trials and tribulations, so there are things in here that are difficult to read and imagine, so read with an open mind. As you read *Transforming Your Life* volume III, you can be assured that everyone who was carefully selected to become part of this book and part of this journey will have nuggets of wisdom to share with you, should you choose to go on the same path with an open mind and daring heart.

This book can open your mind toward what can be achieved with the strength and dedicated focus of the human spirit, if you are open to it.

Finally, the best part of our curation is that we didn't just choose authors from the United States or England. We chose them from across the globe, where stories of human triumph exist, and we found them everywhere! It is my hope and my desire that this book awakens and strengthens your spirit, and I hope you enjoy reading it as much as we enjoyed curating and compiling this for you.

TABLE OF CONTENTS

BORN FOR PURPOSE

Andrew Miller

I am proud to say that I have had three birthdays. Ok, maybe not in the traditional sense, but for me, there are three key dates in my life where my eyes were opened, a new life began, and things were never the same again.

My name is Andrew Miller, and I am the founder of Business Enjoyment. I am on a mission to change the way that success is measured in the world, and I would like to share with you my story, explain how I uncovered my purpose, and hopefully, inspire some people who aren't normally inspired.

Birthday No. 1.

West Sussex, England. 17th August 1971

This is my actual birthday – as we all generally understand it. I think it's important that I start right at the beginning as I believe we are all products of the events of our lives.

The younger of two brothers, I grew up in an average town in England. Reasonably intelligent, reasonably sporty, and reasonably hard working, I just got on and did things. Sure, there were some ups and downs, but on the whole, we were a happy family, had some lovely holidays, I made some great friends, and generally had a really nice childhood.

Not exactly the basis of a major Hollywood blockbuster, I'm sure you'll agree. Despite that, this normality is actually a critical part of the story.

I have become a big believer in uncovering one's purpose in life. The thing that really creates focus and motivation enables you to shift into flow much more easily and generates an important side effect. It allows you to truly enjoy life.

In the majority of cases, this purpose is uncovered as a result of a serious trauma or tragedy.

The equal rights campaigner who suffered awful levels of prejudice and victimization. The anti-drugs activist who nearly died of an overdose. The business guru who built his empire out of the ashes of insolvency. These are the types of stories that we're used to hearing.

While I've always been impressed by the 'inspirational' stories that fill our bookshelves, computer screens and conference stages, I've rarely been truly inspired because I couldn't relate to the person telling the tale. No one in my family has ever gone bust. We had no dramas around anyone being addicted to anything. And the only 'prejudice' I had to suffer was Jane Austen.

I have, therefore, found myself asking the question, "Is it possible to uncover that sense of purpose and meaning without going through the trauma?"

By sharing my story, I want to provide an answer to that question and show you that everyone has the capability of tapping into that internal motivational force. Even those who had a 'boring' life.

A life to which I now return.

We'll pick things up from when I left University, which saw me holding a first-class degree in maths, fluent in French, and no idea about what I wanted to do.

After generally drifting through various dead-end temporary jobs, I finally got a call out of the blue from a recruitment agency asking me if I'd like to go for an interview with the Insolvency department of KPMG.

I asked, "What's an Insolvency and who is KPMG?"

For those of you who (like me at the time) are not in the know, KPMG is one of the largest accounting and consulting companies in the world. I passed the interview and thus began a 17-year journey within the incredibly specific and unique world of Corporate Insolvency.

At this point, some explanation is in order.

Most people are vaguely aware of the concept of insolvency, but, unless you've had first-hand experience (on either side of the fence), very few people really understand what it is. Also, the process in the UK is dramatically different to the rest of Europe and the United States, where it's all conducted by lawyers in corporate offices. In the UK, the work is a lot more hands-on.

For example, you know how there is a mortgage on your house and, if you don't keep up repayments on that mortgage, the bank can call in the loan and repossess your house?

Corporate insolvency works on the same principles, but for companies.

A bank will loan money to a company to fund its growth and allow continued trading. This is often done by way of a 'corporate mortgage' (the technical term is a 'debenture') meaning that, in effect, the bank owns the assets of the company until the debt is repaid.

Should the company get into financial difficulties, the bank has the power to call in that debt and take possession of the company. In real terms, they will appoint a specialist accountant (an insolvency practitioner) who replaces the directors of the company. The accountant's job is then to realize the assets for as much money as possible and distribute the funds to creditors. A company usually retains most of its value by being kept intact, which means that it is very common for the accountants to trade the company whilst looking for a buyer.

A trading insolvency is incredibly intense, involves a lot of hard work, and is thoroughly exhilarating. You instantly become responsible for everything. And I mean everything. From running the production line to making sure the photocopier still gets serviced. You have to quickly assess what is going on; get the employees and suppliers on board – most of whom are owed money; secure the support of customers; and introduce your own systems and procedures so that you know exactly what is going on.

The first few days/weeks are full of firefighting as you wrestle to gain control. As a volley of queries, complaints are fired at you, and complex commercial decisions have to be made on the spot. You often have to take some tough decisions, which can impact a lot of people's livelihoods. Money is the driving factor at all times, but that doesn't mean it's not possible to carry out your duties in a humane and understanding way.

I've been on jobs where we've had Christmas cards from the staff (it was at Christmas, just to be clear) and strangely, it's not unusual for people to thank me when I've made them redundant. This is because I'd kept them updated with what was going on and they knew that I had done my best to keep the business going.

As for how I handled the emotional turmoil personally, I found that I was very good at compartmentalizing and not letting the stressful elements of the work get me down.

As my career developed, the commercial experience I gained was immense. I ran businesses of all shapes and sizes, from bingo halls to shopping centers to the construction of oil rigs and the production of pet food.

As I progressed, I got to work all round the UK, in Europe, and two years in Australia and the far East. I rose steadily through the ranks doing interesting and challenging work, was respected by my peers, and was paid very well with good prospects.

I was, as far as the world was concerned, a 'success.'

That did not mean, however, that I was happy.

Birthday No. 2.

Hampshire, England. 18th October 2005

It was at a team building event that everything changed.

We undertook a number of exercises, one of which was centered around 'values.' You're probably familiar with the concept. We were given two pieces of paper. On one, we were instructed to jot down all of our values – the things that we hold to be important to us. On the other piece of paper, we were asked to note down the values of the firm. Not the ones stuck on the walls of the offices, but the actual values that we saw played out on a daily basis. We then ran through an exercise where we looked at how we could bring the two lists more closely in alignment. This was an exercise I never completed. I just stared at both bits of paper thinking,

"Surely there must be an overlap somewhere?"

As this information filtered through my brain and body, it suddenly hit me,

"Oh yes! I hate my job!"

I realized that, while there were moments of the job I enjoyed, they were actually few and far between. Outside of a trading insolvency, it was mostly administration work: form filling, letter writing, and paper filing. Meanwhile, the projects themselves were all very similar and generally consisted of long hours, huge pressure, and filled with lots of angry creditors shouting at me.

How had I not seen this before?

Over time, I came to realize that this lack of awareness is quite common. From birth, we are conditioned to believe that work isn't meant to be fun or enjoyable. We're told to focus on doing the best we can, to progress as high as we can, and, ultimately, earn as much as we can. That is what success is meant to be. Enjoyment doesn't enter the picture.

Now that my eyes were opened, I was clear that I didn't want to do this anymore. The only problem was I didn't know what I would like to do instead. At the end of the day, I was making good money and I liked the people I worked with. Just quitting and going off to 'find myself' didn't seem like the best strategy.

I was just going to have to work out what I wanted to do while being employed.

The Universe then did what it does at times. It noticed the arrival of the new 'me' and popped in to say "hello", because within days, I was offered a new role. It's only with hindsight that the significance of the event became clear, but it turned out that this role would lead me directly to where I am today.

The title of the role was 'People Management Leader.' Basically, my job was to help team members with anything that wasn't connected directly with a project. Motivation, confidence, conflict, or personal issues. You name it, and I was the go-to person for whatever they needed.

I could rarely take a walk across the office without someone coming up to me and saying, "Erm, could I just ask you something in private, please?" leading to a conversation around some sort of personal crisis that they were facing.

This all had to be done on top of the day job and many of my colleagues thought that I had been given this role as some sort of punishment.

But I loved it.

Sitting down with people and helping them deal with issues that they were facing right now and seeing immediate changes in them was so much better than all the other things I had to do. Plus, I was actually quite good at it.

Part of the role included collaborating with my equivalents in different departments. As I got to know some of these people better, I started opening up about my job dissatisfaction and from these discussions came two important points.

First, the more I talked to people about 'not enjoying what I do', the more people opened up about not enjoying what they do either. This led me to thinking:

"Does anyone actually enjoy their job?"

It was clear that it didn't matter how 'successful' anybody was in their career; it was not the same as leading a happy and fulfilling life.

Second, I got to hear about 'Coaching.' This was a term that I was completely unfamiliar with in a business context, but the more I investigated it, the more I liked the sound of it.

It turned out that my day job in insolvency had been developing some of the key skills. When you go in and take over the company, you don't pretend to be an expert in that industry. Instead, it's about working with the existing team and challenging some of their habits and decisions, ensuring it fits into an overall strategy. Combine that with a humane approach, and I was in a great place to explore the world of coaching.

It was not a quick process, however. The time from the moment of realization to actually getting out took the better part of five years, including enough drama and twists and turns to fill a book by itself. The CliffsNotes version is that in that period, I managed to maneuver myself into pole position for an internal coaching role. The contract was written, the ink was dry, and all that was needed was the stamp of approval. It was at precisely that point, as I straddled the threshold between heaven and hell, that a perfect storm of a corporate merger, a global recession, and the tragic death of a key individual slammed the door in my face and kicked me straight back to where I had started.

To be completely honest, there had been some changes.

I had been promoted and was now heading our trading and property team, a position I used to justify the need for getting some coaching training. In turn, this meant the firm approved my enrollment into two coaching diplomas.

Much of what I learned on those courses, I brought back to the team, pulling together training sessions around team dynamics, goal setting, and beliefs. That put me in prime position to develop some training courses that were rolled out across the country. Plus, I was actually coaching people as part of the practical element of my course.

But all of this was just temporary relief, a lamppost along a long, dark path.

It is hard to convey the emotions you feel when you have everything that you've ever wanted just within your grasp, only to have them ripped away from you with no hope of return; and when you know you are in the wrong job, you come to really hate it, which pays a heavy toll on your psyche.

It would be wrong for me to say that I suffered from depression. That is a serious disorder and the term is frequently used inappropriately. However, I was definitely not in a good place. The eating and drinking increased, and the weight piled on. A knee injury I'd suffered at school started flaring up, and I found myself on crutches almost as often as I was off them.

As a team leader, part of my job was to motivate everyone else and help them with their ongoing issues. So, it was ironic that I was in such a bad place myself. So much so that every single day, as I drove into the office, I would feel horribly sick. I found myself retching, dreading the day ahead.

I finally made the decision to leave on the basis of a conversation I had with a fellow student of coaching. She had decided to quit her job, start up as a coach and damn the consequences, even though she had just found out she was pregnant.

Driving home, I just kept thinking, "If she can do it, why can't I?" Our financial position is pretty strong. No mortgage, savings on one side, and, if I were to leave and it didn't work, I'd be able to get re-employed pretty easily with my experience.

So, there was no real risk.

"So what is really stopping me?"

I decided to wait until the end of the year to make sure I got paid the annual bonus – quite useful if you're about to launch into a world of uncertainty. The fact that I was in such a bad place mentally made it quite ironic that I actually received my best ever appraisal grading, along with a large pay rise. In turn, this meant there was an even bigger shock to the department when I then handed in my notice.

I was one of the longest serving members within the office, on a six-figure package, and working in one of the few industries that was actually growing in the middle of the largest recession the world had seen in a century.

What an excellent time to leave and to set up your own business.

* * *

Deciding to set up a coaching practice is one thing, but what kind of coach did I want to become? There are so many to choose from. After exploring many options, I settled on a niche that basically didn't exist and as far as I am aware, still doesn't.

Combining 17 years of experience at KPMG with my new direction, I focused on working with business owners going through financial difficulty or insolvency and helping them cope with the emotional consequences.

Traditionally, the industry is only interested in the business side of things. The director is treated as an add-on who either helps the insolvency practitioner or is gotten rid of. More often, they are viewed as being obstinate, obstructive or stupid—sometimes all three together.

The external perception, from those owed money or from the media, is even worse. At best, they are considered incompetent. At worst, they are accused of being criminals or inhuman monsters.

The truth of the matter is that, while there are always going to be crooks and incompetents in all walks of life, the majority of directors whose companies fall into insolvency are decent, caring individuals. The business is their child, and they have done everything to keep it going, often by paying out everyone else as much as they possibly can and often at the expense of their own financial well-being.

As they watch everything they've built collapse in front of their eyes, they go through the same range of emotions any parent does on the death of their child: shock, denial, anger, and grief. Is it any wonder that external parties, such as the bank or the accountants, don't get to see them in their best light?

If they do lose the business, many directors end up experiencing intense feelings of shame and guilt. Attempting to do anything new can throw up a crippling lack of confidence. Over time, it is easy for someone to drift into depression – or worse.

I don't know the actual statistics, but there are very few insolvency practitioners who aren't aware of at least one suicide.

I believe that by helping these directors with their emotional stress as early as possible, three potential benefits could emerge.

First, they might be more open with the bank and the accountants at the beginning. When one is scared, the tendency is to put up walls, be defensive, and not trust anyone. The more open they become, the more likely it is that the parties can cooperate, and the chances of saving the business increase.

Second, if the business does have to go, then the director wouldn't sit around at home getting depressed and living off the state. Instead, they would get up and start running a new business, employing more people and contributing to society again.

Third, from my experience, those who went through such an experience gained a better appreciation of what was important in life. They became more mindful, more generous, and more philanthropic. Consequently, by helping these people get through the hard times and become more successful, society as a whole would benefit.

That was the theory anyway. Actually making it happen was, as ever, a different concept.

Going directly to those in difficulty was always going to be hard, as their head is already in the sand. Most of my work was going to have to come from the professionals advising the companies. However, most of them either didn't understand what I was trying to do or didn't keep the advice in mind as they went about their hectic schedules.

Consequently, I found it very difficult to pick up any work.

I remember going to a networking event where there was a presentation from a marketing expert on how to use LinkedIn to connect with your ideal client. Find the groups where your ideal client hangs out, he explained, and get involved. Take part in discussions, add value, and get known. Over time, you'll attract your ideal clients.

That's great, I thought. Works really well in principle. Unfortunately, there isn't a LinkedIn group for business owners who are about to go bust.

However, as I pondered the concept, I turned the thought around and wondered, if such a group did exist, what would it look like? I quickly made a leap to something that might be feasible. Instead of people about to go through it, there may be interest for those who HAD BEEN through it. It taps into the human desire to share war stories and pass on information to others.

Exploring the thought further, I abandoned the social media element and realized that I could just find these people myself. If I interviewed them and uncovered their personal experiences, I could create blogs and articles that would explain what I was doing, why help was needed, and what people in similar situations could do about it.

I sent out word, and it was amazing to see the number of people who were now approaching me to tell their tale. Neither I nor anyone in our network had had any awareness of their experiences. As the interviews progressed, I started seeing similar patterns in their stories. Common threads of emotional reaction and positive action that could be taken at different stages of the process.

Eventually, I realized that, with a combination of the interviews and my own experience and knowledge around the subject, I had enough material for a lot more than just a few articles. There was a book in this.

This was not something I'd ever done before, and I had no idea how to go about it. With a bit of research, finding a few people who knew what they were doing and a bit of discipline on my part, my first book was self-published in October 2012.

Hope Won't Pay the Wages was the first, and to my knowledge, the only self-help book for people in financial difficulty and one that focuses on the emotional stresses, helping people develop mindsets required to make it through an insolvency mentally intact.

Like any business book, it was never intended to be a moneymaker in itself, but now I could explain to people what I was trying to do.

In addition, the book acted as a great intervention tool for advisors and accountants.

"Look," they could say "don't take my word for it. This person was in exactly the same position you are now. See what they have to say about it."

Working with a PR agent, we started getting my name out there. I began writing articles for magazines and was invited for interviews on the radio. Eventually, we even managed to gain the attention of the Government.

I met up with a representative from the Department for Business, Innovation, and Skills and put forth a proposal. A support network of experienced business owners, coaches, and counselors who could offer support to every director of an insolvent company. While funding would be required to run the operation, the benefit to the country overall was undeniable.

They were impressed and liked the way I was interested in the person, not just the processes and systems. A few weeks later, I was formally invited to become a policy advisor to the government in the area of Business Failure.

Once again, things were falling into place.

Once again, my dreams were being realized.

Once again, it all went wrong.

The work with the government never happened. One never expects them to move quickly on these things but, when I followed up their invitation, people had moved on and the focus had shifted. Not long after, there was a general election, a change of government, and that was that. Meanwhile, I wasn't earning much money from my chosen area, despite having done all of the things that the marketing gurus tell you to do.

I had a niche so tight that I had truly created a category by myself – with one individual, with a unique set of skills and experience, offering a unique service. This was a service that was most certainly needed and every person I worked with was incredibly grateful for what I was able to offer them.

I was a published author with (and I don't want to come across as arrogant or biased) a genuinely good book that has greatly helped people in need.

I had a good profile—writing articles for magazines, doing presentations around the country, and talking to the media.

Every ingredient required in the recipe of success, and none of it was working.

One of the messages in my book is that you have to work with reality, not fantasy. Sometimes, if things aren't working you just have to stop, accept it, and move on. Which is exactly what I did.

Birthday No. 3.

London, England. 9th September 2017

While I had some clients in the insolvency sector that I'd created, much of the work that I was actually getting paid for was with ordinary business owners just looking to improve what they were doing, so I shifted my focus toward standard small-business coaching.

At the same time, I started to look at myself and the patterns that I was running. I had all the skills, the knowledge and the wherewithal to be successful. I got great results with my clients and people found me to be approachable, interesting, and engaging. Yet, there was still something missing.

I was spending a lot of time helping people but not seeing much in terms of results. Either people would disappear once the subject of money came up or I would make ridiculous concessions to ensure we carried on working together. Lots of effort, but very little reward.

Was it possible that I was too nice? Did I lack the 'killer instinct' needed to follow up on the leads and get them across the line? I certainly didn't want to be that pushy salesperson that forced people into doing something they didn't want.

Did I have some sort of fear around success? It certainly felt like I was self-sabotaging somewhere along the line.

One specific fear that I knew I had was around phoning people. I just couldn't do it. Even if it was a close personal friend, the only way I could make a call was if I'd prearranged it in advance. Anything outside of that would trigger anxiety and a churning knot in the stomach.

I tried coaching, counseling and even hypnotherapy. Initially, it made little difference but I was able to uncover a deep seated fear of rejection, leading me into becoming a 'people pleaser.'

"What can I do to make you happy so that you'll like me—even if it's at my own expense?"

This attitude had been colored by a few other experiences throughout life, such as my dad yelling at me when I'd interrupted his conversation, a career where I was the person that people least wanted to meet, or even having to call creditors to tell them that they weren't going to get paid.

Eventually, I realized that the phobia about calling people was not actually about the phone. It was a fear of interrupting people.

From my experience, when I interrupted someone's day, it led to them being angry or upset – which I took as rejection. The telephone was just the most common medium of reaching out. When I thought about it, I couldn't knock on doors or break into conversations at networking events either. I even found posting letters through doors uncomfortable.

However, with the telephone, you are completely blind as to what the other person is doing and the brain instantly assumes that they will be doing something important. This means that the last thing that they want is to be interrupted by me. Unless, of course, the call had been agreed in advance.

Having identified the issue, I started exploring deeper therapies to help resolve things and finally progress was made. More than that, I was now aware of new ways to help people and I threw myself into researching and learning the different therapies around.

For most of my life, it had all been about numbers, processes, and strategies. Then I learnt about mindsets, beliefs, and personality profiles. Now I was learning about subconscious patterns, energy healing, and techniques such as tapping.

I wanted to use these new tools to go deeper into myself, remove my hidden problems and be in a position to help others with their issues. It became clear that everyone had some sort of deep block or hidden pattern. By equipping myself with a wider range of skills, I was able to help people at all levels of the 'success spectrum' improve and develop.

Still, I felt there was something missing.

I would read these books, which kept going on about finding your 'why,' and I never knew what mine was. Whenever people asked me what I wanted – you know, really wanted – my answer was vague. I just wanted to help people, and I couldn't really get more specific than that.

At no point could I say what my purpose was or get clear about the direction I was heading in. While I was motivated and felt good about what I was doing, there wasn't any sort of burning passion driving me forward.

Should there be one? What does it mean if I don't find it?

On the advice of another coach, I started to think about the clients that I'd done my best work with. Those that I really connected with and where my work seemed instinctive and effortless. What sort of people were they, what were they looking for, and what did they get from working with me? In addition to helping identify future ideal clients, it might also reveal clues about what my purpose was.

I thought long and hard about those handful of clients who were really magical to work with. After much consideration, I realized that they weren't really coming to me for more sales or a bigger business. That was often the consequence and a fortunate by-product. Instead, they were coming to me because they weren't happy in their business and by the end of our time together, they were enjoying life and business so much more.

This was where the concept of Business Enjoyment came from.

I started calling myself a Business Enjoyment Coach to see how people reacted and, in the main, it was pretty positive. It stood out as being something different and desirable, leading people to ask for more information. Everyone innately understood that if you're not enjoying your business, then what's the point? You might as well get a job.

Over time, I developed a Business Enjoyment model and even the semblance of a purpose: *To change the measure of success.*

Talk to anyone for any length of time and you will find that what really matters to them is something much more than just money. Sure, a level of security is important, but it's also about family, connections, and relationships. It's about knowing that you're doing a good job, adding value, and making a difference.

Ultimately, it's about enjoying what you do.

This made sense to me and it resonated with people, when I said it. Could I have found my purpose, my mission? It certainly made sense in my head, but I still didn't 'feel' it. There still wasn't that burning passion that everyone kept talking about.

What was I still missing?

It would have been easy for me to stop exploring at this point. I believed in what I had to offer, I was authentic, and even had a good marketing message. Was it really a problem that I didn't feel an electric spark when I thought about it?

Well, one thing I know is that it is very easy for all of us to 'settle' and make do with what we've got. 'Don't rock the boat.' 'If it ain't broke don't fix it.'

Playing safe, however, doesn't allow us to uncover those extra bits that make life so worthwhile. I decided not to settle and, instead, to keep exploring. To do that, I needed to dig deeper.

Around this time, I enrolled in a group coaching programme with the international coach, Rich Litvin, author of the book *The Prosperous Coach.* He was someone who I respected a lot, and I liked his approach to marketing and selling, being very service-led and 'non-pushy.' As I was forming all these new ideas and patterns, there was an opportunity to get on to one of his group coaching programmes. It was going to be a lot of money, but it felt right. I took the plunge and committed to it.

Part of the program included a ticket to one of his 'intensives'—three days focused purely on self-development and skills training. At the event I attended, he'd arranged a really deep session, run by some of his associates who specialize in getting people really connected to their emotions.

In the group calls, we had been exploring this concept of me not being emotionally connected to my mission and, in fact, I wasn't that emotionally connected to much else around me.

Remember me saying that I was good at compartmentalizing?

It was more than that. I found that most of the deeper emotions just rebounded off me, without making a dint. When exploring an exercise around 'What makes me cry?' to tap into what really moves and motivates me, the genuine answer was, 'Not much.'

As I got ready for this deep session, I decided that what would help me most would be if I could access those deeper emotions. So I set the ability 'to cry' as an intention for the session and made sure I told lots of attendees. That way, not only was I accountable, but by getting really clear on my objective, my brain would subconsciously start seeking out the opportunities.

We ran through a number of moving and breathing exercises to get us out of our heads and into our bodies. We worked in a succession of pairs and triplets, asking questions that got deeper and more personal as we went on, peeling back the layers and exposing who we really were to the world. As I dug deeper, a memory arose from nowhere.

An event that had taken place when I was only four years old. It was such a minor, trivial incident. My brother played a silly little trick on me that made me cry, and, whilst I looked around for comfort, my entire family laughed. Obviously, they were laughing at the trick, but I felt that they were laughing at me.

For an adult, it seemed completely immaterial. I certainly had had no recollection of it prior to this exercise. However, to the four-year-old version of me, it was a big deal. In order to protect myself in the future, I developed some coping behaviors, seeds that would bloom into set patterns in my adult life.

This was the point where I learnt to fear rejection which, over time, led me to become a 'people pleaser.' The reason that I helped others but not myself.

This was the point where I started building an emotional wall. When I learnt how to compartmentalize. Don't let them see what's really going on inside because they're only going to laugh at you.

This is the truth about human conditioning: the patterns that run our life, our behavior, our drives – our 'why' – is always born out of trauma. It's just that we may not always be aware of it.

What's more, our key drives usually start off with a negative energy. It starts off as a 'fear' of rejection. Taking steps to 'avoid' being seen. Worrying about 'losing' everything. As long as the drives stay like that, we will never fully find what we're looking for as we're constantly hiding and running.

Of course, our coping mechanisms help us develop some amazing skills. This is part of the problem because, subconsciously, we want to hold onto these negative drives as they've got us to where we are today. However, when the things that drive you come from a negative place, the result will be negative.

Our drives and skills may generate 'success,' but it may also create feelings of fear, stress, or anxiety. The greater the 'success', the bigger the fear.

What we need to do is to process that trauma, remove its ability to constrain us, and allow our natural positive energy to flood in. Our skills remain intact but now they come from a positive place. This can then allow us to become successful and maintain a positive state. In other words, to actually enjoy life.

These realizations came to me later. While I was still in that deep dive intensive session, I still had to process my trauma.

In my mind's eye, I pictured my four-year-old self, crying and lonely, and bent down to give him that hug that he so desperately wanted. I then lifted 'me' up onto my adult shoulders and ran around the room shouting about how amazing this kid was. For the record, nobody really noticed as they were all dealing with their own stuff, which allowed me to just shout and shout and shout about how incredible and loved this child was.

Suddenly, there was a breakthrough, something that felt like a huge crash and a 40-year-old wall came tumbling down. Decades of pent up, held-back emotion washed over me and, as per my intention, the tears erupted.

The tears didn't stop, even as the exercise came to an end and the organizers brought the session to a close. As they wrapped things up, a combination of overwhelming emotion, bright lights, and tears led to me seeing things. A vision.

In the style of a 1960s animation, I saw a scene of industrial hell. All factories and smoke. In the foreground, a black blob writhed. I became aware that this blob was a mass of people tied down by nets and chains. These constraints represented the subconscious patterns we develop in childhood and the beliefs we absorb from our parents and society, which continue to hold us in check to this very day.

The stories that tell us to settle, to tolerate, and to be content with mediocrity.

All of a sudden, an arm burst out of the dark mass, ripped the chains apart, and stood up. Tall and proud, the figure stepped away from his constraints, ready to set off on his path to freedom and unlimited potential. However, before leaving, he stopped, bent down, and helped the next person to their feet. One by one, they helped each other until there was a stream of people walking away from servitude and toward a world of enjoyment.

This was it. This was my mission and my purpose, unfolding before me, and I was fully connected to it. There was a surge of energy that flowed through my entire body and the meaning of what I wanted to do resonated not just in my brain, but in my heart and gut as well.

I truly was reborn.

* * *

My New Life

Getting connected with my vision has made a massive difference in my life. My business plans have developed at a pace and with an ambition that I had never experienced before.

My mission stays the same: to change the measure of success away from sales and profits and toward enjoyment. That includes understanding the factors that are required for enjoyment to exist.

Now, however, it actually means something to me.

I have been building a community of business owners who share the same values and beliefs as me, via a network of low-cost, high-value discussion groups called Breathing Spaces, which explore the Business Enjoyment model and create a mutual support group for business owners. The plan is to create a model that can be replicated around the world.

The more people who join the conversation, the more momentum it will gain.

Ultimately, I would like to see business being run on a completely new and different basis. Imagine what the New York Stock Exchange or the FTSE 100 would look like if success of a business were measured on something more than just money?

For the record, I don't know what that looks like either. Not yet, at any rate.

As long as I can move things in the right direction, it does not matter to me whether or not I can see this achieved in my lifetime.

The pain that a money focussed society creates has recently become even more evident. As I write this, we are in lockdown as a result of the COVID-19 virus and the expectations are that we are heading into a deep global recession.

Much of the pain and suffering that will be experienced will be as a direct result of this reliance on sales and profits as being the main measure of success. On the other hand, I'm also hoping that this period will allow people to appreciate how important the other elements of life are: family, community, and contribution.

As devastating as the COVID-19 pandemic has been for families and for business, I am hopeful that some good will come of it. There will be fundamental changes about how we run things going forward, and it is up to us to make sure these changes are for the better.

So, what are the key things I want you to take away from this chapter?

First, I do believe that finding a purpose and being connected to it is important. However, there must never be any pressure on you to find it. Know that this purpose exists, somewhere, and keep looking for clues. Do what you can to uncover it but only from a place of passionate curiosity, never from desperation or stress.

Second, whatever your background or childhood, there will be some deep-seated patterns in your behavior that can be changed. The reason may be something incredibly insignificant – seemingly irrelevant to an adult. However, the deeper you dig, the more you will uncover. The more you understand yourself, the easier it will be for you to find happiness and the closer you will be to finding your purpose.

Finally, be aware that learning about yourself never stops. Be absolutely content in knowing that there is no final destination that you have to reach. It is, as they say, all about the journey. There will always be more to learn, more to do, more to uncover – that is part of the enjoyment of life. Every day is an opportunity to rediscover yourself, to see the world with fresh eyes, and to be born again.

I have had three birthdays to date.

I'm totally open to a fourth.

ANDREW MILLER

Andrew Miller is the Founder of Business Enjoyment. His purpose is to bring joy back into business and create a movement where enjoyment is spoken as one of the key measures of success, along with sales and profits.

With a unique combination of business and people skills, Andrew helps people find success in what they do and enjoy the journey at the same time.

Andrew is the author of seven books, a qualified accountant, and holds diplomas in business coaching, life coaching, and psychology as well as being trained in a number of cutting edge, deep change therapies.

His main focus right now is to build a community of people keen to understand themselves and their business better.

If you want to be part of his community, go to www.businessenjoyment.com and explore the *Breathing Space* events that he runs.

Life is about so much more than just money, and Andrew wants to help people enjoy their business in a life of freedom and true enjoyment.

Contact Details

Website: www.businessenjoyment.com

Facebook: www.facebook.com/BusinessEnjoyment/

Twitter: www.twitter.com/enjoybiz

LinkedIn: www.linkedin.com/in/andrewrmiller

TRANSITIONS AND TRANSFORMATION FROM THE MORNING TO THE EVENING OF LIFE: A JOURNEY TO CONSCIOUS AGING

Ann Moir-Bussy

Between Two Worlds

It is March 2020, and as I begin to write this chapter, the world around is changing in ways some have never seen before. The COVID-19 virus has spread globally, and like many other cities, the small city where I live in Victoria, Australia, is in a state of lockdown.

Everyone has been asked to stay at home and go out only for essential supplies and then to keep 'social distancing'. With limited freedom to move around or to visit friends and family, the familiar daily and unquestioned routines are no longer there. People have to find and learn a new way of adapting, communicating, and how to deal with confinement and limited contact with others. It requires a different mindset, an alternative way of relating, that maybe we did not think possible.

What is it like for you when you have to learn to live differently, to think differently, to find new and different ways of being and relating? In enforced isolation, what reserves can you draw upon within you?

We are in need of a bridge that will enable us to cross from the world of how life has been for years to what it now needs to become.

Are you and I meant to be the bridge between these worlds?

At these crossroads in history, to reflect on the transformations we have been through and the transformations still to come is a powerful opportunity. Transformations are like gates. Each gate that we go through, we leave something behind and encounter something new. Together as we go through the gates, we can become the bridge leading to a new and profound relationship to who we are in this world, to what is our purpose, and what are the gifts that will be our legacy for those after us?

It is an honor to share this story – my story about changes, transitions, transformations, and a story about becoming.

War and Chaos

The last time my mother saw my father for over four years was the day I was conceived. Immediately after that night, he was conscripted and very soon became a Prisoner of War of the Japanese in Changi in Singapore, leaving my pregnant mother and my brother, who was 18 months old. At the time of my birth in 1942, Britain was submerged in dark and challenging times. Those early years were often marked by nights in air-raid shelters with sounds of planes and bombs around us. The initial years at school were also marked by practices of running to a specific place when the air-raid sirens went off. In late September 1944, my grandparents woke me excitedly to

go downstairs, and as I stood in the bedroom doorway and looked at my mother, I blurted out, "Who is that strange man in bed with you mummy?"

It was a new experience having a dad who took us to different places, including long walks to the beach, building sandcastles, and being a family. Just before my 5th birthday, a little brother was born.

From the Known to the Unknown – New Childhood Discoveries

I learned early from my parents to embrace change and to take the risk of stepping in a new direction. As a prisoner of war, my father had met Australian soldiers who spoke of the need for skilled workers in Australia at that time. He was a carpenter and builder and had the qualifications of an electrician as well. My parents applied for immigration to Australia and were accepted. We left Britain in February 1949. The four weeks on the ship – the Asturias – was full of discoveries for us children. Unlike modern cruise ships, things were very practical – schooling, sports, a fancy-dress dance, and of course, no TV or radio to distract us.

My mother became sick, and I was told I could not go to the ward where she was.

Do you remember doing the opposite of what you were told as a child? It's about testing our independence and using our own voice. So, I crept under the rope and up the stairs to see her. Only when I was older did I discover she had lost a baby – a little sister!

I celebrated my 7th birthday, the day the boat docked in Melbourne. My older brother had made friends with the cook, and he produced a cake with yellow icing. By the time we arrived in Sydney, measles had broken out on the boat, and my brother had it, so we were quarantined for a couple of days. When we finally left the boat and

Transforming Your Life: Volume III

were being taken to the immigration center, it was as if we had stepped into another world. Immigration had given us a posting to Cobar – a town far out west of New South Wales, and in those days, a two-day train trip to the last station on the line.

Transitions were not difficult at that age. We learned to be 'Australian' and tried to adapt to the Australian twang, which my mother corrected continuously. A little sister was born in this far-out town, and I learned to wash nappies and help with all the household chores. We had become friends with a beautiful Australian family, and as the parents grew closer together, they asked if we'd move with them to a little bush town 111 kilometers from Sydney. Dad was the builder!

I wonder if young children today would love that old steam train trip back to Sydney. We each had backpacks with tin plates, cutlery, tinned food, etc. Water bags were hung out of the train windows for our drinking. On the second morning, we were all up early and standing at the windows looking out as the train roared past a little station in the Blue Mountains where my grandparents, who had followed us to Australia a few years after we had left, now lived. As the train raced past, we all waved amid cries of delight to see them again. From Sydney, we took another shorter train trip to Buxton, a small village surrounded by trees and bushland. We had no house and tents needed to be erected, so we could all settle for the night. Living in this remote village was fun at that age, except for redback spiders and snakes!

Eventually, my parents wanted to be closer to the Catholic school, and they bought a block of land in Thirlmere. Each weekend, my dad would go and build our house, starting with a small shed in

which we could all live. We moved in when the shed was ready, and the rest of the house slowly took shape.

Changing Lifestyles and Missionary Influences

Can you remember an event in your childhood that became a significant influence in your future, even though you may not have realized it at the time?

This move was a turning point for me. Not far from the place we had moved to was another little town called Douglas Park. It had a big monastery and training school for boys who wanted to join the Missionaries of the Sacred Heart. A priest from there would come to the little church where we lived and say Mass each Sunday. Quite often, they came back to our home for a meal. My parents were devout Catholics and soon became interested in the far-reaching missionary work this group did in Papua New Guinea (PNG). In particular, my brother also became involved and was taken to visit the Apostolic School, where they trained boys through secondary school and prepared them for further training as missionary priests.

The early 1950s was the era when the focus was on reaching out to far-flung places, and we learned about work in Japan, Asia, Australia, and PNG. Seeing my interest, the priest told me about the sisters who worked alongside them, and I was taken to visit them in Sydney. They also had a secondary school in the Blue Mountains, preparing girls in philosophy and mission lifestyle, but it was much smaller than the boys' school. I was fired with enthusiasm, and at age 12 in 1954, I was accepted into this secondary school.

Serious Transition – From Spontaneity to Conformity

As a teenager, did you ever think that your wings were being clipped? You wanted to fly, but you found yourself caged or only able to fly within the limit of the rope? And how did that affect your later life?

This is what happened when I began secondary school. I learned when to keep quiet and not express an opinion, when to "put up" with things, and when to take criticism with an upper lip. But I also learned a deep inner spirituality based on the Missionary of the Sacred Heart mission – that is the power of love. So, when things became really difficult, I went inward to a place where I attempted to touch universal love. Over the next five years, it became more complicated, and I lost my smile and spontaneity. Still, conformity meant I was accepted for the next stage and then in 1959 entered what was called the Novitiate – the formal place of training to become a missionary sister and take vows. I was still committed to the vision – to be the Heart of God on Earth. And so in 1962, I made vows as a religious sister.

After this, my parents told me they were going to Papua New Guinea to be lay missionaries, my father as a builder, and my mother as a catechetics teacher. Their vision still inspired me.

I was trained as a teacher, and with Final Vows, in January 1965, I was sent to Alice Springs in the Northern Territory, where the Order had a boarding school as well as a large primary school. I became 'mother' to over 20 girls aged from 5 years to 14 years; half of them were indigenous girls, and the others came from remote cattle stations across the Territory. After school, I did all the things a mum would do – changing clothes, homework, meals, listening, bathing the little ones, and in the evening sleeping in a room alongside them, wherein the middle of the night the call would be, "Mum, I want to go to the toilet," or "Mum, I'm sick." And in the morning, we would all go to school, and I would teach the class assigned.

Alongside this, I was living the life of a Sister with set times for prayer and meditation, community gatherings, and readings. Something inside me was beginning to question everything. I loved the children and found joy and delight in being with them. Then, as is typical in a Religious Order, four years later, a call came – in the middle of a school year, "You are to be transferred to Queenstown in Tasmania." As a friendly priest said, "You are moving from the sublime to *the cor blimey*."

Yet another transition and transformation!

Dark Night

Leaving the children behind was a wrench. I arrived in Hobart in July late in the evening. The Sisters there met me and then put me on a bus for Queenstown on the west coast of Tasmania, very early the next morning. It was to be an eight-hour trip. I was the only passenger on the bus, and it was snowing! From Central Australia to freezing Tasmania, and inside me it felt like the beginning of the dark night as I tried to make sense of the move. Religious life in those days did not encourage one to mix with people apart from work. I had been instructed to stay on the bus and given a sandwich, while I envied the warm log fire I could see through the window. By the time we arrived in Queenstown, a mining town in a valley surrounded by bare hills (all the vegetation had been stripped for the mines), it was dark, miserably wet, and cold, even though it was only 4 in the afternoon. I longed for the warmth of Central Australia and the smiling children.

I was given two classes to teach. The children were lively, and it was not difficult to be absorbed and watch them learn and grow. I also remember the first landing on the moon and watching it on television—the wonder and amazement of such a breakthrough in our world.

Inside me, the dark night was all-encompassing. Being in a valley, surrounded by the high mountains, which were often covered by cloud and mist, was like being in a pot with the lid on, especially after the wide-open spaces of Central Australia.

Some years later, I learned a lot about Jungian Psychology and the power of myths to parallel the journey.

Inanna, the ancient Sumerian goddess, was a powerful symbol of ancient feminine wisdom for turbulent times. In her book *Descent to the Goddess*, Sylvia Brinton Perera draws on Inanna's story to demonstrate the need for a woman to claim her own inner authority in a masculine-oriented society. Though I didn't realize it then, I was very much a daughter of the patriarchy, trying "to uphold the virtues and aesthetic ideals which the patriarchal superego has presented to us" (Perera, 1981, p. 11). In this ancient myth, Inana, the Queen of the Heavens, decides to visit the underworld to meet her "dark sister" Ereshkigal, the queen of the Great Below. Inanna has a trusted female servant, Ninshubur, whom she instructs to rescue her if she does not return within three days. In this dark journey, Inanna is stripped of her finery and clothing and killed. It is only when Ninshubur secures her release by sending someone to mourn with Ereshkigal and bring her food and water that Inanna is reborn and returned.

For me, the journey meant descending into the dark to let go of my role-determined behavior and find a new way of being. It is a journey we must make not once, but at different stages of our growth, depending on the transitions we need to make.

At turning points of your life, have you ever felt as if you are going into a dark night, and you feel unsure about when or where you will see daylight again? If you look back, you will realize that when you have let go of some limiting pattern of behavior or belief, you were finally free to move forward again.

Into the Light again – Mission Life

After 18 months, I was asked to return to the Northern Territory – this time to an indigenous station called Daly River – 150 kilometers southwest from Darwin. Keeping in perspective the era – the early '70s, missions were common, and across the Territory, Catholics, Anglicans, and Uniting Churches had mission stations where schools were developed for the indigenous children. The young Aboriginal men and women were trained as teachers, so they could eventually take over.

Boarding school was an aspect of many missions – though not what you would imagine, as we lived in remote places, where generators only ran at certain times of the day, and the dormitories were mostly built from corrugated iron. Beds were mattresses on the floor, very close together, and I often thought how difficult it was for them to be confined to this space when their families were only a kilometer away. They all had jobs to do before breakfast like raking leaves, sweeping paths, helping in the kitchen—jobs that were meant to train them in domestic living. I felt these demands on them at such a young age were often too harsh and did my best to soften them and make excuses for them when those in charge called them to account.

It was here we learned to live in awareness of the snakes, frogs, and anything creepy-crawly. The mission was on the banks of a big river, which in the wet season could flood. When lights went out in the evening, small frogs would emerge. You had to carry a torch in the evening to avoid stepping on them or a snake. These slippery creatures would come into the pipes and up into the sink or even into the toilet. We also learned to flush the toilet as soon as we entered it, in case there was a snake under the rim, which I encountered a few times. The sheer joy of youth, resilience, and the ability to adapt to almost any environment!

On inter-school sports day, the children were loaded into the back of a big cattle truck and asked to join hundreds of other indigenous children in friendly sports. On one such occasion, as we passed a tourist bus and the people took out their cameras, the children peered through the truck and cried out, "Mooo, moo!!!", and then doubled up with laughter at the look of horror on the tourists' faces. Indigenous children had a wonderful sense of humor, in spite of the harsh conditions in which many of them had grown up.

I also learned to drive on the airstrip. Planes and mail only came in twice a week, so it was an excellent spot to learn.

Car Crash and Move Back South

It's impressive how quickly we settle into a routine and get used to a way of life until something unexpected happens. Can you remember incidents that became a turning point in your life, and you found yourself jolted into a new and different way of living – just as we all are today because of the COVID-19 pandemic.

In late 1974 on a trip back from Darwin, the driver was speeding along the gravel road when he suddenly skidded to miss a kangaroo.

The car swerved wildly, and as we rolled down a bank, I glimpsed my whole life in front of me, till we landed back on our wheels. It was deadly quiet. When the driver said, "Are you OKAY?", I realized that I wasn't, and neither was the passenger in the seat in front of me. We were both on the passenger side. The two on the driver's side were shaken, but okay.

We were 50 kilometers still away from the mission. Darwin was 90 kilometers back the other way, and the nearest ambulance was 50 kilometers away at Adelaide River. We had passed a roadworks camp on the way, and the driver walked back to get help. When it came, it was a huge roadworks truck. They lifted the front passenger onto a mattress and put him on the back. I had sustained severe whiplash, and we later discovered some damage to the discs but sat up in the front of the truck as the driver drove back to the ambulance station. By that time, I could hardly move, and as we were loaded into the back of an ambulance, the pain seared through. It was late at night, and we were taken into the emergency. The front seat passenger was admitted and had an extended stay in the hospital after surgery. At midnight, I was released with a strong collar around my neck, followed by many days of physiotherapy. The Religious Order decided to send me south to a primary school in Brisbane, and I taught Grade Six primary school class.

Into the Tunnel Again and Surprise Meetings

The person in charge was an unfortunate and fearful woman who was afraid that I might step out of line. So, she started watching and monitoring me, which wasn't easy to get used to. Though I had learned to drive in the Territory, I now had to learn to navigate city roads as I was the only one in the community who had a driver's license. A lovely old gentleman, whose sister-in-law was in the same

Order and working in Papua New Guinea, offered to take me on lessons, and within a week I was making my first solo trip to the airport to meet someone. "Turn left at the old brewery, follow the river, go right at the old pub...," etcetera was how he got me to remember. So, while being in the tunnel, it was wonderful to learn from him and regain a little sense of humor, all of which were needed for the next phase of the journey.

Return to the Missions

At the beginning of 1976, I went to an even more remote station in the Northern Territory on the far west coast from Darwin called Port Keats, now known as Wadeye. Many years earlier, an old Missionary of the Sacred Heart had founded the mission station. Three different tribal groups had come to live at the mission. There were tribal differences and so there was often conflict, and the spears and sticks would come out, and there would be open warfare.

While English was the language in which we taught, among themselves, their own dialects were used more commonly. Here, the plane from Darwin carrying passengers and mail came only once a week. If there happened to be a dense fog, which was often the case in winter, we could hear the plane circling above, looking for a gap in the cloud to land. It would eventually give up and go back to Darwin, and the mail and news we had been waiting for, would be held over for another week. And of course, these areas didn't have a TV either.

The big old church had wooden benches as seats. Mosquitoes abounded, and during the sermons, one could hear frequent slapping to kill them rather than be bitten. An old man died not long after I arrived, and his body was wrapped in a shroud and laid on a bench at the front. There were no coffins in those days to mask the reality of death. The ride to the funeral was on the back of a tractor, and everyone walked behind with the family, wailing in sadness. At the graveside, two men jumped in, and the body was lifted down to their waiting arms, where they laid the old man down gently. The two men were then pulled out, and everyone helped to cover up the body. The old man's faithful dog sat on top for three days, mourning him.

The mission had vast gardens, and sugarcane and fresh vegetables were usually available. Powdered milk became the norm. A large cattle station nearby provided fresh meat and the river and sea fresh fish.

There was a road of sorts that went to Daly River – almost a two days drive, but often not passable if there had been rains. It was a beautiful place to learn self-isolation and self-sufficiency, and all of us knew how to entertain ourselves without modern technology. Many of the mission stations had old film reels, and once a week, everyone gathered in the basketball court, sitting on blankets and pillows to watch an old movie.

Does this kind of lifestyle appeal to you today, when you are quarantined in the middle of this virus outbreak? It's the lifestyle that will make or break you. But, I think it is far healthier than being quarantined in the middle of a big city. In those earlier days, people knew how to communicate, even when the spears came out, with shouting and threats, but rarely carried out.

I was in my mid-30s, and something was continuing to shift inside. A 30-day Retreat opportunity appeared, and I went south into seclusion, where a Jesuit priest led us each day in prayer, talks, and silence for 30 days. For the next few years, as I struggled with the growing darkness inside me, he became a mentor through his letters.

Outside, no one knew what I was going through as I was always in the role of teacher and good Sister.

Are you aware of the roles you are carrying, and how strongly do you identify with them? Wife, mother, professional woman, worker, or whatever role you have taken on? In the first half of our life, it's so easy for us to identify with these roles and lose sight of what could be, unless or until events or incidents set us on a journey to look for more answers.

Back to the Center – Grief and Loss

This time the mission station was 80 km south-east of Alice Springs – Santa Teresa. I was appointed Principal of the School and leader of the community. Today, over 40 years later, this place is a thriving community. The people have developed a huge Santa Teresa Spirituality Center run by the strong indigenous women. Each year, many school groups from southern schools come and learn the art and crafts they teach and do volunteer work with them. It is wonderful to see.

Back in the '70s, the village was surrounded by a dusty desert, dogs ran wild, alcohol had become an enormous problem, and there were many accidents and deaths as a result.

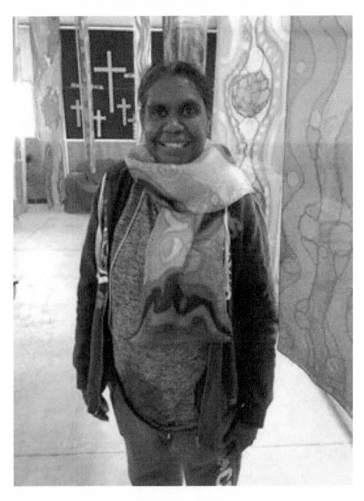

Image from Spirituality Centre Website

There were no phone connections then, and radio was used to communicate with Alice Springs. It was in April 1978 that I got a message that my father was dying of cancer; he was only 62 years of age, but the ravages of being a prisoner of war had taken its toll on him. They were now living in north Queensland, and by the time I got there, he had succumbed to the illness. It all seemed synchronized. 10 minutes from the airport, we had a flat tire, and it seemed that he died at that particular moment!

Santa Teresa in 1976

(Find & Connect Northern Territory,
http://www.findandconnect.gov.au/ref/nt/objects/YD0000015.html)

Work was constant in those days. The philosophy I had learned was to keep going, keep giving, and don't think about yourself. It was no wonder that I began to get sick and needed to have a hysterectomy. There was little time to ponder the ramifications of this as I went straight back to work at the school. I was so conditioned to thinking that this was what I had to do and not fully aware then that I was following the voices of others dictating who we should be and what we should do.

Do you ever hear these voices, both outer and inner, and feel that you need to keep up with the status quo? Do you worry what people will think of you, that you are letting the side down if you don't conform? What voices are you struggling with right now? What are the voices today that keep women trapped inside themselves, no matter what calling they are following?

The Tiwi Islands and the Edge of the Mid-life Forest

The final mission appointment was to Bathurst Island in the Tiwi Islands, north of Darwin. The people here were very different from the shy and quieter Central Australians. This group was quite extraverted and had retained a lot of culture with their dancing and singing. This was the place where 100 years ago, an old missionary, Bishop Gzell, had bought the young girls as "wives" to prevent them from being married off to old men. He was known as the Bishop with 150 wives. He helped the girls to train and get work and then marry men their own age.

Arriving here was the first time that I felt totally exhausted and wondered how I would keep going. It was not just physical exhaustion but deep inner tiredness from the struggle to make sense of it all. Prayer didn't alleviate the darkness. After one year, I was again appointed Principal of the School as the previous Principal had become ill and moved south. By the end of the second year, a glimmer of hope appeared when a Missionary of the Sacred Heart priest came and said they were running a 26-day renewal retreat at their old Apostolic School of Douglas Park. It was for religious men and women from different Orders. I applied and was finally given permission.

What a breakthrough this was as again a wise mentor appeared and helped me unravel some of the tangled mess inside. The Spirituality of the Heart was powerful at that time, and it was the balm to the soul. The love and friendship within the group enabled me to stir the embers again and return to the Islands. Within a few months, the doubts and physical exhaustion returned, and I wondered if there was a way to end it after all.

Have you ever felt that you can't take another step, that to keep going along this same path is like suicide to the soul? It is when we reach that dark place; there are only two options – give up and die, or go down and through. The way out is through. Once that choice is made, there is a little light leading the way. For me, it was the opportunity to go to Brisbane and do my Bachelor of Education.

The story that encapsulates this dark night journey for me was found in Dante's *Divine Comedy*. Dante was a noble Florentine who, as a young adult, was condemned to exile during the strife between the Guelphs and the Ghibellines. During this exile, he wrote the *Divine Comedy* – his own journey to finding the divine center within him. In his first book, *The Inferno*, he begins:

> *Midway along the journey of our life*
> *I woke to find myself in a dark wood*
> *For I had wandered off from the straight path.*
> *How I entered there, I cannot truly say,*
> *I had become sleepy at the moment*
> *When I first strayed, leaving the path of truth.*

He awoke in this dark wood, filled with fear and so much apprehension that when he is confronted by a lion, a leopard, and a she-wolf, he realizes that he has missed his true path. He will only be able to find this true path after he has gone into the depths (the Inferno) and confronted his deepest fears. He then moves on to the mountain of Purgatory, where he learned that he has to take time to go inward and trust in each step as he faces the great unknown until he finally reaches heaven.

For me, this was an eight-year journey that, like Dante, became possible only with the help of guides.

Have you at different times felt these elements of restlessness or discontent with the way life is unfolding? Or have you, with frantic energy gone this way and that, tried to find your way by doing something completely different? The way out is through.

The Dark Night: Meeting Carl Jung... through Dream Work

That two years of study (1983–84) was a time of hungering for new knowledge and understanding. It was alongside the studies that I was introduced to Carl Jung through a weekend workshop on the Myers-Briggs Type Indicator and Understanding Dreams. Jung's powerful legacy in psychology was his understanding of the symbolic life, and that actual growth came through bringing what is in the unconscious to consciousness or awareness.

The unconscious is somewhat like the dingy cellar under one's house that has never been explored. When we find ourselves lost in the dark wood, this is the time to go within and explore this cellar. I found it covered in cobwebs and dust, and as each corner and crevice was cleaned, I learned what needed to be discarded. In addition, I discovered the treasures I didn't know were there, and that needed to be brought into the light.

As with Dante above, it was a time of confronting the shadows and the darkness and the terrible fear of where it all might lead.

The guide appeared as I began the process of Jungian Analysis, searching the underlying meaning of the symbols in the dreams and nightmares and bringing them to light. This continued once I had graduated and posted south to a primary school in Sydney. The year was a struggle – the dreams and analysis were pointing in a different direction to the one I had walked in the first half of my life. The fear of stepping into the unknown was great. I could not go back, but I had not yet found the guiding values for the afternoon of life.

At the end of that school year, I applied for 12 months of leave and went to work in a Center that held workshops and retreats. The 12 months became two years, and then I took the next step and applied to live away, more formally. I began to teach some of what I was learning and also to facilitate workshops. My guides were again a Jungian Analyst and a Spiritual Director, without whom I could have never navigated the dark terrain. The eight years were a liminal time/space between one way of being and another, a time when the views and beliefs we developed over the first half of life seem to be no longer available to us, and childhood faith is challenged and tested. Old skins were being shed, dismemberment took place, and I learned to follow what the poet Rilke said:

"Be patient toward all that is unsolved in your heart and… try to love the questions themselves like locked rooms and books that are written in a very foreign tongue. Do not now seek the answers, which cannot be given you because you would not be able to live them. And the point is to live everything. Live the questions now. Perhaps you will then gradually, without noticing it, live along some distant day into the answer."

The day I finally left religious life, I felt a deep peace, even though I had no idea how I was going to survive financially, or where I would live.

The Afternoon of Life

Recovering personal authority is one of the major tasks as we begin the afternoon of life. This means to find what is true for oneself and to live it. Poet and author David Whyte refers to the story of Moses, who, when told to take off his shoes, discovers that he is standing on holy ground and that he has all his life been standing on the ground of his own experience with the Deity. It takes a while for clipped wings to grow again, and some attempts to fly end in falling flat on the face.

The first task was to find a way and a place to live. For a while, I worked as a housekeeper. I retrained and studied and completed a master's course in Counseling and began to set up a practice and also continue to teach and facilitate workshops. Having been a missionary for so many years, I still wanted to love and help people. I had no idea how to charge for my services and attracted many people who expected it to be free. I accommodated their requests, but it did not pay my rent. It is amazing how unexpectedly advice was given to me, and I learned a new way of being. Very slowly, I found my own voice and support, and I started tutoring at a university.

It was then that I met another traveler who shared similar values, and we realized that we could continue the journey together. We became soul mates and married in 1995. As I write this, it is the day before our 25th wedding anniversary. With the current state of lockdown because of the virus, we have a beautiful day at home to celebrate together.

One day, quite out of the blue, a friend phoned and said there was a job being advertised in the Northern Territory to work for and support four Indigenous health groups who were part of the *Social and Emotional Wellbeing Services* they were setting up. This was a collection of services that helped indigenous people in that space. So many people were living with the heritage of their parents being part of the Stolen Generation – people who were snatched from their families as children because of the then White Australia Policy. So many grew up in institutions, were abused, and had no idea of parenting as they didn't experience it. My husband and I applied, and we were accepted for the job which, while we lived in Darwin, took us to Katherine and down to Alice Springs to the Aboriginal services there.

The incredible thing about this job was that when we arrived and worked at Danila Dilba, an Aboriginal controlled Health service, we discovered that one of the Health workers there had the name of one of the children I had cared for in the boarding school in Alice Springs and I went to check. She and her two sisters had been taken at a young age by the government Welfare as their mother often left them alone for some days to fend for themselves. They were sent to the boarding school. I was fortunate to be able to mother them for a couple of years till I was moved. We met here over 30 years later. The renewal of contact was heart-warming—hugs and the word 'mum' filled me with tears. We soon met her two sisters again.

Wonderful reunion with the eldest of three sisters (then 12 years old) left behind in the Boarding school when I was moved to Tasmania

A similar thing happened when we visited Alice Springs, and one of the indigenous councilmen said, "Do you know Marlene?" "Oh yes, where is she?" "She's my partner, but she's really depressed, will you come?" We went to the house, and she was sitting lonely on the verandah. He said to her, "Hey Marlene, here is someone you know" (she is almost 40). I went up to her and said, "Marlene, oh, your face is still so beautiful". A moment's hesitation and she burst into tears and hugged me tight, and I knew all those years had been worthwhile. These women still keep contact today – a legacy of love and the journey. It was also in Darwin that I was able to lead the Stolen Generation women through a journey of healing via art and also able to teach Reiki healing to the health workers.

Do you realize that even when you are not aware of it, you are having an influence on other people's lives? People are being touched by you, and you are the bridge for them to move from one place to the next – even more so as you go through your own gates of transformation.

When the job ended, it was another transition of "Where now?" and I was accepted to work at the Gawler Cancer Foundation Centre in Melbourne. It was September 2001, and we had only just arrived when I got the message that my mother was dying in North Queensland. We've talked a lot about changing times and transitions, and this was another huge year of world transition. It was the year of 9/11 in America when the twin towers were bombed. We arrived in Melbourne, and the Australian airlines, Ansett, collapsed (my youngest brother had worked for them for years and was suddenly jobless). So, to get a flight back to my dying mother in Townsville was difficult.

The message had come through on Tuesday. The earliest flight was Saturday, and in addition, the house we were to rent became available on Thursday. I left my husband surrounded by boxes. We got lost on our way to the airport but made the plane in time, and I arrived late Saturday. My sister and I spent the last hours with her on Sunday morning.

Two weeks later, my husband's father died, and the first workshop I attended at the Gawler Cancer Foundation was about death and dying. I didn't think I needed it as I had just lived through it. My journey at the Foundation was not long as on Christmas Eve I had a phone call from the University of New England (UNE), and because of my experience with indigenous people, I was asked If I would help develop a Diploma in Aboriginal Family and Community Counseling. While it took me back into teaching, it was godsend as it provided us with a steady income, which we needed. And it was there that I began my PhD journey.

UNE taught a Master of Counseling Course in Hong Kong. What a strange journey and turnaround of events as we went to Hong Kong two or three times a year to teach students. My first trip was full of questions: "How can I teach Relationships Counseling to Chinese students whose values and philosophy about relationships I don't know?" So, I learned and studied Chinese philosophy and practices, and that was wonderful. I'd learned so much from my parents about understanding other cultures and was so enriched by what I learned from these students. We also encountered the quarantine of the SARS outbreak, and for some months, could only teach by distance. My PhD focused on how the Chinese students who had learned all their counseling in English-speaking courses and from English speakers, reconceptualized and transformed what they learned for their own cultures. My primary supervisor was Head of the Department, and as I completed, she asked me to come and teach there. What an amazing experience for my husband and me to move and live again in another culture. I was 65 years old.

A group of Master of Counselling students with me as they completed a course I taught on Solution Focused Therapy - They proudly presented their work at a conference in Singapore just as we were leaving Hong Kong.

It was a refining experience and a special gift as I was nearing later life. Chinese friends we made there have come and stayed with us now we are back in Australia. Below is a picture of an ex-student and his wife and family who welcomed us each Chinese New Year into their family and who have since stayed with us here in Australia.

Conscious Aging

At 70, we knew it was time to return to Australia. I secured a job as a Senior Lecturer at a University in Queensland, coordinating and supporting the little team there and setting up a Master of Counseling course. I really believe that God was behind all this, as not long after I returned, my sister became seriously ill with non-Hodgkin's lymphoma. She was eight years younger than I was, and we had been close. Being in Queensland meant we could travel to north Queensland to see her – as she went from hospital to palliative care and a nursing home. We were so fortunate to be there for the last six days. She was only 65, and her husband of 40 years and son were bereft. I miss her deeply, and her death made me think much more about conscious aging.

At 75, I left the university, and we decided to move to Ballarat, just over 100 kilometers north-west of Melbourne. We wanted to focus on the ways we could use the years of experience to help other women (and men) to begin that journey into the afternoon of life and conscious aging. Setting up a business and practicing counseling, coaching, and teaching and making enough money to live was a struggle, and there were lots of wrong turnings that got me nowhere.

I finally discovered Sai Blackbyrn's Accelerator Program and was accepted to join. I learned what had been missing in my business and began to move ahead. A functional website has been set up, and I'm now developing an online program that enables women to enter their gates of wisdom and move into the afternoon of life, embracing their own power. Showing other women how to break the limitations and barriers that hold them back from realizing their destiny is crucial in these times. Art is a powerful tool I often use and I taught this group of students how to use it for others to express what cannot be spoken.

Healing Through Art

What is holding you back from listening to the whisper and yearnings in your own soul? What is it that you have within that can inspire other women to break free and become this bridge to a new life?

Meditation and Qigong are the daily practices that enable us to be in stillness and open to what is emerging each day. As John O'Donohue in his poem *Fluent* says, "I would love to live like the river flows, Carried by the surprise of its own unfolding." Like a river, you and I follow the twists and turns of our own lives, and we are often surprised by the beauty that unfolds around us. The challenge is to live each day with a compassionate heart, have clarity in our words, and a gracious awareness. This requires courage and constant love.

Aging is another transition, and transitions happen within transitions. They are not linear but circular. I have no regrets, only gratitude for the many paths the journey has taken me on. A friend once said to me that life is made up of fateful detours and wrong turnings, but what a discovery and wealth of new learning is there if we are open to it. The poet Rilke said, "Let everything happen to you: beauty and terror. Just keep going. No feeling is final."

And Lao Tsu, the wonderful Chinese philosopher said, "If you want to awaken all of humanity, then awaken all of yourself, if you want to eliminate the suffering in the world, then eliminate all that is negative in yourself. Truly, the greatest gift you have to give is that of your own self-transformation."

The Invitation is Waiting for You

The invitation to all of us is to open up to life. That means to stand on solid ground, the ground of one's own being. The whole world is waiting for you to take your place, the place that only you can fill. We begin by asking questions that will enable us to move forward. Sometimes those questions begin when something is taken away from us, and there is a spaciousness which then appears, and we do not know how to inhabit it. It may be grief or a sense of disconnectedness, or loss, or a feeling of not belonging. We may even feel imprisoned—be it in work or a relationship or within ourselves, unable to move.

David Whyte expresses this so clearly in this excerpt from his poem:

> *Sometimes*
> *...you come to a place whose only task is to trouble you*
> *With tiny but frightening requests*
> *conceived out of nowhere*
> *but in this place*
> *beginning to lead everywhere.*
> *Requests to stop what you are doing right now,*
> *and to stop what you are becoming*
> *while you do it,*
> *questions that can make or unmake a life,*
> *questions that have patiently*
> *waited for you,*
> *questions that have no right*
> *To go away.*

You are not alone. When you articulate that question and take the first step, you will find a guide, as Dante did, and as I did. The guide will be a witness to your life, listen, and be there and share in your questions and the conversation.

Your invitation is to do the work of transformation, to put yourself in conversation, crack open your heart a little, and let the wind open the door. The horizon may not be clear, but as you welcome each transition and enter each gate, glimpses of it will appear, somewhat like traveling along the road and coming to a crest and seeing it in the distance before it disappears again. The task is to be in a relationship with the horizon of your life, which is waiting for you.

In the beginning I asked,

"What is the bridge that will enable us to cross from the world of how life has been for years to what it now needs to become? Are you and I meant to be the bridge between these worlds?"

Yes, we become that bridge when we attend to our own becoming – our own metamorphosis, our own transformation. The poet Rumi captures this beautifully:

> *Quietness*
> *Inside this new love, die.*
> *Your way begins on the other side.*
> *Become the sky,*
> *Take an ax to the prison wall.*
> *Escape.*
> *Walk out like somebody born into color.*
> *Do it now.*

Now is the time to be still and leave behind the old life of frantic running away from the silence and stillness. Awakened and aware women – and men – are a powerful force in this changing world, a force that will enable new shoots, new growth in a new world, and in new times. Let my story, my history, and your story and your history be an unlocked gate to a new life – not a barrier, but a bridge to our becoming and hence to the becoming of our world.

References

Dante (1971) *The Divine Comedy, Vol. 1: The Inferno,* trans Mark Musa, Penguin: Indiana University Press

Lao Tsu (1997) *The Tao Te Ching* trans. Gia-Fu Feng & Jane English (25th anniversary edition) Vintage Books Edition: US.

O'Donohue, J. (2004) *"Fluent"* in *Conamara Blues, US: Harper Collins Publishers Inc.*

Perera, S.B. (1981) *Descent to the Goddess – A way of initiation for women,* Toronto, CA: Inner City Books.

Rilke, R.M. (1962) *Letters to a Young Poet, trans,* Herter Norton. New York: W.W. Norton.

Rumi (1995) *The Essential Rumi,* trans. Barks, C. & Moyne, J. New Jersey: Castle Books

Whyte, D. (2003) *Midlife and the Great Unknown – Finding Courage and Clarity through Poetry.* 2 CD Set. WA: Many Rivers Press.

Whyte, D. (2012) *Sometimes* in David Whyte, *River Flow – New and Selected Poems.* Langley, WA: Many Rivers Press.

Whyte, D. (2014) *Solace – and the Art of asking beautiful Questions* – 2CD set Many Rivers Press:WA.

ANN MOIR-BUSSY

Ann's rich life experience embraced a wide variety of teaching, counseling, consulting, education, workshop facilitator, and author. From 1965 to the late 1985, Ann taught in many schools around Australia, including indigenous schools in remote areas of Australia. From the 1990s, her work encompassed counseling, coaching, and consulting with both individuals and couples in personal, professional, and spiritual growth in Australia and Hong Kong.

From 2002–2017, Ann was a counselor educator and Program Coordinator for Bachelor and Master of Counseling programs and PhD students in Counseling. She taught them that mindfulness, self-awareness, and courage to grow and change personally were essential elements if they were to help others.

Ann has developed effective and powerful ways to facilitate change and healing, enabling clients to be the best possible version of themselves in order to attain their goals and dreams. She believes in a holistic approach that embraces all aspects of life and integration of mind, body, and spirit. Ann is strongly influenced by Jungian ideas that enable us to explore the inner life and bring more consciousness and awareness into daily living in these changing times. In addition to this, Ann is a Reiki Master and practices Qigong and meditation daily.

Visit www.annmoirbussy.com and sign up for a FREE discovery session to start your journey.

Contact Details

Website: https://annmoirbussy.com/

LinkedIn: https://www.linkedin.com/in/ann-moir-bussy-04b2b715/

Facebook:
https://www.facebook.com/www.embracelifenow.com.au *and* https://www.facebook.com/AMoirBussy

UNSTOPPABLE: A JOURNEY OF BECOMING WHAT I MUST BE

Anna Jiang

There was a spring in my life that I will never forget. That was the spring that I barely slept. Lying awake beside my one-year-old, a little angel drifting off in the darkness, I struggled to hold back the tears. My husband had stopped communicating months ago. I couldn't bear the thought of our son growing up without a dad. How was I going to manage it all? Working at the university and struggling to finish my PhD, I felt like I was living in a tunnel with no light in sight. Vulnerable and full of fear, I began falling into a depression.

Things, however, took a big turn very shortly. In that summer, my husband and I divorced. Before Christmas, I got an email from the university confirming the award of my PhD. Today, I'm an author, a university lecturer, and a productivity Neurocoach. I am independent, happy, and fulfilled.

How did I end up in this happy place? How did I get from that sleepless spring to where I am now—happy, content, and in control?

I believe anyone can rise out of a seemingly impossible situation. Change is not as miraculous as you may think. Often, all it takes is the right mindset and a clear set of steps to set you in the right direction. Let me tell you how I did it.

Dirty Laundry

My husband was a good, traditional Chinese man. He worked as a banker. When I first met him, I adored conversing with him. He seemed to know everything under the sun. I appreciated the different perspectives he offered me. But after I gave birth to our son, things started to change quickly. Eventually, we reached a state where communication felt impossible, but I didn't know how we ended up there. All I know is that our conversations went something like this:

> Me: "I'm exhausted. I need to get up three, four, or five times a night to comfort our baby."

> Him: "Are you suggesting that I'm the one who is leading an easy life?"

> *I did not know what to say. I felt even more depressed.*

> Me: "I need to finish my PhD. My career depends on it! But with the baby, I hardly have any time to write."

> Him: "I told you that you ought to have finished it before you had the baby!"

> *I was lost for words. I didn't know whether to blame him or myself.*

Me: "I think my mom gets tired helping us out. Can you be nice to her? Please don't ignore her when she comes over."

Him: "I'm already nice to her. Don't focus on what I say or not say, look at what I do."

Me: "What did you do?"

Him: "Can't you see what I do?"

* * *

I began to wonder whether I truly knew the man I had married. It seemed like he didn't know me either. To him, our communication breakdown was no big deal. He said he was happy in our marriage. I felt like I was drowning. I didn't feel needed or cared about—let alone loved. My self-esteem evaporated into a haze of loneliness, helplessness, and desperation. Nearly at the point of breaking down, my suffering eluded him. He insisted all was well. At last, I suggested that we go to a therapist—it was a last resort. He said therapists don't solve problems. Besides, to him, we had no problems to solve.

Therapy had been my final hope for my marriage. My husband's denial drove us further apart. I began to see how our core values differed. When we first met, we seemed to understand each other. But we expected different things in our marriage. We lived in separate worlds and spoke two different languages. There was no hope of translating between the two. He was a stranger from a strange land. Ironically, language and cross-cultural communication was my academic expertise. I had studied both for more than two decades. With people from vastly different cultural backgrounds, I spoke effortlessly. But with the person I was most intimate with, communication felt impossible. In my marriage, my skills of communication failed to deliver.

It was clear that divorce was the only way out, but the decision did not come easily to me. I had to consider the consequences on my son. Like most new mothers, I wanted the best for my baby. I had to choose the lesser of two evils.

When I said to him: "I want a divorce," his reply shocked me.

"Don't you dare to threaten me!" My husband said.

He thought I was crazy to throw away the "good" life. But his words made it more painfully obvious that I had never known who he was. I wanted desperately to get out of a marriage that was suffocating me. He didn't want to end the marriage, but he didn't want to work through its problems either. To him, our marriage wasn't broken— so why fix it? Why end it?

Some couples come together because they want to get to know each other. Once they grow familiar, the intrigue vanishes, and the couple drifts apart. My husband and I came together because we thought we knew each other. We drifted apart when it was clear we didn't.

Phoenix Rising

So, there I was: a "crazy" woman who had left her husband and a soon-to-be-divorced woman who had exchanged the good life for the lonely life of a single mother. My husband wasn't responding to my messages. I was scared to hell. I wasn't afraid because of what I imagined he might do to me. I was frightened because of what I imagined his absence might do to our son.

When I saw other fathers on the street take their child's hand, I felt a lump in my throat. I sometimes got emotional. Had my husband disappeared forever? Would I be both the mother and father to our son? I had to provide for him, but I didn't know how I would emerge from the shadows of a failed marriage. How would I finish my PhD? When would I be happy? When would I be strong? I wanted to raise a happy, strong kid. But neither strength nor happiness flourishes in the absence of hope. And I was losing hope.

My fears and uncertainties kept me up at night. Every time I looked at my son, I felt a mix of regret and guilt. After a good cry, my brain seemed to work again. It was only after shedding an ocean of tears that I had an epiphany. For my boy to grow up in an environment filled with happiness and love, I had to be filled with happiness and love. Since I was a mom, I had to create the best conditions for him to grow up in. I had to be strong. I had to protect him from harm. There was no room for negotiation. "To be or not to be" was not a question I could ask myself. I had to be there for my child. I had to take action then and there.

So, I changed the story that I was telling myself. Remarkably, my situation transformed. I began to see the beauty in having only one option. Achieving clarity about what I had to do and who I had to become was the best thing that could have happened to me. It helped me strip away the inessentials and focus on what mattered the most. It empowered me. It made me unstoppable. I may have still harbored fears, but I wore new armor against them. As Franklin D. Roosevelt said at the height of the Great Depression, "The only thing we have to fear ... is fear itself."

Amidst my own great depression, I was determined to take Roosevelt's words to heart. I had to save myself from drowning in my own fears. I focused on the things I had to do. My years of experience as a teacher and as a home-schooled student had taught me that the best way to lead was by example. I had to be a good example for my son. I needed to be the best me possible. I knew that it would be riskier to remain tight in bud than to blossom into a full flower. It was my time to bloom, to fulfill my potential, and to live life to the fullest.

Before my marriage, I had pursued many passions. I have an eye for art and for beauty. I had practiced calligraphy for more than a decade. I am passionate about language and the study of language and communication. The power of education to motivate people, to transform their minds and hearts, has always amazed me.

But when I was struggling in my marriage, I stopped pursuing my interests passionately. I lost my drive. When the marriage ended, I had to rediscover who I was and achieve clarity about what I had to do. I knew I needed to finish my PhD. It wasn't just that I needed the degree to move on in my career. I was researching the nature of learning and teaching; my project was an inquiry into language and human thinking. The topic was valuable, and I was passionate about it. I had already collected the data. I just need to finish the data analysis and write up the thesis.

In many ways, pursuing a PhD is like undertaking any big project. It's easy to get started, but it's painfully difficult to complete. You inevitably feel stuck. At times, it eats you up. It consumes you. I procrastinated. My reading of the literature never seemed sufficient. The writing never seemed good enough. I doubted whether I was suited to do research in the first place.

But when I began telling myself that I had to finish it no matter what, I was unstoppable. I stopped feeling afraid of the challenges and mired in the difficulties. I did whatever it took. I set myself a deadline, broke the work into manageable chunks, and hit my daily writing targets.

Once I had clarity about what I had to do, the only problem I faced was time. For a single mom with a one-year-old, time is the most precious thing. But if you have to do something, you make time for it. So, I went to bed at ten, got up at four in the morning, and wrote until nine a.m. Whenever I had free time in-between teaching and attending to my baby, I wrote. Writing became my daily habit. Two months on, I finished a draft of my thesis. Then I heard from my ex-husband, who had sent me our divorce papers.

The word "divorce" no longer disturbed the peace in my heart. I had let go of feeling like a victim of a failed marriage. I had given up playing a supporting role in my own life. I had taken center stage. I was the leading lady. Failing in my marriage didn't mean failing in my life. Just because one relationship didn't work, it doesn't mean my relationships with others would fail. Besides, I had developed an understanding of what worked in a marriage and what didn't. I saw how I could benefit from my experience.

In the darkest days of living in the shadow of a broken marriage, it would have been all-too-easy to have fallen into a trap of negative thinking. The popular discourse in China of the divorced woman would have told me I was a failed wife—a woman not worthy of love and a mother who let her son grow up without a father only for him to have problems in adulthood. Conventional thinking says that only pain comes in the wake of a broken home. But I didn't have to live my life according to that thinking. I may have let go of my marriage, but in giving up on one path, another unfolded. Having less can offer more. With fewer marital problems to worry about, it was easier to direct my attention to what mattered most.

Books on parenting often teach single moms to make up for a missing father. Our culture is quick to see the absence of a father as undesirable and a single mother as deserving of pity. But two parents do not, by default, parent better than one. If a couple is struggling, the conflicts and underlying tension often negatively affect the well-being of their child. It is hard to find a family where no harm has been done. Even the most protected family environments can leave children feeling vulnerable. If kids are not exposed to the tests and challenges of life, they may be ill-prepared for adulthood. If guided appropriately, they can come to understand loss. They can develop strength of character and resilience for whatever might come. Children who have experienced loss early in life learn to cherish what they have. They learn to appreciate the present.

So, I embraced an entirely new narrative. The old one went something like this: "How are you going to live a happy life without a husband?" and "How is your child going to grow up properly without a father?" The new narrative empowered me. It went like this: "Nothing will diminish my strength and my happiness. I will be a happy and strong mom and will raise a happy and strong kid."

The new story began to work its magic.

I felt strong, and I felt happy.

I was unstoppable.

Discovering the Power of Language

Once I changed the narrative, life turned around for me. I told myself that I no longer lived under the shadow of anyone or anything. I no longer saw my failed marriage as a loss, but a win. I felt less like a victim and more like a hero. I was in charge of my own narrative and at the helm of my own life, just like any leading lady.

Language, I realized, had the power to transform any situation. We are all linguistic beings. We live in language in the same way that fish live in water. The words other people use to describe us can make a significant impact, especially the negative words—the mean ones. If someone you love tells you that you have failed as a partner, you rarely forget it. If your mother tells you that you are always wrong, you carry those words with you. Just as it is easy to remember the insults, it can be difficult to remember the praise. Your partners or parents may have said many kind things to you. But we tend to forget those kind words. It's perfectly normal. Our evolutionary brain has learned to stay alert when encountering anything that threatens our survival. Negative words linger for that reason.

But far more powerful than the words people tell you are the words you tell yourself. Far more influential than the stories others narrate to you are the stories you narrate to yourself. You tell stories to explain and interpret what happens to you. Your stories are not objective truths. They arise from subjective interpretations. They embody your sense of self; they negotiate your identity. A product of how your mind works, stories offer an embellished version of reality, one that appeals to the ways you view yourself and the world. How you speak to yourself can either lift you up or pull you down. If you take charge and change the story, you can change the way you see the world. And if you can change the way you see the world, you can change how you experience your life.

As a young person, I studied English as a second language. In speaking another language, I found the courage to speak my mind. In my new language, I argued with my teacher effortlessly and confidently. I felt like I was dancing. I imagined I was rising above the crowd, floating above all my insecurities. Another person— hidden inside my body—leaped out, lively and intense. I didn't recognize that person. Nor did my parents. Speaking another language had teased a stranger out from under me. I was witnessing the power of words. That power had been hidden within me all along.

That experience gave me a distinct feeling that language entwined intimately with my act of living. It shaped so intricately my sense of meaning. It informed my purpose. So, I spent the next two decades devotedly studying language. The beauty, potential, and power of language drove me to pursue a PhD in applied linguistics and language education. But it took going through a divorce to understand just how transformative language can be. From the depths of depression, desperation, and divorce, I developed into a happy single mom—a doctor—who had new hopes for the future. With a new narrative, I felt like I had taken a new lease on life, one that came with a new mindset and a new, healthy brain.

Understanding the Interaction between Language, Emotion, and the Brain

I have always sensed that language, emotion, and the brain were linked somehow. I took a keen interest in the study of neuroscience to uncover the connection. By accident, I came across a course in coaching based on brain-science. Once I had a clear idea of what the course was, I knew I had to take it. Through that course, I developed an appreciation of how significantly language shapes cognition and the activity of our neural networks. I now see clearly how language constitutes emotional perception and how our brain is driven by emotions. Language shapes how we think, how we feel, and who we become.

Does that surprise you? I imagine you too use words to craft your experience. Have you ever talked to yourself when faced with a challenging task? Didn't the words you used make an impact on how you approached your situation?

It's possible to think without words. For example, when you think you have an idea coming, but you are not certain of the words yet, you may think in pictures or have an "aha" moment. But there are certain types of thought that would be inaccessible without language. For example, you use language whenever you engage in logical reasoning. Soviet psychologist Lev Vygotsky suggests that language acts as a scaffolding in thinking and problem-solving. In his model, logic relates to the conscious mind and non-logical processes to the unconscious. Thinking evolves from, in the words of brain scientists, "vague-unconscious" to "crisp-conscious" — a fundamental mechanism of our brain. That helps explain the interaction between language and cognition in our brain. Language is mostly conscious; cognition is rarely so.

Developmental and cognitive scientists consider language the tool that you use to understand abstract concepts. Your ability to think in abstractions explains why you feel, see, and understand the world in a way that animals, without language, can't. Words that describe emotions—love, joy, or envy—are abstractions. Animals might experience sensations of love, but they don't have an abstract concept of love. Your ability to conceptualize love, according to psychological constructionist approaches, is a critical ingredient in how you perceive and experience love. Under that framework, any word you know that describes an emotion—anger, disgust, or fear—enables you to make meaning from sensations, whether those sensations arise from external or internal stimuli. The perception and experience of a specific emotion develop within a given context.

What does that mean, practically speaking? Have you ever experienced stage fright? If so, you might know the feeling of getting cold feet when you were preparing to get in front of a large audience. You may have said to yourself, "Don't be afraid. You'll be okay." But before you identified that you were afraid, you most likely sensed a vague but intense, generally negative, feeling. Vague, general, and unnamed feelings are called affects. They are conscious but do not have access to language. Like adult humans, infants and animals have core affects. When you acquire language, you learn to transform your vague sensations of either pleasure and displeasure into discrete and specific types of emotion through language. In childhood, you discovered that fear, for example, is different from anger. You distinguished the two with language.

When you develop a rich understanding of how language, emotions, and the brain work, you can learn to train your brain's response to feelings, thoughts, and events through language. You can let go of your attachments to words, especially if those words trigger unskillful action. Jaak Panskeep, an Estonian neuroscientist and psychobiologist, argues that seven core emotions drive the activity of the human brain. Sigmund Freud, the popular psychoanalyst, suggests that we often repress those core emotions, which leads to neuroses. But you can learn to honor and take care of—rather than repress or react to—your core emotions. Instead of getting caught in reactivity or repression, you can use positive language skillfully to support a healthier brain. Healthier thoughts, feelings, and actions arise from a healthy mind. A healthier mindset enables you to experience a deeper sense of beauty, fulfillment, and peace. It can also give way to a deeper sense of meaning and purpose.

Hearing My Calling

How do you realize the connections between language, emotion, and the brain? How do you cultivate a healthier mindset that skillfully responds to thoughts and feelings? The Neurocoach course I had enrolled in taught me exactly those things. When studying practical neuroscience, I learned brain-based strategies that helped me tap into my intuition, creativity, and wisdom. I learned how to shift between different states of mind, to cultivate a healthy mind and an optimally functioning brain. More importantly, I learned the practical skill of coaching, which has helped me guide clients through emotional distress and mental blocks and more readily achieve whatever they want from their lives.

I enrolled in this course because I wanted to study practical neuroscience. I did not expect to be a Neurocoach. But when engaging in practice sessions with colleagues and friends, they told me that I had a natural gift for motivating and inspiring people to achieve their goals. The idea of becoming motivational (or productivity) Neurocoach appealed to me tremendously.

In ways, I have been a motivational coach for over a decade. Coaching happens frequently in an educational setting. I discovered early on in my teaching career that the problem with learning for many of my students lay not in their lack of capacity but in their state of mind. As a teacher, I have developed a reputation for motivating and inspiring my students. Students come to my class and feel elevated when they leave the classroom. For some, all it takes is just an invitation to describe one of their proud moments in life and talk about what it is and how they do it. I believe the true value of education lies in its power to inspire and transform.

For me, several dimensions of coaching and teaching have always overlapped. I see coaching in my teaching and educating in my coaching. It might be easy to see how a teacher needs to coach her students. But it can be more difficult to see how a coach needs to educate her clients. Typically, people don't go to a coach to receive an education or to be taught by their coaches. But each of us can learn from others. Education comes in nearly every interaction. We can especially learn from others who work in different fields. A Chinese proverb says that a rock from a foreign shore might be as valuable as a jade.

Given the rapid changes happening in the world, no one can afford to throw away the rocks they gather from foreign shores. No one can afford to stop learning. If we go about our lives as we always have, tossing away new perspectives, we can't expect change to happen. If we don't know or can't identify the problem, we are hopeless to change it. And if we use the same understanding and the same behavior to deal with our problems, we'll always get the same result. Coaches encourage clients to see with new eyes, to approach problems from different angles using new techniques and strategies. Gaining the awareness of new perspectives and ideas is the first step toward positive change. You might call that inspiration. I think it is the same in the world of education. Great teachers inspire. Great coaches inspire. More importantly, both can transform lives.

By emphasizing the teaching role of a coach, I am not suggesting that a coach lecture her clients. As a university lecturer, I rarely lecture my students. I guide them. I collaborate with them in the construction of knowledge. The most effective teaching happens not when the teacher is lecturing solo but when both the teacher and student actively engage in the co-construction of knowledge. For that to happen, the teacher takes on a role as a facilitator facilitating the process of knowledge-building. In the constructivist theory of learning—which is one of the most influential theories in the field of education—the teacher is a facilitator where students create meaning from their own prior experience and knowledge. In the co-construction of knowledge between the teacher and students, the teacher makes the best use of their prior knowledge and experience. The teacher draws upon what the student already knows to build a new understanding and deepen the students' knowledge.

Neurocoaching applies the same principles. One of the most important things about Neurocoaching is that the coach never forces her own ideas on her clients. Instead, a coach guides her clients to tap into their own wisdom, creativity, and intuition to solve their problems themselves. Sometimes, a coach might offer her own insights, but she does so in a way that is relevant and makes sense to the clients. The way to make the best use of the time with a client is to tap into the deeper potential of that client's mind. It's the most effective and the most efficient.

The coach acts more as a facilitator. The beauty of acting as a facilitator—in both coaching and teaching—is that it can direct attention to previously unknown areas, areas that neither the coach nor the client, student, or teacher had expected. When new areas of exploration are uncovered, the most exciting pathways open up. For a teacher, charting into a new territory of learning might lead to exciting, if not ground-breaking, discoveries. For a coach, those discoveries might mean fresh insights or perspectives that lead a client to resolve difficult challenges.

Connecting the Dots

As I reflect back on my life, I can see profound reasons why the words "motivation" and "productivity" particularly appeal to me. Born into a culture where the game of comparison and competition started in kindergarten, I came to know all-too-well the importance of productivity and achieving results. Throughout my experience at school, I learned that as a student, my success would always be judged by academic scores and academic scores only.

Luckily, I was good at that game. I learned how to produce results in my early years of school, before senior high. I breezed right through all my subjects. Teachers adored me; my fellow students envied me. I had always been the good girl. I never let my parents worry about how I was doing at school. I finished my homework and read books in my spare time without anyone telling me to. I was a model student.

But when I transferred to senior high school, the unfamiliarity of a new school challenged my sense of self and my sense of belonging. A year before, I had been on cloud nine; in senior high school, everything soured into a sad shade of blue. I never adjusted completely to my new school. My self-confidence plummeted. My grades suffered. The only thing that gave me solace was that English still came effortlessly to me, and I was still getting good grades in the subject. But it was not enough to make me happy.

I was deeply depressed. The more depressed I felt, the more my grades suffered. But I was making an effort. Even now, I can remember a scene of me dozing off on my desk late at night because I had been studying for four hours straight. The me who had grown up as a bright, confident young girl knew that she had a strong mind. She would do everything within her power to succeed. Determination was something that was naturally wired in her brain. That girl knew that she would somehow rise again. She was just having a slip. It would only be a matter of time.

She did rise. She inspired me to go onto college and major in English. The choice seemed natural. Speaking English had been my only solace in senior high school. College suited me well. I no longer worried about grades and obsessed over test scores. I felt thrilled by the endless opportunities to read books, write essays, and carry on conversations in my beloved second language. With that new mindset and rediscovered passion, the top A student came back. I was confident and on top of the world again.

My love of English and my interest in bridging two cultures and two languages led me to study for a master's degree in simultaneous interpreting. Simultaneous interpreting is the job of interpreting what a speaker is saying at the same time that the speaker is speaking. I knew the career would come with its challenges, but I imagined all the fun I would have embracing them.

It turned out I was both right and wrong. I enjoyed the feeling of cocooning myself in a booth (a small size room equipped for interpretation) and focusing entirely on the task. When I put my headphones on, the world felt like it was disappearing around me. My worries washed away.

And I did have worries. A lot of them.

I was surrounded by top students who came from many different universities. The feeling of not being good enough and not doing enough haunted me. The game of comparison and competition came back into play, much more emphatically than ever before. I felt a lot of pressure to perform well in every class. I did not want to lose face in front of my classmates. More importantly, I did not want to lose any points on my academic scorecard. I felt the constant looming pressure to achieve results.

Thankfully, I did perform. I achieved high academic scores. With an excellent academic record, I landed a job as a university lecturer. I thought I would be happy being a teacher, teaching something that I love. But I was wrong. I worked at a research-intensive university. Once again, I began to feel the pressure to compete. I felt the pressure to produce not only academic scores but to write and publish papers. I realized that I needed to pursue a PhD at a well-known, world-class university in order to compete in my field. So, I got back into the game. I kicked off into yet another competition. I worked hard on my research. I sought whatever sources were available to read and build my expertise. I wrote research proposals and made revisions. I did that so many times that I lost count. I had to produce a research paper that would win me a position in a very competitive PhD program.

With some luck, I did it. I got into a PhD program at a British university, the one that was my first choice. It turned out that I was talented at doing research within particular approaches and paradigms. I developed a love for applied linguistics, for philosophy, and for anything abstract and highly conceptualized. I enjoyed arguing with the lecturers in my courses and listening to different voices contradict my ideas.

Looking back on the course of my academic life and my career, I have consistently found myself in environments that have pushed me to do my best. I have always been driven to succeed. I have always been obsessed with productivity, with getting things done. It turned out that I have been competitive at nearly any game I have been thrown into. And so, I began to think that my go-getter attitude might be a gift that I could offer others. I could help people overcome their mental blocks, achieve their goals, and get whatever they wanted from life. I wanted to make a difference. In coaching, I had found my calling.

My life experiences formed a picture, a puzzle that I had been putting together somehow with the pieces of my life. Everything connected beautifully.

Seeing How to Serve: Integrating the Power of Language and Brain-based Strategies

We live in a world that is undergoing rapid change. The model that worked in the past might not work today. Everyone needs to take on an attitude of life-long learning. Without self-development, there's little chance for advancement in either career or life. All of us need to learn constantly. We also need to produce results. Productivity is one key to surviving and thriving in today's world.

Unlike many motivational and productivity coaches, I employ my expertise in language and practical neuroscience. I use my talent for productivity to build my clients' resilience. From experience, there are three things I've learned that are critical to reaching whatever goal you wish. First, mindset matters. It can determine whether you succeed or fail. I failed in senior high not because I lacked the ability or the effort. I failed because I lacked the right mindset, just as I succeeded in my PhD because I had the right one. Second, doing what you love is essential for productivity. Accidents may have led me to pursue a career as a university teacher, but I'm now teaching something that I am passionate about. Third, clarity about why you are doing something is crucial for your success.

To help clients achieve their goals, I've developed a process that integrates adopting the right mindset, learning to do what you love, and achieving clarity on why you're doing it. I use a narrative approach that employs brain-based strategies. To understand my clients' unresolved issues, I listen attentively to their stories.

Why do I use the narrative approach? Narrative is the primary form by which we make our human experience meaningful. The stories we tell reflect the stories we inhabit. Listening to clients tell stories helps me see the ways those clients sabotage their own efforts to achieve their goals. Since telling stories is one way that we make meaning and express our sense of self, I use a narrative to elicit from my clients what they value most. Identifying their core values enables clients to examine whether their goals are in harmony with their highest purpose.

Lastly, I use brain-based strategies to help clients overcome emotional challenges, boost their energy, and tap into their intuition and creativity. For example, I guide my clients to deeply relax using mindfulness strategies. When clients feel deeply relaxed in body and mind, it's easier for them to tap into their intuition to help solve their own problem, which most of the time, is very effective and efficient. Since most of us don't like to do what other people tell us to do, it's more effective when we can find meaning for ourselves. I encourage that in my clients.

Unstoppable Happiness

A psychologist I knew once said that if you want to achieve whatever you want for your life, ask yourself the following questions:

Are you a self-initiator?

Are you a self-healer?

Are you a self-discipliner?

Are you a self-motivator?

I think the reason why I found a way out of the shadow of a failed marriage and finished my PhD is because I learned how to be a self-initiator, a self-healer, a self-discipliner, and a self-motivator. I took charge of my own narrative. I used narrative to heal myself and to initiate my goals. I motivated and disciplined myself to achieve results.

Now I'm proud and confident enough to say that nothing stops me from being happy and strong. I am a happy and strong mother to my son, a happy and strong teacher to my students, a happy and strong motivational coach to my clients, and a happy and strong author to myself and to my readers.

ANNA JIANG

Anna Jiang was born and grew up in China. She is a linguist and lecturer at Beijing Normal University. She holds a PhD in language education from UCL (University College London) Institute of Education. For more than a decade, Anna has been committed to teaching and researching education and language from a cross-disciplinary perspective. She is particularly interested in the ways that language plays a role in how we live and learn. After a traumatic life event forced Anna to reconsider her path, both spiritually and professionally, she moved onto a new stage of her career. She's now an educator and speaker, but more importantly, she's a productivity Neurocoach who uses her own experience along with the wisdom of neuroscience to help people overcome obstacles, achieve goals, and live a life in tune with their highest values. She advocates brain-based experiential learning in the educational field.

<u>Contact Details</u>

Facebook: <u>https://www.facebook.com/anna.jiang.180410</u>

Email: <u>annayqjiang@qq.com</u>

COACHING THE SKILLS THAT MATTER
AFTER THE BALL STOPS BOUNCING

David Radosevich and Deirdre Radosevich

Following Our Passion

"Follow your passion; it will lead you to your purpose."
Oprah Winfrey

C hasing your passion in life was easy as a child. It was a time in our lives when fear did not play a big role in guiding our thoughts and decisions. We would often get together with friends and play sports or simply hang out all day. These were people who made our lives so much fun. Playing kickball on the playground during recess or going to the park without a care in the world was a way of life. It was a simpler time, where we could go as far as our bikes would take us just as long as we were back home in time for dinner. In hindsight, following our passion as children seemed effortless. We knew little about fear or a grand purpose at this stage of life, but we certainly knew passion very well.

From grade school through college, athletics was a major part of our lives. We enjoyed the grit, drive, and competitiveness needed to succeed. There was always an internal game, pushing our minds and bodies to new levels. Although fear was a part of our thoughts at this stage, we were able to take a healthy perspective when self-doubt was present. Competing is what made us excited to get out of bed each morning, despite the tired and sore muscles. Ultimately, this early passion became a cornerstone in defining who we are today.

When it was time for us to pursue our professional goals, we often fell back on the lessons we learned as athletes. We are both first-generation college students, and when we started our college journey, we only had vague ideas of what it would take to become psychologists. Fortunately, we were clear about the profession we wanted to pursue, without having to constantly switch majors like many students. We were both passionate about learning how the human mind works and applying those skills to help others. Unfortunately, most of our ideas about psychology at that time were based on movies or television shows, since we did not personally know any psychologists in real life.

We have had great mentors over the years, who have helped diminish our fears and build our confidence to succeed in our chosen profession.

David has followed his passion by motivating people to achieve meaning in their lives and helping leaders in organizations have a clear understanding of the factors that contribute to their success as well as the blind spots that derail it.

Deirdre has followed her passion by extending her knowledge of theories and diagnoses, while building rapport and providing treatment to clients who have varied diagnoses.

Both of us have also honed our craft as professors, where we have a front-row view of the generation that is learning how to fly from their parents' nest, in order to make their mark on the world.

Our early passion was honed in sports, and although we did not know it at the time, sports taught us the critical life skills that matter after the ball stopped bouncing. More importantly, our passion was leading us on a journey to find our purpose.

Putting in the Effort

> *"Nothing will work unless you do."*
> **John Wooden**

One of the most important skills in life is putting in the effort to achieve your dreams. Wandering down a path that no one in our families had traversed before us required us to look fear in the face. Along the way, we had to become comfortable making mistakes, but more importantly, learning from them. Although it did not come naturally at first, life taught us that the correct spelling of *failure* is in fact *l-e-a-r-n-i-n-g*.

We both realized that we had to get comfortable with being uncomfortable in the pursuit of our professional dreams. After a long road of graduate classes, internships, post-docs, tenure, and licensure, we were in the new position of being the coach or teacher rather than the student.

We had paid our dues throughout our twenties by eating way too much Ramen noodles and spending late hours in the library in pursuit of our dream. It was thrilling to begin providing therapy and mentoring students who were fresh-faced and full of ideas and promise. However, the glow of being a newly minted PhD did not last long as a whole new level of effort would be required to successfully apply our craft.

This point was driven home by a business owner whose introductory statement, even before shaking hands, was, "I hope you're not one of those pinhead academics who doesn't know anything about the real world."

After all, beyond an initial competence check, our clients do not care much about our fancy diplomas. They simply want to know that they are in good hands and that we can help solve their pressing issues with an appropriate solution.

So, we set out on our new journey by putting in the effort to learn how to effectively transition from theory to practice in a way that adds value to the lives of our clients and students.

I (Deirdre) am trained as a cognitive behavior therapist, which means that I help clients understand the connection between faulty thought processes, unhealthy negative emotions, and unhelpful behaviors. Through my experiences in graduate school as well as training at both the Albert Ellis Institute and Northshore University Hospital, I gained experience helping children and adults overcome anxiety, develop coping skills for trauma, and learned how to implement new behaviors to help families function better. I enjoyed helping others find strength in areas of darkness. I moved from working with individuals and families to becoming the clinical director of a residential program for adolescents, who were experiencing more significant behavioral or mental health challenges.

My role was to ensure that the children were receiving evidence-based treatment, working with counties to form plans for life outside of our treatment center, as well as supervising clinical staff. Through this experience, I learned to become more comfortable in a leadership role and find my voice to campaign for client and staff needs.

In my (David) consulting role, I have worked with Development Dimensions International (DDI), a global leadership consulting firm focused on helping organizations hire, promote, and develop exceptional leaders. For over 50 years, DDI has worked with first-time managers to C-suite executives in guiding them to tackle leadership challenges. My specific role is to evaluate the potential of top executives for promotion or selection based on personality profiles, cognitive assessments, and behavior in an assessment center. I roleplay business scenarios to assess behaviors relative to defined leadership competencies, interpret personality patterns influencing behavior, and write feedback reports for the leaders' ongoing development, aimed at helping them make an impact in their organization.

My experiences at DDI have provided me access to the inner workings of some of the brightest minds in the business world. Having to evaluate all types of leaders, ranging from a starting sales manager with few direct reports up to CEOs who are guardians of multi-billion-dollar enterprises, is not a trivial endeavor.

It has taken years to develop the level of assessor insight required to provide a "report card" on their performance, relative to predefined leadership competencies. I have to base my judgments on science and observed behaviors, but there is also an art to providing leaders feedback critical to their growth.

How the message is positioned is often just as important as the message itself, especially if we want the leaders to follow through on the action plan to deliver effective outcomes back in their organizations. To continually train my assessor skills, DDI invests a lot of training time to ensure I understand the nuance and sophistication required to distinguish people who can lead the organization to future success from those who cannot. Needless to say, my business acumen grew exponentially and continues to grow after years of experience. It helps to be around highly intelligent colleagues with a voracious appetite to learn and get better each day in the pursuit of delivering high value to our clients.

In the classroom, we both have experience working as professors. Teaching is arguably one of the most important professions in the world. In fact, as we write this chapter, parents all over the globe are realizing the difficulty of teaching as they are required to homeschool their children in the face of the COVID-19 pandemic.

Just like us, our students are setting out on a path of learning how to help others as psychologists and coaches. However, as the years passed, we have noticed a growing and troubling trend in this digital world.

During our interaction with young adults, one trend we have observed is that while they are communicating a lot with each other on their smartphones, they are also more likely to be undermined by fear and continually struggle to effectively solve their problems. This pain point in the lives of so many young people stoked our curiosity, and we put our efforts into exploring it at a deeper level.

Understanding the Mindset Pandemic

> *"Fear is a darkroom where negatives develop."*
> **Usman B. Asif**

The current news headlines are focused on the COVID-19 pandemic that is taking its toll across the world. However, there is also another pandemic that is spreading among people – fear. Like a thief in the night, fear of failure (FOF), fear of people's opinions (FOPO), or fear of missing out (FOMO) steals people's ability to confidently lead a life of meaning and realize peak performance in their profession.

It is natural for some people to rise to the challenge when faced with doubt, while others shrink under the pressure. We have also noticed that some of our students were more likely to reach their goals than others. What is both scary and interesting, however, is the degree to which fear is contributing to their ineffectiveness beyond their academic abilities.

At times, even the most promising student would become crippled with fear, which diminishes their ability to step up when needed or effectively solve problems when faced with tough decisions. At an ever-increasing rate, students engage in counterproductive behaviors, such as procrastinating, social loafing, ghosting peers on team projects, or simply not stepping up with their best effort.

One day, we did an exercise in class where students had to look up their daily average screen time on their smartphones. Shockingly, the average amount of time was nearly six hours a day! Our first thought was that maybe they were using their smartphones to be productive with homework or job-related projects, but they indicated they primarily used it for social media apps. Combined with classes, jobs, internships, and sleeping, six hours a day on one's phone does not leave room for much else. Human interaction is mutating at an alarming rate, and one alarming side effect is the fear of not living up to others' "perfect" online presence.

When coaching our students, we often feel frustrated when we see some people have a head-in-the-phone approach to life where they simply hope that things will pass and magically get better. Given that we only spend a limited amount of time with them, addressing their concerns did not make us feel very confident that real change would occur. This led to personal frustration that we were not making the type of impact that was needed.

We were also startled that the same behavior was occurring outside of the classroom with many of our adult clients. In working therapeutically with clients, we notice a lot of variation in their level of engagement. Some people jump in wholeheartedly, ready to look at what has not been working and try something new. We love seeing the positive impact we have on many of our clients' lives, and this validates our professional worth.

On the other hand, some people have the "I've tried it before approach" regardless of their age. For these people, it does not matter if we focus on changing mindsets, challenging old beliefs, or trying a new path; they are not willing to try something new, despite their deep dissatisfaction with how things are currently working in their life.

As parents of two young children just starting out in the world, we are concerned about the land mines they will have to sidestep to have a joyful life. We started talking with our friends who had children in high school and college, and they shared stories of their own struggles including how to motivate their children, help them tackle tough issues, or improve how they interact with others in an emotionally intelligent way. One common theme that struck a chord was the poor experience their children were having in sports. Unlike the free-flowing playing style when we were young, the modern version of sports involves travel leagues with significant family budgeting, year-long training, and overworked coaches who simply do not have the time or expertise to teach the intangibles of sport – those soft skills that are so hard to learn.

Several stories inspired us to take a leap of faith and transform our coaching business. The first story came from a friend's personal experience. He described how his son was a talented athlete but got frustrated with his soccer team's experience. For example, there was an instance where a senior player did not like the instructions from the coach and started swearing and yelling back at the coach.

Most parents would have been mortified and had a heartfelt talk with their child, but this particular set of parents joined in the boisterous chorus of swearing at the coach. Another example, from the same team, was how the seniors would bully the younger, more talented athletes both physically and emotionally so that they would quit the team and not steal their playing time. This experience took the joy out of the game for this athlete, and he talked about quitting soccer entirely. It was heartbreaking for his parents to watch, and unfortunately, the coach did not offer any support or solve the situation. The fear that the senior bullies had of losing playing time led to a corrosive culture and a poor experience for most of the team.

Fortunately, this story has a happy ending. Our friends talked to their son about what happened, and on his own, he decided to go back and play his senior year so that he could be captain and make some positive changes to the culture. He helped ensure that seniors would no longer rule simply based on their grade level, but rather, everyone would be treated as equal teammates. He stepped up as a leader and helped play a transformational role in creating a team that everyone enjoyed. Other parents complimented him on the job he was doing, and his teammates voted for him to receive the prestigious leadership award. Later on, this athlete told his parents that he was glad that the bullying experience occurred because it served as a springboard to learn about himself and how to be a more capable leader. It taught him to compete with compassion.

This next story really stunned us on a professional level. We were invited to lead a workshop on building confidence for an elite team of female hockey players aged between 13–18. We went into the workshop thinking that these girls would be at peak physical and mental levels.

After all, we watched them go through their drills during the camp and they were impressive. Over one hundred girls were invited to this elite camp from several states. We were told that most would receive full scholarships to play at the collegiate level. We were excited to spend time with this rare bunch of athletes and play a small role in helping them elevate their game.

We started our workshop with great involvement and enthusiasm. Then, we started an activity that required them to write down, on Post-it notes, their biggest fears that were holding them back from being their best. We gave them time to think and the room got eerily quiet, but we saw pens moving in the silence. After a few minutes, we talked generally about their fears, so as not to put any individual on the spot.

Like the seasoned professionals we thought we were, we fielded all their questions with solid action steps to overcome their confidence issues. Some of the questions included: How do I make sure I am confident but not cocky? How do I know when to raise the bar on my goals? What do I do to get over a bad game more quickly? How can I build up my teammates' confidence? Will visualization help me perform better? Can you share examples of positive self-talk?

We were excited about the sophisticated and well-thought-out questions. We thought about how well-adjusted and motivated these kids were at this stage of life. We commented to one of the camp organizers, "Congratulations to them, their parents, teachers, and coaches. These girls are going to take the world by storm!" At the end of the workshop, we gave high-fives and everyone seemed excited about having a new mindset tool to help them elevate their game. Most of the girls left their Post-it notes detailing their fears for us to recycle, as they were off to the ice for more skating time. However, as we picked up the dozens of notes, it was as if someone just punched us in the gut. It was one of those moments that wakes you up out of your status quo slumber. We read several fears such as:

- I'll never be good enough.
- I'm fat and ugly.
- Nobody likes me.
- I will never be a winner.
- I hate myself.
- I'm not as smart as my friends.

We were confused. What happened to the confident, beaming, energetic children who were in front of us a minute ago? As psychologists, we understand that we all have self-doubts and negative thinking, but this was a transformative moment for us. We began to understand the silent mindset pandemic that is negatively impacting too many of our youth today. If this group of girls had these thoughts, what about those who are not on the fast track to a full college scholarship?

Was it the environment of coaches and parents constantly pushing them in ways that increased their fear level? Was it a sign of the times in this era of ever-present social media? Whatever factors are at the root cause of this complex issue, we knew we had to reinvent ourselves and reach this target age group in a way that we had not in the past.

These experiences transformed our thinking about how to make a more meaningful impact on the lives of high school and college students. We had a laser focus on our current occupations and using best practices as we were taught in graduate school. Despite that, there was still an underlying frustration and a tsunami of fear that was taking over our children and creating a pandemic of fear.

We spoke with two friends and set out to do something bold and different. Our vision was to positively impact the lives of student-athletes by teaching them that sports are about more than wins and losses, minutes played, and points scored. Their athletic experience is also about developing a growth mindset, learning how to be part of a team, and learning to interact with people in emotionally intelligent ways.

The million-dollar question was how we would do this without coming off as more boring adults telling this younger generation what to do. In the face of this challenge, we began to follow our passion with greater focus, and our purpose began to become clearer.

Overcoming Bad Advice from Good People

"When you teach your son, you teach your son's son."
The Talmud

One weekend at a local festival, we overheard a conversation between a father and his middle-school-aged son regarding football. The father said to his son, "If you want to keep playing football, you need to stop holding up people when you tackle them. You are bigger than half the kids out there. You need to start hurting people, breaking their bones and shit. If you want to play football for the rest of your life, you have to hurt people."

This is certainly not the best advice for a father to give his son and is quite cringe-worthy for fellow players. The poor kid is going to walk into practice armed with advice from his dad, telling him to hurt people rather than taking advice from his coach who, we are sure, supports safer methods of playing football.

We don't doubt that the father wants the best for his son, but this is not sound advice for a young athlete who wants to succeed in football. While this extreme example is hopefully an outlier, the common complaint we hear from coaches and teachers is that while parents seem to want what is best for their children, all too often, they may provide advice that is counterproductive to larger team goals.

Another obstacle is that most coaches have not received formal training on how to teach young people life skills. They likely continue to teach the same way they were taught when they were kids – assembling all those life lessons (at least those they remembered) from their parents, coaches, and teachers into a blueprint for how they mentor their current students and athletes.

In fact, we interviewed several teachers and coaches about their approach, and unfortunately, this "father knows best" approach to teaching skills was the most common approach. As an example, we often asked how athletic coaches prepare their captains for success.

The prevailing response was they simply told them to be a positive role model and go shake hands with the opposing team at the beginning of the game. This simplistic guidance was surely a missed opportunity for growth and development!

A similar theme we heard from coaches was a "suck it up buttercup" approach to handling adversity. While mental toughness is a key ingredient to success in sports and life, this message often misses the sophisticated nuance needed to first assess the degree of adversity the person was facing and their coping skills needed to effectively handle the challenge at hand. The sad reality is that those who do not learn from their mistakes in the past are doomed to repeat it. The fact that we were preparing a future generation to handle challenges the same "old school" way we were taught was painfully evident, especially knowing that there are more effective techniques that could be taught from psychology and business. We knew we had to take a different approach.

One highlight from our early conversations was that everyone we met agreed on the main problem. Their concerns were our concerns, and we felt like we needed to pivot to make a greater impact on the lives of youth as well as a professional transformation in our business. The struggle was in using our skills, which were effective with adults, but were not quite hitting the mark with the younger generation. We considered writing books, conducting seminars, or using train-the-trainer models for teachers and parents to pass on our best practices. However, these brainstorming ideas would lead to incremental improvement at best, but they would more likely result in simply maintaining the status quo. We had to transform our practice in a meaningful way but realized we needed help. After all, while we were frustrated with the "bad advice from good people" phenomenon, our "good advice from good people" approach was not necessarily yielding significantly better outcomes.

Partnering for Transformation

> "*It is not necessary to change. Survival is not mandatory.*"
> **W. Edwards Deming**

It was both humbling and exciting to contemplate the professional challenge facing us. On one hand, we would have to retool our approach after years of using our time-tested techniques. On the other hand, it was exciting to have a professional challenge that ignited our passion and brought our purpose to the forefront.

To help us with our transformation, we relied on partners who had expertise in areas that we did not. We formed a business with two friends.

Paul is an innovator, who not only brought the idea forward but also brought C-suite business acumen to the table, particularly the power to build strategic partnerships.

Brian is an accomplished software executive with a clear strategic vision on how to meet young adults on their terms. It also helps that he is a basketball coach and made his university's Hall of Fame for his athletic feats.

We both brought the psychological coaching pedigree to build content that was aligned with empirically-based evidence. During our conversations, it was interesting that all of us noted that we would not have dove into this business challenge by ourselves. This revelation alone was significant, as we were trained to be the solo coach and spent a career working as lone wolves in our practice. We realized that there was strength in numbers. We also knew that we would have to become vulnerable in constantly challenging each other so that our respective expertise would result in a coaching tool that had a meaningful impact.

A common mantra throughout the content creation process was, "Will a high schooler understand that scientific word?" Making our psychological jargon more age-appropriate was harder than we thought. Being hip and cool so that the younger generation would actually listen to us was even more difficult.

In the early stages, we were excited about creating our new product, although we did not know the exact deliverable. The constant shining light was that we were fortunate to be aligned on our purpose – to help children and young adults build the skills that matter both on and off the field. In that spirit, we founded a company called The 3rd Element (3E). Our premise was that we were all athletes back in the day and most of us have watched our own kids grow up in sports. But the scene is different today. Rather than playing pick-up games in the neighborhood, kids today have grown up playing in organized leagues and regularly work out with trainers. They start out younger and spend their time developing their skills, trying to get faster and stronger. Skills and performance are surely two elements to building a complete athlete. However, there is a third element that seems to have been lost.

The 3rd Element focuses on being coachable, accountable, and putting the team before yourself, the same skills you need to be successful in your career and in life.

We believe that sports provides a natural opportunity to coach kids to be leaders, help them to better interact with others, and give them an opportunity to develop their emotional intelligence. We believe kids should approach sports with a mentality for hard work and getting better every day – things they can control – and let go of stats, playing time, and wins as the only measure of success.

By doing this, kids will have a better experience, be less likely to quit early, and ultimately build skills that will last a lifetime.

So exactly how do we do that? We spent a long time struggling with how to best reach our target audience before we had our proverbial Aha! moment. We had to reach kids where they spent most of their time, which was on their phones. We clearly knew that smartphones were overused and that too much social media is a bad thing. That said, we thought that if we could create engaging content delivered by high school and college athletes themselves, we could coach valuable life skills. Our goal was to take our empirically validated concepts and let the younger generation speak the message.

We stretched ourselves by dreaming big. If we wanted to scale our impact, we had to leverage technology. Most people have heard the phrase, "There's an app for that." Well, in our case, there wasn't one, so we put our money where our mouths were and created an app that included our best tools – cognitive-behavioral therapy techniques, goal setting, personality assessments, and pulse checks, among other features. We had to be able to do a deep dive in a more easily digestible format. Not only did this process require a big financial investment, but we spent countless hours as a team raising the bar to be better coaches. The status quo was soon becoming smaller in our rearview mirror. We set out on a bold adventure and put ourselves in uncomfortable situations, like pivoting the business with venture capital, overcoming technological barriers with the app, and learning basic social media marketing strategies.

Each of these challenges seemed daunting at the time. After all, we were trained psychologists, not entrepreneurs.

We continually kept our eye on the purpose of our new venture as challenges to the viability of the business inevitably came up. We had to break free from old practices of being a therapist or coach in one-on-one sessions. Stretching ourselves to get into the partnering business was key.

As a result of our efforts, we partnered with local schools, business experts, sports organizations, and philanthropic individuals in our community in order to launch our new coaching solution in both school and sports teams. To impact a larger number of people, we had to scale and still maintain our standards. Step by step, we were able to learn new ways to apply our craft. At this point, professionally, we had evolved from who we were a year earlier.

Impacting Lives

"A life is not important except in the impact it has on other lives."
Jackie Robinson

With our hard work, financial sacrifice, and collaborative brainstorming resulting in a coaching product that was ready to go to market, we started to collect data of our impact. We found a local high school that was willing to let us conduct a controlled experiment that compared a control group with a treatment group over a three-month period. In discussions with the principal and teachers, we would have students take our life skills survey at the beginning and end of the pilot study. Only the treatment group would receive the 30 lessons we had created in the app. The plan was set, and now we simply had to launch it.

We arrived at the high school and were ready to meet the 200+ students who were going to be part of the study. We went into about six classrooms and our presentation of who we were and why we were there seemingly went well. There was one instance, however, that made us wonder if children this age were really ready for this type of coaching.

We were in the auditorium with the largest group of the day, and unfortunately, it was difficult reining in the class clowns and disinterested students. It was like we were the substitute teachers for the day, and they were going to run all over us. When we made it through the painful portion of the orientation, where we had to speak, the vibe in the room changed as they transitioned to using our app.

Silence set in, and the students were fully engaged.

We knew that our work was meeting them in their space, on their own terms. They couldn't care less about the countless sleepless nights we spent creating this app over the past year. The students only cared about what was in it for them, which, thankfully, was a series of engaging life lessons. We felt like the proud parents who watch their children eat delicious brownies, not knowing that vegetables, so finely chopped that they wouldn't be noticed, have been mixed in. At the end of the orientation, we even had one student, who broke away from the herd and shook our hands, thanking us for the opportunity to use the app.

At the conclusion of our impact study, we crunched the numbers and found several interesting results that demonstrated a clear positive impact.

Here's just a highlight comparing the control group from the treatment group:

1. Males reported a:
    - 22% increase in their belief that they have the ability to lead others.
    - 28% increase in confidence to overcome their fear of failure.
    - 23% increase in their likelihood to set goals.
2. Females reported a:
    - 47% increase in their belief that they have the ability to lead others.
    - 41% increase in confidence to overcome their fear of failure.
    - 18% increase in their belief that they can effectively resolve conflict.

We were ecstatic about the findings. It was clear that we were making an impact as a result of our coaching tool. We also heard several anecdotal stories that stood out in our minds. For example, there was a male high school senior who would barely talk to his family and often grunted one-word responses to their questions. He had earned an athletic scholarship to one of the best college teams in the country and had a singular focus on improving his skills. After completing our coaching program, his parents thanked us.

They said they don't know what we did, but he now talks to his sister and even volunteered to show his improved grades to his parents. He told us that he never really knew how to set goals properly and develop a growth mindset. Even if he only took those two messages away and forgot all the rest, that's a huge win in the eyes of his parents.

We also heard from other parents who were skeptical at first, but then shared how a life skills coaching program would be relevant and engaging for a high school kid. One father said, "My son didn't put school as his top priority, and we often had to nag him to the point of exhaustion simply to do his homework. However, your app nailed it with short and relevant lessons. He is now setting personal goals and taking an interest in learning."

It was refreshing to hear this positive feedback that our coaching program speaks to teenagers in a way they understand and will hopefully help them grow both on and off the field. Clients have expressed appreciation for our work with them in the past, but this particular project was sweeter, in that we were impacting a younger and bigger audience in a way that we had never imagined was possible.

Aligning Our Passion and Purpose

"My father gave me the greatest gift anyone could give another person; he believed in me."
Jim Valvano

As we reflect on our journey with 3E, our university teaching, and our coaching practice at Mindful Path Center, there are several key takeaway messages.

First is the importance of harnessing the power of our mindsets. As a human race, we spend so much time training our bodies, whether in the gym or with the latest diet fad. We also exert great effort in honing our craft, right from schooling to continually learning on the job. However, we have largely ignored the need to train our minds. This third element needs to be at the forefront of a balanced life. It was encouraging to see that many of the teenagers we work with had a desire to be transformed, even though they are just starting out in life – that is, they want to be better positioned to have an amazing life.

Another transformative reflection from our experience developing the coaching tool was that we are not the face of the program at all. We were used to being front and center in our coaching experience. However, in this instance, the founders of the 3E team are the hidden coaches, who let others be the face, using their voice to deliver our message.

This fact was unsettling at first. After all, doesn't experience and credibility matter anymore? Now, however, it is refreshing to be the hidden voice while others take the stage and connect in ways that are more meaningful to a much younger generation.

We also discussed the notion of impact. It is a difficult concept to quantify, given the wide range of issues people explore with us. We usually have a front-row seat to our clients' baby steps and little wins in their transformation journeys. However, with an app as a coaching tool, we are mostly removed from the personal vantage point.

Consequently, we have learned to appreciate the small ripples we are creating, which have the potential to pan out and have a lasting impact. If we are able to build the confidence of teenagers and help them see what is on the other side of their fear, perhaps that is the small ripple that will change the trajectory of their lives. Providing a blueprint for how to continually grow and overcome life's inevitable obstacles is a skill that every person needs.

Jimmy Valvano, a famous NCAA basketball coach, once said the greatest gift you can give someone is to believe in them. In our minds, our coaching tool is that gift. It is a key ingredient for the younger generation as they battle to overcome the pandemic of fear, in order to live a life where others not only believe in them, but where they believe in themselves.

Now, we are in our "new normal" after intentionally transforming our coaching practice to reach a new audience. We are glad that we stretched ourselves with our 3E partners to venture into a new world since it has helped us to become more capable as we connect with others, whether it is our university students, executive leaders from business, or clients at Mindful Path Center. The beauty of aligning our passion with our purpose is that not only do we help others to achieve what's possible in their lives, but we are also doing the same for ourselves.

DAVID RADOSEVICH AND DEIRDRE RADOSEVICH

David Radosevich

As a psychologist focused on high performance, Dr. David Radosevich is passionate about coaching people who want to be more than passive spectators in their lives. As an executive coach to C-suite leaders of Fortune 500 companies, David teaches business leaders to accelerate their impact. As a professor who teaches students how to excel in business, and as a performance coach who trains athletes to raise the bar on their mental game, David helps people perform to their very best.

Deirdre Radosevich

Dr. Deirdre Radosevich is a licensed clinical psychologist who helps people find more peace and motivation to reach goals. By using her training from the world renown Albert Ellis Institute, Deirdre has helped clients become more mindful of negative thinking traps that become obstacles to their happiness. As the founder of Mindful Path Center, Deirdre works to find answers to difficulties that arise in life through therapy, assessment, and coaching.

Contact Details

Website: www.mindfulpathcenter.com

LinkedIn: https://www.linkedin.com/in/davidradosevich

LinkedIn: https://www.linkedin.com/in/deirdreradosevich/

THE FLYING EAGLE FORMULA FOR PARENTING SUCCESS

Deborah Canja

In Africa's Himba tribe, when a Himba woman decides to have a child, she goes off and sits under a tree, alone, and she listens until she can hear the song of the child who wants to come to life. And after she's heard the song of this child, she comes back to the man who will be the child's father and teaches him the song. And when they make love to conceive the child, they sing the song of the child as a way of inviting the child to come.

I don't know about you, but that's not how my boys started.

And I'd like to say that their arrival was planned and I was prepared and I knew what I was doing, but that's not what happened either.

Don't get me wrong, I knew I wanted children. I just thought it would be, you know, at "the right time." I now know there's never "a right time to have children." Or maybe the time is always right because once my children arrived, they filled my life with love and delight.

And something else. Worry! Have you ever felt completely responsible for something or someone whose very life depends on you? I don't think I consciously thought of it that way at the time, but I felt *so incredibly responsible.* I wanted to do everything in my power to make sure they were safe and happy and that I gave them the best of whatever I could. In that, as with everything else in my life, I could hear my dad saying, "If you're going to do a job, do it right!" I tackled parenthood like everything else – all in.

But, here's the thing. As I was expecting my first child, my parents packed up and left. Really. They retired, sold the family home in Michigan, and moved to sunny Florida. My mom started a new career. So, when it came to day-to-day guidance, as a new parent, I was on my own.

And I was pretty clueless. I didn't grow up with aunts, uncles, and cousins around or any new babies. I didn't know the first thing about what to do. That didn't bother me, though. Research is my thing. I'm a lawyer. I researched parenting like it was the biggest case of my life. I read everything I could about child development. And while we didn't have the internet and Facebook to share information in those days, we had something else – magazines. They were displayed at the grocery store checkouts, just like they are today, but there were more of them at that time. Every month you could read articles like *"25 Ways to Teach Your Child to Think," "How to Raise Kids Right: Advice From 5 Experts," "Teaching Values: How Good Mothers Do It"* and *"How to Bring Out the Best in Your Child."*

I was a parenting junkie.

Because I'd read the research that shows that tiny kids are like supercomputers and that we learn more in the first six months of life than any other time, I did "bits of knowledge," which are a kind of a flashcard, with my sons. Using them grows the brain's synapses and connections and increases a child's capacity to learn. And they worked!

When the boys started elementary school, I began an after-school program for the entire school to give them fun experiences like dissecting frogs, learning different languages, and how to draw cartoons. I became the PTA president, a Cub Scout Den Mother, and a soccer mom. I made elaborate Halloween costumes and put notes in their lunch boxes. I hosted an "algebra math club" at our house when they were in 4th grade. They started college math classes in 7th grade. I sent them to summer camp and NASA Space Camp. I coached their Science Olympiad team. They had chores, they had jobs. I had us eat family dinners together. And on and on ….

As I look back on my parenting, I can see that I was doing all of those things to give my boys a great start in life. And they turned into fine young men. I did do a lot of things my boys will say they appreciate. But what I know now is that as great as all of those things were, they weren't the most important.

Sometimes, it's only when you look back and analyze things from a distance that suddenly things become so much clearer. I wish I had realized then what I know now.

I kept looking for wisdom when my boys were eight and 10, and even though I had long since graduated from high school, I found myself sitting at a desk in a high-school classroom with a bunch of other parents. Our eyes were glued to a video playing on a small TV, perched on one of those rolling carts they have in schools. I was there to participate in a program about drug abuse prevention called

"Parent-to-Parent."

I was there to soak up every scrap of wisdom on how to keep my boys safe from the unknown territory of middle school and high school.

In Parent-to-Parent, we learned a story about navigating unknown territory. Maritime legend says that in days of old, as mapmakers drew their maps to guide sailors across the seas, when they got to the edge of the world they knew and didn't know what lay beyond, they added a warning in the blank spaces: "Here be dragons."

I didn't want any dragons to get my kids—or any other kids I knew. I finished the class and was awarded a "Certificate of Dragon Slaying Proficiency." It says,

> "Be it known to all persons that the above-named person... is qualified to train others in the fine art of dragon slaying."

Since then, I've spent a lot of time training and coaching parents and teachers. And, along the way, I learned a thing or two about dragon slaying. There can be a lot of dragons lurking in the unknown future, but dragon slaying is all about confronting the unknown with a plan. The trick is finding a plan that actually works. And that reminds me of another story about maps.

In 1513, a man named Admiral Piri Reis created a map of the known world for the Sultan of the Ottoman Empire. Reis said he relied upon twenty other, older maps and that some may even have come from the Library of Alexandria, the fabled repository of the ancient world's knowledge. Only about a third of the map has survived, and that piece shows the coast of Brazil on the left and the coasts of

Europe and North Africa on the right. Scholars generally agree that those depictions are fairly accurate. But, there is a lot of controversy about what it shows at the bottom.

At the far south of the map, stretching across the bottom, is an expanse of coastline that some believe is a match for the pre-Ice Age northern coast of Antarctica. The only problem is that Antarctica was not "discovered" until 1818—more than 300 years after Piri Reis drew his map. If the map does show Antarctica's northern coast, it had to have been surveyed and charted sometime before 4,000 BC, which is the last time it was ice-free. And that would mean that ancient wisdom about the coast of Antarctica had been lost for centuries.

I tell that story because it reminds me that the wisdom of past generations—whether it is a map, a plan, or important knowledge— is sometimes "lost" as fads come and go, only to be found and then lost and found again.

So, when it comes to parenting, it turns out that the thing I wish I'd known, the most important piece I missed, is ancient wisdom. From time to time, it fades from sight, becomes popular for a while, and then fades again. Maybe one day it will become common knowledge, but for now, each generation has to learn it anew.

If you're like me—wanting to get it right and be a "good" parent— this is the wisdom you need to know. Or maybe you are haunted by the thought that we only have a short window of time to make a big impact on our kids.

A friend told me he almost panicked when he realized he'd only have 18 Christmases with his son before the boy left for college. Then he whittled that down to eight, reasoning that his son might only listen to him between the ages of five and 13. He's trying to make every one of those years count. I remember how that felt! Perhaps you are hoping to do all of the things your parents or teachers did well, but somehow avoid all of their mistakes. Or maybe you want to protect the children you love from drug abuse, bullying, gun violence, and sexual exploitation. Maybe you just want to give your children every advantage and do all you can to equip them with the skills they'll need to navigate an unknown world ahead: the job market, relationships, and a lifetime of fast-paced change.

For all of us, the big question is: How do you do that? These days my inbox is filled with advice: "*The One Phrase to Never Say to Your Toddler,*" "*5 Scientific Reasons Your Kids Are Annoying,*" "*7 things Boys Need to Hear from Their Fathers,*" and "*How to Raise Successful Kids.*" Some things never change, do they? From the grocery check-out to my inbox. But, here's the thing: if all that advice worked, we would all be following it, and our children would be perfect and infallible. It doesn't work that way, though, does it?

But there is something that does.

Now I'm on a mission to share what I know. I don't want others to spend years trying to do the right things only to find out later that they missed the most important ones. My greatest wish is that you will have the clarity that I didn't have in order to give your children the real lifetime of advantage. Our good intentions are not enough. We need to combine our good intentions with a specific, proven plan for getting there. And that's what I'm going to share with you.

Ancient Wisdom

Confucius is thought to have said, "Those who think they can and those who think they can't are both usually right."

And therein lies the heart of it:

> Who we believe we are, and who we decide to be,
> determine our life.

> Success comes to those who believe they are successful.

Have you ever heard the phrase, "the rich get richer"? Why do you think that is? Sure, they have a number of advantages. With money, they can buy more businesses and stock, and influencing legislation is certainly easier. But that's not the deciding factor. The fundamental reason that the rich get richer is because they think of themselves as rich. It isn't a goal—it is their identity. That identity, that belief, that very embodiment of richness—they don't just visualize it, they ARE it. They become it. And it draws more of it to them. It's as if they make a home for richness and richness comes home to them—and the experience of being rich repeats and repeats.

It works because the human mind is THE most powerful force for shaping lives, destinies, and the world. That's the message of books such as *The Law of Success* and *Think and Grow Rich*. As Napoleon Hill tells it, he was challenged by Andrew Carnegie, one of the richest men in the world, to interview the most successful men in America to learn the secret of their success. When he published *The Law of Success*, the law he revealed was this: "What the mind of man can conceive and believe, the mind of man can achieve." Hill wrote *The Law of Success* in 1928, but even earlier, James Allen wrote *As a Man Thinketh* and said that our minds are like a garden. Whether you cultivate your garden or neglect your garden, you will end up with something— either a beautiful harvest or weeds.

We don't want weeds—for ourselves or our children. That means we have to consciously cultivate a beautiful garden. The possibility of cultivating our minds or harnessing the power of our minds to grow as a beautiful garden isn't new, but it *is* gathering new attention. Today's athletes use it to perfect performance through visualization. Olympians practice visualization right along with the physical part of their sport. Every swing, every stride, every move is choreographed in their minds ahead of time, all the way through to the award ceremony. They "hear" the national anthem play and see themselves step up on the podium to accept their medals. Many sports psychologists and performance coaches now teach that success is ninety percent mental and only ten percent physical. The idea of visualization is the basis for vision boards, affirmations, and the sale of lottery tickets.

There are probably two schools of thought on how and why this works. One theory is that when we focus our mind on a goal, we naturally begin to prepare ourselves to reach that goal by doing things that will move us closer to it. We are also programming ourselves to look for the opportunities that will help us get there. A famous saying attributed to the Roman philosopher Seneca puts it this way: "Luck is when preparation meets opportunity." It simply means that we make our success by focusing on it and working at it.

The other school of thought says that everything in the world is made of vibrating energy. This energy is shaped into physical matter by our individual and collective thoughts. These thoughts vibrate at different frequencies and similar frequencies "find each other" in order to come into harmony. According to this theory, the deepest beliefs we hold about ourselves are thoughts that have electrical energy. They vibrate and attract the thoughts and actions of other people that are of the same frequency. Some people call it "The Law of Attraction". The *Bible* says, "You reap what you sow." Another way of putting it is your thoughts create the reality you live in.

While both of the theories about how and why this works have merit, the most important of these is the second. Visualization by itself isn't enough. But once you hold powerful core beliefs about who you are, they will attract situations to you that validate what you *already believe* about yourself. It is at this point that your focus on a goal, and your preparation will create a success of the opportunities that come to you. However, without powerful core beliefs, nothing will really turn out as it should, or as you hoped it would.

Every spiritual path teaches this truth in one way or another. In the *Bible*, Jesus is quoted as saying, "If ye have faith as a mustard seed, you can move mountains." That faith isn't about size or how much faith one has. It isn't about how great you are in stature or how blessed your table may be. It's really about a deep sense of knowing who and what you are. A mustard seed doesn't question what it is. It simply is and grows. If we know who we are, if we truly understand what beautiful beings we are, we can step into that same kind of knowledge and power.

And to take it one step further, it means that you are creating the future right now in the present. Whatever beliefs and feelings you hold right now about yourself, the future will bring you more of the same. The people might change, the situations might change, but the feelings you get will be the same. When you apply this understanding to parenting, coaching, teaching, or any endeavor in which you are raising or guiding kids, it changes everything.

Creating a Success Mindset

If, as Napoleon Hill and so many others have said, our thoughts create our reality, then the experience of success, the memory of success, and the emotion of success all change our way of thinking. Having experienced it once, our thoughts turn to the re-creation of success, to doing it again, to reexperiencing the thoughts and emotions that fill us when we succeed. You've heard the phrase "success begets success?" That's why. Our minds remember and know success and create more of it.

By helping children experience success, we help them create a mental pattern of success. We now know that our body and brain react equally to the visualization or mental imagining of a situation as they do to the actual event. That is why reliving a disaster or a bad experience over and over can have as powerful an effect as when it first happened. And that's why the opposite is also true. Reliving success brings more success. That is what is meant by bringing the past into the present and thereby creating the future.

In the book, *The Nature of Personal Reality*, the author says this: "What exists physically exists first in thought and feeling. There is no other rule... The world as you know it is a picture of your expectations." If that is so, we surely want to abandon our thoughts of bad experiences and instead relive and remember our thoughts of success.

That is why, when it comes to raising, teaching, guiding, or mentoring kids, our number one goal is to help them create the pattern of a **"success mindset."**

A success mindset is a specific set of core beliefs that you hold about yourself that are so powerful they attract financial, spiritual, social, emotional, and relationship success into your life. At the heart of it is the rock-solid belief that *"I can do it – I can succeed at whatever I put my mind to.*" It also includes these additional beliefs:

- *People like and respect me.*
- *I can be responsible for myself.*
- *Other people believe I can be responsible for myself.*
- *I bring happiness to others.*
- *My life matters and there is a purpose for my being here.*

These core beliefs are the greatest gift we can give to our kids (and to ourselves, for that matter).

Think about it … how many of us are carrying around the beliefs we picked up from somewhere that suggest we are not okay? How many times have we worried that someone doesn't like us or that maybe we don't have what it takes to follow our dreams? Ask yourself: who would you be if you never had those limiting beliefs? How would your life have been different?

By specifically nurturing a child's success mindset, we create better outcomes for them. We lay a solid foundation for their future success. In the process, we become the most effective parent, teacher, or mentor we can be.

A Dream Comes to Life

In 1956, when I was two years old, my parents bought property on a lake in Northern Michigan and opened it the next year as Camp Flying Eagle, a summer camp for boys. Neither of them had ever been to a summer camp, and they'd never even bought property before. In fact, they didn't even know exactly what they were doing or how they were going to do it. But they had a dream.

It was my dad's dream to create a success mindset within young boys because that was what made it possible for him to survive a really difficult childhood.

If you go back in time to 1932, the United States was in the middle of the Great Depression. In Michigan, times were tough, people were out of work, and food was scarce. My dad was 11 years old and living with his mom and younger sister. His father was gone; he'd left when Dad was only three. And then his mom left, too – to go back to Europe to take care of family business. She left my dad and his younger sister with older half-siblings, but weeks went by and then months ... and she never came back. I'm not exactly sure what happened next, but at some point, someone decided they couldn't support another child and they sent my dad to live at the YMCA.

I know it was a very difficult time because he never, ever talked about it. I realize now that not dwelling on difficult situations in the past was his way of moving forward. This is the reason why he never talked about his WWII experience, even though he landed on Omaha Beach during the D-Day invasion. We know dead bodies were everywhere with the troops still under attack. I think it's also the same reason he never wanted us to make a fuss over his birthday. When he was growing up, he didn't have a family to celebrate his birthday or to include him during holidays.

However, he did tell me one story that gave me a small glimpse into his life. When he lived at the YMCA he sold newspapers to earn a penny a paper so that he could buy a five cent candy bar. It was often his dinner. One day, he stood outside all day selling papers for 12 hours and only made three cents. He never forgot that. Life was tough.

But there was one thing the YMCA did have. It had a swimming pool and a competitive swim team. In high school, my dad became a swimmer and diver and started winning competitions.

It takes a certain inner strength and discipline to be on your own and to motivate yourself to put in the hours and hours of difficult practice to become a top diver. But he did it. His discipline and dedication won him an athletic scholarship to the University of Michigan, where he went on to become captain of the swim team and an All-American diver. And then he went on to become a teacher and a top education administrator for the State of Michigan.

And there's more to his success story, but the real question is, where did his inner strength come from? Plenty of people end up in sink or swim situations and too many of them don't make it. Sometimes I wondered how he was able to keep going. But now I know ...

It was his dream to share his knowledge about what a boy needs in order to have a successful life. He did that by creating Camp Flying Eagle and the unique program we now call "The Flying Eagle Formula" that was designed to embed a success mindset in its young campers. Over a period of 27 years, over 3,000 young boys went through the camp and experienced the Formula.

The brutal truth is that we don't really know if a parenting, teaching, or mentoring approach will work in the long run until we see if it has had the desired effect over time. That means not only in the short run, but also in 10, 20, 30, and even 40 years into the future. That's called longitudinal evidence. The Flying Eagle Formula has that longitudinal evidence – over 60 years of results to prove it works. It's what makes this approach unique and different from the clutter of the latest parenting and teaching fads and the endless (and often expensive) list of things all "good" parents and educators "must do."

As the campers grew into men, they went on to become great husbands and fathers as well as successful businessmen, community leaders, and teachers. And they said it was their Camp Flying Eagle experience that had been instrumental to their success.

With that in mind, the Flying Eagle Formula is designed to teach parents, teachers, and other adults how to send the right messages that build a success mindset. It does so with simple, practical things that anyone can do at any time. More important, it shows how to focus our efforts on *the one thing* that produces future success: what children believe about themselves. It's based on the premise that what we believe about ourselves, good or bad, attracts future experiences that validate that belief. It brings "law of attraction" principles to parenting and the "think and grow rich" mindset to children.

America's most successful people, from millionaires and billionaires to spiritual masters, have used this same approach to bring happiness, meaning, money, and fulfillment into their lives. The Formula provides an easy way to help a child break through to an extraordinary and fulfilling life.

The Flying Eagle Formula

I. Success starts with this

If you've read Napoleon Hill's books or seen the movie *The Secret*, you know they teach that a key factor in creating what you want in your life is to be specific. The more specific you are, the better. That's the first step to deliberately creating success, whether you are running a business or raising children. When you write down what your mind has conceived, it is especially powerful; you begin to believe, attraction begins, and achievement follows.

What result do you want? If you are a parent, have you taken the time to actually describe what you hope will be the result of your parenting twenty years from now? What are you trying to accomplish? What does it look like? Do you have a philosophy to guide your parenting or teaching? Have you ever tried to write it down?

It starts with a long-term goal, a vision of the future day when your child will graduate or leave school or home or move on to a new stage of life. What skills do they need to have? What personal character traits do you hope they embody? What do they need to know? And why? This is where you have to actually visualize what you WANT the future to look like for your child. This is the time to think about the kind of relationship you want to have with them when the future arrives. Will it be different from the relationship you had with your own father or mother? This is another way of saying we start with the end in mind. To start with the end in mind means to be able to describe what that end looks like with all of its important details.

Remember: Your goal is to embed a success mindset, an identity of being a successful person, into a young mind. To do that, you must start with a written plan, a description of the end result you wish to see. That is because, as Napoleon Hill found, the secret of success is a mental one – what the mind of man can conceive and believe, the mind of man can achieve. *YOU* must first conceive it and believe it.

II. "I can do it!"

The cornerstone of a success mindset is the rock-solid belief that "I can do it!" Where does that belief come from? Most often it comes from experiencing success and then forming the belief that "I am a successful person." Your job is to introduce your child to opportunities that lead to that belief.

To do that, you have to ask yourself, "What is my child good at? What are their strengths? What do they like to do?" This is not a time to pick activities or skills that you think your child "should" have. You need to find something that a child wants to do and at which they can be successful. Think creatively.

Keep in mind that your goal is for your child to really believe *and know* that they are a successful person. This is not something you can simply tell them. They have to experience it. It does not have anything to do with competition or being better or more talented than others.

Providing opportunities for achievement is only half the strategy. The impact of achievement is magnified when it is accompanied by recognition. And recognition is always more special when it is accompanied by some sort of ceremony. You only have to look at the many public award ceremonies for adults that dominate the news to know that awards given during a ceremony have an impact, signify a special success, and are remembered.

Think about it. What are three different likes or strengths your child has? For each one, come up with a creative way for her to experience success using that strength and then how you might recognize and celebrate the accomplishment. For example, if your son loves to tell jokes, give him the opportunity to write a joke book with at least three jokes and earn 10 cents for each word (my dad used to pay me a nickel per word). If he completes it, celebrate his success by proudly sharing it with family and friends. Or, if your daughter loves to draw, ask if she'd like to design a family greeting card.

Get thoughtful, get creative, and always remember that you want your child to come to *know*, through successful experiences, that he can tackle something new and succeed at it.

III. "There is a purpose for my being here"

The confidence that comes from believing, really knowing that you have a purpose for being here and that your presence makes a positive difference in the world creates a solid foundation that can withstand the most difficult storms of life. It is especially satisfying when you can see the difference you've made and know that your contribution mattered. It reinforces, in a memorable and meaningful way, that *you* matter.

One of the best ways to embed that feeling in our children is by helping them become part of a group of people working together to accomplish a common goal.

The memory of having a purpose and place, the feeling of belonging that comes with being part of a team effort, and the feeling of self-worth realized when others value our contribution are powerful motivators of adults and powerful teachers of children. By providing that experience, we help young children create a mental and emotional picture of being needed, of having something important to share, of feeling valued, and of succeeding. That picture will draw more of the same to itself and create a future like the past they remember.

The lonely ones are those who see no function in the world for them to fill, no place where they are needed. Loneliness is a killer, the silent enemy. It can lead to depression, escape into alcohol and drugs, and suicide. "Lonely-proof" your child. Recognize the importance of teamwork and contribution and commit to finding opportunities for your child to experience them.

Is there a project at your house or at your school or in your community that needs to be done? Is there something that needs to be fixed? Can you take the time to include the children you love in the effort? Even everyday tasks like doing the laundry can turn into "team" events.

Remember that your goal is to embed a feeling and belief of belonging. You want your child to know that her contribution matters. You want them to know that they can make a difference. The little time and effort you take now will reap future rewards far beyond what you can imagine.

IV. "I can be responsible for myself"

Channeling the high energy of children into achieving, growing, and maturing team players is a lot easier when done within a structure and with a routine. The structure is "an ordered way of doing something" and routine is the repetition of that order.

When you come right down to it, structure and routine help build self-esteem. Think about how frustrating it is when you can't figure out what it is you need to do to please your boss, your teacher, your parents, your friend, or your spouse. What are the expectations and rules, you wonder. Not knowing creates stress and anxiety. On the other hand, when we know what is coming next, we can adjust our behavior to fit in. When we fit in, we feel we belong. When we feel we belong, we feel better about ourselves and about others. The need to belong is so powerful that it changes behavior. Who among us hasn't changed our behavior in an effort to better fit into a group?

This is especially true for children. Young children are eager to learn "the rules" and to play by them because it gives them a sense of mastery and confidence that they understand how the world works.

Structure and routine provide the common rulebooks for them to follow. When used as a part of a strategy for building future success, having structure and routine frees a child's energy to focus on future planning. And when mental energy is focused on future success, it creates that success.

Remember: You are teaching your child who they are; you are training their mind to think a certain way about themselves. Your goal is to instill a sense of confidence and mastery through structure in order to foster a feeling of being in control and competence because they "know the routine" and can "work with it." You want them to come to believe that they are a person who can learn what is expected and can do it successfully. You are seeking to help give them opportunities to learn, to anticipate, and plan.

Through the use of structure and routine, your goal is to give:

- ➤ A sense of belonging, confidence and mastery;
- ➤ A belief that they are a person who can learn what is expected and who believes that they are responsible for doing it and can do it;
- ➤ Opportunities to anticipate and plan;
- ➤ More mental energy to focus on learning;
- ➤ Opportunities to learn how to use "free time" constructively; and
- ➤ An environment where success is much more likely.

V. "People like me"

When we look back on our lives, has not our opinion of ourselves been shaped by the adults in them, especially when we were children? How many of us still struggle to overcome the belief that we are somehow not OKAY? Where did that come from?

An adult who believes in a child can unleash a powerful force of self-worth. Like a seed, it takes root; once a seed of self-worth is planted, the tree will grow, with branches of confidence, satisfaction, and success. Every day can present endless new opportunities to plant a seed of self-worth in a child.

The easiest way is with the words you use. Not words like "you are so wonderful," but words that recognize something important in a child. "You have real artistic ability." "You have a unique way of looking at problems and finding a solution."

Beyond the words we say, another powerful way to plant seeds of self-worth is to show confidence in children to respect their views and opinions—in other words, to validate the essence of who they are, what they think, and what they feel.

Sharing experiences from the world at large with children, discussing them, and valuing a child's input is another important way to show that you respect them and that their presence and opinion are important. Anyone can do this, at any time.

Honoring a child's choice over personal matters is another important way to sow seeds of self-worth by giving them opportunities to choose how to govern their lives. When you let a person choose something for themselves, you are telling them that they, as an individual, are responsible for themselves and that you have faith in their judgment. Your goal is to give your child daily messages that you believe in their competence, and in their ability to be responsible for their life. You want to embed a belief in his mind that they *are* competent and able to take on responsibility.

VI. "I belong"

Structure and routine lead to traditions, and it is the traditions that ground us. Tradition is something you and others "always" do or it is the way you "always" do it. Traditions create a sense of belonging, of being a part of something special, and of something shared. Never underestimate the importance of the memory of belonging to something special.

Reflect for a moment on your own life and ask yourself whether and how the presence or absence of a deep feeling of belonging and security has shaped your life, your relationships, and your ability to reach your full potential. You can help the children around you create a future of success by creating an experience of tradition and a deep feeling of belonging and security.

Starting a tradition is easy. It doesn't have to cost money. Just look at what you "always" do, or will likely do again, and try to inject a little specialness, a little silliness, or a little ceremony. A little bit of fun, a little bit of wonder and the desire to do it again make enriching traditions. A special song sung every time you leave on a trip or come back home, playing a favorite game only when it rains, watching a movie together every Sunday, or camping out in the living room once a month are all easy ways to create the magic that helps create success.

One way to create a tradition is to take a trip to the same place every year. Another way is with a specific song. "Special night" traditions such as movie night, or pizza night, or a game night are all easy to start.

Once they start, traditions can be hard to break, whether you like them or not. The key to changing them is to recognize the important role they play in creating a sense of continuity, of belonging, and of being part of something with history. These are all powerful desires that we meet with traditions, and if you want to change one, keep in mind that you need to replace it with another.

And always keep in mind your goal—to create a deep feeling and belief of belonging and security through traditions.

VII. "I can figure this out"

One thing we can be sure of: the successful among us are creative problem-solvers. Can that be learned? Yes, it can, and in a fun, enjoyable, and easy way.

The ability to solve problems creatively depends on a mind that is free to consider alternatives, to think of options, and to "think outside the box." We now know that when the mind encounters and processes new information, it expands. New neural connections form as new information is absorbed.

The human brain has the ability to take in and store vast amounts of information. If we were aware of all of it, all of the time, we would have difficulty focusing. Instead, every day we tell our own minds what to pay attention to and what to ignore. Our mind then brings to our attention more of what we've said to pay attention to and ignores the rest. But creative problem-solving calls for an ability to consider what we might have been ignoring. By deliberately encountering new and different experiences and opinions, we send a message to our subconscious mind that it is okay to be open to new information.

Childhood presents us with a window of opportunity to grow the brain's capacity to be open to and process new information. It is that openness that will enable our children to seize new opportunities when they appear. Your goal is to send a message to your child's subconscious mind that it is okay to think about, learn about, and consider new information. You can do this by visiting new places or even new restaurants with unfamiliar foods. Or watch different news channels and discuss the different viewpoints. When your goal is to give your child the ability to creatively solve problems, a trip to a museum takes on a whole new meaning.

VIII. "I bring happiness to others"

If our goal is to help kids experience success, a good dose of fun can help. Whether you are at home, in a classroom, or on the job, adding fun into the mix will improve results.

What makes something fun? Sometimes it's hard to remember just how much fun we had as kids or how to create that kind of fun. But, over the years, I've learned a few guidelines.

> ➢ It helps to do something different from the usual routine every once in a while. For example, if bedtime is always at 8, on movie nights, it could be at 9.
> ➢ Anticipation builds excitement – A regularly scheduled special day or night of the week with a surprise activity can go a long way toward encouraging good behavior and fostering joy. Even looking forward to spending a dollar at a dollar store can build excitement.
> ➢ Singing silly songs is always fun.
> ➢ Resist the impulse to criticize. As adults, even though we have good intentions, we often let criticism take the place of encouragement and instruction. When criticism is withheld, effort encouraged, and achievement celebrated, the joy of

trying something new can blossom.

➤ Resist the impulse to "prank" kids. No prank or practical joke should ever embarrass, undermine, or make fun of a child. Think carefully about the message your child may absorb. It will repeat throughout life.

IX. "I am loved"

All children need to feel loved and cared for. It is validation that "people like me" and "I'm okay." No matter what role we play, we all have opportunities to share love and caring with the children around us. One of the best ways is to make your child a priority by scheduling a regular time to spend together each week, doing something he or she chooses and enjoys. Watching the same movie for the 16th time is not always easy, but it will be an investment with a powerful payoff!

X. The Most Important Lesson

The summer after my mom turned 83, she sat down to write the story of the camp and of the Formula. All through those summer days, she sat at her desk overlooking the lake in Northern Michigan where the summer camp once stood and pecked away at her computer – day after day for nearly three months. At the end of summer, she returned home to Florida where everyday activities interrupted the flow of the book writing. But when the next summer arrived, she came back to the lake and kept pecking away at the computer.

And as we began to truly understand why the Flying Eagle Formula was so successful, her desire to write a book of lessons learned became a mission to share what we knew could work for all kids.

In our book, ***Swim the Lake Before You Row the Boat: Awaken a Boy's Success Mindset, Unleash His Confidence and Give Him the Foundation for a Great Life,*** we share the specific ways we applied the Formula to create extraordinary success for the young boys who were our campers. But because the formula is based on ancient wisdom and universal principles, it also applies to girls and we have been thrilled to know that parents, grandparents, teachers, and mentors of both boys *and* girls are finding guidance from it.

We also share some surprising insights, such as:

- Your time with a child, no matter how brief, can have a lasting positive effect that leads to success—as long as you use the right interventions;
- Why rules can lead to failure; and
- *What* you do is not as important as *why* you are doing it.

And the most important lesson? It's what Mom wrote at the end of the book:

"We all, in some way, wish we were better than we are, don't we? We want the same for our children. But neither Alex nor I was or is perfect, and I have learned this lesson: you don't have to be perfect to make a profound and positive difference in the life of a child. You can make mistakes. You can judge yourself harshly and believe that others are just as harsh in their judgment of you. Even so, as imperfect as you may be, you can still be the one who changes another's life for the better.

The most important ingredients are not that you be perfect, or that you get it "right," or do it the way we did, or that you have a supportive partner, or a perfect one or even one at all. What does matter is that you give the young people in your life experiences that will build long-lasting memories of success; that you let them make decisions and give them opportunities to be responsible; that you reward their accomplishments with your recognition; and perhaps most important, when they make mistakes, as we all do, that you not be as hard on them as you are on yourself. Take time to listen to them, respect their opinions and let them make their own choices about personal matters. Encourage new experiences, have fun with them and show your love and caring.

Perfection is not a requirement."

References

Allen, James Allen. As a Man Thinketh. Barnes & Noble, 1992.

Canja, Deborah, and Tess Canja. Swim the Lake Before You Row the Boat: Awaken a Boy's Success Mindset, Unleash His Confidence and Give Him the Foundation for a Great Life. Okemos:Spencer White Publishing, 2019.

Hill, Napoleon. The Law of Success. Wise:The Napoleon Hill Foundation, 2013.

Hill, Napoleon. Think and Grow Rich. Wise:The Napoleon Hill Foundation, 2012.

Oliver, Bill. Parent-to-Parent Drug Prevention Workshop. PRIDE: National Parents

Resource Institute for Drug Education, 1990.

Roberts, Jane. The Nature of Personal Reality: A Seth Book. New York:Prentice-Hall, 1974.

DEBORAH CANJA

Wouldn't it be nice to have a parenting roadmap based on a tried and true formula that works for all kids? One that gives you the peace of mind that comes from knowing you have given them the inner strength to withstand life's most difficult social and emotional challenges? One that puts them on a path to achieving their dreams to be, do and have all they desire? Now you can.

The real secret to successful parenting lies not in what we do, but in understanding that the thoughts our children are thinking today about themselves will attract tomorrow's people and situations that validate what a child *already believes*. The good news is that we can easily help children form beliefs that attract future happiness and success.

For more than two decades, Deb Canja has made it her mission to help parents find the information they need to help the kids they love. Canja is the founder of Bridges4Kids, a comprehensive website of information and resources to help kids from birth through college. She is also the founder and CEO of Success4Kids, which helps adults foster the beliefs that create "success mindsets" in children. Her new book, *Swim the Lake Before You Row the Boat* shows how, with only a few minutes a day or month, a caring adult can help children form the beliefs that attract future happiness and success. Visit http://www.spencerwhitepublishing.com for free resources.

Contact Details

Website: https://spencerwhitepublishing.com/deb-canja

E-mail: deb@bridges4kids.org

Facebook: https://www.facebook.com/deb.canja.9

LinkedIn: https://www.linkedin.com/in/deborah-canja-443b1014/

CO-CREATING MY REALITY: A JOURNEY FROM TOXIC RELATIONSHIPS TO TRUE LOVE

Ekaterina Koretskaia

My new story began ten years ago,
when I discovered that my belief
of never being enough, was not mine at all.
I remember how this pattern jumped out at me
from a book, ironically given to me
by my husband on a rainy day.
He was my jail guard,
yet, the one who inspired me
to escape a prison of inadequacy.
It was the best gift ever,
besides the birth of our son –
a starting point for all my discoveries
in a magic country of my long-encumbered self
that could not wait to be free again.

That is the funny or ironic part of my story: the person who made
me suffer so much also helped me to start healing. This was not

because the sufferings our relationship caused made me realize X or Y, but he literally put in my hands a book that revealed a repetitive pattern to me. And it was repeating in all of the areas of my life: family relationships, including the one with my son, work, and friends.

Escaping without Confronting

It began with a "best friend" when I was eight years old. She was always depreciating and manipulating me, but we had a very strong bond and I was very much afraid of staying alone, so I could escape from this friendship only when I was 16 years old. It was a great achievement by itself. Of course, I did not investigate the reason that made me begin this friendship and stay in it for so long. Thus, this experience made me learn something crucial about friendships (I haven't had any manipulative friends since), but it didn't eradicate the underlying pattern, obviously.

Then, it was about my boss at work who was never satisfied and screamed at me at every slight mistake, while I was a beginner in the job. One year was necessary to find another place and to quit the toxic collaboration, to escape the suffocating space. My next boss was adorable and very encouraging, so I said to myself "you are progressing, girl." This was definitely true, I didn't dig deeper to understand why I tolerated the abusive behavior though, even "just" for one year.

And finally, when my self-assured future husband appeared in the picture and conquered me, I was very far from imagining that this man will push me to work on the stuff I neglected with the previous two chapters in my life!

Awakening

Going back to the book given to me by my husband, I discovered among the basic schemes of the Transactional analysis the "I am not ok/You are ok" pattern. It felt like a clap of thunder in a calm sky. Ok, ok, the sky was not that calm, but I was basically blaming my husband for being the unique source of my sufferings. I was not seeing that I was co-creating my current reality! I was actually the one who jailed myself in false beliefs. This was a starting point of all the other discoveries about myself and my story, which led me from highly toxic relationships (and actually being a sort of magnet for those) to true love, from a state of playing victim to taking responsibility for my happiness.

Can you guess the title of this new story's first chapter? Well, nothing original: DIVORCE. I am one of those people who is convinced that things NEVER happen by chance or accident. I believe that they happen for a REASON that we may not understand at first. And of course, I can see now how new doors opened and healing opportunities appeared ahead of me once I had taken the only right decision (though very difficult, painful, and scary) to leave a toxic marriage. The first support I received was the possibility to learn how to express my emotions through the turmoils of family court & co. This was life-changing.

Starting to Heal

I have often been sick throughout my marriage—chronic colds, streptococcus (several times a year, with the need for different antibiotics to heal, because I stopped responding to some basic ones), back pain, and sleeping problems. Nothing serious, but very energy-draining, and still with some real risks to have serious side effects as well. I was only twenty-nine years old, and my son was two. Seen the energy of a two-year old boy? Yeah, and I had none to give him. Nor was I able to put clear boundaries during the period of the "no" at every question, which goes from approximately two to four years old.

I am not a person who complains, and I have a tendency to handle my stuff all by myself usually (I had to learn to ask for help by the way, but this is another story), but this time I opened up to a friend and colleague of mine who was very satisfied with her doctor. At that time, this doctor was not taking any new patients since his practice was full. But, he was friends with my colleague, and at her request, accepted to see me. I was a little bit intimidated when I first landed in his beautiful office in the middle of the classiest neighborhood in Geneva. He was pretty well-known in the country because of a historical figure among his ancestors. But that was not the only reason. This doctor had made a name for himself and was a renowned health practitioner. He was also a published author.

Our conversation went like this:

"What do you expect from me?" The intonation was provocative.

"Umm... well.. you know... I have these chronic pains and am often sick, and my friend told me that you were very good at that."

"Ah, interesting! So, you think I will be able to fix it for you?"

"Well, yes, I think you can help me at least..."

"Do you know that you are the one responsible for your health? It is a prerequisite to work with me."

You see that life was definitely pushing me in the same direction: taking responsibility for my life. I accepted the terms, and he began to ask me very astonishing questions for a doctor: what is going on in your life right now? Ah, you are in the middle of a divorce? Tell me about it. What didn't work in your marriage? How did your spouse behave? And how were you reacting to this behavior? Why is that, do you think? What do you feel now? What do you do with these emotions? How long has it been since you cried?

I was answering on autopilot and then after a few sessions on identifying my emotions, I gave myself permission to not judge them. Once I accepted them fully and learned how to express them, everything started to fall in place.

There was, of course, sadness. The sadness for the end of a dream to live my whole life with my husband and the father of my child. The sadness for my little boy who deserved to have a full family. And there was the anger, obviously. The anger, because of a feeling of unfairness that this was happening to me. The anger toward my husband who refused to continue the couple therapy. So much anger...

I rediscovered that when we are sad, we need to cry to feel relief (nature conceived us wisely and our ability to cry exists for a reason!) and cry until our sadness is gone, not just crying in tears sometimes here and there in stressful moments. We need to really acknowledge the sadness, honor it, and feel it fully. I had to let my past go out of my body through tears of relief. And this was, as I also discovered, the ultimate act of self-love one can give themselves.

For the anger, it was more difficult. I knew how to cry, but express anger for yourself, not screaming at someone? This was totally new for me. And liberating. I signed up for a weekend retreat in a chalet lost in a forest to learn the tools. There was only one, actually. The same as before: acknowledge the emotion, feel it fully (replacing myself in my imagination in a given context, with the relevant person in front of me, saying something that made me crazy), and express it by yelling it out of my body in the middle of the forest, with a help of a stick tapping on a dry tree with all my life-force (especially effective when you were exposed to violence, either psychological or physical and could never respond).

Sounds crazy? Yeah, I confirm that at the beginning I was feeling like a freak, but after having integrated this practice in my life, I never had streptococcus again. The frequency of my colds also reduced by half. All the high parts of the respiratory system such as the nose/the sinuses, and the throat happen to be the first organs to be negatively impacted when we repress our anger. And honestly, nature gave us the ability to cry to relieve sadness and pain, isn't it logical that there must be a similar way to be relieved from anger? Don't you agree?

The magical thing about it was that it provoked a chain reaction—one expressed emotion unblocking the next one. And then joy became possible. The emotion we would like to feel more often than the other two is actually blocked as long as the other two are.

And the beauty of the process was that not only was the chain reaction acting on my whole emotional spectrum, but it had effects on my whole relational spectrum as well! It meant that all my relationships started to improve dramatically. Of course, it did not happen overnight. Still, I could feel and see the progress I was making through each and every interaction. I was learning to live in a completely different world, a world where I had more choices and where I was the center of my life and no event or other person could take that place anymore! I was in a world where I didn't repress my emotions like before. I wasn't a pressure cooker ready to explode if the lid was not opened properly, I had the freedom to let my emotions be and feel relief.

My behavior and response to my ex changed drastically. Earlier when he would stop by to pick up our son for the weekend and say something nasty, I could literally "kill" my cushion, hitting it on the bed. After my emotional spectrum widened, I began to stay calm and grounded in front of him. Through time, he gave up provoking me because it didn't work at all and he was the one feeling ridiculous when screaming at me, while I was calm and unshakable. And can you imagine the shift it opened up for every difficult conversation I could have at work, with family, or anyone, when I knew I had this way out, whatever happened?

After the divorce, my career at the bank started taking off, very naturally, without me doing something special about it. As I look back at this part of the chain reaction, I understand now that my self-love grew tremendously throughout that period—each accepted and expressed emotion giving me a big hug of encouragement and compassion toward myself. And with self-love came the confidence that everybody was witnessing at the office. I also started new activities that I was always postponing before but that I knew would bring me a lot of joy: theater classes, painting, and yoga. The excuse of not having time or being a single mom dissolved itself in front of a brand-new offering for the employees of the bank of all these courses at lunch break—another gift from life that I received during this challenging time of transition.

I remember the pride I felt for what I was accomplishing when, after a presentation of a tricky file to a Top manager, the latter came to see my direct manager and told her that he didn't recognize me. And how fun it was when I saw him one day at the coffee machine, he talked to me quite differently, while I totally switched from my previous status of being a child in front of a parent (Top manager), which resulted in an adult–adult conversation!

Last but not least, the most important and life-changing transformation at that time occurred in my role as a mother. I was able to help my four-year old son process his own emotions. I could see that he felt a lot of anger and sadness and that it was too overwhelming for him to manage. My "emotional doctor" explained to me that for kids, it was even easier to learn how to express their emotions because they were far more connected to their bodies and feelings than us.

So, with his instructions, next time when I saw anger rising in the eyes of my boy, I asked him if he was angry at mom and dad not being together anymore. At first, he was puzzled, but then timidly nodded. I told him that he had the right to be angry and that he could throw the anger in the trash can to feel better. I told him to scream out as strongly as he could and to let out the ball he was filling in his belly inside the trash can. The walls trembled (poor neighbors)! Then, we went to the toilets, virtually emptied the trash can in the toilet bowl, and I made him press the flush button. The following days, I tried to repeat the exercise when I saw my son's cheeks become red because of rising anger. It was not as effective as the first time, but still, we were progressing. Two weeks later, his eczema had totally disappeared. That was the prognosis of the doctor, but I didn't believe him, or at least I was not expecting the results to be so quick.

And, for the first time in my life, I was able to put clear boundaries to my child without being short-tempered. With the help of a child psychologist, I rediscovered the simple pleasure of drinking my coffee and reading a magazine on Sunday morning without being interrupted for five minutes, then ten, then fifteen, and so on. I was able to have some time for myself again.

New Try

The relationships with men took longer to evolve; the pattern of not deserving the right partner for me was very pervasive for some years. Giving up was not an option though since I discovered the self-help area, I knew that there must be tools for this issue as well and that I will come across them someday. All the men I met at that time were missing something for the relationships to last, until the day when the encounter made me feel "this is him." It happened under the summer sun of Greece, the magic of the surroundings massively contributing to this feeling of meeting my destiny. We were on vacation with our respective children and we "clicked" immediately.

We saw each other in Geneva after coming back and quickly started to date. Our relationship developed very fast (too fast as I was about to learn later), but I wanted to believe in love again and didn't pay attention to the little alerts that my intuition was sending me from time to time. Passion has this effect on our ability to see things; we are hypnotized and, as I understood later, our hormones concretely impede us to see the situation clearly. That's why all the relationship specialists give the advice of not making life-changing decisions when people are at this stage of romance, when the partner appears to be perfect.

We made the decision to live together one year after our encounter in Greece and decided to celebrate this first year in the same place, returning to the dance floor where our eyes met for the first time. It was during a perfect evening on the beach under the stars when I heard a warning of my intuition that I repressed immediately.

On such a romantic occasion, with our common apartment that was waiting for us after the trip, he seemed unsure of something. He broke the moment with strange words: "I cannot understand why you chose me, you are a much better person for a relationship than I am." My intuition told me that these words sounded very awkward and that I must clarify what he really meant. Instead, I reassured him telling him how awesome he was, convincing myself that modesty was another of his qualities. This could not be farther from reality! Now, I know that he told me his truth that night, foreseeing his inability to build a long-term relationship. What a lesson to pay attention to my intuition!

The core of our relationship could be summarized by the two poems that I wrote after our break up, being in a process of grieving and finding a beautiful tool to help me in that process: poetry therapy.

He didn't want a family

He was cheerful to be by my side
when romance was alive,
for travels of the world,
when friends stopped by.
But, what happened when I needed to talk?
Where was he when my son was sad?
A family is not a party every day—
he had to realize that he didn't want one.

Accepting my vulnerability

I thought I was strong,
not paying attention to his rudeness,
when he screamed insanely at me
for a spilled glass of water on his new table.
My God, I was such a punching ball,
relieving him of his unexpressed anger
against somebody I had never met.
It's crazy how we all fall back into old patterns
as long as they are not identified.
He was in my life
to make me accept my vulnerability
and to establish clear boundaries.
Life goes on since, without him,
and I thank him immensely for this lesson.

This was a hard one. I was brought up in a culture of performance, and the Superwoman syndrome is something very common in my country of origin. Not only does it impact our behavior at work where Superwomen rarely ask for help, but it sets the highest standards to demonstrate strength in private life as well. And then you put some false beliefs on top of it, like "only weak people show their vulnerability" and here you are in a love relationship, pretending that it doesn't hurt when your partner shouts at you.

When I suddenly realized that I could not stand it anymore and that my feelings were dying, I worked on accepting the sensitive and vulnerable part of me and on putting sound boundaries. I also understood that my partner was actually mirroring my relationship to myself and that I was once more co-creating my current reality. Very soon after that, my boundaries were not accepted nor respected with a clear "no way, that's how I am" and I felt in my bones that I had to move on because the lessons I had to learn were now fully absorbed and true love was to find elsewhere. Easier said than done. I started this relationship with so much hope and pride in my growth after the divorce! And here I was, hurt and not accepted again, with my son, who was hoping to have a new family.

The most difficult thing was to forgive myself for having exposed my son to this situation twice. He was 12 years old and we could have conversations about this for hours. He could not figure out why we broke up because I tried to protect him from our fights as much as I could by never starting to argue when he was around. This was the period I discovered EFT (Emotional Freedom Technique), which helped me a lot with this feeling of guilt and forgiveness of myself. I can also see now, from my son's comments on relationships, that I modeled something for him during that period, even though he was too small and could not understand when we broke up with his father: the fact that leaving an unhappy relationship was an act of self-love. It is something to be proud of.

Magnet for True love

After processing my grief (I cried an ocean!), I wondered if I could really trust myself for choosing the right partner. One day, I came across a video of a coach on YouTube who proposed techniques to attract true love and I signed up for an interview. My gut told me that this was what I needed, the tools I looked for so many years.

Of course, I had already heard a lot about visualizations, positive affirmations, and the law of attraction, being drawn to all self-help techniques. But this time, someone explained to me how to visualize and what was the right mindset to do it effectively. I also clarified what I wanted in a love relationship and discovered the importance of writing it down. Did you know that research has proven that people who write down their goals are 42% more likely to achieve them? What an easy, free, and powerful tool for everybody to use!

And then, it came to the Superwoman syndrome which in this area was all about: I am the only one who can make it happen, I have to take action, to show up, to go out, to meet new people, etc. I discovered that True Love was a miracle of the Higher Power/the Universe/the Divine and that we humans were not the ones who could make it happen alone—it is a co-creation with the Universe. Our role is to dissolve all the barriers in the way of this miracle and to be clear about what we want to manifest in our lives in this area. A Higher Power will take care of the rest, which makes you relax immediately and trust the process without obsessing about it.

As soon as we practice a certain degree of detachment and a feeling to be already complete without a partner, our energy shifts and we become a magnet for a partner who also feels complete without us. This means that we can build a healthy relationship together based on equanimity. If we are visualizing from a place of lack, suffering, and loneliness, what we attract is logically a relationship of lack, suffering, and loneliness. I started to do more and more things I loved, reconnected with my dream to be an author, and was feeling joy even from interactions with people on the street because what we cultivate grows in our life. It's that simple! I visualized my future relationship from a place where I was joyful and felt proud of myself, and life gave me more and more reasons to feel proud and joyful, which of course maximized my chances to meet someone with the same energy.

I also learned to be grateful for what I already had. Gratitude is a very powerful emotion that attracts even more reasons to feel it. I started a journal of gratitude by simply noting daily what I was grateful for in my life. My challenge was to find at least ten things per day. Seems a lot? Yeah, at the beginning it was difficult to find even five! But with practice, I started to notice more and more of the things that worked in my life, instead of focusing on the ones that didn't (which is how our mind tends to function, unfortunately—concentrating on the positive is not natural, but it is something we all need to learn). From my comfortable bed and delicious breakfast to gorgeous views from my office and apartment—all the things I took for granted before!

And there was also the part about intuition, life tested me several times on that, actually. The first test happened during a vacation on a very romantic beach. Remember the sun of Greece? ;-). The guy had even done the same studies at college as my ex! The stars, the ocean, live music—the atmosphere was all the same. The next day, when he invited me to lunch together, and he said something about the choice of the table, which I would not have noticed before, but it felt odd to me and this time I listened. It was all about choosing what was great for him, the question about what I preferred was not on the menu. When I expressed my preference nevertheless, he seemed not to pay attention and just explained why his choice was obviously the right one. What a small incident! But the feeling in my gut told me that there was something here to investigate. I continued my observations, and it seemed too early to draw conclusions, but the following developments only confirmed my feeling.

Another episode was funny. I was having lunch with a nice guy, and we had a lot of interests in common, including the same type of studies and lifestyle. All the criteria "matched", and I was becoming somewhat more pragmatic, thinking that maybe I was too blinded by my romantic side :-). When the waiter arrived with the salad, I became aware that I forgot to tell him about my intolerance of vinegar. I could smell there was a ton of it on my salad. The waiter had already gone back to the kitchen, and I told my lunch companion about my food intolerance. The guy looked at me and said, "oh, what a pity! Can I have it then?" Well, all the "matched" criteria vanished in the air at these words, simultaneously with his trial to reach my knee under the table at this second date.

Criteria can help, but nothing replaces the gut feeling! I was very sensitive to this topic of food because my ex actually always blamed me for being so difficult at restaurants with my special needs. I had even become almost ashamed of those and felt like I was a burden for people going to dinners with me or cooking for me. After the breakup, I have looked at this characteristic of mine with fresh eyes and realized that there was nothing to be ashamed of—it was a matter of genes and it was not my fault at all. It made my life more complicated and with fewer choices compared to people who could eat everything. What I expected from my partner was an understanding and supporting behavior. And I promised myself that next time I will stay connected to this wish.

Imagine what I felt in a similar situation when the man I was lunching with sometime after this episode didn't wait for the server, got up, and went to change my plate. It seems like a detail, but it meant a world to me—a sign that he would accept me just the way I was and care about me. I didn't fall in love with him right away, but it was a sign for me that I could relax and be myself, and the following dates only confirmed that.

A very powerful exercise has also been writing about fears and finding antidotes to them. So, I would, for example, write "I am anxious about the man leaving in front of a problem with my son because it is too difficult, not even trying to figure out the situation, not even trying to find a solution." And then I formulated the antidote: "I am confident that my partner will always be supportive, share his experience and try to find a solution, whatever issue arises in the education of my son." And I tried to gather as much proof of that being possible as I could (it is important to remember that our mind can only attract situations that it believes are possible).

I would notice a story of a colleague when something like this happened, and I would enquire about how these issues were handled during a conversation with a friend who was happy with her new partner and who was a stepfather to her children, etc. And, of course, I would visualize what it would feel like having this type of partner—meaning, not only imagining the behavior of the man but actually feeling what emotions it would create in my heart.

We've been together for two years and when I look back, I would never have believed five years ago that a man could be so unconditionally supportive, generous, loving, and encouraging. These men were simply not part of my world!

The Calling

After my divorce, I often felt like a failure in the area of relationships because I didn't manage to succeed in building a happy and lasting marriage. And the fact that all the classmates of my son at school were living with both parents (yes, even when divorce hits every second marriage in Western Europe!) made me feel like an ashamed outsider, not fitting in at all at the school gatherings. This is how I can describe my feelings at that time:

Playing both roles of mother and father
is a challenge I have to face.
The guilt of not being able
to offer a complete family to my son
follows me everywhere –
a black shadow, smothering me
from school parties to sports competitions.
I exhaust myself trying to breathe.

Several years later, some of my friends, who I thought were quite happy in their marriages, started to face similar challenges and made the decisions to separate from their spouses. When they opened up about the type of conflicts and atmosphere that prevailed in their relationships, I was understanding and supporting, having in mind all the emotional stages I went through myself several years before and becoming aware that we all more or less go through the same ones in this type of situation.

By that time, I had already gathered a lot of precious information about healing, emotion processing, support of children doing the same and figuring out how to attract the right partner, and felt ready to share it. In fact, sharing my learnings with my close circle gave an empowering meaning to all my struggles as I was witnessing how much value my support and guidance had brought to my friends. I was happy to help them save time and recover faster than I did, searching for the tools alone.

Some time has passed and one day I was offered a very prestigious top management position at work, my career in the banking industry having taken off after all the deep work I did on myself, as mentioned before. And while I was very honored to have the trust of my managers and accepting with enthusiasm all previous managing positions and new challenges, this time something was different. I did not feel any excitement. But why? I knew a lot of people who would kill to have that job!

While I was meditating on this existential question, the answer came quite fast from a TED talk I watched "by accident." A guy was sharing his experience on how someone had once changed his life telling him: "You don't need a career, my friend, you need a calling!" I felt warm energy in my plexus at these words, and all of a sudden it was clear that it applied to me as well! The coach who worked with me on the process of attracting true love anticipated that it would lead me to reconsider all other choices in my life, including my job. This was another chain reaction due to the fact that her work was aimed at lifting the inner barriers to love, and to self-love in the first place.

And, of course, the more you love yourself, the more you connect to your deepest desires and yearnings in all areas of your life. And the more meaningful you want this life to be. I got curious about all these questions and took the MBTI test, which is one of the top internationally recognized tests to assess your strengths and areas of competence to direct you toward the best job possible for you. The results were surprising only to me, and all my close circle reacted as if they already knew it. Well, coaching, teaching, and designing programs to help others were my top three areas. And I was already doing it naturally to some extent in my day-to-day interactions with others.

I must confess that I had once dreamed of conceiving one comprehensive program regrouping all the techniques I learned through my journey, but it was like a sweet dream I would never believe possible to reach. Suddenly, it became more and more tangible and life was inviting me on this path.

One discovery led to another. Sometime after meeting my partner and taking the MBTI test, I came across spiritual coaching for women called Feminine Power, created by a coach whose mission was to empower women to realize their highest potentials. I signed up for what I thought was a seven-week course for awakening women. However, at the end of the course, I felt clearly that I could not stop at this point. All the signs were pointing in the same direction, the one of my calling, so I signed up to become a certified coach and facilitator.

And then, everything started to fall in place. I could practically see all my learnings and other discoveries beautifully integrated into a comprehensive coaching structure like pieces of a puzzle clicking together, to give the highest value possible to women who were facing the same challenges as the ones I had faced.

This was how I came to conceive a program specifically aimed at helping mothers going or having gone through a divorce, as well as their children, to process their emotions and to rebuild a new life, with additional optional modules to attract true love.

My dearest wish is that these women find the support and tools they need to go through this often traumatizing experience, only to become stronger and more aware of their awesomeness, which will be a great foundation for their new brilliant life.

I start my guidance with a focus on emotions because I came to the conclusion, during my own journey and having witnessed and accompanied the journeys of others, that this was really the most urgent need to address through a divorce. Emotions are usually overwhelming during this challenging time, and even after, and impede women to gain clarity on the next steps, while they have to make many important decisions and changes in their lives. First, the women learn how to recognize, feel in their body, and express their sadness and anger which are the main ones, to make the third one possible—joy, of course. The latter happens to be completely blocked if the two others are, they really all function together, as already mentioned before. If you are connected to yourself and express your emotions without judging them, all the spectrum can manifest. You block one of them, and the other two are imprisoned.

I remember when I was feeling angry all the time in the first stages of my divorce, I couldn't even be in the present moment when playing with my son. My thoughts about the unfairness of the situation were obsessing me, and I felt foggy and didn't know how to escape from this feeling. It took me some time to accept my emotions without beating myself up for feeling them and not being present enough for my child. Acceptance was only the first step though, and I still had a lot on my plate. Nearly everything was irritating me in addition to my divorce—from someone who was not polite in the street to colleagues who were talking all the time while I was trying to concentrate on my work.

I was very surprised to discover that there was actually a positive thing about this constant irritability: I could practically start from any of the frustrating situations to express anger, and it would naturally lead me to the core issue. For example, I would be angry at a close relative who judged me instead of supporting me through this challenging time. So, I isolated myself in my room, connected with the anger (immediately after the close relative left, which is always easier, since the emotion is still "in the air"), felt it in my belly and crushed it on the cushion speaking out loud the words I wanted to place in our conversation, but didn't. I realized that the things I said applied to my ex as well, since he judged me all the time without supporting me. I was working simultaneously on both situations! The relief I experienced was very new to me, after several years of living in a constant disappointment and frustration of an unhappy marriage. This experience made me more capable of guiding women in similar situations to express their anger, starting from the situations where it feels easier for them to connect to this emotion.

However, it often happens that we have been disconnected from ourselves for so long that it is not so easy to feel something concrete in our body and even harder to express it. In this case, I propose to start by doing EFT (Emotional Freedom Technique), which is an acupressure technique or "acupuncture without needles", where we tap on points on the body while speaking out loud specific scripts, to build new neural pathways and make us connect to our feelings. EFT processes part of the issue and can sometimes clear it fully. It helps to understand where we feel stuck or to reconnect to the emotions in our body, while fully accepting where we are. In both cases, it makes it easier to express anger and sadness as we fully acknowledge our stuckness, forgive ourselves for it, and allow our deepest emotions to surface without pressure. I guide women in adapting the scripts to their specific situation and that's what makes it even more powerful because as they catch it, they are able to go deeper and deeper with each round of tapping. Then, they are able to come back to the first technique and express anger or sadness in a very relieving way. Sometimes, they feel that EFT only is enough, it depends on the stage of their grief and their sensitivity. That's why it is more effective to use several techniques and "play" with them depending on the needs and issues of every woman and situation. There is also another technique of symbolically getting the emotion out of our body, giving it a color and imagining it being a ball in our belly that we pull out.

These techniques are accompanied with meditation and journaling practices that are also helping to connect to ourselves, to lighten our mind, and even to come up with ideas or solutions, or to gain clarity on the next steps. Sometimes, it also brings back a repressed emotion and helps to get rid of it right away. They can be done separately or in combination, which make them even more effective. For example, writing in a journal can be done after doing a specific type of meditation called "body scan." Thus, all the feelings and sensations that surfaced during the meditation can be laid down in the journal, which is an additional step in gaining more awareness and accepting our emotions.

The next step and urgent need is about reviving self-love. Self-love is a foundation that helps to navigate any situation in life and build healthy relationships; it's a foundation for happiness itself, actually. When you love yourself, you have compassion for yourself when you go through difficult times, and you attract people who love themselves as well, as you are with the same type of energy. This is what allows relationships based on respect to emerge. During my own journey and stories of my friends, I realized that women tend to judge and blame themselves, analyzing divorce as a failure, meaning "I did not succeed in my marriage." Well, first of all, we were not alone in this and the responsibilities were shared with our partner. Secondly, our personal story led us to it, for us to learn something, which is true of every challenge life puts on our path. Divorce is a life-changing experience, and it is our personal choice to take change positively and with curiosity or negatively, with a hopeless mindset. Curiosity and a positive mindset can begin to appear once the emotional baggage is cleared, and every woman has her own rhythm for that. It is often the most moving and magic part for me as a coach, as in this moment I feel that I contribute to something so valuable: the woman starts to feel emotional relief and is gaining perspective about the situation and the possibility to learn something about herself and relationships.

Self-love is revived by identifying and neutralizing self-judgment and negative self-talk and by adopting emotional hygiene as a sustainable practice. It is about creating or restoring a qualitative relationship with ourselves to become our own Best Friend. There is a very powerful set of exercises in the Feminine Power coaching to do so. As a coach, I guide women to identify an already powerful place within themselves, to connect with it, and to begin getting curious from that place. Then, I guide them to feel all the empathy they usually direct to others and to turn it toward themselves instead. From this resourceful place, I make them connect to the younger part of themselves that feels "I am not enough" or "I don't matter" or "I am not lovable". They give that part an age, and then witness and name the feelings and needs of their younger self. Finally, they unite their resourceful and wise adult self with this younger self, as if they were hugging their inner child who didn't receive all the support and love she needed at that time. From there, I midwife the building of a new power statement that overwrites the old belief and results in a powerful transformation.

Then, feeling better themselves, the women begin to feel more at peace and energized to be able to extend some of these practices to their children, depending on their age, and they even love them "better" from a place of self-love and reconnected to their own power.

There is a golden rule that applies here: children cannot feel good if their parents feel bad. So, caring about themselves usually automatically helps their kids. And children have this enormous advantage over adults: they don't live in their minds as much as we do, and they are much more connected to their bodies and emotions. So, especially with the little ones, the expression of anger, which is often very vivid throughout a divorce, can take a symbolic form of screaming in a trash can, like I did with my son. More grown-ups can find it fun to do EFT, with an adapted language, of course. And we can also tap on the acupressure points of our children (even babies), or make them tap with us.

After the most urgent emotional needs are taken care of, this is the moment I suggest women open up to new possibilities aligned with their (re)acknowledged awesomeness. What were their childhood dreams? What were they postponing these years, waiting for their children to grow up? They now have more time for themselves when the children are with their father, so, how could they use it wisely? I invite them through a Feminine Power practice to reconnect with their deepest yearnings and see if there is an area of their lives that they would like to ignite. Some of them feel ready to work on the relationship area, yearn to meet new people, and maybe meet a new partner. Others prefer to concentrate on their career, spirituality, or creativity. Sometimes they want all at once and in such cases, we determine together which area is most "in season" at this moment of their lives and could give traction for the other ones. For example, in the case of a woman who hesitates between the area of love and the one of her career, I make her connect to both areas and feel where the greater energy lies. I make her identify the gap between her yearnings and reality. If she senses that the area of her work is the one she feels greater enthusiasm to embrace, she starts to think about the next level at work or her true calling and what are the skills that she needs to develop to embrace it. Doing so, she is naturally more connected to her soul and the ripple effect of it could be that she will more easily attract her soulmate without even working on it specifically.

I also invite women to connect with a Higher Power/the Universe/the Divine (whatever they call it), as well as to their intuition, to receive the guidance that will lead them to their new lives. We also address the question of new boundaries that will help the new lives to manifest and take space.

For those women who feel ready to meet a new partner, we embark on a journey to discover what the barriers to love around their hearts are and how to change the old stories about relationships. We dive in the ways they learned to behave to adapt to their social environment and culture growing up, as well as parts of them that were stored in their subconscious as non-effective. They have the choice to become fully who they are and accept all of them.

Partners only mirror what our relationship with ourselves is and as I said before, empowering the latter will empower the relationships with the opposite sex. In addition to the visualization technique, I work on developing ten specific behaviors to cultivate and make the miracle of true love enter the lives of my clients, not forgetting to rely on a Higher Power as well.

From an insecure mother being in a toxic relationship to a confident woman who loves her life, my journey has made me understand a lot in life. I could better connect to myself and my emotions, as well as build a better relationship with myself and accept all the parts of me, including my vulnerability. After the divorce, my relationships with my son, family, and at work shifted drastically, opening the way to a new life, where I felt a lot more aligned with who I was, my values, and my yearnings. This has finally allowed me to meet my new partner and attract plenty of other healthy relationships, as well as to dream big. I deeply wish to help mothers facing divorce to do the same and to ease their journey through this complicated time. I simply can't keep my learnings for myself, and it brings me so much joy and fulfillment to share them!

EKATERINA KORETSKAIA

Ekaterina was attracted by the self-help area throughout her personal experience of going through a divorce, being a single mom, building a new life, and trying to believe in love again. She refused to be a victim of the circumstances and decided to take responsibility for her relationships and happiness, which led her to approach her divorce like a catalyst for change that happened for a reason. Her investigative nature made her search for effective tools to go through all these challenges for several years, to process her emotions, the emotions of her son, and understand how she was co-creating her reality of being a sort of a magnet for toxic relationships. The discoveries she made have generated a massive transformation in all areas of her life—in her role as a mother, in her relationships with family, friends, men, and even at work. She learned how to put sound boundaries, process her emotions as an ultimate act of self-love, coach her son to do the same, and attract healthy relationships.

Her willingness to help other women to do the same and never give up on themselves, finding self-love and true love, made her become a coach in the area of relationships, after a career of 15 years as a manager-coach in the corporate world. Ekaterina is offering tools of releasing emotions to mothers going or having gone through a divorce, helping them support their children to process their emotions as well, and build a brilliant new life. She uses the Feminine Power principles[1], as well as tools like EFT and others that she discovered through her own journey, with concrete and effective guidance of implementing them in daily life.

Ekaterina is a happy mother of a teenager, is in a beautiful relationship with her new partner, and beyond writing enjoys reading, drawing, hiking, and traveling.

Contact Details

Website: https://ekaterinakoretskaia.com/

---

[1] Created by Dr. Claire Zammit.

FREESTYLE-YOUR-LIFE – THE CUTTING EDGE OF TRANSFORMING YOUR LIFE

Erneste Carla Zimmermann

I magine yourself being very ill and your kids and parents mourning at your funeral! It sounds unbelievable, right? This was exactly what I went through facing death at the age of 48. Unfortunately, this situation also kept my sons from having an untroubled youth.

Status Quo

Let me share a part of my journey where I transformed my life. For nearly three decades after reaching the age of 30, I faced multiple diseases. Due to Sick-Sinus-Syndrome (extremely low heart frequency), I got my first pacemaker in 2003. After 10 years, the battery ran out, and a new pacemaker was implanted in 2013. In addition to my heart deficiency, I was diagnosed with uterus and breast cancer. I also had lymph nodes and tumor cells in the gums, which had to be removed through several surgeries. I was prescribed painkillers in the highest possible doses to stabilize a thyroid dysfunction and to cope with the pain due to Fibromyalgia as well as two disc prolapses. This then led to problems in my stomach and gut. Finally, my body reached a critical level of toxicity. I had developed a wide spectrum of imbalances and intolerances. My body collapsed and refused any intake of nutrition. For more than a year, fresh smoothies made with greens from my garden were the only nutrition it accepted. From my studies on how I could possibly heal myself, I already knew about the health benefits of secondary plant substances. They are a key element to detox, prevent cancer, and improve overall health.

Today, I understand that my wise 'Inner Healer' helped my body cope and detox. By only accepting those smoothies, it flushed out the copious amounts of drugs in my system. You are probably not familiar with the term 'Inner Healer.' This results from a higher spiritual practice. Good health is our normal state. When stress levels go up, things get worse because the system is not aligned and falls out of balance. The body itself in the form of the 'Inner Healer' resolves many problems, and we then don't realize them. We are happy to feel better and go on with life as usual!

But going on as before is tricky. This is when things really got worse for me, and more symptoms started showing up. When I was down to 47 kilos at the height of 180 cms (almost 6 feet) I got space food that normally supports astronauts during their missions to outer space to ensure that I do not fall apart. I had tried countless healing approaches of different faculties such as Chinese medicine, alternative medicine, homeopathy, as well as functional medicine, but nothing really seemed to help.

As a divorced single mom of two sons, running a full-service real estate agency, and also being occupied with the start-up of my coaching company, I was constantly maxing out my limits. At that time, I was working long hours, almost 24/7. Being a multi-tasking genius helped me to deal with up to seven things at once. But, I was still not able to check off enough tasks from my to-do list and therefore tried to work even more.

On top of that, I am a highly sensitive empath gifted with being able to feel other people's emotions. All of this activity and pressure, as well as being a people pleaser, led me to be permanently exhausted without being able to give my brain and body a rest. After a point, I even hated being such an empath because I could not even distinguish which feelings were my own. Well, I knew that whatever we resist strengthens, as energy flows where attention goes. Despite that, it was hard to cut off my daily tasks. I was running my own business while building up a new one. My life was overwhelming.

Game Over

I felt like a marionette, run only by the sympathetic nervous system in fight-or-flight survival mode. At that point, I was unable to slow down. This led to needing more drugs in the form of sleeping pills, which were not effective. I finally ended in a burnout state, increasing the overall inflammation in my whole system. Neither I nor the doctors had a clue on what to do next. My body was no longer capable of running these 'marathons' on an ongoing basis, and at the same time, dealing with all the toxins. Wake-up calls in the form of the mentioned diseases and several accidents, such as a fall where I broke my right wrist seven times, finally forced me to give my body a rest. And if all of this wasn't enough, everything got worse when I started to see double pictures, and my eyesight deteriorated significantly in 2015. Brain scans showed a Glioma. The four brain surgeons involved had no clue. I had a feeling that whatever they saw was not another form of a tumor, but a result of outrageous inflammation in my body due to ongoing stress. And finally, the health struggle was followed by a financial collapse.

Time to Change

This time I did not have any other option but to listen to the call inside from my 'Inner Healer' for immediate change. Despite not knowing what to do, I refused to proceed with brain surgery. The surgeons calculated the risk of my vision being impaired as very high. It was one of my boldest stands to completely trust my intuition and step into the unknown. Instead of the surgery, I decided to do a very high daily dose of intravenous cortisone therapy in the hospital. That helped a bit.

Being afraid and shocked by all the diagnoses I received, and the estimations about what all this could lead to, like epilepsy or falling into a coma, I prepared everything for the unfortunate case of not surviving it. I wrote my bucket list again, specified my body's disposal, and updated my testament and last will with the lawyer to make sure my dad could take me off the ventilator and machines. I was totally clear on the fact that a life based on long-term life support was not the life I wanted to live.

My 'Inner Healer' told me to quit traditional medicine. I already had been through 18 surgeries. Despite feeling powerless and helpless and without any control, this time, I did not resist what I had been feeling for so long. The quest was to skip conformity and to break free from living unauthentically, and to stop the betrayal of lying to myself by putting other people first. I needed to prioritize myself. I was so fed up with giving the responsibility for my health and life to doctors who were treating my symptoms with more and more drugs and now had no clue how to help me. I felt like a guinea pig. My life was pure hell. I knew I was totally overworked and had to stop it, but I didn't see a way out. How could I shift things around? I was a solo entrepreneur, and the cost of health care was through the roof.

New Healing Approach

I also knew that I had to heal the emotional childhood trauma that had gotten me stuck and was forcing me to relive my horrible past over and over again. Despite not having any certainty that the new spiritual and soul approach would be the right way for me to heal, I knew I had to get my body unstuck as I could hardly move. I booked in with an energy healer for the next four weeks. I felt that I had to approach my diseases from the spiritual and soul level. It was time to acknowledge the unconscious patterns and emotions that were running in the background—keeping me living in the past. It was time to finally let them go.

I had tried all sorts of healing methods in order to heal myself, and no stone was left unturned. One hour with the energy healer felt like a week of hard work in a quarry. My dad, a graduated chemist, and his girlfriend, a heart surgeon, do not believe in any spiritual approach. They were unable to understand my decision to try a whole new healing approach and tried to talk me out of it, to no avail. Seeing his daughter in such a horrible and uncertain state was very challenging for my father. He had driven me to all the medical appointments for such a long time since the first symptoms with reduced eyesight had appeared. It was horrible for him to see his girl's health getting worse day by day and preparing all the documents for my possible end. What made matters particularly hard for him was my attempt to prepare and ask for euthanasia, should I fall into a long coma. But, he remained strong.

I'm forever grateful for my dad being by my side. I remember begging him to drive my car, so I could visit the energy healing sessions as I couldn't see clearly, and I couldn't drive anymore. As my health got worse, my final wish was to spend some time together with my sons and him. So, he booked a flat for us near the healer's village. Just the five-hour ride down there was horribly painful, and spasms in my legs forced us to stop every now and then at resting places. Imagine me lying down in my dress between the parked trucks as my legs would not stop shaking. Eventually, we got to the flat. All three of them were shocked to realize how bad my condition really was.

Ready to Break Free

I surveyed the way I had lived, and I knew for sure that I could not go on with my life half-lived and with my message dying within. For the last few years, I was mostly living in survival mode, which finally blew my head.

I yearned for living authentically in the present moment, as well as the wonderful future where I could be the creator and victor of my life, instead of living unconsciously in the traumatic past. No matter what, I was ready to break free and to transform my whole life and business. I had studied many spiritual and evolving principles with the best evolutionary mentors worldwide, such as Derek Rydall, Gregg Braden, Eckhart Tolle, Bruce Lipton, Deepak Chopra, and especially Dr. Joe Dispenza. I was impressed by Dr. Dispenza, who had healed himself from back injuries after an accident.

We are conditioned to believe that the outer world is more real than the inner world. We then tend to give our responsibility away and trust other people more than ourselves. My research and studies with the most amazing mentors in this field showcased living from the inside out to be the only way to live a happy, healthy, and authentic life. It is essential to become aware of our thoughts, emotions, and limiting behavior in order to reframe it for the better. Neuroscience has found out that until we awake and become conscious, we usually live about 95 % of our life unconsciously on autopilot, and therefore in the past. The unconscious patterns rule our lives based on anticipation of the known past and predictable future and business as usual. In fact, our brain and body are the anticipations of the known. I knew that in order to heal, I needed to think greater than I could feel. I had to stop living the unconscious life every day.

Letting Go of Everything

I was ready to break free and to let go of all the burden in my backpack. I got rid of anxiety and everything that did not make me feel good. Change for me was inevitable! I had to transform into living in the present moment and the unknown. I knew epigenetics had found and shown the physical evidence in the brain and body that by thought alone one can change the body, biology, and state of being. Getting ready for my rebirth and the reinvention of my true authentic self as my guiding force was my number one goal. I had to take back my power and responsibility, and I had to save my life. I knew vibrant health is the natural state and expression of life. I just hadn't felt it for so long. The quicker my health went downhill, the more I was reminded of the health challenges and imbalances in my childhood.

The Boldest Decision

Can you imagine what it meant to conquer my greatest fear of losing my eyesight, facing death, and stepping into the unknown when I decided to go on this spiritual path and refused the brain surgery?

The surgery, due to its risk, was not an option for me, and I do not believe in chemotherapy or radiation either. I believe this to be extremely harmful to the body. And I probably would not have survived it either because I was too weak. It was a nightmare, but I was committed to doing whatever it took. I trusted my intuition, even though I was paralyzed with fear. I reminded myself of Winston Churchill's saying, "If you're going through hell, keep going."

As I began to select a new vision for my future, I started to see double pictures again. I was shocked and doubted this new way of healing to be right for me and asked myself if it would have been better for me to stay with traditional medicine. But, then I remembered the risk of harming the center responsible for eyesight in the surgery that the brain surgeons had told me about.

Blackout

My feeling of total chaos, frustration, hopelessness, and desperation exploded when things spiraled to the most dramatic moment. I experienced a complete visual blackout. My eyesight was gone, and for two days, there was only darkness. I prayed and meditated even more. There was nothing else to do.

Those were the darkest nights for me. I knew the only way to possibly survive was to let go of all and focus on the brighter future that may arrive. Well, by now, I had changed my way of thinking about death and assured myself that there would be another life in another form and that death, should it be my fate, was not the end. But, I was still very clear that it could mean the end in this dimension, and that I would possibly not be able to see my sons and dad anymore. It was pure hell!

There was nothing left to see, fix, or do! Can you feel the situation?

The sign showed again in big letters, "Game over!" When I became aware of thinking for a moment of how bad the situation was, I forced myself to focus on the brighter pain-free future. The delirium with falling unconscious lasted for two days of complete darkness.

Surrender

My boldest decision, in spite of my fear of death, was not to rush into the hospital emergency room, but instead to stay calm and to lie in my bed begging my 'Inner Healer' to step in and assist me. To surrender was my only option. I totally accepted the situation, and whatever would occur out of it and gave my life into the hands of God and my 'Inner Healer.' As Steve Jobs said, "Sometimes life hits you in the head with a brick. Don't lose faith."

Suddenly, all the pain and shaking of my body stopped. I became the observer of it all, and no longer was I the matter trying to control matter (my body). Before that awakening, the stress hormones caused me to focus my attention on the material world, which equals living by the symptoms of stress. I can't say where I was now, but it felt like being somewhere out in space and time. I felt more like myself. Then there was a voice telling me that I didn't have to go through all this for my own sake only, but for the sake of all and the healing of the planet. I was asked if I was committed to become and show up authentically and ready to help transform humanity into authenticity. All of what had happened made more sense now, and I gladly accepted it. Then, after two days of surrendering, by the leap of faith, out of nowhere, a bright light illuminated the room.

Become Somebody Else

Everything had changed. I was completely conscious and aware, being the observer of myself and the world around me. It was a transformation from being focused on external matters before to now pure consciousness, and I was very grateful for the change. If we want something to change, we need to become conscious and change our mindset, expectations, beliefs, emotional behavior, and lifestyle. Lasting change is impossible if we want to stay the same, as we then live in the known past and, therefore, a predictable future. I had to become totally conscious and become somebody else, in order to survive and continue my life on a whole new level of awakened consciousness. It took me years to figure out how to heal myself and to uncover my authentic self. I knew I had to become authentically me and let go of all the rest that was conditioned. The death of my old ego-based self and my old life, mostly run on unconscious autopilot, was necessary for the rebirth of my true authentic self.

Back into a Whole New Life

After returning back home, I slowly adapted to the new authentic self that I had chosen. Everything else had fallen apart. My subconscious was still not back after I had lost it during my visual blackout. I had to relearn all behaviors that normally happen automatically on autopilot. Can you imagine that simple things like doing the washing, driving my car, etc. had become a big deal now? This did cost me an enormous effort on concentration, training, and time. Additionally, I focused on the daily inner healing work that I had studied years ago with Dr. Joe Dispenza to rebuild my body and brain in the best possible way. It was really tough to stay focused on this healing regime. Interfering thoughts were part of the strong force that wanted to return back to normal and the known past. It felt almost like the quarry in which I had been before. But I was very disciplined and always returned back to my desired feelings and plan to set up everything in the best form. I practiced this for more than two months until I finally realized changes in my brain and body.

My eyesight got better and better, and the chronic pain and spasms got less. In the meantime, I continued detoxing my body with a daily smoothie made with the fresh herbs out of my own garden and enjoyed the recovery on my terrace.

Stepping into the Unknown

I had skipped my former ego-based autobiographical self. Things like playing roles, wearing masks, the fake play, and trying to fit in to belong had now stopped. I had transformed into a 'new being,' and people didn't recognize me anymore. Well, I took this as a good sign, and as most of them had not been willing to be by my side in my darkest times, I anyway stopped being in contact with them. But, I must admit this process did hurt enormously. Let me point out here that the environment is crucial for any transformation. You might have people in your life who will probably hold you back if you consider a transformation for yourself. You can easily detect this once you become aware as the observer. I assure you, you'll be astonished by how gridlocked situations and people are. Whenever you want to transition to a higher state of consciousness, you need to surround yourself with people who are living there and mentors who have done it. Anything else will hold you back. To not risk any relapse into the old system, I only was willing to surround myself with my sons, my dad, two best friends, and my amazing mentors.

I'm pretty sure that my last co-dependent relationship (which I had left shortly before the diagnosis) was the final cornerstone of my soul forcing my body to stop me. The brain challenges had been a clear sign that the relationship I stayed in was wrong. I did learn my lesson of never ever compromising my true nature for anything in life again! I needed to prioritize myself, no matter what. I finally did, but it was almost too late!

Whenever we are unable to find a solution for a problem, that really bothers us to the bones, we tend to prolong. Sometimes we don't become aware of the root cause that then can manifest in the body. Cancer researchers have found that it takes approximately two years for a tumor to manifest and show up. The root cause, in my case, was seeded in my childhood and reliving the traumatic past. We attract what we unconsciously believe to be true. The brain has a memory of the past and, from time to time, will bring up evidence to prove that your beliefs and thoughts are right. It's very tricky to break free from that automatic pattern of self-sabotage, and the only way to master and breakthrough this automation is to become the outside observer, let go, and start with a new slate.

Heal Yourself

Being reminded of 'my old life' while writing this, I'm filled with indescribable gratefulness for my awakening into my true authentic self and a new way of life. I now have the freedom of doing only what I love, and being surrounded only by the people I love most, as well as my dog Joli. Anyway, the saying, whenever you are ill, you will discover true friends, is absolutely true. In those darkest times, only true friends showed up. Everybody else was scared.

The goal is to evolve and make yourself feel the desired outcome now and forget about the old stuff. No matter the circumstances, I harnessed my experiences of aliveness and abundance, the wonderful relationship with my beloved sons and dad, and the beauty of nature in my garden. I tried to find the good in all and was ready to feel all my feelings no matter what came up. They have been imprisoned deep down in the cave for so long, and I had to heal and release them. Whenever you face similar challenges, my tip is to not go on denying them. They always try to remind us of a similar case in the past, where we first had this feeling. The only way through this is not to resist but to feel them. That's when you get ready to heal and elevate yourself. I am a fan of Les Brown. Knowing his whole life journey, I especially love his quote, "Life has no limitations, except the ones you make."

Accept it and allow the unlovable shadow to be. It is a part of you. Look for a mentor who has gone through it. The healing comes from acknowledging, embracing, and releasing the emotion. The stuffed down emotions only want to be seen, heard, and acknowledged, and after a while, they disappear. We call them the shadows because they hide in the dark until you bring them into the light by acknowledging and accepting them. We also consist of different aspects, the female, the male, as well as that of a child. Without mentorship, it's nearly impossible to balance all those existing opposites within you. It's like Yin and Yang, and they need to be balanced to co-exist. Remember the parable of the wolves? The one you feed wins. It's either the fear, anxiety, or neediness, or the faith, gratitude, joy, and love. But, whatever you choose stays. It can either make your life or break it. In most cases, they are related to childhood trauma and had benefits at that time. For example, illness could be created to get attention when without it there was none, just like in my case.

Evolve Yourself

Make sure you watch your emotional state. Bring yourself into a high vibrational state of love, hope, joy, and gratitude every day. You can do this throughout your day by simply reminding yourself of lovely situations or people when you experienced those feelings. Just by doing that, you catapult yourself into these wonderful feelings and can immediately change your emotional state. I'm doing this on a daily basis. I have realized that positive thinking alone is not enough. You need to combine the positive thought with the same positive emotion. By the way, this is the same principle that worked for me in my healing journey (according to Dr. Joe Dispenza). It's called healing by thought alone in the first place. But it only works properly when you combine it with feeling the amazing feeling that you want to feel in your future.

That's why I totally get it when so many people who have been reading *The Secret* say it's just not working for them. By focusing on the positive mindset alone, telling yourself "I am healthy" when, in fact, you feel horrible, you can't get past your body's mind. It quickly detects this as not being congruent and will not believe it. What you think and what you feel is always a match. Your body will not believe you, and the dominant feeling always wins!

"I am" statements are strong affirmations and have a big effect on you. That's why it is crucial not to beat yourself up with negative self-talk. To watch your words is very important! To feel happy on a consistent basis in the now when, in fact, everything is horrible, is crucial to transformation and making the quantum leap. In other words, to feel the desired emotion by reminding yourself of wonderful happenings leads to feeling as if your life is pure happiness. But, it all depends on our attitude and how we see things. The two sides of the coin are always in play. Either we see things as an obstacle or as an opportunity and evolve from them. Either way, we will be proved right.

Enjoy Each Moment

I'm sharing these insights with you to remind you that your life and health are your most precious assets. Nobody knows how much time is left, and therefore worrying about things you can't change doesn't make any sense at all. It is a waste of time and unhealthy. My best tip is to change what you have control of and to accept what you don't have control over. Remember that we all are incarnated here for a special reason. The quest we came here for is to discover our true nature and to share it by living. It's our choice to accept the call and to evolve.

If you don't love areas of your life, and if there are things eating you, it's time to change! Blaming or judging others on the outside or being in grief only means that you are giving your power away to other people or circumstances. The outside, according to the Law of Attraction, is only a mirror showing your own limiting beliefs, emotions, expectations, and behavior. Just like I did before my awakening, most people relive their past life over and over again every time they get triggered by somebody or situations which remind them of a similar emotion in the past. Until we become aware and mindful, our mental, emotional, spiritual, or physical bodies act as a storage medium of our old life and lead us back to experiencing the same old feelings and life.

Only you can change your life. The longer you resist change, the longer the pain will show you that you don't follow your true purpose and right path. It's our decision to embrace the status quo, skip the fake role-playing, conformity, and trying to fit in, and finally be authentic. Otherwise, illness, accidents, or other challenges may take you out of the race!

The Queen of Transformation

Let me finish my story first. The two days of darkness, surrendering, discovering my life's purpose, and accepting my life's agenda still have been the most mysterious and impactful days of my life. I am more than grateful for my life's Golden Ticket and the awakening into living my true authentic self. I have been pushing myself for decades listening to my inner talk of 'not being good enough' and therefore was running faster and faster while trying to fit in.

Today, leading by example, I follow my mission to remind entrepreneurs to discover their true nature, and to express their purpose as an awakened leader in the world by sharing it. Investing in my health, happiness, freedom, and knowledge was the best decision I could take. It will also always pay back for you, should you choose to. I could elevate myself not only because of my awakening, but because I planted the seed for real transformation in my long-term mentorships with the best spiritual, mental, behavioral, and high-performance coaches in the world. For nearly two decades, I have studied with Bob Proctor, got my trainer license from T. Harv Eker, and evolved my thinking and behavior with Eckhart Tolle, Dr. Joe Dispenza, Gregg Braden, and Derek Rydall, just to name a few of them. To transform my business, I was additionally trained by high-performance coaches such as Brendon Burchard, Darren Hardy, and Robin Sharma. The mentorship with Brian Tracy started out with him being my sales coach, then my personal development coach, followed by book coaching, and till today he is my stagecoach.

I finally understood why most of the so-called life-changing seminars or programs were failing to change people's lives. To be able to gain a life-changing transformation, we need the right assistance on the implementation from coaches who live what they preach and have mastered it themselves first. More information or just to know concepts without implementation doesn't change anything in your world. Over the years, I did not see lasting change with the 21-day courses either. Science has shown that the changed mindset, emotions, and behavior need to be implemented for at least 60 to 90 days.

With the guidance of the best worldwide mentors, I have totally transformed myself over and over to now being seen as a role model for ending anxiety and transformation into authenticity. This named me the **Queen of Transformation**. Today, I'm living a healthy, happy, and fulfilled life on my own authentic terms. I follow my soul's purpose of being the guide for those longing to get real and living their best authentic life ever and leading their authentic business. There are always two sides to the coin. My health challenges and my life's journey often have been a nightmare. What I have gained is the treasure of my awakening, the serenity I was always searching for, and the trueness of being real and authentically me.

I have also transformed my business from an agency style where I needed to be at a certain place to an online business that just needs my laptop. This is the only way to have my business always with me because I love traveling. It provides me total freedom in terms of time and location. Today, my life consists of a never before known freedom to be truly who I am and being my own self-expert. The greatest gift of all is to be healthy, happy, fulfilled, and in peace being authentically me.

Authenticity Leads to Happiness

True and lasting happiness and fulfillment only come from the inside out and not from material things. My statement, therefore, is, "Being authentic is the only way to be sustainably happy and fulfilled in life." Unfortunately, we never got a manual to handle ourselves or life!

The Washington Post reports the latest data from the General Social Survey. According to it, Americans are getting miserable. Even the world happiness report states that more and more Americans are unhappy.

Even though we live in the most technologically advanced time in history and have every reason to be happy, unhappiness resides. The main reason is that most people don't live authentically and up to their life's purpose. In our fast-growing world, with an increasing amount of stress to cope with, we are constantly overwhelmed and running in the rat race. We yearn to live authentically and be happy and search for it outside. Both can't be found outside. It's nothing we become but connect to. It's an inside job and awaits you to tap into it. And when you learn to connect to your inner joy and authentic self, your days start to be filled with ease, serenity, and a feeling of freedom and laughter. What you do for a living, matters. It's not only the fact of getting paid but the sense you feel while working. This is essential for good health. May this be the moment you, maybe for the first time, truly love yourself. The benefit of being your own best friend and treating yourself better can't be overestimated! But for all that to happen, you need to master connecting to your own inner joy and authentic self. It comes down to how you see yourself. It's time to relight your fire!

Lifetime is Limited

Why am I telling you about my hero's journey and sharing the darkest nights of my soul and my awakening? Part of my promise, given in my darkest nights, to be the guide for those longing to get real and living their best authentic life ever, is to share the inspiration that everything is possible once we find back to our true self.

Healing also comes from being motivated, inspired, and learning how others could overcome their obstacles and find their way back to health, happiness, joy, and an authentic lifestyle! Therefore, I have created The FLY-Freestyle-Your-Life System. On the FLY-Freestyle-Your-Life podcast, the most authentic experts and speakers share their best tips and strategies to inspire my listeners in FLY-Nation with free mentoring on how to approach challenges in their lives and business and how to heal themselves. It is the number one podcast inspiring you to live and lead your authentical greatness and to be the hero you were meant to be.

Become Your Own Self-Expert

Probably your life isn't always a blue sky either. Times of crisis and challenges are part of life. This is the time when we can grow out of our old life. Unfortunately, we miss out on many opportunities that are often hidden behind the difficulties in a crisis. Most of the time, we are afraid to take a leap of faith and miss the chance to evolve. We mostly prefer to stay in our well-known comfort zone. I always call it a familiarity zone. As you know by now, most of my life was not comfortable at all. For a long time, I regularly kept going to doctors. Surely you agree that the challenges I have faced led to my awakening and evolving into a higher state of being and consciousness. I doubt that I would be here if I had chosen the surgery. From there on, I would have most likely had another surgery claiming to save my life. I could also be dead. Was it scary? Hell yes. Was it worth trying to heal me by trusting my intuition and giving me over to my 'Inner Healer?' Yes! Stagnation, on the other hand, is a slow way of dying. I can show you how to train and tame not only your brain and body but to tackle your challenges and evolve from them. Pushing through boundaries is often where self-initiation starts.

Transforming Your Life

Creating the FLY-Freestyle-Your-Life System was a step closer for me to fulfill my promise, made during the darkest nights of my life. It is the holistic transformational system to overcome anxiety, become your own self-expert, and authentically you. It is the home base for your hero's authentic journey. I am the guide for those who are longing to heal, become real, and who are ready to create, live, and lead their life and business on their own authentic terms. Experts stated that it is not only a life-transforming system but a way of living.

The benefit is living intentionally and with optimized health and happiness from the inside out, and fulfillment on a whole new level. You become a self-expert in all areas of your life. Once you learn to become aware of your limiting thoughts, emotions, and behavior you are able to heal and master your emotions once and for all. Now is the time to create, live, and lead a healthy, happy, and fulfilled life on your own terms.

How to Not Only Survive but Thrive in the Crazy Times of COVID-19

The world is changing faster than ever, and that change is accelerating. This creates a lot of uncertainty and stress. If you rely on the same strategies you used before these chaotic times, you're almost certain to run into problems. Rapid change and uncertainty require different methods of operating in the world. Those who learn and apply these methods will experience health, happiness, fulfillment, and financial success instead of financial hardship.

By now, we have experienced a total breakdown of life and economy worldwide. These major wake-up calls are seen almost every century, followed by smaller crashes coming up in decades. Every day, we experience the anxiety and fear of the virus that might kill us but also has a big influence on our health and rights. We now get declarations on how to behave and face insecurities on a daily basis. While waiting to go back to normal as quickly as possible, most people don't understand the message this wake-up call has for us. Since we were unable to slow down as humanity, we were now forced to. It reminds me of my own life story. The quest we are all up to is to become authentic and live purposefully. We didn't take climate change seriously, and now we got the bill. In fact, in my consideration, we have a responsibility to save this paradise called Earth for our grandchildren and future generations. But, exploiting and polluting nature was more than ever on the rise.

Nature now is at rest and flourishes in the breakdown. We could do the same. By simply changing our attitudes, mindset, and behavior, we could not only save ourselves but also our beautiful planet. We are witnessing within the crisis the unfolding of the greatest opportunity of our lifetimes—Spiritually, Emotionally, and Financially. You must move out of conditioned habits and into experiments, exploring new possibilities for your interactions with yourself, others, and the world. This generates opportunities for new pathways to arise that will lead you to the future you feel called to create.

The New Economy

Now more than ever is the time to dig in, level-up, and invest in yourself. The way you respond today to these challenges will ripple through your life for decades. The New Economy is already here. It's up to you, whether you participate or grieve, and wish for your past life to come back. There is no turning back to normal. It's gone. The better you prepare yourself now for the time after the crisis when the dust settles, the better you will be positioned for great success. Take the leap of faith now to put yourself in the game. Get ready to relight your fire and create, live, and lead authentically on your own terms!

I want to ask you to reflect on three to four big moments in your life where you had to go to the edge of your comfort zone, take a risk, and step past your own self. Did you get the right assistance to surpass and grow from your challenges, or did everything still remain the same? I don't want you to suffer in a way that I did just because you don't know how to heal yourself. You could risk your life by going on with 'business as usual.' When you constantly feel unhappy or already have severe symptoms or diseases, it's time to change! Don't wait for your own wake-up call that might cost you your life. Every passing moment is gone and will never come back. I can tell you from my experience that nothing matters more than you stepping up to live the dreams you have delayed because you have been too scared, let the negative input from others win, and therefore settled for less. You are amazing and you matter just the way you are!

Relight Your Fire

Do you feel called to live a greater version of yourself? If you yearn to live and lead a healthy, happy, and fulfilled life and business on your own authentic terms, I might easily help you out. Enjoying life being present in each moment and only doing what your heart brings to shine is key to tap into the happiness within. As you see, to Freestyle-Your-Life, means to break free from what is not you, doesn't feel good, and to restyle your life. In times of the crisis we now face, it is more important today than ever to reduce stress, confusion, emptiness, and this overwhelming feeling of being stuck! You need to be able to welcome more impact, love, peace of mind, and joy that you crave and deserve.

In my mentorship, I focus especially on the implementation of the best shortcuts and strategies to evolve consciousness, and real transformation from anxiety into authenticity, so you can restyle your life on your own authentic terms and become your own self-expert. I'm your guide, arm-in-arm, by your side. Together, we could get you back on track and to rethink what really matters to you. You are your own prison guard as I just described, and you can learn how to fire him! Ask yourself what Bob Marley suggested, "Open your eyes, look within. Are you satisfied with the life you're living?" If not, but if you are ready to bring ease into your life and enjoy the freedom of being the real YOU, I am more than happy to share more of my insights with you. For the moment, I hope you have gained some takeaways on how to make bold decisions. It's actually fun to embrace your greatness and to become the best version of Yourself. You are here to make a difference. Don't let your story die unshared.

ERNESTE CARLA ZIMMERMANN

Erneste Carla Zimmermann, MBA, is featured as a speaker, author, and internationally known anxiety and authenticity coach. She holds degrees in business administration, shamanic healing, and hypno-coaching. As a certified trainer, she guides you on your transformational journey of breaking free from self-sabotage and self-oppression and leads you into greatness and owning who you are. Erneste Carla has walked the path. She discovered that being authentic is the only way to be healthy, happy, and fulfilled.

After facing death, she transformed totally and now is known as the role model showing that everything is possible once we find back to our true authentic self. This earned her the name the Queen of Transformation. She is the founder and CEO of FLY-Freestyle-Your-Life and ECZ-Consulting and the creator of the FLY-Freestyle-Your-Life Systems. These worldwide unique holistic Mentorship Programs, The Anxiety Freedom Formula, and the Authenticity Blueprint, are the step-by-step systems you can follow to heal, discover, align, and leverage your life's purpose as an awakened leader in the world. You'll learn easy implementable next-level techniques and shortcuts enabling you to enjoy a healthy, happy, and fulfilled life and business on your own authentic terms.

She is the author and co-author of three books. The life-changing book about the FLY-Freestyle-Your-Life Systems inspire you to heal and heroically step forward and claim who you are meant to be. It is an open invitation and a must-read if you dare to uplevel your health, mindset, heal your emotional wounds, and live as a happy and fulfilled self-expert leading your own destiny. The FLY-Freestyle-Your-Life Best Practice Book of life's greatest lessons from the world's top experts reveals how to turn your life around and liberate.

The FLY-Freestyle-Your-Life stages such as the FLY-Podcast and the FLY-Summits are part of the epic FLY-Freestyle-Your-Life Movement and Authentically Me Tribe and help you take your life to the leading edge of healing and authentic evolution. Experts, speakers, and Erneste Carla share their best tips and strategies on how to end anxiety, become authentic, and uplevel your Status Quo beyond the fear of being YOU.

Erneste Carla is the go-to expert for entrepreneurs, coaches, and those who commit to showing up authentically, in life and in business. Besides guiding you on the process of becoming your own authentic self-expert, she equips coaches, health, and wellness business owners with the FLY-Freestyle-Your-Life Methodology. In all she is doing, she follows her mission to help you heal, live authentically, and to stop the misery of living a life that is not yours.

For more information about her systems, stages, books, consulting, and coaching, to download the Shortcuts to end anxiety or to break free and FLY as well as to schedule your free transformational 'Anxiety Freedom' or the 'Discover your authentic greatness' session, please go to https://freestyle-your-life.com/ or https://www.facebook.com/freestyleyourlifecom.

<u>Contact Details</u>

Website: www.freestyle-your-life.com

Podcast: https://freestyle-your-life.com/podcast/

Facebook: https://www.facebook.com/freestyleyourlifecom/

LinkedIn: https://www.linkedin.com/in/erneste-carla-zimmermann/

CHANGE IS THE RULE, BUT IT'S NOT YOUR RULER

Hugh Todd

Our world is constantly changing, sometimes at breakneck speed, sometimes quietly so you'd hardly notice. Change happens to us – and we make changes happen. It can be traumatic, and it can be a relief. We don't always make good choices. There are times when we know we should make something change – and we let the opportunity slip away.

Change is simply unavoidable. That being so, how do we consistently turn it to our advantage and make it a source of inspiration, progress, and growth?

Episode 1: Torn Away from Family

It is 1962. I'm nearly 8. My father is picking his way carefully through the potholed, dirt roads between our village in Uganda and Entebbe airport. When we get there, my parents are about to bid me farewell and send me unaccompanied on an eight-hour flight to a boarding school in England. I think that's north of Africa somewhere.

I'm quietly terrified. I'm already grieving for home; I've had to say goodbye to my friends, and my dog. My mother has a serious heart condition, and I know I might never see her again. It will be another 10 months before I can come home – air travel is both new and expensive.

1959. Childhood in Uganda and Somalia

I know that this has been a tough and expensive decision for my parents. They see it as being in my best interests.

Were they right, or were they wrong?

So many children have been taken from their families, their communities, their culture, and their roots. They have been orphaned, sent away as refugees, or for a host of other reasons. I guess they would share that same gut-wrenching fear that settled deep in my stomach as they faced the unknown. They would also share the natural resilience of the young, the inbuilt ability to learn quickly and adapt to new circumstances.

Which of us sink, which of us swim, and what makes the difference?

This chapter is the story of a lifetime of changes. Some are planned choices, and some come out of the blue. Some work out well, some are devastating – at least initially. Each contains learning that has, without doubt, shaped my development as a person, as a family man, as an educator and coach, and how I, in turn, influence others.

A Shocking Way to Unearth Values

I don't remember the journey, but I've somehow arrived at this new school. I'm given a locker, and I've been shown my dormitory. I can't find a toilet – language differences. Such a huge building, so many boys everywhere. It's overwhelming.

I come across a group of older kids. It takes me a minute to comprehend what I'm witnessing. They are making fun of another boy. They seem to think it's amusing. It's not just teasing though, it's abusive, and they are pushing him around. Why on earth would they be picking on this young lad? I simply have no idea. Then it hits me, and I'm shocked to my core.

He's black.

All the emotions that I've been bottling up for the last 48 hours blow to the surface. I can't control myself anymore. I've no idea what I'm saying – yelling, probably. Never in my life have I felt so angry. Now, I'm the one being pushed around by these older kids, and I fight back.

We're separated by staff and taken to the headmaster's office. There he serves us each a few strokes on the backside with a thick leather belt.

This is how I discovered some important things about myself.

In many of the schools that I had attended in different parts of Uganda and Somalia, I was the only white kid – and I had never been teased or abused for being different. I had no idea whatsoever that color prejudice or racism existed. I was, in a way, color-blind.

However, the episode at this new school changed me. I learned right there that I couldn't tolerate injustice. It was so unfair that this lad was being targeted just because of his skin color. Furthermore, it seemed unfair and wrong that I should be punished for standing up to these bullies.

I learned that I was on my own, for real. No other student had stepped in to support me in any way. The group of older kids warned all the other newbies that if they saw any of them talking to me, they'd also get some special attention. My parents were thousands of miles away and could only be contacted by airmail letter. It was now down to me to survive this.

In Africa, I had loved going to school. Everyone there knew that education was essential, and we all wanted to understand things, so schooling was based on satisfying our curiosity and problem-solving. There was no need to force us to learn. Here things were different. Learning was by rote, memorizing vocabulary, history, and rules, and if we didn't recall enough in tests, we were punished. I hated it with a passion.

Out of pain, fear, and loneliness, I learned:

- Never to judge people for superficial, irrelevant reasons.
- I'm passionate about challenging injustice and unfairness.
- When you don't have a choice, you just have to get on with things.
- Education and learning should never be forced on people.

I didn't then know how relevant these would be in my future life. I had five years of this pain. However, if I hadn't gone through the experience, what would I have learned about myself?

Like me, you probably know people who espouse certain beliefs, then behave in a completely different manner, when put to the test. For example, apparently devout churchgoers who listen to sermons about tolerance before raging at a cyclist because he slowed their car journey by a few moments, or the very same people getting angry about refugees trying to enter their country.

Whatever we believe about ourselves, I think we only truly discover what is in our hearts when we face a tough choice, a tough situation; how we respond in those moments defines our values.

For example, what are we learning about ourselves, and how are we redefining our values during the COVID-19 pandemic lockdown and aftermath?

I suspect that each of us has values that have never really been put to the test, the kind of things we hope to be true about ourselves. But, until push comes to shove, we won't actually KNOW which of those values defines us.

"Even the helpless victim of a hopeless situation, facing a fate he cannot change, may rise above himself, and by so doing change himself. He may turn a personal tragedy into a triumph".

Viktor Frankl [1]

Episode 2: Discovering My Tribe

It's still 1962. It's just been 3 months since the harsh introduction to boarding school. Here's this eight-year old kid, wrenched from his family and East African childhood. An only child, and alone in a vast crowd of school pupils, his world is turned upside down again. In a very different way.

I'm getting used to traveling on my own! It's the start of the Christmas holidays. I've managed to get to London, then onto the train taking me north to Scotland. In Edinburgh, farming relatives will be waiting to meet me.

They were amazing. It turns out that my uncle and aunt had 10 kids, all packed into a cottage on a hill farm. There was no heating, and it was below freezing most of the time, so we packed around the open fireplace in the evenings to chat, and to share tea and crackers. Everyone was busy all the time; they knew all the jobs that needed to be done on a farm. The place was buzzing with energy and fun.

Me? I was like a fish out of water. They seemed to be using a different language. Their strong Scottish dialect and accent combined with farming terms, and with so many conversations going on simultaneously meant that it all went over my head.

I was in awe of them.

It was a shock to be part of a *family*. Lots of kids, warmth, fun, energy, and teamwork everywhere – preparing and clearing up meals, farm work, washing clothes, looking after the babies.

Farming in The Pentland Hills, Scotland

Going to the farm would be my pattern during school vacations for the next 10 years.

I didn't always cope well. I never felt good enough – I never fully grasped all the complexities of farming. I continued to have a very different education in the south of England. I arrived with an English accent and left with a broad Scottish accent every time!

In spite of all that, they accepted me wholeheartedly and – for the most part – tolerated my sometimes odd behavior incredibly well.

"You can always tell a real friend: when you've made a fool of yourself. He doesn't feel you've done a permanent job."

Laurence J. Peter

More than five decades later, and after living on the other side of the world for several years, I still feel the bonds, the acceptance, and the friendship of my cousins. They taught me the strength that can be found as a member of a close, supportive tribe, and inviting me to be part of it was life-changing.

So, when I moved to secondary school, I was able to make friends, to take on leadership roles, and to feel part of the school community.

Captain of School Rowing 1972

The strength of acceptance into the school 'tribe' came through to me in a very unexpected way.

It is 1971. I'm in a school play, a comedy. The hall is filled with over 700 students. My first line is deadpan, "I come from Siberia." And the audience erupts into laughter and keeps going. It turns into a standing ovation, with people crying with laughter. Onstage, we just have to wait, caught completely by surprise. Puzzled, I lift an eyebrow. And that sets everyone off again.

We were all completely connected and engaged, at that moment. It reflected acceptance, respect, and even affection. I know it wouldn't have happened if I hadn't been well-liked.

It was a humbling, joyful, and powerful moment.

Episode 3: When Good Choices Turn Bad – Take Action!

"Take the first step in faith. You don't have to see the whole stairway, just take the first step".

Attributed to **Dr. Martin Luther King Jr.** *by Marian Wright Edelman* [2]

Have you ever chosen a path for all the right reasons, then found yourself stuck in a nightmare situation that bore no resemblance to your possibly naïve expectations? How far did you let that situation crush your spirit before summoning the courage and inspiration to break out of it?

It is 1972. Coming to the end of my time at school, I won a place studying Law at Dundee University. I genuinely believed that the Law would be all about helping real people to get justice, to solve problems, and to right the wrongs.

Idiot. I was so naïve.

It wasn't like that at all. I found myself back in an educational system that was a torture for me—learning parrot fashion—and I was surrounded by students who had totally different motivations for being there. Money, career, family expectations. Justice? No. Challenging unfairness? No.

I felt completely disengaged.

However, I had *chosen* to do this course, so it was down to me to make it work. I decided to persevere. I didn't know what else to do.

Let's go forward nearly two years to 1974. I was still on the course, hanging in there by my fingertips. I had a permanent, silent scream going on in my head. I immersed myself in extra-curricular activities like sport, drama, and drinking too much. It didn't work. I became clinically depressed.

Walking home after lectures one afternoon I was so detached from my surroundings that it was like watching a movie, instead of living in the real world. I was mentally and emotionally numb. I became aware of an inner voice telling me that it was time to do something about this.

So, I made an appointment to see a doctor, and he prescribed anti-depressants.

One thing about me is that I do *not* have an addictive personality. Growing up, I had watched my parents chain-smoking, and in my mother's case, into the grave. I knew I would never allow myself to become that dependent on anything.

However, I found out that anti-depressants can quickly become addictive. That was the spark I needed to decide to take responsibility, to step up, and change the situation before it turned inevitably into a slow-motion car crash.

How? What could I change? I had no idea.

Then a French flatmate, Bernard, helped me to get a part-time evening job in a youth club in one of the rougher parts of Dundee. I loved the banter with the teenagers and lapped up everything I could learn about their lives and challenges.

A few months later John, the manager at the youth club, asked me the question that would change my life.

"Hugh. Do you know that you could do this full time?"

Huh? What? How?

"There's a three-year College course called Youth & Community Studies. Then you'd be qualified to do this professionally."

Really?

Right there and then, he called the course leader. I interviewed the next day, withdrew from Law, and a week later turned up for the first day of my new course.

I had found an escape route from the situation that was crushing my spirit, an exciting, fascinating new path that would define the rest of my life. I loved every minute, combining all kinds of practical work experience with classroom learning.

One of the concepts I learned was *"the non-directive approach to community and youth work."* It was all about empowering others to make their own choices without imposing our own values and assumptions.

Nowadays, we'd call that *"Coaching."*

How valuable did that one little gem of an idea turn out to be? Well, it turned into the fundamental principle that would go on to drive the rest of my career. One way or another, I have now been a professional coach for more than four decades and spanning three continents.

I had found a different way to tackle unfairness and injustice, and to empower others.

My first professional role was intensive. We pioneered new approaches to working with young people "at-risk", creating individual-, group-, and peer-coaching techniques to help them tackle their life challenges in empowering ways. There were just four such projects in Scotland at the time. One of my counterparts, at the Easterhouse project in Glasgow, was Jack Black, the founder of Mindstore (https://www.mindstore.com/). He has since then enhanced the lives of hundreds of thousands of people.

The Youth Worker

Taking the leap into youth work also created another life-changing moment that wouldn't have happened otherwise.

In 1979, I took a group of 'at-risk' teenagers for a week in a remote Scottish forest. On our last full day, we had arranged to go horse riding at a local farm. It wasn't an ideal day – we had rain, mischievous horses who decided to abscond while we had a lunch break, and other challenges for the trek leader.

On our return and without my knowledge, two of the boys approached the trek leader, Elspeth, and invited her to our final evening barbeque. She took this in good humor and enquired who was asking. As a unit, they pointed toward me and said, "He is!"

It seems the group had reckoned we were a good match. They were right – we married the following year, and we're now approaching our 40th anniversary.

It's fair to conclude that I had made the perfect, life-changing choice when escaping Law school and took a different path!

Breaking Free of Bad Choices

I have met many people who, like me, had made apparently good choices only to find themselves stuck in a nightmare. Some of them managed to find the strength to break out of situations like these. Others, sadly, did not.

What's the difference?

One key factor is *confidence*. The longer we remain in any toxic situation, the more our confidence in our own ability to deal with the change, with the unknown, and with the consequences of our choices, diminishes.

Another is creating and noticing *alternatives* that might open up for us. Often people stuck in dreadful job roles, for example, are so overworked and crushed that they simply don't have space to notice an opportunity or search for a new role.

A third is *support*. Supportive people provide the strength that empowers us to take action and to stick with it. I had friends suggesting alternative paths, and when I summoned the courage to call my father to tell him I'd decided to drop out of Law School and why, I was shocked by his response.

There was a pause. It took him the length of one breath. Then he simply said, *"How can I best support you?"*

Thinking about situations that you've chosen to escape from in your life, what strengths did you draw upon? What gave you – or could give you – enough confidence to feel that you're making the right choice, even when you can't know for sure how it might turn out? How might those strengths, and what you learned, serve you going forward?

"You've got to follow your passion. You've got to figure out what it is you love - who you really are. And have the courage to do that. I believe that the only courage anybody ever needs is the courage to follow your own dream".

Oprah Winfrey [3]

Episode 4: Life-changing Illness

Dealing with life-changing illness is something that most of us can only imagine. Those who have lost the use of limbs, suffered cancer, a stroke or a heart attack, or any other such traumatic event will understand exactly what I'm saying: we take it all for granted until we lose it. I can say with experience that dealing with the loss is very, very hard.

Here's what happened to me.

It is 1985. It's 3:00 a.m. I come out of a deep sleep feeling strange. I'm covered in sweat. I head to the bathroom for a drink of water. I fall sideways into the wall. What's happening? I stagger through to the bathroom. By the time I get there, I realize that something is seriously wrong.

A nasty little virus had somehow caused permanent damage in my middle ear, destroying my sense of balance. The virus also caused a complete loss of mental and physical energy.

You know how we assume that we'll recover within a week or two when we get sick? I thought exactly that to begin with. In reality, my recovery was so slow that it would take another 10 years before I could begin to enjoy physical activity again.

Overnight I had lost almost everything that made me ... me.

My career, the work that made my life meaningful – gone. As far as I could tell at that time.

The physiological health that I had always taken for granted – gone.

I learned that all of the 'friends' I had made through sport were simply teammates, not friends. With the exception of close family, my social health – the network of people I thought of as friends – was gone.

My sense of humor, feelings of love, and affection, even my ability to feel fear – all gone.

Where did I find the psychological strength to survive and recover? Simply put, I found it in *the mindset* I had chosen.

My attitude was that every difficulty, every crisis, contains something valuable, something that we would not discover without such experiences. That is still my mindset today, and it's stronger than ever.

This experience helped me to learn how to be *patient*. I realized that any progress I made would be at a snail's pace, so there was no point in beating myself up for not getting over it in a day, or a week, or a month. I learned to take a much longer-term perspective.

I learned that I am, by choice, an *optimist*. I believed that I would recover, that I would have value as a person, that I would still be able to contribute to the family, work, and community life, and that I would be stronger in some way from the experience.

I learned that *I am not indestructible*. I have limits that must be respected, and that abusing those limits is likely to bring a reckoning. Others suffer heart attacks, relationship breakdowns, mental health disorders, and other costs. I've been lucky – I've been able to regain my health. I will never again be complacent and take it for granted.

All of this gives me the chance to be a far *more insightful coach* than I could ever have been, otherwise. I recognize that my friends and clients also tend to make a lot of assumptions about what can be taken for granted, so I am constantly looking out for such blind spots. I might ask them something like this:

'What makes you think that you need to get better at coping with stress? Isn't that just getting in the way of you doing something to eradicate some of the things that are causing the stress in the first

place?'

The COVID-19 pandemic, sweeping the world at the time of writing this chapter, is serving as a reminder that we cannot take our health for granted. How long will that mindset last before we go back to our default attitude, feeling indestructible or that "It will never happen to me."?

Episode 5: Breaking Free from My 'Comfort Zone'

"When you go out of your comfort zone, and it works, there's nothing more satisfying."

Kristen Wiig [4]

It is 1998. I'm a lecturer, a course tutor in a BA degree in Community Education. By now, I have 23 years' continuous, salaried, full-time employment as a professional coach, community worker, and college tutor under my belt. I'm accustomed to knowing exactly how much I would be paid, on the same day of each and every month.

However.

However, I was utterly sick and tired of the way I had been (badly) led and managed for the last 15 of those years. I couldn't stomach any more office politics and petty jealousies. I loved teaching and coaching, which meant that I had little interest in trying for promotion into an administrative, managerial job.

When an opportunity to escape this comfort zone came along, I was ready and willing to consider it.

Elspeth had the opportunity to step up into a challenging role in the business world, which would take her away from home more often. I was commuting 20 miles daily – so who would take responsibility for our two daughters?

The Stay-at-home Dad Who Got to See the World!

I chose to resign. I became a stay-at-home dad, looking for occasional freelance coaching and training work in the gig economy. From here on, I would no longer be the family breadwinner with a career. Instead, my wife's career would take precedence.

Remember, at that time it was almost unheard of for men to make this kind of choice.

How would it work out?

To my astonishment, it opened an incredible range of opportunities and experiences that I would never have contemplated – in business, as a parent, and as the 'trailing spouse' in the relationship. Here are some examples.

Becoming a Business Owner

Our girls had been attending an after-school club in the local community nursery school. Almost the moment that I became a stay-at-home dad, the owners confided that they were moving overseas and would I care to make an offer to take over the business?

Woah! Me, a business owner? Nope, not something I was prepared for at all.

People kept twisting my arm. "You'd be perfect." And the killer, "Why not do it?" I had the perfect answer to that one – no funds.

Until, suddenly, another duck lined up. My father found the perfect retirement flat, sold his home, and offered the funds from the proceeds to buy the business.

Suddenly, I was responsible for 12 staff and 35 pre-school kids, plus the after-school service. There were a lot of unexpected and very challenging problems lurking just under the surface. For example, it wasn't as viable as the accounts had made out, and I hadn't anticipated the level of suspicion that would come my way as a man choosing to work in childcare.

It was scary. The responsibility of having to ensure that all our staff got paid at the end of each month through cash flow ups and downs kept me awake at night. Yet, it was wonderful to have the chance to put my ideas about leadership to the test in practice.

Within five years, our nursery school had won a "Best Small Business" award in Scotland. In my last three years there, we had zero staff turnover. Both were down to the nurturing, coaching culture we had built. I had been able to step progressively back from managing the business, handing responsibilities over to the team, as my freelance work had grown.

The Coaching Practice

Meanwhile, I had built a great coaching practice with terrific results with clients in the construction industry (I am not a tradesman), among others, and I acted as NATO's solitary leadership coach (I don't have a military background either!) in Europe for 10 years.

How about the family?

I'm not going to pretend that everything was rosy all of the time.

Like many senior executives, my wife often found it difficult to make the transition from work to home life, especially when she was away on a Monday to Friday basis and came home exhausted and stressed. Understandably, being away so much meant that retaining her sense of significance in the home, and feeling appreciated, was also a challenge.

While one of the girls settled quickly into the local school with new friends, it proved much more difficult for our younger daughter, who found herself facing an impenetrable and quite nasty clique, who had already been schoolmates for several years.

We had invested in a large, crumbling sandstone house dating back to 1840, with an overgrown walled garden. It turned out to be a daunting challenge.

We muddled through somehow.

10 years passed.

Our daughters were by now following their passions, studying at the Royal Scottish Academy of Music and Drama (RSAMD) and Marine Biology. My wife's career had gone from strength to strength, and she had become an amazing role model for our girls, and women everywhere.

Life was good. And then … change happened. Again.

I went from having a thriving practice to zero, almost overnight. By choice.

Episode 6: Life as a Trailing Spouse

It is 2008. Elspeth's company has offered us a once in a lifetime opportunity to move to Sydney, Australia. The timing seems perfect.

Let's go!

What an exciting challenge! I envisaged a fallow six-month period while I introduced my amazing track record and abilities to Australia – a chance to draw breath, jump once again into the unknown, and find fascinating new challenges and clients.

While Elspeth headed off to start her new role, I wound up my UK/European practice, put our house on the market, and followed her to Australia.

Did you notice that this was 2008? Right when the world was heading into a massive global financial crisis.

The Family in Sydney!

It would be 10 more years before we managed to secure the sale of our house after two contracted purchasers failed to complete. Those failed deals led to a local rumor that there was something wrong with the house – and a decade-long nightmare.

The recession also made it even more difficult than it should have been to win business as a freelance coach and trainer in a new country, without connections, referrals, or recommendations.

People in the coaching industry know how hard it is to explain what we do, how hard it is to build credibility and trust, and how hard it is to ask people to invest hard-earned funds with a vague belief that somehow it will be well worth it.

I had no niche in mind, no ideal client, and no social media presence. But, I still believed that I'd know them when I found them at business networking events or through making connections, by making a difference where I could.

You guessed it. Six months down the track, I still had no paid work.

I had gone from being an award-winning business owner, a parent, and a successful coach with a stream of delighted clients to someone who was bringing nothing to the party. No income, no job satisfaction, no kids to parent. I wasn't a native Australian, and effectively, I was an immigrant, competing for local contracts.

I realized I had no clue how to start a service business from a standing start, with zero referrals or momentum. Have you been there? Maybe you're in that position right now. It's a humbling realization.

When we reinvent ourselves in any way, we give up the security of knowing what we're dealing with. We're sure to discover some blind spots about ourselves.

When we reinvent our business, our career, the same thing happens.

How naïve could I be? How blind, how complacent?

Relaunching My Practice

I knew I had to get off my butt and get involved, learn, experiment, and try things.

Such as *networking*. Let me use this as one example of the various ways I tried to relaunch my practice.

Going to business networking for the first time in my career was an eye-opening experience.

Let me say that I'm not the most extraverted person, and I don't enjoy walking into a room full of complete strangers. All the same, I went ahead and signed up for all kinds of networking events.

I discovered that hardly anyone loves such events, and, weirdly, most are run in ways that make it hard to actually connect with anyone else there.

I figured out some ideas that would make networking events more effective and volunteered to host a meeting of the Sydney Business Networking Group. The organizer was delighted. And over the next couple of years, it grew from a membership of 70 or so to over 1700.

I'd found a way to build credibility and presence in the local business community. Job done, right? Did it help me rebuild my coaching practice? No.

Everyone saw me as a brilliant MC. Not as a coach. Ironically, I was hugely effective at helping other businesses to thrive but not my own. I was too busy organizing, hosting, getting to know exhibitors and members, keeping events moving and dynamic, and ensuring that people learned how to have effective networking conversations in 10 minutes or less.

It achieved my objective of quickly connecting with all kinds of people and organizations, but conversely, it held me back from the real task of promoting myself as a *coach*.

Having the freedom to explore and get involved with so many interesting people and projects was a real privilege, and I did learn some fantastic skills.

After seven years, I was reasonably busy, enjoying the experience of working with a wide variety of clients in a new country. I had earned a regular spot crewing on a successful racing yacht. I gained Australian citizenship while retaining my British passport. Our older daughter had also moved to Sydney. I was loving this new life.

Then, it happened again.

Another International Relocation

It is 2014. We're moving to Hong Kong, where Elspeth is going to head up a global project transforming anti-money laundering procedures for her company in the financial sector.

Time to wind everything up and start all over again in a new country, a new continent, a new culture.

Exciting? Of course.

This time I knew what was coming. I was determined to hit the ground running.

Before we moved, I recorded a complete suite of videos covering leadership skills – team leadership, communication, and conflict, inspiring and energizing staff, and more. I asked my connections for introductions to Hong Kong-based leaders and arranged coffee meetings. I reckoned I would be adept when attending networking events.

Surely I'd crack the code this time. Surely I'd quickly find serious clients and get my practice up and running.

Volvo Ocean Race Activities, Hong Kong

Well, dear reader, I can say that I did do better restarting this time. It still wasn't easy, and I had a number of disappointments along the way.

My reincarnation this time led me to become a sought-after coach and mentor for start-ups and young entrepreneurs. I became an accredited Marshall Goldsmith coach. The third branch of my new practice was in developing coaching skills and culture in schools.

Precisely what kind of coach was I? What was my special area of expertise, my niche?

You're right. I was an expert in everything, for anyone. I was able to indulge my endless curiosity about all these new projects and learn,

learn, learn.

I was still as blind as a bat. I still didn't get the message that I was doing potential clients a disservice through my own lack of clarity. The people who could have gained most from me would, more than likely, never hear about me.

Meanwhile, I was meeting potentially amazing coaches on a regular basis. I became something of an 'uncle' (to use the Hong Kong expression) to many of them.

I responded to their needs in various ways. One was by creating educational videos. I developed a set of competencies for school-based coaching. I researched attitudes toward coaching among parents, staff, and students. I took time out to travel on business trips with Elspeth to her teams in India and Poland so that I could write and record training videos in those locations.

Educating and mentoring other coaches was now the *fourth* branch of my coaching activities.

Can you tell what I was overlooking?

I still didn't have a marketing strategy or campaign. I didn't have a database. I didn't have a funnel. I didn't have a clear offering. I didn't have a target niche to focus on. Those are the transformation challenges I'm now addressing.

A Final Relocation?

Let's bring this story up to date. It is 2020, and we're back in the UK.

I'm deeply proud of the three amazing women I've loved and

supported in my family.

Elspeth has completed her final project for her company and has taken early retirement. We've moved house to be near our four-year-old granddaughter and her mum.

After all these years, we have so much freedom, so much choice. We have friends all over the world. We have a retreat in Spain. My Australian passport means we could move back down under, or to New Zealand. Moving closer to our families in Scotland once more would also be appealing. I can work as much or as little as I choose.

Life and Career Focus

As you suspect by now, I'm not likely to settle quietly into a comfort zone. I'm still passionate about coaching, and I intend to see if I can build a bit of a legacy by sharing some of what I've learned over four decades with people who are now at a similar stage to where I was in my development, earlier in my career. I now have the focus that I lacked, and I'm learning how to help others to discover what I have to offer.

23 years ago, I wrote down my life priority: *to be great friends with my future grandchildren.* That meant committing to a lifetime of investing in my physical health, my mental agility, my sense of fun, my relationships with my family, and more. It has acted as a beacon, continually motivating me to keep moving forward. Today, I love being part of my granddaughter's life and watching her growth as a human being. With luck, more of this new generation will follow!

What's the guiding light that will help *you* to transform, and to do so as often, and for as long as you can?

SHARING WISDOM FROM EXPERIENCE

Here are some takeaways from these experiences. I hope you can gain something from them.

Strategies for Whole Life Balance

If you take a snapshot of a typical day in your life, you will be able to identify where you are spending too much time and energy, and too little time and energy. That's a relatively simple rebalancing choice.

The story I've shared covers nearly six decades of ups and downs. The ideas I want to share relates to a much longer timespan than we normally consider when thinking about life balance.

To make the most of our time here on earth, we should manage three states of being. Acceleration. Recovery. And … Stop. Just stop.

Rapid Acceleration is when we can really stretch ourselves. Think of athletes in training going further, faster, for longer, lifting more weights than before, students on courses, children rapidly learning new skills, knowledge, abilities. Or, the first six months in an exciting, challenging new role, in a new company, or living in a new city or country.

However, if we continue at that pace for too long, we are going to break down in some way. For athletes, recovery time and protocols are just as important as the training. Children need fun and play, not just school and homework. Employees and bosses need to settle into routines, to follow long-term strategies, rather than trying manically to solve everything in a single day. Constantly stretching my limits caused me to lose my health and vitality, and it took 10 years or so to regain it.

We need *Recovery*. We need times when we go with the flow, when we cruise, when we allow ourselves to recover from the 'burn' experienced in the rapid acceleration mode. High-level athletes say this is when they actually gain fitness. We let our minds, bodies, and spirit reenergize. We have space to reconnect with the world, with friends, with life.

The danger here is that it gets too comfortable. The pace slows. The walls around the comfort zone get thicker. If we don't push ourselves and accelerate regularly, we're going to get rusty! We need to make the best use of these two states by regularly switching from one to the other, building energy, then burning it.

In recovering from my own illness, I tried to stretch every day, in every way – it didn't work! I had to learn to pace myself, to give myself permission to rest when I needed it.

The third state, *Survival,* is when we experience unexpected traumas—the kind of event that stops us in our tracks. It could be an acute, sudden loss of health. Or bereavement. Or a marriage breakdown. It could be the loss of a job. Losing one's home. Or witnessing or being the victim of violence, an accident, or crime.

Almost every client I've ever coached after such an event expects the impossible of themselves. They insist that they will continue to deliver everything that they normally do on a daily basis – at work, at home, in their normal lives. When (of course) they can't keep this up, they add further layers of stress by beating themselves up for being so weak.

During my illness, I couldn't accept that I couldn't continue as normal with my life and blamed myself for a long time – until I learned to forgive myself for something that wasn't, in reality, something I could control.

I've learned to observe clients carefully and to challenge them when I sense that they are trying to pace themselves inappropriately, using the wrong mode for the situation. They might need a bit of encouragement to get out of a comfort zone, or to take a bit of time out to recover, or to lower their expectations of themselves when what they really need is to simply survive a trauma.

In Summary

Life balance is an ongoing, lifelong, *whole* life process, not a snapshot.

- **Accelerate and Stretch:** When we can, put the foot down on the gas pedal.
- **Recover:** When we need to, use the brake pedal and coast.
- **Stop:** Sometimes, step out of the vehicle!

Comfort Zones, Sticky Floors, and Authentic, Sustainable Growth

Being thrown out of my comfort zone, or choosing to escape one, are recurring themes in my story. Learning how to thrive, and how to build a lifelong pattern of growth, as a result, gives me some insights that I'd like to share here.

A lot of writers tell us that life begins at the edge of our comfort zones. While that may be true, I've learned that it's also important to have a clear process which leads from that point all the way through to building growth into our individual DNA, our locked in, default patterns of response.

This diagram from my book summarizes the steps we need to take. A fuller explanation follows.

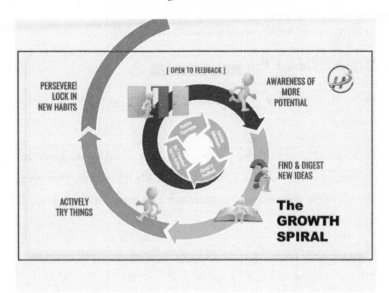

The Coaching Handbook - Pressure & Stress, Hugh S Todd [5]

From time to time, every one of us gets into a *comfort zone*, or finds that we really want to change but can't (*stuck in a rut*).

Whenever we duck out of a challenge because a little voice inside tells us that we're not good enough, or not ready yet (*"Maybe next year"*), we are hiding in a comfort zone. I call this sticky floor syndrome: we fail to make breakthroughs because we undermine ourselves. The glass ceiling is there, without a doubt. However, many women never reach it for this reason.

When we stop growing, we start going backward. That comfort zone is seductive – we know we can do okay within those limits, don't we? What we don't notice is the gradual erosion of our self-confidence. Bit by bit, we start to persuade ourselves that we are no good at taking on new challenges. It's "just not me." And then we're on a downward spiral that gets ever harder to reverse.

So how can we break out of these limiting patterns?

Authentic Growth Patterns

There are a number of elements of authentic, sustainable, lifelong growth.

First, we need to find the *motivation*. This could be triggered by a trauma, by anger, or as a result of a loss. Or it could be that we get some positive encouragement that makes us realize we have potential for growth.

Then we need to get curious and find *new ideas* – how to do things differently, how to be different, what else is out there – and to digest those ideas so that we really understand what they mean and own them. So, write them down in your own words, explain them to someone else, and picture how you might use the ideas yourself.

Which leads us nicely to the next step, *active experimentation*. We need to get over our fear of stuffing things up if we try something new – okay, maybe it won't work perfectly the first time, but so what? From the experience, we can refine, develop, and tweak it into something even better. So, go ahead and try things!

We need to lock the growth in. Otherwise, no matter how great these new ways turn out, the next time you're under pressure, you will default to your old ways. You need to be prepared to apply the new strategy again, and again, and again (maybe 21 reps!) until it becomes *second nature* and an automatic reflex.

While on this kind of journey, pay attention to *feedback*, both critical and positive. It's all a source of new ideas! In the right frame of mind – a growth pattern – you appreciate feedback, whether it is positive or critical.

How to Self-Coach: The Gift of Feedback

I've learned that it takes enormous courage to step up and give honest, open feedback to others. Why? Because almost all of us are so close to receiving it – even if the comments are intended as praise.

Skillfully eliciting all kinds of feedback is one of the most powerful ways of building high-quality relationships, full of trust, active listening, and understanding. We gain permanent access to a stream of insights and learning, and to people who care enough that they will give us support when we really need it.

We all block feedback by changing the subject, by shutting our senses down, by going on the offensive, by finding a way to escape the situation, by making light of praise with a joke, or by passing the credit or blame to someone else. Weirdly, we wonder why we don't get more constructive criticism or praise.

Pay attention: all of these responses are, quite simply, *disrespectful.*

How can we change this?

Show the other person the respect they deserve and listen using one of these approaches. They work like a charm.

1. Check Understanding. Assume we haven't fully understood the praise or criticism. Open our ears and minds. Then ask for more information, for a fuller explanation, for examples to illustrate what they mean.

    That gives us time to recover our poise. Listen carefully; check our understanding. If we agree, ask for their suggestions. If we disagree, calmly offer an alternative view based on our own perspective (we've set the tone, so they are likely to match our example by responding the same way).

We can also recruit the other person as a temporary coach to help us to develop and carry through improvements, and to let us know how we're doing.

2. Focus on the Future. Instead of falling out over what may or may not have happened, turn the conversation to the future. Something like, "If this kind of situation comes up again, how do you think I could do a better job?" Dr. Marshall Goldsmith calls this 'Feedforward.'

It's so much easier to discuss how best to handle a future event objectively. There's a separation from the subjective, personality-based, possibly blaming arguments about a past event.

Don't wait for people to offer you feedback—ask for it, and practice both of these strategies.

Building Social Power and Resilience

How and when do we come to realize the importance of creating and investing in strong, dependable relationships for our own well-being?

Social strengths develop at three levels. One is about trusting *ourselves*, knowing that we are our own best friends. The second is about *tribe or family* – those who are closest to us, and who we know are there for us, whatever happens. And the third is about our *wider social network* – unrelated friends, colleagues, teams, and others who are prepared to offer support when we need it.

The massive culture shocks that I experienced when aged eight were to generate two of these. I had learned that I had to rely on myself and that the bonds in a healthy, close-knit family or tribe can be an amazing source of strength.

Being Your Own Best Friend

What happens when our inner self only pays attention to our failings, real or imagined, or only notices how great we are without observing the flaws?

A real friend tells it like it is – they help us to recognize our shortcomings and blind spots, and they encourage our best features.

Some people learn – or are taught – to be harsh self-critics from early on, and it's hard for them to grow to be their own best friends.

Here's an example. *It's 2007, and Natalie (not her real name), a beautiful former ballet dancer now in her forties, has asked me for help because she can't stand to look at herself. Long story short, Natalie is still hearing her late mother's voice telling her, over and over again, that she is 'ugly' and a 'good for nothing.' This negative script had been drilled into her throughout her childhood.*

We changed that. Have you ever had the unique experience of having a ballet dancer leap across about 10 feet to give you a hug? I still smile when I remember her telling me that she had noticed a gorgeous woman in the foyer, then realized ... it was a mirror. That's the moment that she truly started to believe the truth instead of the ugly script she had been fed.

Her key action was to ask for help.

By contrast, some people are protected from criticism or from failure.

They may come to regard themselves as superior and bulletproof, and their minds are completely closed to any alternative realities. Their narcissism is really a kind of comfort zone.

At least the self-critic is motivated to try and improve – the narcissist 'knows' they are already perfect.

It's far healthier to be somewhat self-critical, to be aware of the scope for improvement. People with this kind of critical self-awareness can be an absolute joy to work with – they make the best leaders, teachers, coaches, and parents. They just need help in building a balanced picture of themselves along the way. Yes, that's another reason why I love being a coach.

Dear Reader: Keep Changing, Keep Growing!

Over to you,

Hugh Todd 2020

Testimonials

Hugh is my guru. He's the ideal coach - easy to bounce ideas around with, always positive and totally solution-focused. Hugh has so much knowledge, and experience collected over time, which means that he can always lay his hands on the right approach for the person or situation.

Louise Kadri-Phillips – South Africa and Hong Kong; Teacher, Certified Performance Coach, Marshall Goldsmith Stakeholder Centered Coach

Hugh is a great coach and an excellent thought partner. He combines years of experience with a creative mindset to bring innovative ideas to the world of coaching, coaching training, and organization development. A meeting with Hugh is always thought-provoking and filled with insights.

Henry Chamberlain Reg. Psychol, ACC – Hong Kong and SE Asia; Director & Founder, HC Global https://www.hccglobal.net

Hugh is special. He is more than just a mentor to me. He makes me feel like my close friend committed to my growth and development. On top of his vast experience to share, he demonstrates honesty, integrity, and he can be trusted to give objective and frank advice so that I can see my blind spots.

Hua Koon Tan – Singapore; CEO & Founder, LEAPP Pte Ltd http://www.leappmobile.com

Hugh is an inspirational coach and mentor, who empowers you to take ownership of your own aspirations. He really makes you feel valued and resourceful. Hugh challenges my thinking in a professional and thought-provoking manner.

Dr. Grace Kew. (Ph.D., ACC) – UK; Director & Founder, Grace Kew Consultancy https://www.gracekewconsultancy.com/

I've certainly gained insight into my own transformation and growth in collaborating with Hugh! He's a great resource to tap into.

Eric Speirs, CEO – Arizona, USA; Elevated Leadership, LLC ElevatedLeadership.jmt@gmail.com

References

[2] Edelman, Marian Wright 1988 "And Still We Rise: Interviews With 50 Black Role Models", Washington DC, USA Today Books: Gannett Co Inc, Edited by Barbara A. Reynolds, Chapter: Children's Advocate – Marian Wright Edelman, From conversations with Martin Luther King Jr, Pages 74 and 75.

[1] Frankl, Viktor E. 2006, "Man's Search for Meaning", p.142, Beacon Press (first published 1946)

[5] Todd, Hugh S 2018. The Coaching Handbook: Pressure & Stress (How to Master the Art of Coaching Conversations) United Kingdom, ISBN 978-1-9993515-0-2, IngramSpark

[4] Wiig, Kristen, 2012. Vogue interview "Funny Business" by Eve MacSweeney

[3] Winfrey, Oprah, original source unknown

HUGH TODD

"Transformed people ... transform people" embodies Hugh's life and career. He's been empowering people to transform their lives and businesses for over 40 years, and is a real pioneer in the field of professional coaching. The very embodiment of resilience, he has lived on four continents and has taken every life-changing event (and there have been a few) as opportunities to grow and to explore new ways of making a lasting difference.

Hugh brings out leadership qualities everywhere he works - such as with NATO, young people at risk, young entrepreneurs in Hong

Kong, housebuilders, women affected by 'glass ceiling' syndrome, and more. His 13 years' service as a community worker keeps him grounded and informs his work as a coach.

Nowadays, Hugh's mission is to make a positive difference in the field of coaching by sharing whatever wisdom he has accumulated over the years. He loves talking with people who "get" coaching, competitive sailing, keeping up with his family in the UK and Australia, and he is always prepared for whatever challenges might pop up next!

Hugh's previous publications include an Open University-validated distance learning module in Self-Management and Personal Effectiveness for a BA in Professional Development, and *The Coaching Handbook: Pressure & Stress (How to Master the Art of Coaching Conversations).*

Hugh's Ultimate System for Coaching Stress & Resilience is a 7-week accelerated learning program for high potential life and executive coaches who aim to step up to a new level of professional practice.

Contact Details

Website: https://coachingwisdom.org/

Email: hugh@coachingwisdom.org

LinkedIn: https://www.linkedin.com/in/hughtodd/

Facebook: https://www.facebook.com/procoachingwisdom/

A WEIGHTY PROBLEM

My journey from being overweight, anxious, and exhausted to an upgraded version of myself

Jacqui Carrel

It's a bright, sunny morning, but I cannot appreciate it. I've taken my children to their respective schools, and now I'm slumped in an armchair. The radio is off, the windows are shut, and the curtains are drawn. This is because I cannot cope with the stimulation of sound or light. My muscles and joints ache and hurt. I am in my early 40s, and I am exhausted. Incapacitated with a painful and debilitating multi-system disease known as Myalgic Encephalomyelitis or ME, I see a stark contrast to the fit and active woman of a year ago. A single parent to children of 11 and 9, I'm struggling to cope, and I live away from my family.

If I go upstairs, I must make sure to do everything I need to before coming back down, as I will not be able to manage the climb for another two hours. I cannot stand up long enough to even peel and chop a carrot, so I'm resorting – with tears in my heart for what I am doing to the children – to buying ready-made, microwavable meals.

This story is about what led me to this day, how I searched for the answers, and how I eventually found strength and resilience. It is also about how I finally lost my excess weight and embarked on an exciting new chapter in my life.

Let's roll back four years from the armchair and take it from there.

After a failed and ultimately damaging marriage to a man who had huge issues and used alcohol to cope, I moved in 1998 from England to my old home in Jersey – a small island near the coast of France – with my children, their cats, and anything else I could fit into our car.

My wonderful parents welcomed us with love and support, and we began to settle in quickly. Arriving during the school holidays meant we had time to arrange schooling for the children and a job for me. I wasn't happy about having to work full time while my children were young – that had never been in the game plan – but I nonetheless enjoyed my new position as a science, psychology, and ICT teacher at a girls' secondary school.

As the days moved on, I began to feel relaxed, safe, and contented. The children made friends and settled down well, and, despite my work hours, we spent plenty of time together. Whenever we could, we'd go to the beach after school and run around together, splashing and laughing, finishing our trips with ice cream from the beach kiosks.

Surrounded by the love of my family, and having a secure job and lovely outdoorsy life, you'd have thought I would have felt fulfilled, but I missed having a partner. While I was in no way debilitated or lonely, I was open to romance.

One day, my mother came into my room with a slightly startled look on her face, and said, "It's RJ!" and handed the phone across to me. My eyes opened wide, too, but I took a deep breath and bade RJ hello.

Let me explain.

RJ was a serviceman I had met in Cyprus in 1980 when he and my father were working from the same Forces' base. I was a naive 18-year-old, still at school, and he was a sophisticated 24-year-old officer. Within minutes of our meeting, we not only discovered we both hailed from Jersey, but we felt a definite spark between us. We spent as much time together as we could, and it was a heady, exciting period.

RJ was posted to a station in an eastern county of England, while I started my science degree in Plymouth, in the south-west. Although the distance meant we could only see each other at weekends, to me, it was worth the time and travel. We shared many lovely times, and I was happy. I thought RJ was too, but two years after we'd met, and with no ceremony, he ditched me. I was heartbroken and grieved for a long time.

Fast forward to the spring of 1999 and our phone call: my pulse was racing with mixed feelings, but I sounded calm. We chatted for a little while, and then he got to the point – he was back in Jersey for a break, and did I fancy meeting for a coffee and walk? And, by the way, he was separating from his wife.

Having not an ounce of sense in my head, I said yes, and we did; my feelings rekindled, and I was in love again. RJ had to return to England to work, and we carried on a long-distance relationship for a year – it wasn't easy, but we could phone and write (there was nothing like FaceTime or WhatsApp then) and sometimes we flew over to see each other. Once again, the times spent with him were heady, and I was happy.

As RJ and I slid into a new normal of visits, walks, meals out, and a holiday in the sun, I looked forward to a time when we would live together and convinced myself that the delicious anticipation of visits was worth the waiting.

Then, in an echo of 18 years earlier, and equally without ceremony, RJ phoned to say he couldn't cope with a long-distance relationship and that it was all off. I was not ready for our relationship to end and was distraught. With hindsight, I should have cried it all out and told him never to contact me again.

But we take the path we do, and mine was to convince him – successfully – to stay in our relationship; again reunited, we decided we needed to live together. It was much easier for me to pick up a teaching post in England than it was for RJ to get a job in Jersey (we have some strange regulations here), so I prepared to move with my long-suffering children back across the water.

Shortly before leaving Jersey, I visited La Corbière, a beautiful, granite headland guarded by a proud, white lighthouse. It's one of my favorite places; I remember standing with the sun on my face, and the sounds of the waves and perfumes in the air, delighting my senses. I also remember thinking, "I must be mad to leave!" I should have listened to that voice, but I pushed it down, and the children and I went to England in August, 2000.

We gained two beautiful kittens and an energetic puppy, and enjoyed walks and talks, socializing and exploring the countryside with the children. RJ continued working with the Forces, and I did supply (substitute) teaching, which I disliked, but we needed the money. RJ, emotionally unsupportive of my feelings around work, still made a welcome end to the day as we chatted over our evening meal and red wine.

Work-wise, things improved when I landed a part-time science post at a lovely local upper school; I settled in quickly and got on well with the pupils and staff. Despite that, I was beginning to feel depressed. My doctor diagnosed SAD (Seasonal Affective Disorder) and prescribed antidepressants. I don't like taking medications, but I felt I had no choice – in the early 2000s, we didn't have easy access to information about SAD and non-med ways to help, and the doctors certainly didn't seem to know either!

The antidepressants helped, but they caused me to put on a dress size in weight; RJ complained about my increasing size and was not at all supportive. Knowing what I know now about his childhood and upbringing, things make sense. I didn't get it then; all I knew was that things were suddenly changing, and our relationship was deteriorating. Savvier and much more emotionally intelligent now, at that point in my life I didn't know how to cope with his moods, nor identify the causes, and the good times became punctuated by arguments.

I should have seen it coming, but didn't. Once again, and with no preamble or compassion, RJ baldly announced it was over, and that was that. Once more, I was devastated and grief-stricken. I felt utterly rejected and diminished and spent the next week barely functioning or eating. Then I realized my children, despite being upset, were trying to cheer me up – who was the adult here? Brought to my senses, I began to eat and started to plan my life.

Liking the small cathedral town where we lived, the children and I decided to stay there. I signed a lease on a house that was close to the lovely, medieval center, and we moved in during the Easter vacation of 2002. Worried I would not have enough income to pay the bills, and knowing that several members of the staff would be there preparing for the next term, I went to my school to ask for extra hours of work.

I walked as calmly as I could into the staff room, smiled (sort of), and flapped my hand in welcome, but before I could speak, three of my colleagues exclaimed, "What's the matter? You look dreadful!" So much for my poise!

I had smoked for a short period in my student days, though not since, and weak tea was my beverage of choice. However, before I could blink, I was sat down with my lovely colleagues who patted my arm and offered hankies, and a cigarette and strong coffee were thrust into my hands. I left with a promise of more work and, my stress response being what it was, with a new smoking and coffee habit.

And so, two children, two cats, and I started life anew in our new rented home; we missed our beautiful dog, but RJ was best placed to look after her. The house was Victorian, impossibly cold in the winter, and cramped downstairs. But it was our space: we set our own rules and timetables and started a new chapter of our lives.

I almost lived as two separate beings then: there was 'normal' me, happy with my children, friends, and work, and cheerfully making the most of the limited resources we had – and then there was the other me who felt an underlying sense of guilt and loneliness. My guilt centered around the children: they had bullying issues at school, their father was causing emotional distress, and I didn't yet have the mental strength or know-how to sort things out. My loneliness was because I hadn't yet learned to be happy once more with my own company, and I wanted a man in my life to share things with.

My thoughts were often scary and unhelpful; they left me feeling inadequate and anxious. As a result, I did everything I could to ignore them. Instead, I did what I could: I buffered. Buffering took the shape of reading, studying, seeing friends, helping people before myself, smoking, and drinking wine every evening. I was also trying to lose weight – but trusting and following the government health edicts to eat high carb, low-fat foods only meant the fat continued to accumulate. My self-esteem also continued to fall.

It wasn't all bad; parts of life were lovely – there was time to be with my children, I enjoyed my teaching, and our friends commented how much at ease they felt in our welcoming home. Despite our second-hand furniture and lack of money, we became a hub for get-togethers and sleepovers. Family and friends from further afield would also come to stay, and these were happy, fun occasions.

But locally, I was attracted to people like me – we were a bunch of friendly misfits who all had problems. I value that part of my life, but while we supported each other, we didn't have the right emotional tools to help ourselves get to a better place.

I began to busy myself even more with projects and helping others; while I was genuinely invested in these activities, my full-on schedule also helped me stop exploring my thoughts. I suppressed my emotions and used up valuable energy resources. My doctor upped my antidepressant prescription; while I didn't like taking them, these meds did help me to function, and for that I was grateful.

One side effect of the meds, however, was continual weight gain. I renewed my efforts in following official advice to eat little fat and mostly carbs, and, of course, that approach remained as ineffectual as before. In desperation, I read and tried the Atkin's Diet that a friend had embarked on. This diet advocated a different approach and encouraged readers to dine on low carb, fatty foods; my weight began to shift! However, because I still didn't quite understand about carb addiction, I soon began to crave sugars and starches and gave up my new way of eating, believing the common mantra that it wasn't sustainable. What I had lost quickly went back on and more besides.

So, the weight gain continued, but I was generally peaceful, or at least superficially. While the meds got me through the days, they didn't help fix the root cause of my issues, and I simply pushed my fears and emotions even deeper. Now I know if you don't cry or talk out loud about your feelings, your body and mind suffer until these things manifest as emotional or physical illness or both, but I didn't know it then.

One day I woke up with a swollen neck and a raging sore throat. I went to work but was sent home later when it became apparent that I could barely speak or swallow. Eventually, I went to see a doctor; though the blood tests didn't corroborate his diagnosis, he diagnosed my problem as glandular fever. He explained this discrepancy by saying I'd gone to him too late after its onset; he was, however, convinced that I had the virus. Guilt about my neglected students fueled a quick return to teaching, but not giving myself time to properly recover meant my energy and immune reserves were far too low.

My anxiety also remained. Despite the extra hours of teaching I had,

I was still struggling to pay the rent and bills. I cut back on everything I could, including taking the cheapest option available on car insurance. A week later, I skidded on an oil patch. Although I walked away from the crash, the car was written off. I did not have enough insurance coverage to get a replacement.

As I had whiplash and a bad shoulder from the car accident, I couldn't cycle to work, so I started walking instead. This was stressful and exhausting in terms of delivering the children to their respective schools on time, getting to mine, and reversing the process at the day end.

But even when my shoulder and neck improved and my wonderful family clubbed together and bought me a car, I just became more and more tired and found it hard to get through the days. I am sure the smoking and drinking and high-carb diet didn't help at all, but it wasn't just that, it was more – and I couldn't work it out.

My anxiety, guilt, and anger levels were climbing because I was also having to regularly explain to the children why their father had reneged yet again on coming to visit them. Sometimes he would turn up, and I'd spend the day in a panic, as on previous occasions he'd threatened to disappear with them – they were empty threats, but I didn't know it then. Bullying at school just added to children's troubles, and I took on their pain. Overall, I felt emotionally disabled and certainly had no sense of self-worth or self-empowerment.

Yet it wasn't all horrendous! I have many good memories of that time. Sometimes I would get to see my family, and that was always lovely. I had supportive friends and regular, happy social occasions. Despite my fatigue, I was still getting into the countryside and going to the gym.

And of course, my children – my wonderful children – were there. They were just a pleasure to have around and were a major source of pride and comfort for me. They got involved in writing and drama (my daughter) and chess and the Cathedral choir (my son). While I felt guilty that I could not pay for any dance or music lessons for the children, I also felt okay giving them time to 'be' rather than shoveling them off to classes every evening like some parents were doing. We also enjoyed family time with walks, books, lively conversations, and board games.

But, overlying all the good things was that patina of anxiety and an increasing sense of brain fog and whole-body fatigue. I tried to convince myself I was imagining things, but, at the same time, I was becoming worried about my sanity and health. Then, one day at the gym, I could not press even the easiest of weights and decided enough was enough. I went to a doctor who said I had something called ME (Myalgic Encephalomyelitis). I had never heard of it!

She assured me I wasn't imagining my brain fog, fatigue, and physical pain, and that my illness was most definitely real. Straight after, I walked the short distance to the town book shop and picked up two books about ME. Settling down with them in the lovely upstairs café, I opened the first book, which started by declaring, "You are not going mad!"; this wonderful pronouncement was followed by a list of symptoms, including severe brain fog, debilitating joint and muscle pain, and fatigue. I cried from relief; I wasn't pleased to be ill, but now I knew where I was, I could explain it to people.

It was summer, and my fixed-term contract with the school was nearly up. The doctor's prognosis was it could take me many years to recover, even with rest, and that teaching was unlikely to be a viable option. I didn't wish to sign a new contract knowing I would not be able to return after the holidays, so we parted our ways with regret, and I felt my teaching career was most likely over.

Because I'd not had a permanent contract, I had no sick pay, so I registered to get benefits and help with my rent. It's not something I have thought about in a long time but, as I write this chapter, I can once more feel the helpless, impotent fury I had felt in the face of the obdurate, unhelpful, unfriendly people and systems that made up our Social Security. The more stressed I got, the more I buffered, and the more my weight climbed.

I went to my bank and asked to make a claim on the insurance policy I had to cover me should I lose my job. They looked very carefully at the contract and told me that as the exact test for glandular fever cited in the small print did not show me as positive, I could not make a claim. And that was it; there was nothing I could do to make them change their minds.

To do anything apart from resting took an immense effort of will, and I would sleep for up to three hours every afternoon. My capacity to cope with any stimuli dropped precipitously, so even when I did get to the shops, the noise, along with the smell of washing powder or anyone's perfume, overwhelmed me.

So, we come back to the beginning of this story, where I was slumped in an armchair — overweight, in pain, and exhausted. Then, sitting there and wishing I could just be better by tomorrow, I found myself thinking, "No! If you got better that quickly, you wouldn't know what put you here in the first place."

It was an unwelcome thought, but a revelation. I was determined there and then that I would solve the puzzle, start to mend, and move on. I did lots of thinking and reading, and as the weeks passed, I was able to do one activity for myself a day. I started going to the bookshop, a ten-minute walk away.

Something inside told me to let the right books present themselves, so each time I visited, I picked out a couple at random from the reference shelves and pored over them in the shop café. Although I had hitherto ignored – even slightly sneered at – the 'self-help' culture, I read voraciously through many books in this genre. Several of the concepts were new to me, and they needed repetition to start breaking through my unhelpful thoughts and behaviors. But I began to see light! I also became happy to be a single person, which was liberating.

We were lucky that year to have a warm spring and hot summer, so I spent plenty of time reading outside, sharing cups of tea and chatter with friends, playing with my children, and I started cooking once more. Gradually, I began to emerge from the pain and fatigue, and it was time to start thinking about working part-time.

I was already qualified in aromatherapy and massage, and also in Thought Field Therapy (TFT) to diagnostic level, which I used to treat anxieties, phobias, and addictions. I did not have the physical energy to pursue either of these as a business, but, as I also wanted to be a business writer and copywriter, I decided to follow the latter route. However, while I knew my craft, I had no clue how to work for myself. After asking around, I enrolled in a government-funded scheme to learn the ropes for starting a business.

The advisors were lovely people, and a group of us who started at the same time became friends. I began to remember what it was like to mix with people who weren't riddled with insecurities, problems, and debts! Furthermore, they appreciated my skills, which did wonders for my self-esteem.

During this time, I also signed up for internet dating, which was still in its infancy. I met several men for coffee and began to feel my self-confidence increasing, although, mirroring most of my adult years, I was still attracted to the wrong sorts and rejecting any relationships with the nice, stable ones!

While some of it was fun, the whole process was tiring and, in the end, tedious. As I was now happy with my own company, I decided to take a rest from dating. I messaged this intention to a man I was in email contact with but hadn't yet met, and he requested to at least meet up once. Since he had asked so nicely, I agreed.

Enter Roy.

That first meeting led to another and then another; I found I liked this man very much, and I knew the feeling was mutual.

Our relationship grew; with a lovely smile and a friendly, patient, calming nature, Roy was a wonderful complement to my life, and the children also loved him. 18 months later, on a beautiful summer day, we were married in a lovely ceremony where my daughter read the lesson, and my son sang a solo.

While I was happily working part-time in writing and marketing, my income was erratic and limited. My work came through referrals, and I didn't have the energy to consistently generate and follow up leads. Needing the money, I decided to try a little teaching once more.

I was offered a part-time, permanent teaching job at a school for pupils with special needs, which I happily accepted. Just as I was about to sign the contract, I discovered I had cervical cancer and had to have an emergency hysterectomy. Legally I could have signed the contract, been secure, and then gone straight onto sick pay; morally, I just couldn't, so I regretfully phoned and explained why I wouldn't be joining them.

The operation went well, but I am sensitive to touch, pain, and noise, so the next few days in the hospital ward are best forgotten! Once home, however, I was able to think much more positively, rest up in loose dresses, and just let the world happen at a gentle pace. I'd had my ovaries removed at the same time, so went straight into post-menopause and hot sweats – not nice! On my doctor's recommendation, I took HRT but stopped after gaining 14lbs in just one month.

Over the next few weeks, the post-operation pain diminished, and I could start moving again. I soon recovered enough to start working again part-time, but from home, not at schools. Roy worked night shifts in a profession he had been in for over 30 years, and the shifts were beginning to tell on his health and well-being. Fed up with his job and seeing what I did through rose-tinted spectacles, he came home just before Christmas, announced he'd handed in his notice, and would henceforth be working with me.

What?! I wished Roy had found an alternative job first. He was an excellent writer but had no idea about business, and I hadn't the energy to up my game or help him. I felt my precious day-time space had been invaded, money became a real problem, and my anxiety began to regrow. Nonetheless, we supported each other as best we could and happily we kept our relationship intact and strong.

But the HRT and anxiety had started another cycle of weight gain, one that was all too familiar and disheartening. Finally, despite what the health officials said, I started to cut out bread, pasta, and sugar from my diet. Looking back, I believe I was pre-diabetic but, whatever my status, this simple dietary change meant my heartburn disappeared, and I stopped needing to visit the toilet at night; in turn, I slept better, which cheered me up immensely. I also started to reverse my weight gain – I still had a way to go, but after ages of feeling frumpy, lumpen, and lethargic, I was delighted!

Although I eventually shed two sizes and was gaining energy, my weight and ME were still an issue for me; apart from some occasional evening-time wine and some daily chocolate, I was eating healthily, or so I thought, so I was mystified and frustrated over my inability to lose more weight.

I don't believe you can lose weight simply by exercising to 'burn it off'; our bodies are much more complex than the simplistic calories-in-calories-out proponents would have us believe. However, this was a moot point as anything more than gentle exercise was still beyond me, so I had to do this through diet. I was still following the high-carb, low-fat mantra, so all my attempts lead to either just a stabilizing of weight or weight gain, and I felt like a failure.

One day, I was complaining to Roy about my lack of progress. Usually supportive, his unexpected reply, "You keep going on about it, but you always do the same, and nothing changes" shocked me – but, through the ensuing tears, I knew what he said was correct.

Over the next few days, I started thinking about what I was doing and eating now and compared it to what I was doing and eating back when I was slim and energetic. Was my past way of eating with occasional starch, low sugar, and plenty of natural fats—the one the government said was bad for my health—actually the right one after all?

I ditched the diet books that advocated a 'high-carb, low-fat, eat six small meals a day' regime and re-read the few that were left; I also began to explore the papers cited in the references of the books. As a result, I cut right back on other dietary carbohydrates, particularly processed ones. I also introduced more natural fats into my diet, which I loved. With this new way of eating in place, it became easy to stop having wine and chocolate in the week.

At the same time, I started seeing the surgery's practice nurse every week for a weigh-in and chat. This simple check-in every Friday morning was valuable and helped me keep on track; going by my past attempts, I'm not sure I'd have kept going through that first few months without this support and accountability.

Because I was losing weight and still unaware of the bad effects sugar has on one's body other than mere weight gain, I would 'treat' myself with whatever I wanted at the weekends, so my need for the sweet stuff, although diminished, hovered in the background.

Work-life went on: Roy set up a company assembling flat-pack furniture, I added website building to my mix, and we ran writing workshops. By now, I'd been back in England for 12 years, my daughter was working, my son was going to university, and Roy's adult children and their own children lived a long way from us. While I loved the town we lived in, I was missing Jersey and my lovely widowed mother, and this seemed a good time to return. Roy had come to love the Island and was eager to go too. In 2013, with our respective children agreeing to visit when they could, we moved across.

Once back and settled, we resumed our businesses, but I quickly regained all the weight I had lost and more besides. I finally tipped into the 'obese' category on the BMI scale, which was a huge blow to my pride. In addition, my heartburn returned, my feet ached, I could not get my long boots on, my thighs rubbed very uncomfortably together, and my self-esteem took a bashing.

What was I doing wrong now? After pushing aside self-denials, I realized I had remained in the holiday eating mode we'd been in when we first came back to Jersey; my latent sugar need had been re-awoken, and I had slipped back into eating a starch-laden and sugar-heavy diet with snacks and wine most days.

I realized that if I went through the process of losing weight in the same way as last time, I would always be susceptible to another bout of weight gain, so I returned to the books and the online papers. I came across recently published insights and discoveries that answered crucial questions and finally began to see a clearer picture. Putting a plan into place, I made the necessary changes and lost five dress sizes over the next couple of years. Weight loss can be quicker, but this gentler approach suited me. Muscle mass can reduce on diets, but I kept my lean tissue and built up my strength and energy. I also stopped having to wear glasses, which was an unexpected bonus!

This is an outline of what I did: First, I made a gradual transition to a low carbohydrate, higher fat diet. This was surprisingly easy, and the meals were satisfying. I made the move to ditch all grains rather than just wheat, ate fewer root vegetables, included more leafy, fibrous vegetables and added avocados, oily fish, and fattier cuts of meat. I ate three meals a day and rarely needed to snack; if I did, I had a small handful of nuts or olives. The hardest part was weaning myself off milk chocolate! Now, however, I find it far too sweet and am instead easily satisfied with the occasional square of 95% dark chocolate.

Once I was sure my body had adapted to using fat for fuel rather than sugar, I started to shorten my eating window. First, I introduced butter and coconut oil into my morning coffee, which served as a breakfast replacement and got me through to lunch. After a couple of months, I found I no longer needed even that, which meant my eating window was now six to eight hours.

This was an inadvertent and gradual shift into intermittent fasting; occasionally, I would go a whole day before getting hungry, but just having two meals in a smaller eating window suited me well, so that's what I did most.

As the weight loss continued, I began to feel mentally and physically better and found I was naturally moving around more. My feet, instead of aching all the time, kept me going on walks that I hadn't been able to manage for a long time. I had joined a choir, and even singing became easier as I could stand up longer and fill up my lungs more easily!

During that period of weight loss, I studied to become a nutritional therapist and passed three diplomas with Distinctions. I began to write a newspaper column around nutrition, aiming both to give facts and tips to readers and to call out the outdated, damaging advice still peddled by many health professionals.

And so, in my 50s, mentally and physically re-energized and wanting to make a difference to women who were also yo-yoing with their weight, I started on my third career, offering nutritional help coupled with weight loss coaching.

This went very successfully ... to a point. Certain clients, even though they were following plans correctly, would just reach a plateau or even regain a little weight, and others would still occasionally crave and binge on junk foods. Even using TFT did not help all of them. I believed them when they said they were eating well and following their plans, so what was I missing?

As I began to walk more, I started listening to podcasts at the same time; one day, my feed recommended a recording by Marisa Peer. I'd not heard of her before but was at once entranced. She did something called RTT™, or Rapid Transformational Therapy, and I couldn't hear or watch enough of it over the next few weeks.

I discovered how we create and keep beliefs from past events and how those affect our actions in the present; I saw how RTT also helped replace the bad, limiting beliefs with good, empowering ones. That was it! Here was my answer to finding the missing pieces of my clients' jigsaws! I added RTT to my professional mix, training partly online and partly in London with Marisa Peer; it was an amazing journey, and I learned so much.

As a bonus, my confidence and feeling of self-worth flourished. I forgave myself for my perceived past weaknesses and inaction and lost all negative feelings about my first husband and RJ. All these things freed up mental space and energy, and the subsequent decrease in stress levels aided further weight loss.

RTT is now part of something I use with most clients within my coaching packages, and the transformations around weight problems, eating issues, and addictions are amazing. I love watching clients grow into their new, empowered selves and lives. Because my waitlist is growing, I have introduced group work, workshops, and online courses so that I can reach and help more people.

So now, in my late 50s, I am healthier and fitter than I was 15 years ago, I value myself and have a unique approach to helping transform clients' lives. My life is happy, fun, and fulfilling, and I thank you for coming on this part of my journey with me. The next chapter in my life will see me learning more, developing my business further, and helping even more people. What will be your next chapter?

* * *

Top Tips

Here are ten concepts I have learned along the way that I wish I'd known or taken on board sooner; if even one helps you, I will be happy. Do let me know!

- Carbohydrates and highly processed foods are addictive, and being overweight is largely a hormonal imbalance issue caused by excess sugars and processed foods, even savory ones. People who are overweight are not greedy and lazy; they are being controlled by a complex phenomenon known as insulin resistance. The cycle of persistent weight gain can also be rooted in the past; RTT can help find the cause and take away the associated beliefs and self-sabotaging behaviors, replacing them with up-to-date, empowering beliefs that very much help with weight loss.

- You can reverse insulin resistance, excess weight, and associated problems by eating natural, non-processed foods that are low in sugars and starches and rich in natural fiber and fats. You can speed up weight loss and energy gain by not snacking and by shortening your eating window. Cut out grains too (it's easier than you may think), and your overall health and brain will thank you for it. Eating real food also helps you develop a good gut biome, which in turn rewards you by making more happy hormones and keeping your gut wall and blood-brain barrier healthy. Please note, if you are taking any medications, you should consult a health professional before making dietary changes.

- You cannot run off a bad diet! Exercise will also make you hungry, so don't use it to 'burn off calories'; instead, use it to improve your overall health and well-being. If you are too tired to exercise much just now, know that as your body starts to recover, you'll find you become naturally motivated to move around more.

- Helping others is good and can bring many rewards, but don't do it to avoid your issues or to such an extent that your health suffers. Make sure you ask for help when you need it, know it is okay to be vulnerable and that it is always okay to ask for help and to say no or take time out. You are not showing weakness; instead, you are empowering yourself.

- An illness or problem does not need to define you; look inside for the real you and start building from there. If you do have something you wish to see the back of, don't 'own' it, as the mind tries to hold onto something it thinks it is losing. For example, instead of saying 'my fat,' say 'the fat,' or instead of talking about 'my addiction,' say 'the addiction.'

- You are you, a unique, lovely person. Take stock of where you are, remember in the past you acted for the best reasons and let any lingering guilt or annoyance about your actions and issues go. You are where you are: start loving yourself now and decide what step to take next to start addressing your issues and empowering your life.

- While on your journey, if something isn't working for you, research, and experiment until you find the right way for you. There is a lot of contradictory information out there, so choose your sources wisely; it was only when I delved around that I was able to change my diet and mindset to become so much healthier in body and mind.

- All feelings are telling you something: you don't have to like them, but you can be at peace with them and not fight them. Take a few deep, calming breaths and observe them from a distance; acknowledge them, and let them pass on the message as to why they are there – then you can make empowered decisions about what you will do next. Whatever you do, explore what is the matter and release it through exercise, talking, singing or tears, because if you push a problem down, it will hurt your body and psyche.

- What you tell your brain in words and pictures, it will believe you. So, make sure you anticipate success instead of stress – lie to your brain if you have to until it becomes natural to think those empowered thoughts. Remember, you are enough, and you are perfect, so when you are describing yourself, use words like phenomenal, brilliant, skilled, resilient, and fantastic. Use power feelings too, like excited, happy, energized, and strong.

- It's part of human nature to experience a range of emotions, so if you're feeling a bit down or scared, add positive words alongside negative ones. For example, say, "Yes, I am anxious, and I'm also resilient;" "Yes, I am jittery, and I have phenomenal coping skills;" "Yes, I am tired, and I have amazing skills to help me through until I can rest;" and "Yes, I am scared, and I can choose to feel excited."

Wishing you all the best on your own amazing journey,

Jacqui Carrel

JACQUI CARREL

We've all been there: out of sorts, down on ourselves, filled with doubt, below par, self-sabotaging our best efforts, and often without knowing why; this is where Jacqui Carrel can help you.

Therapist*, author, speaker, teacher, and environmental scientist, Jacqui Carrel uses her extensive knowledge and unique approach to help individuals lose weight, overcome fears, phobias, and addictions, and to regain emotional and physical health and confidence.

Not afraid to stand up for what she believes is right, Jacqui regularly appears in the media talking about health and environmental issues. She also writes books, creates online courses, has a column in Jersey's leading daily newspaper, and speaks at events.

In addition to helping people to lose weight, addictions, anxiety, and phobias, Jacqui's passion is helping people find their own inner strength, peace, and joie de vivre. To get your own head start, visit www.jacquicarrel.co.uk/hello, where you'll find free resources and a helpful reference section.

Jacqui lives in Jersey, a small but beautiful island off the coast of France; in her spare time, you'll find Jacqui, camera in hand, exploring Jersey's beautiful coastline.

*A few of her many qualifications include the multiple award-winning Rapid Transformational Therapy (Jacqui trained in RTT with the founder Marisa Peer), the famous Thought Field Therapy (Jacqui trained in TFT with the founder Dr. Roger Callahan), and Nutritional Therapy.

Contact Details

Website: https://jacquicarrel.co.uk/hello

Facebook: https://www.facebook.com/JacquiCarrel.blockbuster/

LinkedIn: https://www.linkedin.com/in/jcarrel/

You can also find Jacqui on YouTube.

NEVER GIVE UP

Lis Manson

Discovering My Voice

I sit with my elder brother, almost three years my senior, in the back of our father's Ford, my 8-year old eyes open wide as I lose sight of our Manchester home. We are going on holiday, all the way to the south of France, and I am so excited!

It's going to be a long trip. First, we drive all day from Manchester to London, stopping midway for a picnic lunch and then on to Dover to ride the ferry across the English Channel to Calais, France. As we drive, Dad and I sing; my father's wonderful baritone voice harmonising with my sweet, clear soprano notes. We sing all the songs I know, and it always raises spirits and passes the time more quickly.

At the Port of Dover, men direct Dad to drive the car right into the bowels of the ferry. We excitedly climb the stairs up to the deck to watch the coastline and the white cliffs disappear into the distance. Then Dad and I walk the deck with the wind blowing around us. We disembark the ferry and head for the train station where our car is driven right up onto the second level of an open train carriage stacked with vehicles. The four of us sit facing one another, gazing out the window at passing scenes of the French countryside – the next exciting part of the journey south through France.

At our coastal hotel, my brother and I meet other holidaying children. After playing all day on the beach, we children eat dinner earlier than our parents. The grown-ups dine elegantly later in the evening, accompanied by soft, live piano music. One such evening, as we eat our dinner, my brother dares me to ask the pianist to play an Italian song that I know well in English, *Santa Lucia*. My brother and I had performed this song at home – my brother playing the piano – to entertain my grandmother's friends when they came for tea. They were a kind audience, and their applause made me feel special. But, singing for an audience of strangers would be a completely new experience for me – would they be as kind? Am I good enough to sing for these sophisticated people?

I don't want to show my companions that I'm scared. I don't know how I find the courage to ask the pianist to play the one song I had performed before. Not surprisingly, he knows it and asks if I can sing it, to which I nod. Oh my goodness, what have I gotten myself into? Do I have the courage to perform in front of an entire audience of adults? What are my parents going to say? I stand in front of a microphone beside the piano.

The notes of the piano fill the air. As soon as I begin to sing, the nerves and fear disappear. I concentrate on singing the piece as best as I can, focusing solely on the words, the music, and the sound of my voice drifting out to the audience. When the song finishes, and I hear loud applause, a new realisation dawns on me: my voice is a gift, and I can share it. From that day forward, music would play a central role in my life.

Growing Up in England

Born into a society still repressing deep emotional trauma from World War II, I was brought up in a protected, privileged environment – a lovely home, private school, piano lessons, singing lessons, ballet, tap and modern dance. Our house was always abuzz with guests and friends.

My maternal grandmother lived with us; her husband had died when my mother was two years old, leaving my grandmother alone with her two sons and a daughter. She remarried, but her second husband died three years later. Later she lost both her sons. One died of rheumatic fever at age 14. My Uncle Harry was killed in World War II; he was a radio officer aboard a Merchant Navy Ship which was torpedoed while carrying TNT gunpowder from Montreal to England. My mother was the only one left.

My grandmother's parents had come to England when she was a

child – one of nine children. They were well-to-do, living in a large house with paid help. As a result, she had high expectations. Despite losing her sons, she was the matriarch of a large extended family; relatives regularly visited my grandmother. We often had guests for lunch, afternoon tea, and dinner. As her only grandchildren, my grandmother doted on my brother and me. However, when it came to discipline, it meant we had three parents rather than two.

Our father, the second-youngest of seven children, came from a rather harsh rule-based upbringing, despite never having known his own father. His mother emigrated from Russia to England at 17; she married an Austrian man who ended up in an internment camp in the war. She never spoke good English, but she made up for it with hard work and determination. In 1911, she started her own business selling braiding, buttons, and buckles. Three of her sons took over the business and dealt in sheeting, ticking and textiles. My brother took the business in a new direction, manufacturing bedding, curtains and cushions. In 2019, my brother sold that business – it had supported three generations of families for 107 years!

A workaholic like his mother, my father brought work home with him every night. He would sit in imposing silence at the head of our dinner table while my mother and her mother chatted openly. It seemed my grandmother disapproved of my father, and I'm sure he felt the strain of two against one in our household. As uncommunicative as he was at home, he was an excellent salesman – I recall marvelling at his charismatic charm when I tagged along with him on sales calls. That business was in his blood. He had the most fabulous singing voice and he sang at home every Sunday as we all helped with chores, though he rarely sang elsewhere. I was brought up understanding that it was all about doing the 'right thing' – whatever that was – after, all, whose rules were the 'right' ones?

At four-and-a-half years old, I entered a private girls' school and discipline was the order of the day there too. I did very well in junior school. One year, I received all 'As' with one exception – a 'B' in music, which was my very best subject! I had no idea why; maybe they thought that with my previous education, I was able to do better. I recall getting a comment on a report card. "Elisabeth has no imagination." Not a particularly helpful comment.

Every year, leading up to our school Christmas concert, I anxiously awaited the announcement of who would get the solo part in the classic carol, *Once in Royal City*. I wanted that solo but was refused it because I wasn't the right religion – you see, we were Jewish, not Christian.

I regularly sang in our synagogue services while my brother played the organ. I was never simply a choir member – I was always waiting to get the solo! I loved the music; in later life, I would introduce this music to new choirs in a new country. Being in a choir and learning the music became my passion, rather like knowing lots of hymns by osmosis!

In high school, my passion for music continued; singing madrigals, playing the cello and piano. I did it all. When I turned 16, I started private vocal training which continued into my college years. By then, I had a strong and powerful voice. Once, when singing at a school event, they asked me to move from the front row to the back because my voice projected farther than all the others.

In England, we had to take national exams at ages 16 and 18. I wanted to 'fast-track' my music education by condensing the final level of music into one year instead of two and then passing the exam early. But the school's headmistress, a rather straight-laced lady, bluntly refused my request in a private interview in her office. I became angry, replying, "But, it's my life; I want to sing." To which she replied, "You may only end up in the back row of a third-rate opera chorus!" (Perhaps I would have been happy there.) She ended with, "Your parents and I will decide your future." (In actuality, she was likely protecting the school's success rates rather than mine; they would have been negatively impacted if I had done poorly in the exam as a result of rushing the preparation.) I had to write a formal letter of apology to her for my angry outburst.

At age 17, I played the lead role in a school production of *Dido and Aeneas* by Purcell. At the last performance, I lost my voice; on stage, I had to walk over to the understudy and whisper, "You sing it." I was devastated, not understanding why I had lost my voice.

My father rarely came to hear me perform, but he did attend one special performance when I sang in a band that auditioned for a British talent show called *Opportunity Knocks* with Hughie Green. Like the school headmistress, he also discouraged me from choosing the stage as a profession, saying, "It's a terrible life, travelling from place to place, staying in awful digs and hardly earning any money!"

Upon graduation, I had two choices: go to the *Northern School of Music*, Royal College in Manchester or train to be a teacher. My parents wanted me to become a teacher, to have something to fall back on. Without any support for my own ambitions, I feared I wasn't good enough to become a professional musician. And so, I bowed to my parents' influence and studied to become a teacher instead.

Coming of Age

I grew up in a defined culture – that of my family and my country. And I felt constrained and limited by the strict rules and narrow beliefs enforced by my parents and teachers. Of course, they did not create these rules and beliefs, they inherited them – passed down through their own families and assimilated from the society in which we all lived – a society deeply affected by two world wars. At a very young age, I recognised how I could shine, but as I grew up, I also internalised the 'rules' – do what you're told; do what's expected; don't question authority; don't take unnecessary risks. It would take much of my lifetime, and many trials and tribulations, to become aware of these limiting patterns – and even longer to learn to release them, to find real independence, and truly shine.

Whilst at college, I had a serious boyfriend, of whom my father did not approve. They told the boy and his parents, "We don't want you to have anything to do with our daughter." That day, I had arrived at a residential teaching school; my father appeared unexpectedly, told me to collect my things, and took me home. I suffered the loss of that relationship miserably. However, my father decided for me; I was to do as I was told. My family never really conversed about feelings or what mattered to me.

Later, I met another boy whom my father found even more unsuitable. But this time, I was determined to stand my ground. My new boyfriend was very intelligent, having achieved a double honours Bachelor's degree in economics and politics. He planned to leave England to do a Master's degree in Canada; at that time there were no grants available for a second degree in England. He was accepted at three universities, but the University of Alberta offered to pay part of his voyage and a paid position as a teaching assistant.

We wanted to get married and move to Canada together; I knew my mind and thought I was grown up. The night I got engaged turned into a very traumatic and sad occasion because my parents didn't support the marriage. The family lawyer informed me that my father had taken my bank account passbook and that he was going to do anything he could to stop me from leaving for Canada as a married woman. My father openly disliked my husband-to-be and his family. But, he never told me the real reason for this intense dislike. In the meantime, my husband-to-be left for Canada without me. I felt very alone and struggled with my painful emotions. Many years later, when I discovered my husband's true nature, I realised I should have listened to my father. But, lacking that information at the time, I was simply an angry know-it-all young person who wanted to prove my parents wrong.

Relations with my parents degraded from bad to worse, and I did not have the emotional skills to deal with the fallout. Rows and arguments ensued. My father and brother blamed me for my mother's illness, saying, 'Look what you're doing to her.' Unbeknownst to my family, I applied to emigrate to Canada on my own. My fiancé and I had applied together, but now I had to reapply individually as a teacher. When my family found out, my father told me to leave the house. My mother was distraught because she didn't know how to handle my father when he had made up his mind. There was no conversation. My grandmother was the only person on my side. I remember my father standing at the bottom of the stairs as I carried all my possessions out of the house. It was unnerving, to say the least. I moved to a rather miserable rooming house that my fiancé had helped me find before he left for Canada. Sharing a bathroom with strangers was a shock, and I had no idea how to cook. However, I had a job and, for the first time, I was living on my own. My mother visited me there once and told me I was ruining my life, but I wasn't in the frame of mind to listen to her.

Painful Parting

When I received my immigration papers, I determinedly followed by husband-to-be to Edmonton, Alberta. What was I thinking? Only that I wanted to escape. Honestly, I was a nervous wreck. I had no idea what it meant to leave my family and sheltered life behind. Nevertheless, I had love on my side and a man to support me! So, I arrived in Canada ... and stayed for many years.

Life began in Edmonton, Alberta, with a freezing and difficult first winter. Standing outside for more than a minute in minus 30 degrees Fahrenheit was painful, and the clothes I had brought with me did not suit Canadian weather! My family home had always been a centre for parties; now, I was alone in a new country. To my surprise the customs and values were quite different. I was a fish out of water – unhappy and lost. Though I would not hear from my family for another seven years, I received numerous letters from my family's Rabbi (likely urged by my father), attempting to convince me not to marry this man, but I still had no idea why. When the local Rabbi we met in Edmonton contacted the Rabbi in Manchester, he reported back to us, that he saw no reason why we couldn't get married as were of legal age to do so.

I got a job as a salesperson in a ladies-wear shop in the city. My mini skirts were too short for Alberta fashion and the shadow-and-pounce method of selling in which I was instructed didn't sit well with me. I was fired. However, at this store, I met an English lady who took pity on me. Amazingly, not only were we from the same city in England, but we also discovered that I used to walk home from high school with her nephew! Talk about a small world. When she and her husband heard that my family had cut me off, they took me under their wing and gave me a sort of 'wedding party' – though, since we hardly knew anyone, it was a rather sad affair.

Within a short time, I began to see the man I had chosen to marry in a very different light. I found living with someone I didn't really know extremely stressful. We had no money, and he became disenchanted with his university program, changed courses, and lost his teaching assistant position. To top it off, I realised that he was a philanderer – he had been with other women, and he didn't see anything wrong with it. I was naïve, so naïve. I had a choice: go home with my tail between my legs or make the best of a bad situation. Pride got the better of me and I stayed. After all, I had been raised to 'do what was expected' and wives are expected to stay with their husbands – I had certainly made my bed.

New Life and Trials

We stayed in Edmonton for 20 months. I worked as a typist and then a substitute teacher. I recall entering a geography classroom to teach about the Northwest Territories; unfortunately, I didn't know where they were as Canadian geography was not part of the British curriculum!

Eventually, I earned a position teaching drama and some music in a junior high school. If only the subjects (I was to teach) were the other way round. In fact, had I actually learned how to teach in college? I don't think so. I qualified to teach music, art and drama, but I am not sure that I had any idea what I was doing. I really didn't know how to teach drama, so I had to figure it out as I went along.

The Edmonton Board of Education put me in touch with other Drama teachers, and two of us created and ran a circus-themed drama workshop. With the help of appropriate music and lots of ad-libbing, we managed to bring our circus to life. It was an exhilarating experience.

I also joined a group of teachers who organised and performed an annual review. That year's production was based on the musical *Oliver*, and I played the main character, a teacher, Miss Oliver. Standing on a huge stage at the *Jubilee Centre* in front of a massive audience of teachers, I sang, *As Long as They Need Me*, with all my heart. Yes. I had finally made it onto a big stage, and they heard my voice.

My husband completed his Master's degree and, despite my success as a drama teacher, we packed everything we owned into a small U-Haul and drove across the Prairies to Toronto in pursuit of a new adventure – all riding on a promising job interview my husband had landed. Almost penniless, we spent three weeks in a disgusting weekly-rental apartment. We spread our still-packed boxes around the apartment to cover up the dirt and grease. Fortunately, we soon found a much nicer place, but we had to turn to my father-in-law for financial help to afford it. Unfortunately, my husband didn't get the job we came for.

We found work together, selling frozen pizzas in a shopping centre. We cooked the pizzas in a small oven in the centre aisle of the mall and served free samples. An excellent salesman, my husband was far better at this than I was – I think he could have sold ice to Eskimos. Then, for a few months, I worked in a travel agency. An acquaintance told me about a teaching job, and I found myself teaching music in a junior high school in Toronto.

Still very young, I found it a challenge. However, I started a choir, learned how to conduct with the help of the visiting instrument music teacher, and led successful performances. Unfortunately, I came up against authority. Without my principal's permission, I attempted to form connections directly with other music teachers in the area to do joint performances between schools. The principal took offence. At the same time, I experienced issues with my wrist, which led to two small surgeries. The required physiotherapy led me to leave the job.

Next, my husband and I entered into a retail adventure. At a party, we met a lady with a retail space for rent above a convenience store in midtown Toronto. Before I knew what hit me, my husband had rented the place without even checking it out. When we got the keys, we found the space in a dreadful mess; all the fixtures had been removed, but the garbage remained. We set to work cleaning it up, building dressing rooms, painting and wallpapering to make it look presentable. We had a new sign made, in an attempt to encourage customers to walk up the stairs to the second floor – it had originally been an apartment.

We printed flyers and snuck into apartment buildings at night to slip them under doors and we held parties, catered with my own treats, as I loved to bake. Over time, we built up a clientele. My first trip to source merchandise – by train to Montreal in the dead of winter – was stressful and fearful. I had no idea what kinds or sizes of clothes to buy, and then I had to carry the heavy boxes back to the hotel through a freezing cold snowstorm. Yet, we ran that store for over three years and met many wonderful people.

Next, we managed to acquire retail space from a furrier in a store located in the lobby of a well-known hotel in downtown Toronto. The management certainly did not want us in their hotel – we weren't successful enough or exclusive enough. Nevertheless, after some refurbishing, we opened and kept this location for over nine more years. We met people, including celebrities, from the far corners of the world. I acted as the operation's public relations person, while my husband was the salesman par excellence. We worked long hours, seven days a week, relying on weekend tourists and convention guests, and also providing in-house alteration services.

During this time, I miscarried twice before doctors identified the medical problem. On my 30th birthday, I lay in bed, trying not to miscarry and my husband commented that he thought I was doing it deliberately. When I did successfully carry our first child to term, I recall finishing shortening some hems in the early stages of labour and cashing up before we drove to the hospital. Eventually, a sort of truce transpired with my family in England. I'm glad to say that my parents occasionally came to see my children, though communication between my father and husband remained very strained.

Later, we moved out of Toronto to start a side hustle – buying, renovating, and selling houses. We also integrated into a small community and joined a tiny synagogue. I learned to be a cantor, singing many of the prayers and music in services. The Rabbi was struggling to teach people to sing with only a prayer book; I commented, "You can't teach people to sing like that." Next thing I knew, I had taken responsibility for forming and conducting a small choir. This effort felt like breathing to me – I loved it. I got to sing, and I helped others to find their voices too. Together we created beautiful harmony and provided pleasure to the congregation. We sang at choral festivals and stood out. In fact, this small group sounded so good; we entered a CBC (Canadian Broadcasting Corporation) radio competition. We made it to the finals in the ethnic category and were awarded airtime. What a proud achievement!

After ten years of working hard, we now had two children and I began to work less. Singing and conducting brought joy to my life. On the flip side, my personal life was fraught with tension. Some weeks were good; others, I could do nothing right. I reeled from my husband's constant verbal blows, with no ability to stop them, rather like being run over by a tank. Saying 'stop' didn't have much effect. I now had two children but no money personally and however unhappy I felt, my pride and lack of resources prevented me from returning to England.

After eleven years in the fashion business, and four stores, the lease expired at one of the hotel locations. The ladies-wear business had become very competitive, so we decided to close. Next, we ventured into the food business – importing real cream frozen cakes from England and Germany. I continued to escape from the tension in our house through singing and conducting. I loved helping groups learn to deliver beautiful music. After travelling on my own to Israel with a group from Toronto, I also started a musical group of six women, all professional Toronto singers; we put on some incredibly good concerts. The *Globe & Mail* newspaper even featured our photo on the front page under one of Ronald Regan!

The Return

In early 1990, despite twenty-four years of building a good life in Canada, we decided to return to England. We wanted our children to benefit from an English education and European travel. And my father was also very ill with cancer. We closed the cake business, sold our house, and packed all our possession into a large shipping container. Walking away from everything we had worked so hard to achieve and enjoy, including all my good music and conducting, wracked me with fear.

The first three weeks in England we lived in a hotel. We asked my mother to store some suitcases for us; my father, who was very ill, apparently misunderstood our request and he demanded we leave their house and never come back. He died soon after without ever speaking to me again.

I found the first few months in England very difficult, and I mourned the loss of my good life in Canada. We rented a house for six months and awaited the arrival of our possessions. My husband and I fought a lot. Finding employment, or a good business opportunity, proved difficult. I found some work as a dance-lesson pianist. I also worked for a caterer. Both my husband and I loved cooking and we had been in the food business, which often meant catering dinners. Eventually, we bought a house that required a lot of work and considering our renovation experience, it seemed a good opportunity. Yet, I felt really unhappy in this house probably because I was unhappy generally with my lot and circumstances.

Completely unconsciously, we had become quite North American and didn't know how to be British again. Former friends and acquaintances made little effort to draw us back into their social circles; I felt quite ostracised. So, I started another community choir! One of the members called me the *Pied Piper* because the group attracted so many people and gave joy to both the members and our audiences. Based on the success of the choir, I became the music director at a synagogue. I found great joy in singing as a cantor, teaching, conducting, and using my own voice. I loved the musical harmony and atmosphere we created – times the congregation joined in and moments for musical reflection. These were my gifts, independent of my husband and despite his criticism – to communicate and to find my voice, through musical expression.

Breaking Down

The next three years of my life were fraught with stress and hardship – everything I knew fell apart. My relationship with my husband continued to deteriorate; his verbal abuse increased, and my children had grown old enough to witness it, which humiliated me. I finally found the courage to leave him – however, without any money of my own, it meant leaving my children as well.

My mother, with whom I had only just reunited, grew ill. Before she died, she commented that I had ruined my life. But, I disagreed; I had learned plenty of skills and achieved many successes, which I could not have experienced without moving countries and beginning over so many times. When my mother passed away, I discovered that I had been removed from her will – officially cast out by my family; being disinherited felt like another bitter blow. I had no idea how to continue.

I rented a humble house. The government's housing benefit fluctuated depending on whether I earned a few dollars more or less; I wasn't earning enough money to live on nor was I eligible for much help. I felt scared, like a pariah, scraping the bottom of society. Against her father's will, my twelve-year-old daughter decided to leave and started living with me. As much as I desperately wanted her with me, I stressed over caring for her. Conversely, my son, assumedly, negatively influenced by his father, did not want to visit or see me, which pained me intensely.

Negotiating the divorce initiated more than five years of legal wrangling and litigation. It was like playing chess with a person who changed the rules weekly. I didn't have the emotional skills to deal with my husband's tactics. Responding kindly opened me to vulnerability. Disagreeing required jumping through a fire of ridicule. A friend advised me, "You have to keep going no matter what is thrown at you because you are in a game that ends with who has the most control – you can't give in. A lawyer and good friend counselled me, "Don't give up: there's a light at the end of the tunnel." Unfortunately, at the time, I couldn't see any light at all; however, through patience, I did eventually see the light and a new chapter.

Over time, I entered into a new relationship that ended badly. On my birthday, I returned home from shopping to find he had packed up and left. I felt like the Munch painting, *The Scream*. How much more was I to endure?

Building Up

In my desperation, I turned to a Rabbi for help and solace, but his advice shook me to the core. He suggested that I go to the mental ward at the local hospital. I felt like I was swirling around in a silver milk churn and realised that no one was going to pull me out. The *fact is, you have to do it yourself.* As I walked away, *I made a decision;* I was not going to have a nervous breakdown. It was time to pull up my socks and find my own way out of this misery. **What is courage? We can struggle for a long time based on the fear that we're not good enough.** *Fear is False Evidence Appearing Real.* **I have concluded that courage is simply** *making the decision.*

I stumbled across something called Neuro-Linguistic Programming and studied it for the next two years. NLP helps people to learn the language of their own mind and then positively change unconscious programming. At the time, I don't think I was a very good student – I loved helping others, but I felt so raw that I covered myself with protective armour that kept people at arms-length. Nevertheless, the training helped me to become aware of unconscious patterns in my thinking – patterns that I had inherited from my family and internalised from the society in which I lived – patterns that were repeating through me. It gave me a process for reprogramming my mind to release those old patterns and embrace love – the love for myself.

And then, the training prompted me to ask the Universe, "What will you have me do?" And it replied, 'work with young people', which I had not considered returning to. In addition to working nights as a typist and continuing to conduct musical groups, I passed a qualifying exam to take over a *Kumon Math Centre* and started work to grow it. Hard work dulled the pain. I managed to triple the number of students at this centre before selling it.

Two years later, a newspaper ad headed, 'Teachers Wanted', led me to jump from one ship to another. I applied to buy the children's drama school franchise in South Manchester. I thought I had the appropriate skills; I had taught drama, and I knew how to run a business. However, nothing prepared me to climb the steep learning curve; to learn how to teach drama using a particular methodology, while simultaneously growing a franchise business.

Worst of all, I had to cold-call secretaries in the local schools to gain permission to advertise the programme to their students. (I once tried a temporary job scheduling appointments on behalf of consultants with CEOs of large companies. One day, I called a CEO with the same last name as mine. You could have blown me down with a feather when a man answered, "Manson here." I responded, "Well, from one Manson to another ..." and I still didn't get the appointment.)

Though running the drama academy was hard work, I personally learned skills that still stand me in good stead today. The franchise training taught me that communication is about so much more than just the voice – we taught the art of 'commanding the room'. They said, 'You have to up your energy.' Like a vibrating tuning fork will transfer its vibrational energy to a second tuning fork, you will share positive vibrational energy with the whole room of students, raising everyone's frequency in the process.

I literally met thousands of children and teenagers; I hope that I helped many of them. I learned how to teach improvisation, vocal techniques, how to think creatively, and most of all, how to have great fun with young people. I worked with the very shy and withdrawn, the very outgoing, talented, not talented, and children with all kinds of mental, emotional and even physical issues. The academy's goal was not to teach people to act, but to teach them to communicate; through fun 'play-acting' and improvisation, they learned to speak and act confidently. Many of them impressed me deeply.

I remember a five-year-old little girl who simply did not want to join in the fun. She sat on the floor, holding onto a chair leg for dear life;

her mother hovered outside nervously. I kept encouraging her mother to 'give her time'. Eventually, the little girl exchanged holding the chair leg for my hand, and then to holding an older female student's hand. After three years of continuous practise, her grandmother attended a class and declared, "Thank you for saving my granddaughter's life!" I responded that I had simply loved and supported her until she felt ready to let go of the fear. This girl progressed to successfully delivering a speech on stage at her private girls' school.

A boy with dyspraxia or Developmental Co-ordination Disorder (DCD) – then simply considered extreme clumsiness – joined a class. His parents told me that he wanted to end his life because he was bullied so horribly at school. He tried to play football but had two left feet, and the other boys laughed at him mercilessly. Convinced that his talents were verbal rather than physical, I persuaded his parents to try two classes. The boy blossomed. He loved improvising and inventing characters. He attended classes for several years.

Within a safe, supported environment, these young people *released their fears and found the courage to truly play themselves on the stage of life.* **Be yourself.**

Seeing the Light

Determined to attain independence, I continued to bury myself in work, effectively distracting my mind from thinking about my circumstances and the loss of my son. **Though slow to start, I diligently persevered,** repeating positive affirmations such as 'I'm going to reach the top five per cent.' I didn't know how, I just kept working, **never quite giving up, always moving forward, step by small step.** In five long years, I built the most successful drama academy franchise in England with 650 students in 32 classes per week, across 13 locations.

Around this time, the legal battle with my ex-husband finally concluded. The judge awarded me the matrimonial home and my daughter and I moved into it. I remember opening the front door after being barred from it for over five years; ghosts charged at me. Unfortunately, by this point, the house was in terrible condition, but it was ours nevertheless. Sadly, any elation I felt faded quickly as I realised that it had pushed my son ever further away. After all, my son and his father were ordered to leave the family home when it was awarded to me. I would have joyfully welcomed my son to stay and live with us, but he chose to move with his father. I suspect he was very angry with me.

Aware that I still carried much fear, I went to see a hypnotherapist. We explored a vivid nightmare I had as a child. My mother and grandmother were great knitters; I would hold up my hands and they would wind the skein of wool around them. In the nightmare, the wool string transformed into a heavy, rusty chain that made a horrible sound as it turned. The hypnotist instructed me to wrap my arms around the frightened little girl in the dream. I returned to that place in time, and then I travelled past it to the place we all come from. I knew I was connected to every single thing. I felt an incredible feeling of peace and love. I knew we were all connected. **If we allow ourselves to let go of fear, the magic inside us radiates out.**

I attended several self-improvement seminars and courses. At one of these courses, I stood on a piece of paper with the word 'fear' on it. Feeling wracked with the fear that I didn't measure up, I felt the pain, cried intensely, and finally let go. In that exercise, I saw a white light and felt pure joy. At the same course, we were instructed to hold another person's hands, look deeply into their eyes, and say, "I am here to be seen, and I see you." By the end of the day, I couldn't get past the words, "I AM." Perhaps, finally, simply 'being' was enough.

After five years of working incredibly hard, I felt burnt out. I decided to sell the drama academy business. But what next? I trained to become a coach. I also turned to supply teaching. The techniques I taught in the drama school came in very handy teaching at very difficult schools. I supplied at one school for six months – long enough to start another choir! The small group grew quickly and began singing in two and three-part harmony in a short time. The first time they sang in front of the school, they were terrified of being criticised; but they received the opposite reaction – applause. They now had a voice too. **We take all the skills with us into the next chapter of the journey.**

Out of the blue, I received a call from my son. Overwhelmed with both excitement and concern, I left a choir rehearsal to answer his call on my cellphone. He told me he was engaged to be married. He hoped his father and I could make amends sufficiently enough to both attend the wedding I arranged to meet him and his fiancé, along with my daughter. Much to my surprise, his father attended the meeting as well and the fallout was disastrous. As a result, I was not invited to the wedding.

On his big day, I felt a deep sadness, however, my heart was with my son. Some communication between us was much better than none and knowing he was happy and settled gave me some peace at last.

Second Return

After being back in England for 18 years, I began to wonder what I was doing there. My children were now grown up and leading lives of their own. Yes, I considered England home because I grew up there, but I also missed Canada and the freedom it offered. This time, making the decision to leave was much easier. I had discovered that courage is really about making the decision and after that, following through is easy. I had no idea what I was going to do in Canada, or how I would make a living. But, with help from my brother, I began yet another new life back in North America.

True Independence

I feel like a cat with nine lives, having started new adventures in both England and Canada not once, but three times – learning and internalising many lessons and skills along the way. However, I am content and happy. I enjoy working but not so frantically now, and I still sing and make music. I am grateful that I can teach and be part of others' journeys. Life is a series of chapters; some are good, some are bad – there is always another one. You can't go back, you can only go forward – you can take a side route along the way, but that is all.

Today my grandchildren are my pride and joy, particularly the one who lives close by, here in Canada. My daughter does not have a relationship with her father. My son has a very tenuous relationship with his sister and me. I don't fight it anymore; I focus on my life and well-being on a daily basis. **You can't change people; you can only change yourself.**

I did finally discover why my father disliked my ex-husband and his family so intensely; my father and my ex-husband's father had transacted business together, but my ex-father-in-law had not paid what was owed, and my father considered him dishonourable. This understanding helped me to forgive my father and let go of the anger that had fueled me for so long.

I have wondered, "Why don't I have a normal family?" But, maybe other people don't either. Both of my parents grew up without their fathers; my daughter grew up without her father. I felt emotionally abandoned by my family; my son felt abandoned by his mother when I left his father – repeated *patterns*. Very few people left their families (in the era) when I did, but now many people do it, just like the 'rules' change over time, so do our concepts of 'acceptable' and 'normal'. These belief systems can enslave us at a subconscious level; **attaining *true independence* requires becoming consciously aware of these patterns and then finding the courage to break them. We must release what does not serve us. Patterns evolve.**

I gained true independence when I returned to Canada. Based on my training in England, I provided life-coaching services. I also helped an entrepreneur to grow her franchise, an area in which I certainly advised from experience. I fell into teaching piano. These connections have helped me to find my own 'tribe' based on sharing common interests and goals. In the end, I think we are all 'tribal' – we are all interconnected – we desire the comfort of being in a family or community. Forming choirs always fulfilled that need for me. I am lucky because I have always enjoyed meeting new people.

A while ago, at a concert intermission, I chatted with the gentleman next to me; we talked about the concert; he also came from England and he had also lived in the same town as I did. (When he handed me his card and I looked from it to him, stunned, saying, "Didn't we meet in Toronto 47 years ago?!" He responded, "Oh my goodness, my wife and I came to your home for dinner!" That kind of connection blows my mind. Isn't the Universe interesting?

Having been in a BNI (Business Network International) group in England, I joined one locally and was elected President. I ran the group and supported all the members in their endeavours to give and receive referrals. My drama and communication skills helped create good energy in the group, and it grew. A good friend within the group suggested that I teach speaking and presentation skills. With that encouragement, I embarked on creating a business called *Winning with Words*, to help business people and entrepreneurs be heard in a professional and powerful way that helps attract more business through great communication skills.

I also wrote a book called <u>Winning with Words</u>. I never thought I would ever write a book. It contains lots of interesting stories that illustrate techniques for creating effective presentations and the skills required to speak confidently. I have created and enjoyed filming two online courses, videos of 20 short tips, and a webinar that covers some of the most important aspects of speaking and presenting. Like so many people do, I thought, "Who am I to write a book? I'm not good enough. There are many more qualified people out there." As a child in Britain, I was taught never to boast. My mother said, "Don't show that you can do something that someone else can't." We internalise these 'rules' so deeply that breaking out of our own restricted view of ourselves makes us feel like a 'fraud; we experience a form of 'imposter syndrome.' But everyone loves and deserves applause! Who am I not to write a book? Or even this chapter, for that matter? I'm qualified to do it because I have done it.

I love helping people to find their voice in an authentic and powerful way – to release the fear that has stopped them from speaking in public and communicating fluently. (In the same way, I helped hundreds, possibly thousands of young people do the same, earlier in my career – and learned so much about myself along the way.)

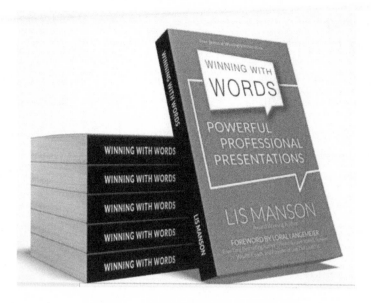

Peace

My parents wanted me to teach; I wanted to perform. I have achieved both. And, today, teaching a step-by-step process that helps students understand, practise, and achieve new skills is ultimately the greatest pleasure for me. I love being on my student's team– it is a team effort – and I enjoy being in the moment when we reach out and feel truly connected. It brings me to life to win the hearts of an audience, and I hope I can help you to do it too.

As Marianne Williamson said so succinctly:

"Our deepest fear is not that we are inadequate. Our deepest fear is that we are powerful beyond measure. It is our light, not our darkness that most frightens us. We ask ourselves, 'Who am I to be brilliant, gorgeous, talented, fabulous?' Actually, who are you not to be? You are a child of God. You're playing small does not serve the world. And as we let our own light shine, we unconsciously give other

people permission to do the same. As we are liberated from our own fear, our presence automatically liberates others."

What have I learned on this long journey? Never give up. Be determined. Use the gifts you have been given. Shine brightly.

I hope you will allow me to lend you some light to shine brighter and reach farther in this busy and complex world – and to find your voice to communicate confidently and bravely, in a powerful and authentic way.

Shalom.

LIS MANSON

Lis Manson is an expert in helping business owners, entrepreneurs and those in the corporate world who have to speak in public and deliver presentations. She has spent several decades building her speaking and presentation skills through teaching music, drama, and conducting choirs.

Today, Lis enjoys singing in small chamber groups, playing the piano and spending time with her family. Lis loves to entertain guests to enjoy her cooking and baking. She also gives her energy to networking and supporting others in their endeavours, particularly using her many years of experience in both business and education.

In her early years, she trained as a singer and a music teacher. After moving to Canada from England, she discovered her love of choral conducting and used her energy to bring together people who loved to sing and create a wonderful sound singing in harmony. A proud moment was being a finalist on CBC radio in their choral competition.

After many years in business, meeting people from all over the world in the retail sector, she returned to England. During that period, she started a drama academy which helped thousands of students to be confident with their verbal communications skills and unlock the fears that stopped them from simply being the best people they could be. This led her to become a trained Life Coach and an NLP Master Practitioner.

Returning once more to Canada to begin yet another chapter in her life's journey, she has created a business called Winning with Words. As President of a BNI Network group, a member suggested that she create courses and offer coaching to help others speak in public, with energy, passion and authenticity. Lis also teaches and practises the important skills that are the basis of achieving powerful presentations.

Lis's philosophy in coaching is the synthesis of business, personal development, and sports. The support of a sincere and dedicated mentor who believes in you and helps you set the big goals; the manager to set the strategies that work; and a personal trainer to keep you in action and a sports trainer who helps to finetune technique, Lis is a coach who is all of these rolled into one so that she can support you to speak, communicate and present your way to success!

UN-SOLITARY SUCCESS

Mike Jasper

My parents were teenagers in high school when I was born. Yes, I was an accident. My parents had to grow up fast and become responsible adults to raise me. For most of my childhood, my family struggled with finances and my parents would fight about money often.

At a young age, I could see that successful people had a strong drive to succeed and a good support team around them. I was lucky to have both. I also remember my mother and father always encouraging me to push myself and telling me that anything is possible. I always had a drive to be successful. Even as a child, I was dreaming big. During my first grade, my mother was called into the class after school to see my Christmas list.

What I want for Christmas:

- Red Corvette
- Motorcycle
- Bicycle

- Race boat
- Jeep

My mom just started laughing and said, "Yes, he dreams big."

My father would always tell me that anything was possible if I was willing to work for it. As a kid, he gave me the opportunity to work in his machine shop and I loved it. I worked full-time during the summers and on the weekends during the school year, from when I was eight years old through high school.

When I was eight years old, I would sweep the floor and clean the machines. My father would pay one of his employees to pick me up in the morning to take me to work at six a.m. I would wait by the glass door in the morning and could see the driver show up. I would work all day until my driver was ready to go home in the evening, around 5 p.m.

When I was ten years old, I was cleaning parts and sanding the sharp edges off of them. My father explained how this was not just work. I was his son and the only way to earn the respect of everyone in the shop was to be the hardest working person there. I was at least twice as fast as everyone else. My father was very proud when he could see that no one could keep up with me. By working harder than everyone else, my days were never boring and I was learning more than I imagined.

By the time I was thirteen, I was programming CNC mills and lathes to make highly complex parts. It was a dream. One of my father's friends was Bob Fox.

Bob had invented a new shock absorber for racing motorcycles in the dirt with big jumps. With his new technology, motorcycles could go faster and jump higher. He also started a company called Fox Factory. I was programming the machine that made the new breakthrough shocks for racing motorcycles. I thought that was the coolest thing in the world. We built other things, like the mainframe computer disc drives for Hewlett Packard. They were huge and I could barely lift them into the machine, but I loved it.

By the time I was 16, I was making more money than my mother and I knew my career lay in the machine shop business. During this time, I had a Toyota truck 4x4 and a Datsun 240z. The most beautiful girl in our high school was my girlfriend, and I thought I was the luckiest person in the world.

After high school, I went to work for my father full-time in his machine shop. He had about 30 employees. Within a few weeks, one of the foremen quit and I was the only person that knew how to run all of the machines and programs. So, I jumped right into a leadership position. This meant that I was responsible for about one-third of the work going through the shop. I would run the day shift and the night shift. Some of the machines would run automatically for approximately an hour. So, I would load the machines with material and then sleep on my dad's couch for 30 minutes at a time. Then, wake up and load more material and do it all over again.

I soon found out that my father had a problem with alcohol, cocaine, and gambling. It didn't take long before he ruined his life, ruined his relationships with his customers, and was out of business. He had a hard time dealing with that, so the police chained up the building and changed the locks on his house. He was left totally broke and reduced to living in his car. Soon, he was hanging out with the wrong crowd and went to jail for dealing drugs for six months. He was about nine months away from having everything paid off and lost about $10 million.

I thought it was time for me to start my own company. I called my stockbroker and told him that I needed to take out my money to open a business. I heard silence on the other end. Then, "Didn't your father tell you?" "What?" I asked. "Your account and your father's account were linked. He lost all of your money on a bad investment."

Overnight, I went from being the rich kid with two cool cars and money in the bank to the poor kid who owed back taxes and had to move back in with his mom. I had to sell the cars to help pay a part of my taxes. Then, I had to borrow money from my mom to buy an old Datsun 210.

The car was so ugly and slow; it's actually funny when I think about it now. My friends were shocked and felt sorry for me. I wasn't sure what to do. I had to get a job, but I was so young that the people who hired me would only pay me minimum wage. Nevertheless, I took up the offer and decided to be the best machinist in that company.

The owner could see how hard I was working and that I had some skill, so within a year, he started grooming me to take over the company. I was flattered but wasn't sure how to pull it off. At 20 years old, this was a much bigger opportunity than I could handle on my own. How could I run this company? After weeks of trying to figure it out, I realized I needed help.

Sometimes, we just need someone to tell us what we don't know, to point out the gaps in our knowledge. I needed to find someone smarter than me to help me find the answers. So, I started researching marketing consultants and business coaches, and soon, I hired a business coach to help me figure things out.

Together, we made a plan on how to take things forward and the owner agreed. In my plan, I proposed working 40 hours per week as an employee, and in turn, he would let me do my own work at night in the machine shop to grow my company. When I had enough revenue from sales, I would buy his company. This was exciting! The first thing I did was to meet with my business coach to figure out a marketing plan. Within months, I had brought in so much work, it was crazy.

When I would walk into a customer meeting, the buyers would ask, "Are you Mike?"

They couldn't believe that a 21-year-old could own a machine shop. They would ask me some questions and quickly found that I knew what I was talking about. Even then, they were reluctant to give me work. The thing was, no one could compete with me. I had no overheads or fixed cost of employees. I didn't even have to pay rent.

No one around could beat my price or my terms of delivery. If a normal delivery was due in four weeks, I would tell them that I could deliver in one week. If I didn't deliver in one week, they could give the job to someone else. I basically gave them a deal that they could not refuse.

A couple of years later, I was getting ready to buy the company from the owner but the economy was in terrible shape. I could get work, but no one was paying their bills for 90 to 120 days. That was too long for me to carry the costs, so I could not buy the company. The owner was 74 years old and wasn't willing to wait around for the economy to get better. He just closed the company.

I really liked sales and business development but needed more training, so I went to work for an insurance company. They would pay me and train me to sell! I was also waiting for the economy to turn around and thought I might try the machine shop business again someday, if the economy improved. I treated the insurance business like anything else I ever did: I dove in headfirst. The first year in sales, I spent all my money on seminars and business coaches that specialized in insurance sales. Soon, I was one of the top producers in the office, but I did miss building things in the machine shop.

A couple of years later, my father and I reconnected. He had changed his life. He was humbled by his experience of losing everything. He had found a job working in a machine shop. However, he wanted more. He wanted to try his luck again, opening up his own shop. He found a partner with money to buy two machines and get a lease on a small building. My father was going to do sales and his partner was going to run the shop. Though within two months, they were going out of business because his partner was not good at running a shop. My father offered me a partnership if I could run the shop. I went for it.

With a bankruptcy and felony, my father's credit was terrible, so I had to sign for all the leases. My father didn't even have a car, so I had to let him use mine. The first year was very difficult and we almost went out of business every month. We made just enough money to pay ourselves minimum wage and sometimes we didn't cash our checks for weeks until they could clear.

The second year, we had a breakthrough. They say if you work hard and keep pushing, invisible forces will come to your help. I experienced that.

I was able to get an order at a large semiconductor company that should have never been approved. However, there was a special part that was made out of Molybdenum. This was a specialty material that almost no one knows how to work with.

They kept going out for a quote and no one was bidding on it. This was my make or break moment. When they asked me, I said, "I specialize in that." So, I got the order. I had never heard of the material but knew that I better learn fast. The reason no one could bid on the job was because it required a special coolant that was not approved in California.

The material has a weird property of shrinking while cutting tools were used on it. For example, if you try to drill a hole in it with normal coolant, it will shrink down, break the drill, and ruin the part. The other difficulty was that the material was very expensive. Each part costs $10,000 in material and sold for $20,000 when done. My order was for six pieces. That was $60,000 in material, and I only had about $10,000 in the bank and no credit.

At this point, my miracle job was looking like it was about to go bust. I didn't have the money to pay for the material or the skill to make the part. However, I knew there was a way to make this happen. Instead of quitting, I called my business coach and he called some other people to have a brainstorming session. Together, we figured out how to solve the problem. As long as I could pay my vendor making the part within 30 days, I could maintain a good relationship.

In order to do this, I had to have a meeting with my customer and negotiate for them to pay me within 10 days of delivery. For doing this, I would give them a 2% discount. They loved the idea. In fact, they loved it so much that I built that clause into all of my future orders. I never had to go out and get financing to grow my company because my customer was financing everything. At the time, this was a new idea and this solution was a turning point for my company. If I were just counting on myself, I would have struggled for a long time.

Instead, I hired a coach and called a group of smart people together and asked for help. From that single idea, I was able to grow my company a 100% every month for years without ever needing financing. Most of my competition had millions of dollars in bank loans and their growth was limited by the cash flow and loans they could get.

That single idea changed my business. The year before, I was making minimum wage. The next year, I was making over $100,000 in profits. Four years later, I was making almost $8 million in profits per year. A few years later, I sold the company for over $50 million and became financially independent at 35 years old.

The first year after selling my company was great. I was traveling, spending time with my family, and buying the toys that I always wanted. After a year, I was feeling disconnected and bored. People always say that money can't buy you happiness, and I was starting to see what they were talking about.

I was actually starting to get depressed. I started visiting a therapist to see what was going on. I made some progress but wasn't feeling complete. I found myself bored and alone most of the time.

I started thinking about the turning points of my business and a light bulb went off. I needed to ask successful people that have gone through this before what they did to enjoy life after becoming financially independent.

I asked the people around me who had retired how they were enjoying their life. Most were bored and disconnected like me, except for one person. One of my friends was really enjoying his life and seemed truly happy. I asked him what he did after selling his company. He said he went through the same crisis as me and turned it around by hiring a life coach. That made so much sense to me. I supercharged my business by hiring a business coach. If I want to live an extraordinary life, I should hire a life coach.

I was a big fan of Tony Robbins, so I found a life coach who was trained by him and worked for him. It didn't take long to start breaking my life into areas of focus, like health, wealth, and relationships.

For me, my health and relationships were struggling the most. While I was building my company, I didn't pay much attention or effort in these areas of my life.

It was amazing how fast I was able to create meaning once I decided to build a meaningful life. I learned that I love connecting with and helping people, and I really like talking about business. So, I combined the things that make me happy and became a business coach.

When I look back at my life experiences, there are a couple of decisions that really increased the speed of my success and happiness. Asking other people for help and finding a coach saved me years of grief. While I could have reached my goals on my own, it may have taken 30 years instead of 10 years. Over the years, I have spent nearly $100,000 on coaching, which has in turn led to millions in profit, elevated happiness, and a more meaningful life. If you are not sure where to start on your business journey or want to take your business to the next level, I am here to help.

MIKE JASPER

Mike Jasper has been an entrepreneur for over 30 years. He started a machine shop business when he was in his mid-20s and grew it into one of the largest contract manufacturing businesses in Northern California, which he eventually sold to become financially independent

Mike is also a certified business coach working closely with other entrepreneurs to help grow their business. He currently lives in Silicon Valley and when he is not working, he can be found relaxing at Lake Tahoe where he likes to ski, ride mountain bikes, and explore the mountains.

Contact Details

Website: www.jaspercoaching.com

FIGHTING DEPRESSION AND RESTORING PASSION AND LIFE BALANCE

Peter Abrahamsen

Nobody knew

How it all began only became clear several years after it was over. A little boy got scared. Nobody knew, and it was nobody's fault.

We often think of personal development and transformation as something spectacular that happens in leaps and bounds, a breakthrough of some kind. However, that is not always the case. When a transformation is gradual, it is easy for it to go unnoticed. We might even think that it has not happened. My transformation happened in two stages. First, I gradually sank into what became a 25-year long depression, and I never noticed. Then, my recovery was slow, to begin with, until it dawned on me that I had found a passion for life. Not just for my own, but also to help others.

I made it through to the other side, and only gradually did I realize the subtle or obvious signs along the way that something was changing for the worse and later for the better. This is the story I'm sharing with you. I hope that you can relate to my story and recognize the signs of your own transformation and either take steps to make changes or simply congratulate yourself for having taken another important step in the right direction.

When I was probably about five years old, I overheard my parents have a discussion about something that they must have been emotionally involved in. Their voices were raised and agitated above normal. My young and developing brain perceived this as mum and dad arguing and being unhappy. In my mind, it could only be because I must have done something wrong. This explanation of how it all began only came about almost ten years after I had conquered what was, in the end, a severe clinical depression. I was studying for a degree in psychology and stumbled across a section about childhood trauma in a textbook on child development. Then it clicked, this was where it all started. Assuming the textbook was right, I had suffered a childhood psychological trauma. I put the theory to the test and spoke to my parents about it, and they confirmed that they had noticed that I was very sensitive to hearing them discussing things. They had actually begun to keep discussions for when I was not around or asleep. Whether my parents had an argument or a discussion is not important, but it is worth noting that I have never heard my parents have an argument.

My childhood and family life in my native Denmark was safe, loving, and mostly joyless. I adored my elder brother but never quite understood why he was so energetic and hungry to try new things. I had become quiet and afraid of making my parents unhappy and was busy convincing myself that nobody loved me. I remember thinking how great it would be if I were lost, and they found me and told me they loved me and had missed me. This sentiment developed into a desire to being lost and not found. I wanted them to regret the way they had treated me, knowing that it was too late. Nobody knew anything, but my brother and mother noticed something. My brother once asked my mum right in front of me, "Why is Peter always sulky?" My mum replied that I was just "serious." We all left it at that.

Life in school wasn't great either. Being the youngest and the shortest in my class, I gradually became the object of bullying. Not the physical kind. I was just consistently excluded from what everyone else was doing. I didn't speak to my parents about it but instead confided in a teacher. He raised it with the class one day when I was out of the room, and when I came back, the air was icy, and everyone was eyeing me in a rather menacing way. "So we are not good enough for you?" was the only comment I got from one of the boys. According to him, I could only redeem myself if I was naughty toward the teachers. I didn't take his advice and just lived with the situation. From this, I learned not to ask for help. Today, as a practicing psychologist and coach, I spend a lot of time and effort encouraging people to do the exact opposite. Keeping issues to yourself that you do not quite understand or have realized you can't fix yourself will only make matters worse. Furthermore, it didn't help that I could sing. It wasn't a hobby to be accepted by the stronger elements in my class.

My brother and I both sang in a highly respected boys choir, 'the Danish Radio Boys Choir.' I liked it there because we all enjoyed singing, and there was no teasing. Singing in this choir for nearly six years gave me the most amazing experiences very few boys can claim. Before the age of 16, I had been performing in several countries, including Soviet Russia, Bulgaria, France, Germany, Iceland, and the USA. There were 20 of us on tour, and since I was one of the shortest, I always had to stand in the front at concerts. There was nowhere to hide. This didn't bother me at all, and I enjoyed being in front of an audience. I still do. However, I have to admit that singing the American national anthem in an American Football stadium in front of a sell-out crowd of close to 60,000 plus millions of television viewers was intimidating. Whenever the Royal Opera in Copenhagen needed boys for their performances, they came to our choir, and I was fortunate enough to perform in operas such as La Boheme and Carmen. It was hard work singing in this choir, and I liked it, but I wasn't excited about it like the other boys. I just took it in my stride. I quickly learned that talking about my choir experiences at school made me look big-headed in the eyes of the bullies, so I decided to keep quiet. I didn't like the idea of being perceived as big-headed, so I developed a very low key and self-deprecating approach to my achievements, which I know has held me back a number of times in my career.

At some point, someone at my school must have spoken to my mum, who taught entry classes there. The Danish education system of the 1970s was quite different from what it is now. Students were split into an advanced or general level at the end of year seven. The teachers thought I had the academic ability to progress through the advanced route, but the amount of work would likely mean that I could not continue with my singing. As a result, my parents and I had a long conversation. I wanted to continue singing, and I also really wanted to move to another school to get away from my so-called classmates. I wanted to go to the same school as one of my best friends in the choir. That, however, was a private school, and my parents couldn't afford it. As they later explained, it would have also sent a very wrong message of favoritism to my brother. We arrived at a compromise suggested by my school's headteacher. I was to repeat year seven at the same school in an already well functioning and harmonious class, and the class would be informed about my circumstances. In short, they would be told that he isn't stupid but has had a rough time in his old class. All of which was true.

My new class made me feel extremely welcome, and I was accepted into their established group with a generosity for which I am forever grateful. As you can imagine, meeting my old classmates in the corridors of the school was never easy, and their snide comments were painful. But, soon they lost interest in me and I in them. This decision was incredibly tough, but it made the last four years at school bearable and prepared me for the next three years in the Danish equivalent of high school.

Still, nobody knew how unhappy I was and how every activity was just another chore. The early desire to please my parents had developed into perfectionism, and I approached everything with considerable diligence. Academically, high school was not much of a problem, and I was coasting a little in some of the subjects. Looking back, I think that I was getting exhausted and tried to use my energy where it was needed the most. My grades were solid but not exceptional, and in year two, I decided I wanted to become a doctor. This meant that I had to give a little extra to get my grades up to where they needed to be.

After graduating from high school, I took a gap year. After 14 years of non-stop education, I needed a break from the books. This was and still is a common thing in Denmark. To give yourself a breather before embarking on university or some other form of education or training. I already had a weekend job as a cleaner at one of the teaching hospitals in Copenhagen, and Monday to Friday, I topped that up with a job as a furniture warehouse operative. Later, I even took a position as a substitute teacher at my old school. So for a full year, I only had every third weekend off. In Denmark, you can improve your high school grades by work experience, and this was my real agenda, as I knew it would be very difficult to get into medical school.

Applications to the three medical schools went in, and I lost out on a place by the narrowest of margins. I took the news relatively well since I was already in the frame of mind that good things would not happen to me anyway. But something inside me shifted, and I realized something about myself. I wanted to be a doctor, but I was actually not interested in becoming one. What I really wanted was recognition and respect. Since that is what doctors usually get, being a doctor had to be the answer. My craving for respect and recognition resembled that of young teenagers who want to be famous without knowing what they want to be famous for. Today, I would actually like to have the knowledge and skills of a doctor, but have no interest in practicing medicine. The lesson I had learned was important. I had just described my problem. I felt that nobody recognized and respected me. I know now that was not true, but that was how I saw the world.

My parents and I went through the options of what to do next. I could do another year's work experience and be guaranteed a place at medical school, or I could find something else to study and get started right away. I was now keen to get started on academic work again, so I dismissed the medical school option. Fear of failure also played a big part in that decision. In the end, I enrolled in a six-year master's course at Copenhagen Business School to become a Translator and Interpreter (MA in English and BA in German). At the end of the first two years, I had to decide whether to continue with both languages for the next two years to BA level or drop one of them. Doing two BA courses at the same time was a big ask, and

I ran my concerns by my brother. In his usual optimistic style, he just looked at me and said, "Of course you can do both languages." He had faith in me, while I had none. So I owe my full-sized qualification to my brother as I did not want to let him down.

During my student years at Copenhagen Business School, my depression got worse, and I was now at a stage where I thought my family was against me. I didn't handle my brother's graduation from university and a new job very well. I felt left behind. I wanted to be where he was. I very much felt like the little brother. How could I be envious when it was only natural that my three years older brother would finish his education ahead of me? I saw the world through quite distorted lenses. Deep down, I loved my brother, but I had got so tired of being "Henrik's brother." Why couldn't he sometimes be "Peter's brother"? This actually was not about him. It was about status, respect, and recognition. I wanted to be recognized for being me, not for being his brother, so quite unfairly, I took my frustrations out on him.

Not only was I busy getting used to being a student (year 1), I had also managed to buy a cheap, 90-something-year-old flat in Copenhagen, which I was renovating at the same time. On top of that, I met a girl who became my long-term live-in girlfriend. It was a lot to take in. She represented pretty much everything that I was not. She was self-confident, bubbly, and openly ambitious. The ups and downs of our relationship are not important in this context, but a couple of aspects are. Over time, she disliked my parents more and more, and I felt I had to make a choice between them and her. I already felt a fair amount of parental control and interference, especially from my mum, so I chose my girlfriend and saw less and less of my parents. It was a choice I made reluctantly, but the build-up of anger inside me made it possible. The other important aspect was my girlfriend's high degree of initiative, action, and ambition. She wanted to start her own business. That was not something I had even considered, but she was very convincing, and it also became my ambition. So, as a pair of translation students, we started our own little translation business. By the time it was all set up and complete with business cards, stationery, and an accountant, she seemed to have lost interest and was already thinking about the next thing in true entrepreneurial style. I was the one doing the bookkeeping and any translation jobs we managed to get. Her next significant grand idea was to move to London after graduation. Again this was not something I had given any thought to, but the more we talked about it, the more it also became my idea. We agreed that whoever graduated first would go to London, find a job, and pave the way for the other. I know it sounds wonderfully ambitious and quite naive. But we did it! Albeit not in a straight line. I have been in the UK for 29 years now and have no regrets.

In the final year of business school, I regularly woke up in the morning and kicked myself for not having taken my own life the day before. It was not a great place to be, and despite that, I managed to write my Master's thesis, teach English evening classes for adults, keep my weekend hospital cleaning job, and pass the final lot of exams.

I graduated, and nobody knew. As was customary, exam and thesis grades were posted on a noticeboard at the school. I had to wait a bit longer than everybody else because the external examiner of my thesis tragically died in the process, and the school had to find another one and give her a bit of time to read. On the day I went to have a look and found that my final grades had now been posted on the noticeboard, I was the only one around from my class.

Now, let's move onto the plans of going to London. I applied to numerous companies for jobs that, in hindsight, were completely out of my reach. But as a newly graduated chap full of technical ability and ambition, I had an insufficient grasp on the realities of the world I wanted to enter. My letters of rejection matched the applications I had sent out. All of them politely explained that although my CV was impressive, they had identified candidates whose qualifications and experience were a better match to what they were looking for. I concluded that it was impossible to look for work in London if you did not live there and that potential employers found it too complicated to get a candidate over from Denmark for interviews. It was years later that I realized I was simply way underqualified for all the jobs I had applied for. During the job-hunting process, I did a number of short-term translation jobs, and one of them was translating the Executive Summary for one of the consortiums that were bidding for the implementation of Denmark's first mobile phone network (1991). One of my classmates was also on the job and she knew I wanted to move abroad. She gave me a job ad she had spotted for a Danish translator based in a town called Blackrock, just South of Dublin, Ireland. This threw the cat amongst the pigeons because I had never considered Ireland as a place where I could live and work. Ireland simply did not exist on my map. Furthermore, I had to run this by my girlfriend, who was completely set on going to London. Also, working as a translator for a translation company was not part of the plan. In the end, we agreed that Dublin was a step closer to London for me and that I should apply for the job. We would then have to see how I could get to London later on. I received a translation test, which I completed and returned. Shortly after, I had a phone call from the Translation Manager who interviewed me and offered me the job there and then. I accepted and two weeks later on 06 May, 1991, I was on a plane to Dublin on a one-way ticket. I had packed up my life in two suitcases and left my girlfriend behind to finish her degree. I said a very brief goodbye to my parents, and I'm not even sure if or how I told my brother.

Early on in my studies, I knew that I would not retire as a translator. I wanted to use my communication skills, rather than just the translation skills. This was why I applied to all those wonderful jobs that I was not yet ready for. So, here I was with a translation job I didn't really want in a country that wasn't part of the dream and plan, and where my girlfriend told me she would never go and live. If we were to meet up again, it had to be in London. Whilst in Ireland, my parents and I exchanged some very difficult letters. They wrote to me saying that they would come and visit. Everything inside me just screamed NO. How dare they, could they not at least have the courtesy to ask if it was OK that they came over. I wrote back and told them that I did not want to see them. This was the beginning of an unpleasant exchange of letters.

Ireland turned out to be a brief encounter and a detour that I'm so privileged to have experienced. There wasn't much for me to do at work translation wise, so I did ad hoc admin jobs instead. However, I did receive a number of test translations from people who wanted to be considered for freelance translation work. With one exception, I failed all of them. I thought the quality was consistently too low, and I dug out the test translation I had submitted to compare and contrast with what I was receiving. Having read my own test translation, I failed that one, too. My perfectionism was getting out of hand. The only translation I did in my five months in Ireland was a test translation for Microsoft. The translators from the seven languages that the company supported were asked to do the same translation, and mine was the only one that got accepted. That earned me a handshake from one of the Directors. My time in

Ireland was tense. The Irish are wonderfully laid-back and completely unstructured for a Dane. Having never lived in another country before, I was in for a massive culture shock. I realized all the things they never taught us in Business School. I got on well with my colleagues and the people I met and got to admire the Irish impulsivity and hospitality. If the sun was out, they would go to the beach, quickly throw people and some food and drink in cars, and hit the beach. On the other hand, I would have spent so much time planning this that the sun would have been and gone by the time I was ready. Back in Denmark, however, my girlfriend was running out of money to pay the rent, the phone bill, etc., and I was not earning enough to support her. We tried to keep things going in weekly phone calls and somehow managed to find solutions to the various problems. I wrote letters to friends back home about my Irish adventure and realized who my real friends were. I lived alone in a flat and had a lot of time to myself. I could not afford to go to clubs and bars or make excursions to explore Ireland. Instead, I went to places accessible by local train and bus and enjoyed long walks along the coast. I tried to collect my thoughts about myself, my family, the relationship with my girlfriend, and the future during those walks along the coast. I had isolated myself from my family and was in a rocky relationship with my girlfriend, who I knew would go to London with or without me. I never came to any conclusions but just sank into a deeper and deeper hole.

My employer provided a way out of the country issue. They had opened an office in the UK and wanted to transfer me to that office. So, I packed my bags again, and by October the same year, I was in the UK and only a 45-minute train journey from London. I rented a studio flat and had established what would become the home for my girlfriend and me for the next five years or so. As soon as she graduated, we sold our flat in Copenhagen and squeezed into our new home. Our relationship deteriorated further. She struggled to find work, I found a new job that was a total disaster, and I was fired after six months. At one point, we were both out of work and struggled financially, to say the least. I managed to get some freelance work as a translator, and she also found employment again. But, by then, my depression had taken complete hold of my thoughts. I had somehow acquired a motivational tape by Brian Tracy, and I played it religiously again and again. But, nothing helped. One day I found myself sitting on the floor, backed into a corner of the kitchen, not wanting to live anymore. I decided to take action and seek help. I booked an appointment with my GP, and I wanted him to refer me to someone I could talk to. This was the point when my transformation for the better started. It began by asking for help. And once again, I wasn't surprised when I was disappointed by the result. At least initially.

My GP listened to my list of reasons for wanting to talk to someone, and he immediately wanted to start me on a course of antidepressants. I resisted and insisted that I did not want medication, but someone to talk to. He then talked disparagingly about counselors for a bit, especially those in the private sector, and eventually agreed to refer me to one of the psychologists at the local hospital. There were two, and he reckoned I would not get on with one of them. I remember leaving that consultation feeling angry and frustrated. I wanted someone to talk to, and he wanted to put me on medication. I made no connection between the fact that the doctor mentioned antidepressants, and that I could have been depressed. I just wanted to make sense of why my family was so domineering. The doctor was great at spotting exactly what the problem was, but he was not at all great at explaining his diagnosis. This was my second attempt at asking for help, the first one being back at school, and this one, too, did not live up to my expectations. Eventually, an appointment letter came through, and I went to my first counseling session with a psychologist, which was my third attempt at asking for help.

Sitting in a bleak room on an uncomfortable chair with the sun shining straight in my face from a window behind the therapist so I could hardly see him made me question how this was going to go. The psychologist listened to my story about my domineering family, especially my mother, and concluded that I was not assertive enough. He recommended that I buy a book on assertiveness. I ended up having three sessions with six weeks' interval, and then I gave up on therapy. I had learned a lot about my therapist's Taiwanese culture and family dynamics, which was interesting but not particularly helpful, and I had learned that in his words, I was strong but not tough. Still, nobody knew about my depression, with the exception of the doctor who didn't tell. I have no idea if the psychologist suspected depression, and if he did, he certainly kept it to himself. And I was still trying to figure out what was wrong with me. I had tried and gotten nowhere, and I took that to mean that I was a lost cause. The only logical next step for me was to take my own life. Not that I wanted to die, but I also did not wish to live. So, I planned everything, the place, time, and method. As I was about to carry out my decision to end it all, I took a mental and physical step back. Bizarrely, it was my perfectionism that saved me. I realized that I did not want to be blamed for not having tried hard enough, and for not having tried everything. So, I decided to put my suicide on hold and find another therapist. I have never told anybody how, where, and when I wanted to take my own life. In the beginning, I was ashamed, but it became a way of protecting the people closest to me. Today, it is a piece of information that adds no value. When I work with suicidal counseling clients, I don't ask them about those details either. If they volunteer to share the information, it is their decision. I am more interested in discussing the life leading up to that decision.

After some research and phone calls, I turned up for the first session with my new psychologist. This was a completely different experience, far from the impersonal hospital setting. I told my story one more time, and she asked me to fill in a questionnaire. There were 15 questions in total. She looked at my answers and said: "Peter, you describe yourself as rather depressed." Somebody knew, and now I did, too. I will never forget those words. I left the session feeling a ton lighter. I finally knew what was wrong. I had a diagnosis. I knew what I was up against and that it could be fixed. It sounds weird, but I was happy knowing that I was depressed. I realized it was the not knowing that was gradually bringing me down. The psychologist lent me a book, which she said explained the basis of the way she worked. It was *The Feeling Good Handbook* by Dr. David D. Burns, a brilliant American psychiatrist. This book became my *Bible*, and straightaway, I bought my own copy. At the fourth time of asking for help, I experienced true help. My problems weren't over, but I had confidence and hope that I was now on the road to recovery. After the first session, I popped into a pub on the way home and sat by myself reading the various leaflets my psychologist had given me. I thumbed through the *Feeling Good Handbook*. I found the questionnaire, and carefully in pencil, so I could rub everything out again, answered the questions in the same way I had in her office. The result was: Severe clinical depression. Eight sessions at two weeks' interval later, I was ready to fly solo. The sessions were good, and I worked hard in between sessions. For me, CBT (cognitive behavioral therapy) certainly worked. Today, I'm using the same questionnaire when I need to check out if a client is depressed. Needless to say that I trust its efficacy.

I had been treated by two chartered clinical psychologists who clearly came from different theoretical backgrounds, and in my case, one method was more effective than the other. My first psychologist was right when he said that I was strong but not tough. It took enormous strength to get to this point, and getting tough was a gradual learning curve helped along by CBT. Today, I prefer the term resilient as it describes me better. Resilience is also the goal that I get my business and consumer clients to achieve. I overcame my depression so quickly because I was unbelievably motivated and worked hard between sessions. I learned to think differently and move away from my all or nothing thinking and extreme perfectionism. Getting that diagnosis was the turning point from existing to living.

I was born in 1961 and learned to live in 1993.

Being ready to fly solo does not mean being fully qualified. Although I now consider myself qualified and cured, I'm still learning and sometimes resort to the techniques I first learned when I experience a low mood setting in. I sense check my thoughts, put things into perspective and balance, and move on. Depression is a diagnosis, a label, but how it affects the person is a very individual thing. I had always thought that depressed people couldn't do anything and spent all day in bed, so the realization that you can be an active and high-performing depressive came as a big surprise.

Life now began to move at pace. My girlfriend and I had gotten to the point where we were just two people living under the same roof. We supported each other financially until we both had an income and could physically split up. We were testament to the fact that relationships are usually over long before they finish.

My biggest and hardest task to date was yet to come—reconnecting with my family and explaining myself. As luck would have it, I got a translation assignment for a few weeks in Copenhagen, and I decided to contact my parents. I wasn't yet sure how to deal with my brother. Meeting them again in their home was an experience that is hard to describe. Both were apprehensive, defensive, and my dad, in particular, was ready to go into battle. They probably expected to get another barrage of insults and accusations in line with my letters. The elephant in the room was enormous, and you could cut the tension with a knife. Normally I wouldn't recommend whiskey as a therapeutic tool, but on this occasion, it worked a treat. We were all sufficiently calm, and I told my story, making sure they understood that I was not there to further blame and moan. It was not until I found the passage in my psychology textbook all those years later, that I fully understood how it all began. And that is what I explained to my parents. A little boy got scared. Nobody knew, and it was nobody's fault. Now, my parents knew.

Soon after, my brother invited me to celebrate Christmas at his house with the rest of the family. He just asked to focus on the future and not talk about the past. I have always respected his wish and have only recently managed to sneak in a bit of an explanation for my past behavior. Today, everybody knows. My family invited me back with open arms, and my parents and I have since destroyed our letter exchange. It no longer serves any purpose.

At first, life post-depression was strangely optimistic. I could walk down the street smiling for no apparent reason, and I noticed that other people no longer looked so glum. I really must have looked like a walking storm cloud before. Now, I also felt physically lighter. Three things happened—a breakup, moving houses, and starting a new job. Three of the major life stressors all at once. No bother. I was looking forward to all of them. Looking forward to something was a completely new experience, and I loved it—and still do.

Life as a single person lasted for about seven years and began with a realization. This was the first time in my life that I was on my own. Being truly single was a significant chapter in my new life. I could now develop my own identity—a very important, and until now, an underdeveloped piece in my jigsaw puzzle. I didn't have to adapt, bend, or compromise. Nothing wrong with that, but that was all I ever did. So many of my clients struggle with their identity, and it destroys their business and private relationships. Always searching, always struggling to be authentic.

I was alone but not lonely. I had spent so much time moving away from what I didn't like that now I felt this strong motivation to move toward something new. Great colleagues, lots of parties, a change of career, and gradually lots of dating, too. Got all of that.

My experience of working for family-owned companies was not great, and I wanted to try the corporate sector. The UK operation of a large American corporation hired me as a change agent. Together with a colleague, I structured their project management processes across all the European operations and completely eliminated overtime in one department. I was even part of the team putting a corporate global project management methodology together. All of a sudden, the walls of resistance to change came up everywhere, especially from the very people who had hired me to introduce change. I didn't understand why and wanted to find the answers.

Some people, as inexperienced in change management as I was at the time, would have bought a book on change management. I, however, signed up for a degree course in psychology. Working a full-time job whilst studying in the evening was bliss. I really loved the evenings when I came home from work, had dinner, and then sat down with my books and a glass of wine. What a treat. Then it dawned on me. When I was first a student back in Copenhagen and went through a period of being totally fed up with the course, I had considered switching to Psychology. Now I was simply doing what I had wanted to do for a long, long time.

Looking back at my career, I had always been more interested in the wellbeing of my colleagues than in the actual work I was employed to do. I had found my true passion—people and their wellbeing.

In 2003, ten years after conquering depression, I graduated with an honors degree in Psychology. It was also the year I met Anette, a lovely Danish lady. After a couple of years' long-distance relationship, she took the plunge and started a whole new chapter of her life by moving to the UK. We are now 13 years into our marriage, and we have still not had our first argument. Life is just too short for that.

During the next few years, I added qualifications in DISC personal profile analysis, coaching, and Thought Field Therapy.

My career took a few twists and turns. I got reorganized out of the American corporation, found a job in a smaller UK plc, and from there, made the jump into supply chain consultancy. First, as a self-employed consultant and later as an employee. I stayed with the same small consultancy for 19 years. It gave me a fantastic insight into different company types, industries, cultures, and countries.

I often wondered what a linguist and psychologist was doing fixing factories, warehouses, and transport. My skills in people and processes actually proved to be a great addition to the engineering and finance-based skills of my colleagues. I got a chance to develop and deliver training courses on communication, leadership skills, problem-solving, project management, and a few other topics. Some of the courses were on aspects of Lean Manufacturing.

I enjoyed the steep learning curve of all the techniques that were completely new to me. Combining that with making a real difference to people in the workplace was what I had been looking for.

The world seemed to change, and many of our clients were increasingly focusing on getting rid of people to save money. The exact opposite of everything I believe in. Obviously, an organization should only employ the number of people required, and that always needs adjusting up or down. But to just cut costs by making people redundant and letting those left behind lift a heavier burden will never sustain any business.

The decision to go solo and resign from the consultancy firm was gradual and certainly the right one. Now I have the freedom to work with business owners and MDs to future proof their organizations by focusing on their employees.

People will work their socks off and go the extra mile if they feel appreciated and valued as a person rather than for the work they do. That too is important, but we really must look at the human being first.

A business does not exist without people. Therefore, every company is simply a subset of society in general. The same problems we see in the general population, we also see in businesses. Mental health is one major aspect that has been ignored for too long. The tradition of taking good mental health for granted and hiding poor mental health is thankfully losing its grip. Slowly, but it is happening. The vast majority of my personal counseling clients are worried that their mental-health issues will harm their career and therefore keep quiet about it at work. Once in a while, I meet people whose employers supported them through a period of poor mental health. They are so humbled and grateful. They have become raving fans of the organizations and voluntarily go to any length to pay back the support. The concept is simple, but it takes an effort to put in and maintain.

I have met so many business leaders who refuse to accept that they have a problem. Pride and ego get in the way. But without recognizing that there is a problem, we will never find a solution. Doing nothing works for a while, but will always come back to haunt us.

There is no shame in asking for help or advice. It is a question of image. Do you want to be known as the one suffering, or do you want to be known as the one who took action and won? It is the difference between victim mentality and survivor mentality. Asking for help is not a sign of failure. It is a sign of strength.

Investigating what is wrong in your life or in your business can be painful and a lot of work. But you have to ask yourself: "Would I choose to be miserable?" or "Would I choose to have a disengaged workforce?" The answer is always no. But some people are afraid of breaking out of what they already know and therefore stay in a bad situation.

When I work with business leaders today, I focus on two main topics.

Human dignity and self-responsibility. With those in mind, it is amazing how you can reduce employee costs, and at the same time, retain a talented, engaged, and resilient workforce. I have worked my way up from planting lettuce in my summer holidays, through cleaning in a burns intensive care unit to being a director and business owner. The concept is the same everywhere.

The business owners and directors who are at ease with themselves and understand the value of people will lead by example and have an engaged and resilient workforce. They are open to asking for help and advice when the business does not perform to expectations or its full potential. They set the supportive yet professional tone, and the followers will follow.

My job now is to support the business owners and their top team so that they, in turn, can support the rest of the organization. It is often lonely at the top. Having experienced this kind of loneliness myself, it is such a thrill to work with the top people and see how the benefits filter down through the organization.

I had to go back to basics to sort my life out. I tried to jump ahead by applying for jobs way out of my reach. It didn't work. The approach in my Healthy Minds for Business coaching program is the same. Get the basics right first, then add the more exciting bells and whistles when the time and the foundations are right. Discovering what goes on in your life or your business is critical to finding the right way forward.

The fear of failure, I understand it. My past perfectionism and procrastination were based on the fear of failure. You just can't run your life or business successfully if you are afraid of getting it wrong every now and then. So, be brave and try something small first.

When it works, you will have the confidence to try something bigger. And remember to congratulate yourself and your employees on achievements. When something fails, learn from it, and move on. Forget the blame game.

When we manage expectations, communicate well, understand the context we live and work in, and approach everything with a degree of humility, amazing things happen.

It takes strength to get there and resilience to stay there. The respect and recognition that I now enjoy because of who I am are authentic. And I make a significantly positive difference to those who ask me for help.

I have come a long way since I was diagnosed with depression. That was the point at which I took responsibility for my life and went from existing to living. Before, I was idling in victim mode, letting things happen to me. Now, having taken charge of my own life, I thrive in survivor mode, with plenty of energy left to help others do the same. My life experience is an invaluable tool in understanding other people's personal or business distress, and amazing things happen to my clients when they too take the route of self-responsibility.

PETER ABRAHAMSEN

Peter is a seasoned psychologist and coach with a thorough understanding of business and the often very lonely life at the top of the company tree. He is a sought-after speaker on mental well-being in general and business in particular.

He works with ambitious business owners and senior business leaders who want to future proof their organizations. Peter focuses on nurturing and growing the internal strength of an organization – the employees. His coaching program Healthy Minds for Business opens the business owner's eyes to the significant losses suffered when employees are absent or turn up for work unable or unwilling to put in the required effort. His program also addresses disruption and cost associated with too high staff turnover as well as the damaging aspects of burnout and feeling isolated.

Having seen too often how a neglected workforce brings a business to its knees, Peter is passionate about helping business owners and senior business leaders create and maintain a professional and productive business culture with engaged, committed, and resilient employees at all levels. Peter has first-hand, personal experience of how the well-being of the employees directly affects the well-being of the business. And as a director and business owner, he understands the pressures and demands facing the top levels of a business and how important it is to look after the people in the business.

Peter has gained his experience from working in a variety of positions in very different types of organizations, both in the private and public sectors—planting lettuce, cleaning in a burns intensive care unit, translator, project manager, supply chain consultant, business owner, and director to mention some. Often working in different countries or within a multi-lingual and multi-cultural environment, he seamlessly adapts his approach to suit his client's culture.

When an organization is in crisis, with the bottom-line worsening or when a business leader can see trouble ahead, that is when it is crucial to have an engaged and resilient workforce. Such a workforce will become part of the solution and actively and willingly contribute ideas and effort to pull through a rough patch.

"The monthly demands for pay rises have stopped," "there is a lot less tension around," "she just put in loads of overtime without being asked and never complained about it or asked for money," are just some of the comments Peter receives as business owners and senior business leaders see business and humanity working hand in hand.

Contact Peter now to start your transformation and start enjoying happy and motivated employees, reduced staff costs, high retention of talent, increased productivity, and satisfied customers.

You can schedule a free 45-minute transformation call as well: https://peterabrahamsen.com/book-in-a-call/.

You can find Peter's book on emotional health *Breakdown Your Emotional Brick Wall* on Amazon as an e-book from Amazon or you can contact Peter for a paper copy.

Peter is also available to be contacted on a personal basis for counseling or coaching.

Contact Details

Business coaching

Website: https://peterabrahamsen.com

Email: peter@peterabrahamsen.com

LinkedIn: https://www.linkedin.com/in/peter-abrahamsen-4822271/

Personal counselling

Website: https://better-lives.co.uk

Email: peter@better-lives.co.uk

Facebook: https://www.facebook.com/Better-Lives-1622239238005084/

FAILURE: THE KEY TO SUCCESS

Russell Frazier

Have you ever felt like your failures were preventing you from success? Failure is easy to repeat, difficult to acknowledge, and seemingly impossible to let go of. But what if your failures held the keys to your future? Failure is what allows you to paint yourself in the shadow of your mistakes. It enables you to emerge bolder, brighter, and more beautiful than you could have believed.

There was no way I was going to *jump*. I was going to die, and I knew it. As I stared down into the murky depths of the water below, I felt the impending chill of death on my shoulder. I imagined how slowly I would drown, sucked beneath the water that would soon be invading my lungs. I didn't know how to swim, and I was standing at a height that terrified me. I was in over my head mentally and would soon follow the idiom in the physical world.

I heard the yells behind me, but they were largely muted by my terror.

"I said JUMP, recruit!"

A beefy hand touched my upper back, launching me forward with the force of a cannon. I was hopelessly airborne, thanks to the helpful swim instructor. The water rushed up to meet me as I crashed through the surface and kept going down. Struggling fiercely, I kicked repeatedly and threw my arms to my sides in an attempt to rise. After an eternity, I broke through to the surface and sucked down a delicious lungful of air. I kicked my feet in a frenzy to keep my head above the surface, but I was doing it all wrong. Panic set in and I slapped my arms against the water to assist with the futility of my legs kicking around. I slid down below the surface, sucking in water.

After several seconds of bobbing and choking, I was grabbed roughly and deposited to the side of the pool forcefully. The trained rescue swimmers had seen enough of my pitiful attempt at surviving. I had successfully failed the Navy swim test. I clung on to the side of the pool for dear life, coughing water and thankful to be alive.

My thankfulness quickly drifted into embarrassment as I lined up behind the others who had taken their swim test. Seated at the table ahead of us were certified sailors who held our training cards. There were several mandatory training items that had to be completed before we could pass basic training as certified sailors. This was one of the big ones. I stepped up to the table and announced my name. The giant rubber stamp held by the sailor holding my card made a thud against the paper, indelibly staining my swim test results with large red letters. FAIL. I grabbed my card and headed to the showers, feeling ashamed.

As I let the warm water run over my body, I thought about what I was here to do. I had come here to change my life and become a better version of who I was before I arrived. I wanted to be here, despite my defeat just minutes ago. Whether I liked it or not, I owed it to myself to try again, and perhaps again, until I passed. I pumped myself up mentally as I got dressed and prepared for my march back to my divisional barracks. It was one of those rare moments when it felt good to be so accustomed to failure.

As a struggling student, there was little I enjoyed about high school. The constant influx of reading assignments, homework, and pop-up quizzes was enough to make me very aware that school was not my "happy place." As I bounced around from desk to desk, my mind wandered constantly. I stared listlessly out the window, the buzzing drone of my teachers fading into the singular background noise that I associated with school and boredom.

I had too much on my mind to pay attention to schoolwork. Unanswered questions were bouncing around my head. "Why do I have to be here?" was a question close to the top of the swirling pile. I felt like everything I was being forced to study led to a dead-end of disinterest. I discovered a secret weapon: avoidance.

I began skipping class with other delinquents, my errant behavior slowly reaching new heights. During my freshman year of high school, I had my first beer. Eventually, I began drinking heavily on weekends, going to parties, and falling into the party scene.

I quickly advanced to marijuana, jackhammering my grades into the ground. Smoking gradually turned into an everyday habit. I looked forward to drifting into the dreamy, listless embrace of the high it gave me. It helped me forget the painful discomfort of not knowing which direction I was headed in life, or how to figure it out.

As much as I tried burying my head in the sand, I still felt the void of uncertainty reaching out to me. It grew larger every week, with every bad grade I moved closer to failing out of my senior year of high school. I would go home after school, dreading the next day when I *knew* I would be asked to hand in an assignment I hadn't completed.

It wasn't that I wanted to do poorly in school. I sincerely wanted to do well. I could not, however, take command of myself well enough to align with my unknown needs. I lacked focus and resolve. I felt stuck. Anxiety and hopelessness overwhelmed me, preventing me from trying. I was a boat adrift in an ocean of uncertainty, with no oar to paddle. Even if I had one, I had no destination to move toward.

One day, snooping around my mom's room, looking for loose change, I found a discarded book that seemed interesting and decided to "borrow" it. The book was *Feel the Fear and Do It Anyway* by Susan Jeffers. It was interesting but also absurd to me at the time.

It dove into the process behind expanding your comfort zone, letting go of a victim mentality, and prospering in the face of adversarial circumstances. It covered dynamic techniques to face fear, while strengthening personal power. I didn't understand all of the concepts at the time, but I remember the deep impression that it left on me. It indelibly branded in me a new thought—that I could control my response to life, regardless of what happens. To this day, I recommend this book to anyone looking to advance in life.

I didn't change my actions immediately, but near the end of my 11th-grade year, I decided that I truly wanted to graduate. My grades didn't reflect this desire in any capacity, but I wanted to do better. My mother was a key component in my decision to change direction.

When I asked her if it was possible to still graduate, she shrugged noncommittally. "Do you want to graduate on time? It's up to you."

The "yes!" inside me imbued me with confidence.

Her question was a Yoda-esque parry that changed my life for the better.

Later in life, I was able to use the power of questions to help myself and others find footing in the pursuit of future goals. Questions demand answers, creating a bridge linking desire to fulfillment. I have learned that the power of questions holds more power than the answers they evoke.

I enrolled in summer school, passed all of my classes, and began my senior year with renewed hope. At the end of March, I was blindsided when my girlfriend told me she was pregnant. I remember the panic in her voice as she spoke to me, unsure of how things would play out. I stood in the kitchen of my parents' house, holding the phone to my ear, not knowing what to say. I was scared and felt the familiar sensation of things spiraling out of control. I had no clue about what to do next, and I felt trapped in the town I had grown up in. I couldn't see a way past my problems.

One day at school, I saw a table with the typical military recruiters looking to get people to sell their life to the government. I already knew I wouldn't last in the military. I was a dreamer, and I liked to do things my way. One of the sailor dudes in the shiny white uniform called out to me. "Let me ask you a question," he began.

I nodded. "What's up?"

He looked back at me, a slight smile on his face. "What are you going to do once you leave this place?"

"Well, I am going to go home and take a nap" I responded, rendering a sarcastic salute at the same time. He let out a hearty laugh and grabbed my shoulder. "I like you, young buck. But I want you to seriously think about my question. If you don't have a plan for life after you graduate, you could end up stuck with no plan forever. And I can tell just by looking at you that you don't want that to be the case."

I laughed. "I already have a plan. I'm going to move to Columbus and get a good job once I graduate." The smirk stayed on his face. He could smell the lie. He asked where I was going to work, and I had no answer for him. He handed me his card and told me to call him, Officer Tyson Persona, when I wanted to talk. I placed his card in my pocket and went to lunch.

His words stuck with me for the rest of the day. I knew I wanted to leave my environment, provide for my coming child, and develop skills that would allow me to create my future. The problem was, I sincerely didn't know *how*.

I continued to do well in school, while secretly panicking about how unprepared I was to have a baby. I felt like I was too far behind to get to a position where I would have been prepared for this. My mind raced constantly, hitting a dead-end with no available answers. I felt like a lobster in a pot, slowly being cooked, knowing I would not make it out.

I kept in touch with Officer Persona occasionally, continuing the task of powering through the rest of the school year. I passed my classes and got approved to graduate. I had barely scraped by, but I had done it! I remember picking up my graduation robe, feeling as though there was still a last-minute chance I would get the call, that

I didn't actually have enough credits to walk. The call never came, and I felt the weight of uncertainty fall from my shoulders.

My parents, brothers, and girlfriend came to my graduation. It was a beautiful, perfect summer day. As I walked across the stage to receive my diploma, I felt on top of the world. I had focused on this goal for over a year, and my moment was finally here. Feeling the diploma finally in my hands unlocked something special in me. I had connected my goals to reality. I had brought myself to this moment.

After graduation, I worked long hours, trying to save money. Around that time, I got kicked out of my parents' home for having my pregnant girlfriend spend the night.

I got another evening job at a telecommunications company, where I worked the second shift after my warehouse gig. I saved up a decent chunk of change and began to think it could become a longer-term solution to my financial woes.

One day, Officer Persona gave me a call, and I met him at my parents' house. He asked me to tell him what I ultimately wanted in life. I told him how I wanted to provide for my family, be financially independent, and move out of the town I grew up in. After I was done, he looked at me from his chair, a slight smile playing across his face. "Do you ride public buses?"

I was thrown off. "Yeah."

He grinned. "When do you get off the bus?"

"When I get to wherever I am headed."

Nodding vigorously, he said "Exactly. Let's say you decide to join the military. You don't have to stay for 20 years. Maybe you'll want to. The only thing you have to decide is where you want to end up. You can just get off whenever you feel like you've reached your destination. That's up to you. But this could be the ride that takes you in the direction you want to go in your life."

Two months later, I got fired from my second job. They did not appreciate the lack of zest I had for annoying people who were trying to eat dinner with their families. I sat in the meeting where I knew I was going to get canned, trying my hardest not to laugh. It was very difficult. I handed in my keycard and was escorted to the front door. I was told to expect my last check in the mail.

I was at the point where the rubber meets the proverbial road, and I didn't enjoy the living space it offered. I started applying to other dead-end jobs, knowing they weren't long term solutions to my growing concerns.

Soon after, my older brother Ray was arrested. He called me after the arrest, and I went to visit him the following day. We talked on the hard phone receivers, separated by the thick, dirty glass partition between us. He told me that he was going to do 25 years in prison. I was distraught, but I held it together. We finished our visit and I walked outside, eventually sitting on a bench. I sat heavily on the seat, tears welling up. I let them come.

Sitting on the bench, my mind moved toward my future. I knew that some of the things I had been doing along with my brother warranted jail time. I was lucky I hadn't been arrested while I was repeatedly breaking the law. I thought about the changes I wanted to take place in my life, and the conversation with Officer Persona. I still was *waiting* to do something about my situation.

My daughter was coming in a few short months. I could keep my head in the sand and wait for the inevitable suffering, or I could make a decision to change my trajectory. Sitting there in the cold of the evening air, with the hot tears still fresh on my face, I made the decision to join the military. It was the best chance that I had, to achieve my plan of personal success. No amount of traveling in the wrong direction could take me where I wanted to go.

I felt a fire in me as I came to this conclusion. I was all in. I was ready to pay what I owed in order to get out of my own way and reach for something better. I felt a resolute strength in myself that I had never felt before. For the first time, I felt that my direction in life was completely up to *me*.

I called Officer Persona a couple of days later and told him I wanted to talk. He invited me to his office. When I arrived, we sat down and I told him I was ready. I volunteered for submarine duty. It seemed challenging and capable of providing me with new skill sets I could take advantage of, when I eventually got out after my first term.

Only my girlfriend knew what was going on through the entire time leading to the decision to join the military. I had decided in my heart that it was the best move for myself, and I wanted nobody else to have a say in the matter.

November 10th, 2008, rolled around, and I was set to go. Maria's stomach was larger than ever, and I knelt down to talk to my soon-to-be arriving daughter. I told her that I was going away for a while, but that I would see her in two short months and she better stay put until then. I kissed Maria's tummy, not wanting to let go as she sobbed in my arms. I gave her a kiss and told her I would write to her as soon as I could.

I spoke with Persona before leaving. "You'll do well," he said, smiling.

"Just pay attention and watch your smart mouth." We shook hands and I climbed into the waiting van, which took us to Columbus. After I arrived at the hotel, I called Maria and let her know I was okay, then settled down for the night. I couldn't sleep, so I stared at the ceiling and focused on the fact that I had made it so far. I had a long way to go, but I was proud of myself for being where I was.

The next morning we were woken up obscenely early, then piled into the waiting buses in the darkness of the morning. The buses groaned to life, turning out of the hotel parking lot and onto the highway. I sat in a seat near the window as we drove toward Great Lakes, Illinois, where I would be completing boot camp for the next eight weeks. I remember watching the bright highway lights blink past under the dark morning. The incredible feeling inside me was building as we moved closer. I felt like I was waking up to a dream. Deep inside of me, I knew I was going to be okay. I felt at peace with my decision, and on the brink of something spectacular. After all of the difficulty trying to straighten out the jagged direction of my life, I was here. My plan was unfolding in front of me.

I was still in training a month and a half later when Sakhia was born. I lay in the top bunk, staring at her picture. It was a surreal moment. I felt a surge of fondness for the beautiful tiny angel peeking back at me. I smiled, knowing in my heart that I had done the right thing with my life. Things were going to work out okay.

After several weeks of near-death experiences in the pool, I finally passed, completing training in early January. Maria came to my graduation ceremony along with my newborn princess. Immediately after the ceremony, Maria gave me a huge hug, placing Sakhia in my arms. I looked down at my daughter and was overcome with adoration. She cooed, staring up at me with her giant eyes. I kissed her warm cheeks and hugged her close. From that moment on, I was wrapped around her finger.

I headed to Groton Connecticut for Submarine School for 16 weeks, graduating second in class. It was a special moment for me, and I was absolutely surprised I had done so well. At that moment, I knew that as long as I made and stuck to a plan of action I could come out on top. I soon received my official orders, designating me to a fast attack submarine, the USS Buffalo, based out of the tropical island of Guam. I said goodbye to my friends, and packed my bags to go home before departure.

Two weeks later, I stood on the pier in the sweltering Guam heat, waiting for my boat to arrive. I watched her draw closer, silent and powerful, escorted by two deeply rumbling tugboats. I watched in awe as the little men stood on the deck of the mighty warship, like little figurines. The captain was in the sail, giving orders to the invisible crew inside who were steering the ship. The men on the deck moved around smartly, yelling strange words and commands. They threw the huge mooring lines overboard and onto the pier in unison. When it was time, they heaved on the lines to tighten them fast across the cleats and secure the boat to the pier. It was fascinating to watch.

When all the mooring lines had been tightened, the crew assembled onshore. I was introduced to my division chief, and he shook my hand, welcoming me to the crew. He introduced me to the rest of the division. It was intimidating to know that I was the greenest crew member aboard. I had none of the "saltiness" they possessed, and it was apparent. Their coveted "dolphin" pins across their chest made me feel unaccomplished. The dolphin pins, or warfare insignia, are only given to "qualified" submariners who had undergone all of the rigorous training required to be considered a full crewmember.

All of the hardship I had undergone during basic training, submarine school and my specialty school had brought me right to this beginning, where I would be put to the ultimate test. In order to attain the desired dolphins, I would need to learn all of the operating systems, cross-train with the ability to perform the basic functions of every station on board, complete supervised training in my job, and gain the knowledge to operate independently. There would be frequent tests at each step to ensure I was up to speed.

The next year went by in a blur. I trained, studied, went out to sea, studied, trained, and trained some more. It was exhausting, and I came close to my breaking point more than once. I moved my daughter and girlfriend to the island, and we got married in Guam soon after. I was excited to be married to my high-school sweetheart and have my daughter close to me.

I was deployed constantly. It was hard being away from my new family, and I know it was difficult for them as well. I stayed on track to getting my warfare insignia, and after almost a year, I scheduled and passed my board. The board was hard, long, and exhausting. I answered question after question, drew detailed schematics of various operating and weapons systems, and was timed on random drills. I had to utilize every ounce of training I had absorbed over the year of preparation. I passed my board and would be a certified "dolphin" wearing sailor.

To this day, earning my dolphins has proved to be the most difficult preparation I have ever encountered, and I am proud to be among the few who have earned that distinction. The process taught me more about myself than I knew and imbued me with the confidence that any challenge can be overcome with persistence, action, and proper planning.

I continued to learn this crucial lesson several times over during the course of my five-year experience on the mighty USS Buffalo. The journey after earning my warfare insignia did not end, but it was the beginning of many more difficult challenges, obstacles, and dilemmas I faced along with my wonderful crew. I will be forever grateful of the power these challenges gave me, and the lessons I learned from pushing myself to the limit and discovering the reservoir of personal power within me.

After about four years of constant sea deployments out of Guam, my ship and crew received orders to do a full change of homeport to Pearl Harbor, Hawai'i. I was thrilled. Hawai'i was beautiful, and I instantly fell in love with the island. My time there went by rather fast. My wife got pregnant several months later, and we prepared for another baby girl. My daughter Sakhia was very excited to become a big sister.

We ended up losing the baby after complications resulted in a stillbirth. The pain of this event was the hardest thing I have had to endure in my life, and it left us reeling. I was out of focus, and felt like I was drowning. I was in a haze of pain I could not escape, and it affected my work, and my family relationship. I tried to silence the hurt with work, avoidance, and exercise. It did little to block the anguish I was suffering through.

I wanted to exit the military that year, but the constant deployments had left me with little time to prepare for this. I didn't want to jump out with no parachute. After some serious discussion, my wife and I decided that it would be better for me to reenlist for an additional three years and try to stay in Hawai'i for shore duty.

With no available billets to stay, I chose an opening in Connecticut. My shore duty billet there was great, compared to the frenetic pace aboard a seagoing vessel. It was an amazing feeling to be able to spend every night at home with my family. During sea duty, I had spent upward of 80 percent of the year at sea. Even when the boat was pierside, every three or four nights entailed overnight duty status. I felt elated to finally feel a sense of routine and normalcy in my life.

Despite all of the great things happening in my life at the time, undercurrents of trouble grew. My marriage was rocky, and the new time we were spending together was not always constructive. I dove into school and my new job with zest, hoping to ride past the issues. No surprise, they did not go away.

The unresolved marriage issues began to mount, leading us to marriage counseling. In the end, it didn't work out. We had both made the internal decision that things were not going to work out between us. We decided that separation would be the best option. She would be moving to Ohio with my daughter.

A couple of weeks before their departure, I headed home from a friend's Halloween party after having too many drinks. I was arrested and jailed for the night, after being charged with a DUI. I felt the familiar presence of the old spinning-out-of-control state from my past. I was beyond embarrassed and angry with myself.

I spent my thin savings on an attorney, then painfully watched my daughter leave for Ohio. My heart was broken, my marriage had failed, and I was in legal trouble. I was already in debt after moving my daughter and her mother back home, and the legal fees began piling with an unprecedented alacrity.

I was still making a bit of money with my rental property, but it would not be enough to pay the mortgage once I left the military in a few short months. I was stressed and overwhelmed. My life was crumbling around me, shaking the very future I had worked hard to build. I felt like I was out of control, watching a horror movie with myself as the main character, unable to yell through the screen to make myself aware of the next potential danger behind the door.

The sky kept falling. I went to nonjudicial punishment with the military and was dropped down to the next inferior pay grade. What little hope I had of recovering financially was left razor-thin. I completed my transition out of the military as scheduled when I finished my contract and became a free man.

I was exhilarated to have completed my service and looked forward to the next phase of my life as a civilian. However, I was behind the eight-ball financially, emotionally, and mentally. More bombs dropped. With no real source of income besides the monthly allotment for school that the military paid for with my GI Bill, I could no longer afford to pay the mortgage. I was still going to school full-time, so I couldn't work a full-time job during the day.

I got a job at Foxwoods Casino, working at Shrine nightclub as security on nights and weekends. The money was minimal, so I got another night job working at a gas station. Between work and school, I was exhausted. Still, I was not making enough to feed me, pay my mortgage, and have enough left over to send to my daughter and wife, who were also struggling. I knew I didn't want to fall behind on child support when it came, so I sent money when I could. This resulted in more missed mortgage payments.

Winter was approaching, and I had no money to fill the oil tank to heat the house. The gas station I worked at shared space with a Dunkin Donuts. They usually tossed out the donuts from the previous day, but the night shift managers liked me, so they allowed me to take them. I was stuffing myself full of donuts on a daily basis. It made me feel nauseous, but I was so hungry and desperate I had to eat them anyway.

Meanwhile, I continued with school. It was difficult because I was constantly hungry, and my poor diet removed the ability to concentrate at full capacity. I was also unable to sleep well because my house was so cold. My home was an antique, and it was very drafty. I couldn't heat my entire home because it would drain the rest of the oil in my tank quicker than a knife fight in a phone booth. Since my upstairs was heated by electric zoning, I kept the heat on in my room and continued to fight the good fight.

I turned on the heat in the rest of my home when I knew I was in danger of my water pipes freezing over. I noticed that the oil was dipping dangerously quickly. I called an inspector, who happily took the last $150 I had to inform me that my boiler was broken and needed to be replaced. Cost for replacement? $10,000 dollars. I laughed aloud. I was beyond feeling sorry for myself at this point.

The boiler was out of order and when the electricity bills came in a week later, I couldn't pay it. I bid the little remaining comfort goodbye and piled on the blankets into my room for warmth. I stayed in my bedroom, throat sore from breathing freezing air, tired because I couldn't plug in my sleep apnea machine at night, and hungry enough to eat fish feet.

In accordance with Murphy's Law, things went further south. I came home from a shift at the casino to hear what sounded like the roar of applause inside. Stepping into the front sitting room, my feet were instantly wet as water from unseen buckets rushed down the ceilings and walls, passing through the wooden floor and into the basement. I looked up the stairs, and water galloped toward me. I ran into the basement and shut off the water supply valves. The basement was full of water.

Upstairs, both bathrooms were full of water. My tub piping in one of the bathrooms had broken, flooding the house. In the kitchen downstairs, the walls bubbled with water damage; the ceiling paint drooped, with long strips of paint eventually falling onto the wet floor. I stood in the sitting room, wet, tired, and exasperated. My world was literally falling around me.

I continued to stay in the freezing house. Since the water was no longer working, I washed clothes at my neighbor's house. I told him that my washer was broken. It was only half the truth. I didn't want to let anyone know about the conditions I was living in, and I was too proud to ask for help. I didn't want to be anyone's burden. I would survive.

The remaining water in the toilets froze, and I could no longer use them. I walked a half-mile in the snow to the Dunkin Donuts or grocery store down the street if I had to go. Usually, if I had to urinate, I would climb out from under the mountain of blankets in my upstairs bedroom and pee out of the window. On one occasion I remember opening the window and peeing into the snow from my upstairs sitting room. As I relieved myself, I thought about my entire living situation and how everything had led to this point in my life. I began to laugh uncontrollably. Life was funny like that sometimes.

I was glad I still had a sense of humor to hold onto.

I knew I needed a new plan and agenda to adhere to. I was tired of pinballing around, leaving my fate to be decided by factors outside of my control. Whatever I was doing was not working, and I desperately wanted change.

I thought back to my success at getting into the military and leaving my crumbling environment. I had planned for my future, taking the necessary steps to see it through. Life after joining had been no different. Every challenge I had faced as a sailor had led me to achieving success, where it had seemed impossible to hold. I knew that even though I was down, I could get up and hit back. The more I thought about what I had endured and conquered in the military, the more I realized I could bounce back. I needed to face my problems and cut through them.

I spent several weeks mapping a plan for myself and asking questions only I could answer. I knew I wanted the ability to get out of my staggering debt. I also desperately wanted to move closer to my daughter. I missed her terribly, and knew I wanted to be in her life physically, spiritually, and emotionally. I was scared and I didn't know how it would work, but I decided to set my goal to move.

I had been searching and interviewing for full-time positions. One evening, I received a phone call from an unrecognized number. It was a representative for a company I had interviewed with several weeks earlier. They offered me a job opportunity with a salary paying over $100,000! That was huge to me and could definitely solve my financial issues. The only problem was that the job offer was out of state. I couldn't take it since I had determined I would be moving closer to Sakhia. I politely declined, ending the conversation.

The woman on the other end told me to call back within the next couple of days if I decided to change my mind.

I sat on the bed in my cold house and stared at the blank ceiling. Was I an idiot for saying no to such an offer? I *had* to be! There was no way anyone in their right mind would decline such an opportunity. Going against my character I decided to call some people and get their opinion on the matter. Without fail, everyone I called told me that I would be foolish not to take this opportunity. I thanked them for their advice and got off the phone.

Somehow hearing their words made me feel better about my own decision to turn down the job. I had made my decision within my own heart, and it resonated within me.

One day, my friend Josie came over to my house and saw the squalor-like conditions I was living in. She was upset and told me to pack my things because I would be staying in the unrented in-law suite at her house until I figured things out. I thanked her and told her how I had everything under control, but she informed me she wouldn't be leaving until I was ready to go. I knew she was as stubborn as I was, so I grabbed a few things and I followed her to the home.

I felt weak for accepting help, but it was necessary and humbling for me. I felt my spirit being slowly brought back to life. The warm running water was a new blessing that I will never take for granted again. The feeling of taking a private shower not at a dirty gym was blissful and rejuvenating. Laying down to sleep in a warm bed with my CPAP machine was wondrous. I began to feel like a new version of my former self. I continued to look for jobs, eventually getting hired as a consultant in Corporate America. The job was not one I chose because of the enjoyment factor, but it helped me regain my footing financially. The work was hard, but I was good at my job and stuck to it.

I graduated in the early summer. My daughter and parents came from Ohio. I was proud of myself, but when I graduated I felt no closer to living the life of my dreams than when I first started college. Besides, I already had a PhD in suffering and an MBA in making wrong decisions. I wasn't going to settle for mediocrity. It was time to go after the things I desperately, truly wanted for myself.

Two weeks before my move to Ohio, I got called into my manager's office and was laid off. He kept profusely apologizing, but I stopped him, a huge grin on my face. I told him not to worry, and thanked him for his time. I told him I would gather my items and go. He looked at me like I was a crazy person.

It must have seemed strange, him firing me and me looking like I had won the lottery. He mentioned to me several times that I could not, under any circumstance, attempt to come back and try to enter the premises. I'm sure he thought I was going to come back unannounced and angry!

I enjoyed some time off before my move to Ohio. After arrival, I was promptly sued for back child support spanning the two years my daughter had moved away. The judge had been wrongly told that I had not been sending monetary payments. I lost joint custody of my daughter and was ordered to pay the "delinquent" child support in full, plus the now mandatory monthly support, even though I had no job. I went home feeling hurt and humiliated. I felt the familiar sense of having lost everything. AGAIN.

I felt like I was living in a revolving circle of torture. I jumped into legal trouble, following another arrest. I had no friends to relate to here, I missed Connecticut, and I was jobless. I felt like a complete failure. I stayed inside my house for weeks, laying in bed and watching movies until I felt my brain turning into mush. I was depressed.

I needed a reset button. I was tired of bouncing around like a paper bag, being blown nowhere and everywhere. I needed an internal destination, a course. Thinking back to my days on the boat, I remembered that the destination was the most necessary portion of sailing. All of the countless missions, sorties, and training underways we went on began with a destination and a purpose in mind. If I wanted success, I would have to plan for it accordingly.

I decided to climb out of my bed of misery and move forward with my life. I talked to other veterans and slowly let myself be vulnerable. I told them that I was suffering and felt upside down, and asked them how they had fared after separation. Surprisingly, many felt the same, reflecting my thoughts of uncertainty after departure. It was humbling to know that I was not alone in my attempt to navigate the new reality of my life.

I felt an intense desire to help veterans like me. I met some veterans in my locality. We talked about our transition, discussing the many similarities in our stories.

I talked to more and more veterans, looking to find out if there were many who struggled to gain clarity and direction after getting out. I was excited and saddened by the resounding "YES" I received. I knew I wanted to help ease the discomfort of my fellow veterans because it was something that we were facing together, whether we knew it or not.

These conversations taught me about the shared obstacles stemming from life outside of the military. Most veterans felt alienated, cut off from the close-knit family in the military they had relied upon, grew with, and faced death with. It was easy to jump into a traditional, cookie-cutter way of living. The focus on getting a job, paying bills, and simple survival suffocated the deeper needs of the spirit, something I could emphatically relate to.

I thought about all of the learning, training, and drills I had undergone in the military. Preparing for the unknown had always been the optimal way to train. No situation or obstacle I faced in service had been void of solutions. There were plenty of times when an unforeseen casualty disrupted the crew, but we had always overcome them. I had faced impossible odds, unfavorable conditions, and miserable circumstances. I had fought to overcome these challenges. I was still a warrior, just in a different fight—not helpless, just unfocused.

I began moving toward the values that meant most to me and held myself accountable for moving toward better. I stopped careening off course. As I focused, things began to positively develop. I landed a great job in a field that related to my experience in military service. It was exciting, demanding, and challenging in a way that was familiar to me. I enjoyed the work, and it provided me with an increasingly escalating income. I grew quickly in the organization and was promoted rapidly.

I was still intent on being able to help struggling veterans, or those that simply needed a fresh take on their path after discharge. Almost as an answer to my thoughts, I met Sai soon after. He told me his story and offered to be my mentor and show me how to serve those I desperately wished to help. I knew I could help others maneuver around the potholes I landed in, helping them steer more quickly toward a personalized road to success. I began to wake excited everyday, happy to work toward helping my fellow servicemembers. I put my time, effort, and energy into creating a program that focused on the unique tools most veterans already possess—providing them with resources and new strategies for satisfying their ingrained thirst for personal excellence and achievement.

Since my veteran coaching business 'Boots to Beyond' has been up and running, I have been able to successfully offer my experience to others, helping them discover their own unique pathways to achievement. Some of my client triumphs include:

- Assisting a combat veteran discharged with PTSD and suffering through a painful landing after 14 years of active duty. When I began working with him, he was employed as a contractor making minimum wage. With a game plan and mindset change, he went from a literally negative bank account balance (trying to earn extra income by painting home addresses on the curb for $10 a house) to generating a cleaning business making $16,000 dollars a month.

- Helping a former enlisted Marine client land a position he had dreamed of. He was able to make more money in his first months out than when he was in (and getting paid to be deployed overseas).

- Aiding a Navy veteran who transferred from active duty service after eight years (while turning down an ample reenlistment bonus) adjust his mindset and use prior skills to begin making an extra passive income of 30k a year, all while attending business school and traveling with his family during his breaks from college.

- My biggest success was taking a grizzled nine-year military veteran from being depressed and losing his home to following his passions, not settling for less, and making over $12,000 a month (TWICE) within a year.

If you didn't catch the last bullet point, I'll give you a helpful hint: that grizzled veteran was me.

These samples of success are definitive and quantifiable. However, the real wealth of these examples is the simple fact that none of these individuals did anything extremely drastic to change their direction. They started where they were, listening to their inner convictions and making the *decision* to move toward their needs. As essayist Dorothy Mendoza asserts, "When faced with a decision, choose the path that feeds your soul." To truly shape your world is to water the seeds of possibility already inside you. I tell all of my clients this simple truth: success starts in the mind.

It has, and continues to be an incredible feeling to witness these ordinary heroes emerge as the leaders they established themselves to be, this time in a different uniform: one of their choosing.

I am humbled by the fighting spirit they carry with them, earned by protecting their loved ones and their country. I am also forever grateful for my errors and failures, for I would not have been able to aid others without my experience of falling flat onto my face more times than I can count.

RUSSELL FRAZIER

Russ is a proud Navy Veteran and the founder of Boots to Beyond, a personal coaching practice dedicated to assisting military veterans chart a new course in life after military service. His program has helped vets from all branches and walks of life tap into their invaluable service experience to craft lifestyles that meet their deepest personal needs.

Russ had a successful nine-year career as a U.S. Navy Submarine crewmember. Through numerous transitions in his life and career, he discovered a passion for mentoring veterans and was inspired to teach others to step into their future.

He lives in Ohio, where he can be found (usually) eating, reading, cracking bad jokes, or lifting heavy things and putting them back down.

Contact Details

Website: https://beyondbootscoaching.com/

LinkedIn: https://www.linkedin.com/in/russell-frazier-7010a189/

AWAKENED PURPOSE: I OWN MY LIFE NOW

Shemsheer A. Lallani

Introduction

My life has been filled with business and personal wild adventures expanding the globe and, more importantly, has been blessed with revelations that the "Universe" gave to guide me on my path of life. These revelations or doors of opportunity were answers to what I internally indirectly or directly asked. I will go into more detail about how my transformation happened, how my purpose was awakened, and most importantly how I own my life now. The slow discovery of my gift, the learning process, the educational lessons, and the periodic presentation from the self to the world changed the course of my life to take me where I am now. Yet, it was not until I came face to face with a life-and-death situation that I embraced the discovery and confirmed my calling as a coach.

Learning about New Cultures

I grew up in the city of Bukavu, in the Democratic Republic of the Congo, where I lived a simple life of innocence and discovery. My city was a lost paradise in the high hills, with a misted Shangri-La of wide, bougainvillea-laden streets that had lakeside villas with swimming pools and lush gardens sloping to the shore of beautiful Lake Kivu. The volcanic soil of the surrounding hillsides was so fertile and the climate so good that there was scarcely any flower or vegetable that didn't thrive there. My very first best friend Godee and I had our own garden where we grew passion fruits, papaya, corn, sweet potatoes, and cassava.

Godee, who was 10 years my senior, was an important friend in my childhood, and he always accompanied and protected me in my adventures. The vast jungles allowed us to learn how to hunt small animals and do a lot of fishing for tilapia from the shore and sardines from canoes. We also did snorkel diving in the lake for munitions left by the last wars or whatever we could find in the hidden depths of the lake. Once he said to me something that really means a lot now, "You will become a great person in the life that you choose to live".

Bukavu was where I discovered many passions, one of which was riding my motorcycle, a Zundapp 450. We would escape the city to ride in the hills and go from village to village while enjoying the local food and people. I was studying in a French School, and languages became another passion. I learned how to speak Swahili and Lingala so that I could communicate and have fun with the local community. I can say that my childhood was one of absolute innocence with the luck of having beautiful parents who worked hard to give me and my sisters an amazing life.

From Bukavu, my family and I moved to Kinshasa, the capital of Zaire, where I attended the American School of Kinshasa, TASOK, for my high school. I was a good student, and my score was always in the As, but I was also a very wild boy because my crazy habits gave me the rush of adrenaline and made me feel on top of the world.

This is where I had my exposure to the high-end society, where they had luxury cars, chauffeurs, cooks, etc. These times gave me the so-called ambitions of making my life big by using my skills and education to succeed. At this time, everything made sense in my life. I was exposed to a world that had a lot of wealth, and it enchanted me. Money brings a false sense of power, and at that moment, it was all I thought about. While I was having a lot of fun and enjoying the high lifestyle, I did not really pay attention to one important lesson that the people of Zaire were showing me. With a low salary of $100 a month, they had learned to be happy with a simple life that consisted of food on their table, a roof over their head, and small parties with the full knowledge that it is all they would ever have.

I had been exposed to the concept of power, yet the locals were indirectly showing me that money should not have such a high cost of loss in happiness and integrity. It never crossed my mind that the exposure to this part of the world and to this culture was also a part of the teachings I would understand much later in life when I realized that money does not buy happiness. Instead, it is a commodity that we are almost forced to venerate as a deity; by abiding to its laws, we lose sight of what is in front of our eyes.

Wildlife in My Personal and Business World

When I graduated from TASOK, I was accepted at the University of Toronto where I took up Arts and Science. At this time, my life was a big question mark because I had an inner drive to succeed as a powerful, rich businessman and another to live and do everything that gave me the rush. I had not found the career that I wanted, so at the University of Toronto, I went from Arts and Science to Forestry, and then I quit my studies and decided to work in different career positions across the world.

The first event that changed the direction of my life trajectory was when I was living in Toronto and had a car accident. This was in 1988, and I had just turned 24. I was preparing for a trip to Cancun, and it happened when I was taking a bus to go downtown. I was hit by a truck that was running a red light at an intersection. I stayed in a coma for 10 days with a 50/50 chance of survival. My parents, who were living in Congo, flew to Canada to be by my side. I know that I survived this accident because they gave me their love, care, and prayers. With this and all of the support from family and friends, I finally came out of the coma with a total loss of memory.

When I lost my memory, all the knowledge, the recognition of people, the awareness, and the feelings that I had for different moments and times was lost as well. I lived a life of total loss with the only purpose to remember, and I was in full battle mode all the time because I wanted to first find out who I was and then who were the people around me. As time passed, I wanted to bring back and remember the places and events and all the things that were important to me. I still recall my first memory when I stood in my condo bathroom looking at my reflection in the mirror with a huge black eye and a loss of 12 pounds and was asking myself "What the hell happened to you?"

My days were a continuous battle with many moments of rage and the wanting to remember my life. My subconscious memory, of all that I had done in my life, was helping me muster the energy I needed to make my conscious mind remember the memories that I had. At the same time, I was being shown that life can take a different direction if we understand the path and have a purpose to follow. My only purpose was to remember the important parts of my life and the people who were a part of it so that I could start living again.

This loss of memory lasted three months, and with the thirst that I had for life and my passion to live, I came out of occupational therapy by recovering in one month instead of three months, with an 85% return of memory. This went to a 99% recovery within six months. Once I finished all the medical procedures of rehabilitation, I went back home and slowly got back the energy and strength I needed.

Six months later, I applied and was accepted at Seneca College in Toronto, where I pursued an International Business Co-op Degree. This was what I thought to be my final career and destiny. My quest to live to the fullest was reignited because the thirst for life had become more prominent since I was reborn with a second chance in life. My life objective was to live it with the sole purpose of reaching the wealth, the high lifestyle, and power in the business world that I had always wanted.

I was so involved with the adrenaline rush it was providing me that I did not pay attention to the many doors of opportunity the

Universe was showing me. You are probably asking what were the doors of opportunity? Well, I was already indirectly helping people around me in college and also when I traveled the world on business trips. I have helped some people change their lives by showing them that life can be full of happiness if we pay attention, communicate, and share with those around us.

The unfortunate thing was that I was not practicing what I was preaching; I was a one-man team who did not need anybody nor did I want to share anything. I just wanted to have fun and live in my own world and not the real outside world. At this time, I was very lucky because I met the one who would become my brother in life. Tyron was always watching my back, and he was there to put me back on track and made sure that I did well.

Although I was intoxicated with the monetary wealth I could have, I was paying more attention to things and people around me. I was participating in activities such as lending a hand to the neighbors, helping the elders, and volunteering. This allowed me to internally appreciate what I had. However, the part of me that wanted to have fun and do crazy things was bigger than this feeling.

In my 3rd year at Seneca college, I was accepted in a one-year Co-op program with the Hogeschool Voor Economic Studies, in Amsterdam, Netherlands. There, I spent six months studying and six months working for a company that did international tenders with West Africa. I will never forget Amsterdam, the city that never slept. I chose to live a life with the energy and passion that this city offered to whoever paid attention to its secrets. The secrets of Amsterdam were its people, its location that provided quick access to any city in Europe, the museums, the food, the beers, the parties, and their different celebrations. There were also events such as the UEFA soccer championships and Queen Mother Birthday, where all the stores are closed for the weekend and the city becomes a flea market offering anything and everything on its streets.

Amsterdam was known for its legalization of marijuana, and the only time I ever smoked weed was when friends visited, otherwise, I did not need to have these drugs to have fun. I was enthralled with all that the city had, be it the restaurants, the nightlife or the culture, and living in Amsterdam was already a high for me. I made a lot of friends and was known as the international Canadian because I mixed well with people from different parts of Europe. After Amsterdam, I graduated from Seneca College with a High Honors Diploma.

For the next twenty years, I pursued my business ambitions by following my flair in commerce all over the world. I held managerial positions in Kinshasa and Angola for brief periods until I realized that I needed to venture out on my own. Whenever I heard of commercial possibilities anywhere in the world, I packed my bags and went. I would go to the country where there was an opportunity and would sit back for a couple of months and just watch how the economic and political statuses influenced the country and its people. I listened to what people felt and thought of the government, participated in the local community events, tasted different foods, and asked questions. This would always give me the background of what was really going on and helped me to decide how and to what extent I could implement my business projects.

I traveled all over the world, from South Africa to Canada to the USA, setting up business ventures and companies. I had dealt with people from different facets, from the very poor living in ghettos to the ultimately rich living in villas and mansions. I had succeeded in some ventures and miserably failed in others. My life during those twenty years was a whirlwind of passions on a professional and personal level. I was moving so fast, always thinking that there are better opportunities in other places, which goes with the saying: the grass is greener on the other side. I never considered stopping and taking a step back to reflect on what I was doing and where I really wanted to go. Now, I know that the grass is never greener on the other side, it is just as green where I stand if I choose to look carefully.

On the personal side, I had met my soulmate in Toronto. She was a very beautiful person with a beautiful heart. Our relationship was also a whirlwind of passion, love, wants, and desires. Unfortunately, I was so involved with my ambitions that I rebelled at any notion to take the needed time to make it work. There had been one very hard situation where the circumstances had negatively affected the feelings and thoughts we had for each other. The relationship ended and left a mark of regret on me. My life and my ambitions were the priorities, and I was ruthless in the quest of my goals. Upon reflection, there are always two sides to every relationship problem and the only cure to this is communication. If I had communicated and tried to understand where she was coming from and vice versa, there is a probability that our story would have been a beautiful one.

My First Fall Out

At this point, my personal relationships were not stable and everything was draining all of my energy. I was physically, mentally, and emotionally exhausted. I was 44 years old and was on the highway with a burnout as a final destination. When the recession of

2008/2009 hit all markets, my whole life crashed due to the speed I was cruising in the business world. I was running three companies at the same time, one in the USA, one in Canada, and one in South Africa. So, I decided to take a step back and stop everything. I told everybody, including my family and friends, that I was taking an absence from work and my personal life and there would be no communication from me. I really had to stop and review what had happened to me and rediscover who I was, where I wanted to go, and what I wanted to do so that I was never in this kind of situation again.

As I reviewed my last years, I first and foremost realized that my life had started taking a turn for the worse in the last three years. I had been drinking a lot and running very high expenses by doing things such as buying fast cars and taking expensive trips that I thought would give me what I needed. I was playing dangerous games in the market by taking high risks with customers who were working in countries that had political volatility and could take my actions as personal attacks on them and their companies. I was not paying attention to my physical and mental state, and I was not stable in all the relationships I had because I considered myself above the rest and anybody with me had to have the same status.

Once I took that step back, I knew that I had to find a place where I could review my entire life. I did a lot of research before choosing a retreat and I found two good options: Kopan Monastery in Kathmandu, Nepal, which was a Buddhist Temple or the Vipassana Meditation Center at Mount Sutton in Canada. In the first one, I would stay far away from home, without any contact for two months. The second one offered two weeks of zero contact in the same country that I was living in. So, I decided to go to Vipassana

Meditation Center.

The first Vipassana Meditation Center was started by S. N. Goenka in 1976. The technique that Goenka taught was the teachings used by the Buddha that went back 26 centuries; it represented a tradition where there was no requirement to convert or change to any religious belief system. The Buddha, or the "Awakened One" or "Enlightened One", was a philosopher, meditator, and a spiritual teacher who never preached a sectarian religion; he taught Dhamma – the way to liberation – which is universal. The teachings at the Mount Sutton Vipassana Center encompass a 10-day intensive meditation retreat with courses that start with observation of natural (i.e., not controlled) breath that allows the mind to become concentrated, and this practice is called Anapana.

Goenka described Vipassana Meditation as:

"An experiential scientific practice, in which one observes the constantly changing nature of the mind and body at the deepest level, through which one gains a profound self-knowledge that leads to a truly happy and peaceful life."

This center offered a monastery-like atmosphere for meditation courses, and the application procedure had strict rules of acceptance. I applied and was accepted. The only thing that I was requested to bring was my personal items. To my surprise, there was no money requested. I was informed that the center followed the same rule which the Buddha used: he never charged any money to his students. The amount received by the center was through donations given by the students after their 10 days of learning and meditation.

I arrived at the center, and the first three hours were spent in my room, which was a small container converted into a room with two beds. I had a long discussion with my room partner and then we went to the main classroom for a discourse where they did a presentation on the rules, the objectives and the techniques used to practice meditation. Right after the meeting, we started the ten days of "Noble Silence." We could not talk, read magazines, watch TV, or do anything that can be a distraction. There was no communication with anybody except yourself and God.

During the meditation sessions, we were taught to create our internal world to observe all our sensations. This is the practice of continued close attention to sensation through which one ultimately sees the true nature of existence. In today's world, we lack mindfulness and we do not put aside any time for silence or self-reflection. Many of us would rather go out and seek different sorts of entertainment rather than looking within ourselves. By following the instructions of using the state of equanimous mind, I was able to go into the depths of myself and see the similar patterns of stress that had kept on emerging. Now, I could correct these automatic stress reactions which then allowed me to have more freedom of the mind and soul.

My daily routine was this: I woke up at 4:00 a.m., and meditated until 5:30 p.m. with breaks for a vegetarian breakfast and lunch that were held in the cafeteria. This room held approximately 50 people, and it was divided with a blue curtain to partition men and women. With the Noble Silence code, I did not ask anybody for anything. If I wanted something, I pointed it to the person next to me and he would pass it to me. I also did not say sorry if I bumped into anybody. This was a very strange and different way of communication because it solely relied on each other's respect and integrity. At 7:00 p.m., there was a discourse on the teaching of the Buddha and at 9:00 p.m., it was lights out.

My first intent for coming to the Vipassana Meditation Center was to get out of the spiral downfall I was going through and find answers to the why and the what. I knew that I needed closure for certain parts of my life, and I also wanted to discover "me" without the opinions or influence of others.

This was the awakening that I experienced with the act of self-observance. When I sat in a meditation pose and started to observe my breathing, I slowly realized that it encompasses all that I thought and felt. Every breath took me away from all that was such a burden and allowed me to discharge the weight that I had been carrying on my shoulders for such a long time. I acutely observed and felt all the sensations that were happening or going through my body and mind and eventually my soul. This awakening showed me that I had to settle and build a new life with all the things that make me happy. The happiness could not be bought, and the rush of life could be enjoyed with the simplest things that are and have always been in front of me.

After the Vipassana retreat, I knew that I had to make some major changes in my life so that I would not crash again and be lost. I decided to reduce my traveling and settle down more permanently in Montreal, Canada. The family business, Photoflash, a global photo passport maker company, was still on the go, and I was still scanning the different zones of business in Montreal. There was a part of me that was still looking for something that would financially fulfill me. Although I had been through several exposures of what my gift or aptitude was, I still had not fully looked into that part of me.

From Montreal, I opened several branches of my company TTerravida Consulting Inc. TTerraserve was an arm that extended in the repossession of real estate, and TTerralinx was an arm that extended in the bad debt industry. Both markets were located in the USA. I had analyzed the consequences of the recession and found that if I find the right venture to invest in the USA, I could be very successful, no matter what the political or economic situation was.

In both of these business ventures, while dealing with different entities, I was dealing with people in very difficult situations whose lives had taken a turn for the worse. Their unfortunate debt circumstances or lost ownership of properties allowed financial possibilities gains with a certain amount of risk for the buyers. As I was working in this world, and directly communicating with sellers, I often found myself comforting and listening to people who were in a bad situation. Most of the time, I offered different possibilities to better their lives by suggesting them to take a new path where they concentrated more on the good things they had and not what they had lost.

These business projects were short-lived because I found out that it was very hard to manage businesses in the USA from an office in Canada. I applied my exit strategy to get out of these ventures because I realized that dealing with businesses entwined with other people's emotions was not making me feel good in the long run. This was another instance where the Universe was showing me the direction and this time, I was actually following my intuition. I was slowly and surely getting closer to finding my purpose.

As I moved on in my life, I met Monisha who became the amazing and beautiful mother of our baby girl Mishaal. My baby girl's presence in my life was a blessing and anchored me to the ground. She was my main link to life, and she showed me the happiness and the joy of living. There are certain things that Mishaal did that reminded me to live in the "Now". I shall never forget the laughs, her first word "Papa", the first steps, and the total concentration when she drank from her bottle. These were her "Now" moments, and all of these taught me how to be a father and a better person. Today, 10 years later, she is my little baby girl discovering the world and being raised with freedom of thought to be a strong and independent woman in the future.

I had taken the path of settling in Montreal, running the family business, and doing the things that made me feel good and alive such as riding my Harley, enjoying the outdoors, connecting with Mother Nature, and organizing get-togethers with my closest friends. I was not a world traveler anymore; my little Mishaal had really grounded me. My life had become a whirlwind of living with simple passions, yet, I knew that there was more, and I was getting closer to finding my purpose.

Awakening My Purpose

I was approached by some colleagues to start a company in Montreal that would deal with selling natural products and commodities through Amazon. They had approached me because of my vast negotiation experience and my capacity to communicate at all levels. I accepted, and we started working in the basement of one of my partner's houses. This was a trial run because I knew that we were very strong-headed and very individually oriented. One of the two partners had been a CEO of a company that had gone from a $35,000- to $125-million company in the .com explosion. The other gentleman was an IT genius who mastered the world of computers and had very good skills on the net with a vast experience of dealing with markets such as Amazon Inc. We tried to divide the workload and unfortunately as time went by, I was seeing signs of what is usually called head butting between associates.

There was a power struggle and lack of communication amongst ourselves and after six months. I tried to communicate with them about the possibility of overcoming the personal barriers we had. I wanted to move forward using a very distinct motto that I constantly try to apply: always have fun and do the best you can in everything you are involved in. If I don't have fun doing what I do whether it be work, relationships, or hobbies, it will eventually exhaust me, and I never do my best if I am not having fun. Unfortunately, the attempt at finding a balance in our work relationship did not materialize, the opinions were very different, and it was going to be impossible to work with them and have a great time.

My very best friend Zul, who was a good listener and supporter, showed me that there is always a silver lining to any bad situation. He showed me that I was getting out without suffering a financial or integrity loss and that there was something much better for me in the near future.

After all of this happened, I decided to again take a step back and review everything. This time, I had concluded that the world of business did not appeal to me, and there was no thrill in closing deals and contracts anymore. I asked myself two important questions: "What do I want to do and what is my purpose?"

As I reviewed my whole life, where I have been, and what I had done, there was a continuous factor that was always present wherever I was and whatever I was doing. I had always helped or assisted people indirectly by communicating with them and sharing their space or just listening. I did some research about better ways to help and assist people who had different problems, and after many weeks of search and filtering all the possible outcomes, I found a possibility that really resonated well: Health Coaching.

I found an online coaching school called Health Coach Institute (HCI). The core curriculum was based on psychology, brain science, intuitive listening, habit change, and healthy lifestyle design. Their following anthem was totally in sync with me:

> "Just do what you love 'cause it's most advantageous
> The passion that you share will truly be contagious
> Deep down you might be scared, but decide to be courageous
> Outside we're kind of square, but inside we're all outrageous.
>
> So let's say a prayer for those free souls kept in cages
> Feel it coming in the air, their stillness turning into rages
> Drop the someone who stares, be the one who engages
> Be the person that's rare, the one who writes their own pages
>
> And always be aware our value is greater than our wages
> You can be the millionaire, but money ain't the thing that gauges
> No doubt things are unfair, just take them on and small

stages

And just do what you love and just do it with love, no matter what your age is"

— **Health Coach Institute**

According to the HCI, a health coach is a master of habit change. Healthy habits create healthy results, and the most effective health coaches help people make better choices for themselves. The course is delivered in four pillars: Nutrition, Health & Wellness, Transformational Coaching, and Personal Growth. I joined the HCI and truly enjoyed the courses, the trips I took to their conferences, and the layout of activities they offered online. It was through the interaction online with other students using web portals that I learned that this was a platform that concentrated on finding the best possible ways to help all sorts of people. I was on a path that was going in a direction that was making me feel good.

As I progressed through the course, I was already opening the door to use my coaching skills with friends and relatives who were in difficult situations or just needed somebody who would listen. As I coached, I was learning that there were different aspects of coaching for different people. Some clients that I coached had problems with clarity and purpose, some had problems with being overweight, and others had issues with values and beliefs. They all centered around pillars that were health, life, and spirituality. For me, these pillars provide the balance I needed to have so that I can live with what society and life throw at me daily.

Since I wanted to make sure that I had all the tools and knowledge in my bag so that I could help people in any situation, I decided that

I had to further educate myself in Life Coaching with Neuro-Linguistic Programming (NLP). NLP works on the principle that everyone has all the resources they need to make positive changes in their own life by bringing and developing communication in any given situation. It is the study of excellent communication – both with us and with others and it is an attitude and a methodology of knowing how to achieve your goals and get results.

Taking this NLP training course was like learning how to become fluent in the language of our mind so that the ever-so-helpful "server" that is our unconscious will finally understand and dictate what we actually want out of life. In everyday life, 10% of decisions are made by our conscious mind, and 90% of them are made by our unconscious mind. We have already been programmed to do a lot of things, and I learned the language of the voice, body and mind that our subconscious will listen to. With NLP, I discovered all the different ways to read languages of the voice, body and mind, and this enabled me to reach out and understand others.

The world we all live in is influenced by politics, entertainment, economies, financial capacities, family, hobbies, and so much more. The problems that we encounter will always be centered around how you are and how you live your life. The unfortunate thing is that we are so engrossed in what is around us that we forget the most important part of living: ourselves. I have learned that the first priority is me because if I take care, respect, and love myself, I will be the support that others need. This is what I have been teaching my clients to do. My goal is to help them find peace and balance for mind and body so that they can live a simple and happy life and live in their "Now".

Educating myself in Health Coaching and Life Coaching allowed me to expand my knowledge, and it helped me understand and confirm that the material part of life will never give me absolute happiness. It will be very momentary, yet true happiness is how I live and why I live. I thought I was living a full life, but it is only when I took the path of coaching that I found out that I needed to have a purpose so that I could own my life. In the material world, we are born with nothing and we die with nothing; during my life, I have been in search of something that will make it worthwhile to live. Today, I have found my purpose, and it was only realized to the fullest extent when my papa Amir Lallani passed. My father was a man of valor and life. He was my superman. He had reached the height of his accomplished life with my mother being his main supporter and friend. Through them, I had learned that life is one that has to be shared with love and compassion.

When I buried my papa, I made him a promise; I will always be there for mama and I will make him proud of me with my accomplishments as a coach and any other work that I do. By making this promise, I have fully embraced my destiny of coaching, volunteering, and helping humanity.

I Own My Life Now

All the different doors that the Universe showed me throughout my life have led me to where I am and what I am doing today. My life is to help and touch as many hearts as possible so that they can live a life they want filled with simplicity, love, and passion.

I am 55 years old, and I am very happy with my life of simplicity and faith.

I have a purpose, and I own my life now.

"Free yourself from the complexities and drama of your life. Simplify. Look within. Within ourselves we all have the gifts and talents we need to fulfill the purpose we've been blessed with."

Steve Maraboli

SHEMSHEER A. LALLANI

Shemsheer Lallani graduated from Seneca College in International Business Co-op and worked for 20 years as a corporate businessman with companies in several countries such as South Africa, the USA, and Canada.

Shemsheer has been volunteering in the Muslim Ismaili community for the last 20 years and donates his time to raise funds through different venues such as the World Partnership Walk and Focus.

Since 2016, Shemsheer has been working as a Health and Life coach, helping people around the world. He is also CEO of TTerravïda Consulting Inc.

As a Coach, his main goal in life is to contribute to humanity by assisting and helping people to awaken their purpose and own their lives.

Contact Details

Website: www.shemsheerlallani.com

Email: shemsheer@shemsheerlallani.com

Instagram: https://www.instagram.com/shemsheerlallani/

LinkedIn: https://www.linkedin.com/in/shemsheer/

Facebook: https://www.facebook.com/shemsheerlallani/.

I AM IN TRANSITION

Sonia Saïdi

*"The two most important days in your life are the day you are born
and the day you find out why."*
Mark Twain

May 1980. I symbolically entered the stage and screamed,
"Hello, I'm here and I have a purpose."

We are constantly searching for the meaning of life and human
fulfillment. This requires working hard, being on the lookout, not
giving up, being curious, and always asking "what's next?"

At the end of the day, it is all about our fundamental and true
purpose in life. It is from this moment that the transition of life
begins.

I am the third child of immigrant parents. They left their country to
come and live in France. My mother never had the luxury to read or

write; her destiny was to support her family by working at the farm. She did not receive a school education, but my father was lucky enough to be able to continue his studies up to the baccalaureate. Afterward, he served in the navy for a few years.

I always liked going to school. The pleasure of discovering the world in all its facets fascinated me, and I would stay locked up in my room for hours—reading, listening to music, watching wonderful nature documentaries, and asking questions. I was thirsty for life. The only fear was the harmful environment that some people could create in your existence. It also meant that you could see the doors that shut you down. You could decide to choose which one to open to release your full potential or keep it locked.

During my childhood, I lived through traumas—being verbally belittled by my school teacher at the age of eight, being humiliated by classmates at school, having heart surgery at the age of 11, and a few more. These scars—both visible and invisible—cost me a lot. They further resulted in very poor school results repeating a grade and many annotations from my teacher, "Sonia can do better, Sonia must concentrate more, Sonia must pull herself together." And it goes on and on for years with the same speech. Sometimes this can motivate you or lock you into your own shell.

Life brings you small gifts during your existence, and it's up to you to honor it. Mine has been translated in the most beautiful way possible. My parents had a house built, and we moved to a nicer environment. And I had the joy and happiness of meeting one of my charming neighbors who brought me knowledge through books, gave me private lessons, and introduced me to the world through world history, poetry, and geography, and where I had developed a fondness for philosophy and English. She gave me the greatest gift I could hold in my hand, a book. It was *Sophie's World* by Jostein Gaarder. This particular book opened my vision of life when I was 15 years old. Everything changed at that moment.

September 3, 2000. It was a Sunday afternoon and only a couple of days before the school year started. I remember it distinctly because it was the hardest time of my life. I was with my mother when we received a phone call from my uncle telling us about a serious car accident involving my father. Half an hour later, my uncle came to the house, but this time to tell us the sad news of my father's death. My world collapsed.

"If you can't fly then run, if you can't run then walk, if you can't walk then crawl, but whatever you do you have to keep moving forward."

Martin Luther King, Jr.

How to deal with life changes? How to face it all when everything is pulling you down? What if this happened? What if that did? This is how our mind nurtures us; it makes us doubt our capacity in dealing with major transitions.

A year after my father's death, I stopped school for a while. I had a variety of jobs and experiences, including working as a shelf clerk in a sports store, cashier in a local supermarket, a photo framer, and a salesperson in a fast-food restaurant. My goal was to help my mother financially, like my brothers did, and pay the bills my dad had left behind. However, I mostly wanted to be independent, which would allow me to pay for my driver's license, buy clothes, hang out with my friends, and put some money aside for the D-Day that would unexpectedly come knocking at my door.

But deep down, I felt that I had to go back to school and to refine the learning that I had accumulated through the jobs. But at no time did I want to cut the cord of my professional life, so I chose to enroll in a two-year course at a school where I could benefit from both work experience and academic training at the same time. I felt an attraction toward working in sales, but above all, I wanted to be surrounded by customers who could ask me questions. To see a customer happy and satisfied filled me with joy. I contacted many companies and spoke to various people until a few replied with a positive answer. All I had to do was to pick the right company.

Thus, a new journey started. I was so happy, and things turned on my side. I excelled at my work, easily reached the daily targets, met great colleagues, and impressed my manager with my agility to adapt and learn. In a few months, she promoted me to manage a small group, where I had to train them on sales. I felt so grateful and respected by my elders for being trained by a young person like me. This is how it pays off when they start to generate great results. I was the youngest in the team.

At school, I developed a great environment with my schoolmates and teachers. Results went from "Sonia could do better" to "Sonia is doing good." The school, from time to time, invited many successful managers and CEOs to share their work-life environment. I was always very attentive and captivated by their speeches.

My teacher introduced us to his friend Daniel who worked for an international company. We had the pleasure to interact with him and ask many questions. He told me, in confidence, that he was very interested in my personality. Later, he gave his business card and said, "Contact me when you are done with school, a place is waiting for you in my company at any time."

What a blessing! I felt so thrilled about his comments and even more confident about my career direction.

Months later, I started to get bored at work, which also affected my motivation to go to school. After a long introspection, I took the initiative to stop everything. I felt that I was wasting my time sitting all day at school for something that doesn't improve my learning. Apart from that, my manager also couldn't offer me more since I was in a student position. I went to see my teacher, and he understood my decision. He said, "Sonia, I sensed that you are increasingly demotivated and I spoke to your manager, and she felt the same. But in six months, you could obtain your diploma." I remembered saying to him, "How can you develop your skills when there is nothing to hold you? What to do more where the learning I am getting is not sufficient? What will be the difference if I obtain a diploma or not?

What needs to be done to use this time more profitably? If you're deeply aware that your worth is much more than a piece of paper, then I'm confident about my skill and want to discover my real potential. And if it's not here, then it will be elsewhere."

He couldn't argue anymore because he knew I was right. A month later, I left.

"You have to trust in something - your gut, destiny, life, karma, whatever. This approach has never let me down, and it has made all the difference in my life."

Steve Jobs

There was a new adventure in store for me. I was all set to move on from being a student to looking for a job.

I was so happy and excited. I was seated in front of my computer and was refining my resume. I decided to call Daniel, who had earlier given me his business card.

He remembered me straight away, and I explained to him about my decision. He wasn't surprised at all and added that he was waiting for my call. My teacher had earlier spoken to him about my choice. Nonetheless, he was impressed by my initiative and felt honored that I contacted him. He spoke more about my roles and responsibilities in my new job and explained it along with an offer. I said yes, and asked when I should start. The following week, I started my new career as a sales representative.

After three months, I was disappointed with my job. I didn't like it much. Being on the road every day and trying to sell products to clients wasn't that exciting. Again, I was bored, and I knew it wasn't for me, I resigned. Daniel told me, "You could be a top manager in a year or two, Sonia, you are talented!" Unfortunately, I didn't feel empowered in that job. He wished me good luck in my career.

I spent a few weeks checking other job listings, sent over my resume, interviewed at a few places, but nothing really pleased me. That was until a day when a job listing in a newspaper arrested my attention. I immediately called them, and an interview was scheduled the day after. I ensured that I had everything ready to put all my chances on my side.

The next day, I dressed well, felt motivated, and left the house. I parked my car, entered the office, and met Gilbert. He offered me something to drink and asked if I had my resume with me. Believe it or not, but I had forgotten it at my desk. I said to myself, "Oh, Oh! What have you done young lady! What he will think of you?"

I apologized to him and explained that I left it at home. In a very cool way, he said "Perfect! I believe more in understanding someone in person than reading a resume, so tell me what is your story?"

We spent almost two hours talking and shared a great rapport. He said, "You are hired, when can you start?" I replied, "Tomorrow, I will be here." Done deal!

Back in my car, I drove for about 10 minutes and stopped on the side. I screamed loudly how happy I was, put the music on at the highest volume, and felt incredibly powerful. I was so grateful that I had forgotten my resume, so grateful for the conversation I had with Gilbert, and so thankful to the Universe. I donned the hat of a real-estate agent, and he taught me the tricks of the trade.

Again, there was a lot of driving. Even though this was something I was not so keen to do, I put it to the side and focused on my new job position and gave myself a chance.

A month later, I sold my first house! Gilbert was so impressed by my adaptability and approach to the clients. I was the youngest in the company, and my colleagues didn't like it all that much. They felt that it was a competition against me. I didn't care at all. I enjoyed that particular moment.

I remembered what Gilbert said to me on the day of my interview: "Faith, as tiny as a grain of sand, allows us to move mountains." That's what happened; I put all the faith on my side. It was years later that I discovered that Paulo Coelho had written this.

I worked with Gilbert for over six months until I resigned again. He was very kind and believed in me sincerely. He wished me a life full of success when I decided to seize an extraordinary opportunity to fulfill two of my biggest dreams. I met someone who was gathering all the information to prepare his next trip. I asked him if I could join him and once there, everyone will go their own way. He agreed. There are signs that show you the right path through a message, a song, an advertisement, a quote, or a person. Gilbert was one of those people. He taught me a lot, and I am more than grateful to him even today.

December 31, 2005. I left France for Australia. A new chapter turned in my favor.

With only 600 euros in my pocket and my working holiday visa, I landed into an unknown place, which was exactly what I was looking for. I wanted a fresh start. I was about to achieve two of my cherished dreams: travel abroad and speak English! For the first time, I kept a diary, and I had many little inspiring thoughts.

After two weeks in a hostel, I moved to a shared apartment and found my first job. I became a waitress, one of the most common jobs when young expats arrive here. Gary, the manager at the restaurant was so kind to me, and he gave me a chance to prove, not to him, but to myself that I could convert any of my wishes to reality. I felt blessed and fulfilled by these opportunities since my arrival in Australia and by the beautiful people who came into my life. During my time there, I understood more and more every day, my learning improved, I saw new things growing inside me, I was never afraid to be alone in this country, I saw my intention manifesting itself in my life, and I saw and felt the flow of energy flowing in me and my environment. I breathed freely, and I felt alive.

I strategically used my daily expenses through the tips I received, and I managed to set aside the amount from my salary. A few months later, I took five weeks off to travel around the country. I booked my train ticket to Melbourne. My diary allowed me to see how my life changed and how I blossomed the way I wanted to. I feel inspiration flowing toward me and through me—my thoughts were inspired, and my actions were inspired.

I spent a week visiting the city while exploring incredible street art, walking from one museum to another, listening to beautiful live bands, meeting fascinating people, and even had the pleasure to experience the myth about four seasons in a day, which by the way is completely true! I found in myself a spectacular person who was growing all the time.

To keep my journey alive, I booked a new train ticket to Adelaide.

I ended up at a backpacker's hostel, where I stayed for five weeks and met incredible people. I felt the consciousness of my journey, and I attracted many amazing people in my life: Tobias, Claire, Adrian, Jim, Stacy, and several others. I felt blessed in the city and was thankful to everyone who crossed my path as I learned from everyone.

Tobias was interested in meditation. I took him and his friends to a public park, made them sit near a tree, and helped them to be in the moment by breathing in and out in order to embrace their environment. They all lay down, eyes closed, opened their hearts, and released their inner blocks by using all their senses. They were amazed to hear the birds singing, to feel the wind in their skin, to smell the grass, to appreciate the touch of a piece of wood, and to taste the water in another dimension. When they came back, they felt alive and generously expressed, "Life is beautiful." Tobias was so grateful, and he deeply felt a state of being and accepted the changes. I knew I was born for this. I loved what I did, and I was deeply aware of myself. I finally discovered my 'why.' Helping others is the purpose of my life.

Next, I landed in Sydney. I had a new flatmate, Saban, who came from France, and we rapidly became friends. He stayed with us for a short period, as other flatmates did. The number of people who streamed in and out of the apartment was unbelievable. In this apartment, I met fascinating people from countries across the world.

It was around the same time that I lost my full-time job and had to switch working part-time. I reconsidered my living expenses, looked for a second job, and so on. But I wasn't that stressed or even worried because I knew I was going through a phase that allowed me to slow down and appreciate my environment.

Before Saban left, he told me to get in touch with the Hilton Hotel he was working for. I applied for a job there, and a few days later, the manager called me for an interview.

I met Pradeep, originally from India, who was very kind, and we discussed the job profile. I got the job as a waitress for the breakfast service. I said to myself, "Well done, Sonia!"

"Where Attention goes Energy flows; Where Intention goes Energy flows!"

James Redfield

Two days later, I came in through the staff entrance, registered my name, and the guard told me to go to the management department. I remembered the name of the HR manager, Nick, an Australian in his thirties. Despite an authoritative attitude, he didn't impress me. I firmly shook his hand, sat in front of his desk, and looked him straight in the eyes. I listened to what he had to say. He felt unsettled by me and the flow of energy I was sending. I was in a state of certainty. He understood that he wasn't going to impose his domination on me, and he concluded by congratulating me on being part of the team.

Another voyage began.

I found balance in my journey. I could breathe easily, my finances were growing, and I moved into a new apartment.

A month later, I met the French chef, Fred, who had returned from his holiday. I was just finishing up, and I remember the moment like it was yesterday. He entered the kitchen, turned his face to me, and we looked at each other. That guy became my best friend and partner in crime.

Then, I met my second partner in crime, Ula, from Poland. She is like my twin sister, and I could read her mind. I met her through my second part-time job, where we didn't stay long, and the business partners of this Greek restaurant were crazy.

Ula and Fred were almost like family to me.

At my work, there were regular customers who came to the hotel: office employees who worked close by, retired couples who wanted to enjoy a nice breakfast, and the batch of unsuspecting tourists from abroad.

Steve was one of those business tourists who stayed often. He was very kind and liked to interact with me, especially in French. One morning, he asked if I had visited Dubai and later suggested that I work for him and gave me his business card. I thanked him for his job offer and said I'd think about it. It was going to be a year since I came to Australia, and my working visa was going to expire soon. I had to find a solution to stay longer. A friend told me to convert for a student visa and find a school where I could extend my stay. And, I chose that option.

In a couple of weeks, everything was finalized, and I was shifted to a new status, which changed my legal working hours down to 20 per week. Still, it was better than nothing.

I started looking for other part-time jobs while working at the Hilton. I responded to a job offer and met Michael, who was the co-owner of the restaurant. We had a great connection and he decided to give me a try.

The very same day, I came to work in the evening shift, and I was amazed at how powerful I was. My work was just perfect, fast, and I wisely guided the clients about their choices. My French accent charmed them, and the chef liked my attitude. Positive energy was floating in the air, and everyone could sense it. I knew I had to give my 100% for this job.

Michael was astonished by my vitality and the atmosphere I brought on the first day. He simply said, "Sonia, welcome on board, you are hired to be the new restaurant manager." I was thrilled! He later said, "We will sponsor you to work for us and change your visa status." I couldn't imagine anything better. I felt so grateful and thankful to the Universe.

"We are what we repeatedly do. Excellence, then, is not an act but a habit."

Aristotle

The next day, I was flying in the air and was so happy about my new achievement. I resigned from the Hilton hotel to start working for my new employer.

Michael's associate was a Russian guy from a certain era, and I didn't like his sneaky attitude. My intuition told me to stay away from him, and I didn't think he was trustworthy. I took over my new responsibilities, which included hiring and training staff, coordinating employee schedules, and ensuring company protocols were being followed. I also planned menus with the chef, ordered supplies, managed budgets, and resolved customer complaints among other duties. I enjoyed leading and bringing a great spirit to my work environment.

The restaurant was going to be closed for a few days in order to change its interiors. So, I took that opportunity to move to a new apartment that was closer to my workplace and later traveled to celebrate Christmas and New Year's with my family back in France.

On my way back to Sydney, I stopped for a few days in Dubai and met Steve. He introduced me to his employees, co-business owners, and showed me around along with his friends Scott and Martin.

On my return to Australia, things took a bad turn. My landlord proposed a rent increase, and I found out that my employers never applied to sponsor me. The Russian owner refused to pay my salary in full. He even had the gall to say, "Take this! It is for your participation, and we only used your services until we reopened. Now, leave." I was shocked, and I couldn't believe it.

I wasn't going to fall into this trap. Who did he think he was? I took the money he was brandishing. He even suggested that if I didn't accept the situation and caused any discomfort, he would report me for misconduct. I was shocked, all over again.

I hit the table and looked him straight in the eyes and said, "That's not how you make fun of me, and I don't care for you or your attitude. Save it for the weak-willed. Now, you're going to reach into your pocket, find some extra cash, and give it to me." He was surprised by my reaction, and managed to squeeze an extra 100 bucks. That was it. When I came out of his office, I went to Michael and I told him about what had transpired. He said he was sorry about the way things turned out and gave me 500 dollars. And that was it. Blimey.

I was so angry, pissed off, and devastated. I said to myself, "No way! I am not going to let anyone treat me this way."

I decided to move to a new place, closer to the city, and find another job. I strategically targeted hotels to apply for. I believed that my work experiences would help me get a job. In a short period, I received a call from a hotel and was asked in for an interview. I was right to trust my intuition.

The very day after my interview, I got the position along with a good salary. I finally felt relaxed and proud that I was going to work as a waitress at Shangri La. Only one more thing was missing. My previous landlord wouldn't give me my deposit back. It was frustrating. I asked my friend, Lee, to help me out of this mess.

I organized a meeting with the landlord and showed up with Lee. Lee is half New Zealander and half Mongolian, and he is impressive in both size and muscularity. The landlord was intimidated. Lee grabbed him by the collar of his jacket, and the guy was so scared. In 10 minutes, everything was done. I took some money back and a TV along with a smile on my face. Before I left, I made him realize it was wrong to take advantage of people's kindness. I reminded him that the next time it will not end the same way. Perhaps it's not me, but he will definitely meet someone who will make him understand the hard way.

Joseph, one of the top managers at the hotel, was kind to me. He liked talking to me in French and Arabic. He also mentioned that if he had the power to make me the restaurant manager, he would. But because of my student visa, his hands were cuffed. I thanked him for his faith in me and mentioned that I already felt grateful for having a job.

I feel a sense of self-discipline building in my life as I was taking one step at a time. Soon, everything was falling perfectly into place.

I felt inside me that my life here had to come to an end. My career was not going to evolve any more than that, the status of my visa limited me, and I wanted to see more of the world.

Four months later, I contacted Steve to see if there was still a vacancy at his company. Turns out there was. Weeks later, I had a farewell party with my close friends and bid them goodbye, knowing I'll only see them when I come back to Australia.

May 13, 2017. I landed in Dubai, and it was unbelievably hot. I took a deep breath and prepared myself to tackle a new life.

Steve's company was a social platform where people gathered through events that he organized from time to time. I became the Event Manager and also filmed/interviewed interesting people from diverse areas. I worked for him for almost eight months, and I discovered and developed new skills, met incredible people, and shared a house with just women. I became good friends with a few of them. We created a way to look after each other, like a family does.

The French attract the French, even if I wanted to avoid such a situation. I met Frederic at Bert's cafe, and he worked in communication and sales. He told me his story. Then, I met another French guy in that same cafe, Henry, who was young, interesting, and funny. When I went there again, I saw a guy entering the cafe. I said to myself, "Hmmm, he has a kind of a surfer style, maybe is American or German."

Henry introduced me to him "Sonia this is Medhy – Medhy Sonia". He replied in French! Really, how many of you are out there?

Medhy later became my boyfriend, my employer, my husband, and the father of our two boys. Who knew it would all start in a coffee shop. I worked with him for more than 12 years and became the project director. Our destiny began at that little cafe.

Medhy started his show production company 26 years ago as a stuntman at Universal Studio. He has built his reputation through top-level shows all over the world. I spent hours familiarizing myself with his field of activity by researching the different styles of shows, clients, and artists. I also took care of logistics, marketing, administration, IT, photography, sewing, etc. I am someone who can be called resourceful, and I can adapt to any situation.

Few months later, we got our very first contract in Bahrain. It was a success for both of us.

With time it pays off all your effort. It's very rewarding.

In 2008, when the financial crisis shook the entire world, our industry escaped unscathed. We closed a new contract deal in Dubai and worked with the same theme park for eight years in a row. Our mission was to deliver high-quality shows of an international standard. We faced challenging moments, but it's nothing compared to the smiles you can bring on people's faces.

February, 24, 2013. A tragic day. Medhy was training with his friends to compete for a motocross challenge in the desert. His best friend Henry-Michel, who was visiting us from France, was with him. Around 6:00 p.m., he called to tell me that Medhy had a bike accident against a 4x4 car, and a helicopter was about to take him to the hospital. I listened to each and every single one of his words, and I was very calm. I didn't panic. At that time, I had only Jay who was only five months old. I took him and a friend who was with me at home and rushed to the hospital.

The emergency door opened, and I saw my husband's friends. Henry-Michel was devastated. At twenty years of age, he had a motocross accident during a competition and was now in a wheelchair. He prayed that his best friend would not become like him.

I was so impressed with myself that I could control my emotions in such a situation. I had no choice but to do that.

I left Jay with our friends, and I entered the room. I saw Medhy, and he was obviously in a very bad shape. His wrist was dislocated, and he had multiple fractures and several broken bones. The doctor informed me that he was lucky to even have survived this.

I saw Medhy in this unbearable pain, but I knew he would recover. This was not the time for him to leave us. And he slowly did. Four weeks in a hospital. Three weeks in a wheelchair. Three weeks on crutches. Months of rehabilitation. And years of forgiveness. What disappointed us the most was the guy who caused this accident informed the police that my husband was guilty. We took this to the court but decided to keep quiet after our lawyer informed us that his father was the chief police officer.

"Turn your wounds into wisdom?

Oprah Winfrey

After 10 years in Dubai, moving houses six times, producing great shows around the world, my second son Lenny was born; we met unforgettable friends and moments, and it was time for us to move to a new healthy environment. We bid our dear friends goodbye and left for a new adventure.

December 29, 2016. We set down our suitcases on the island of Palma de Mallorca.

Our sons, Jay and Lenny, have never been introduced to Spanish, so you could imagine how it was at the beginning. 10 days later, Jay and Lenny started nursery school. The first week was a bit too much for them. Moving to new surroundings, a new house, a new school, a new language, and a new culture was daunting, but they did well. In the second week, they started to express in Spanish so easily like they were fluent. I remembered one morning Lenny asking his dad to pour more cereal and said, "mas papa, mas." Medhy looked at me and said, "What is he trying to say?" I responded, "He wants more cereal."

As far as I was concerned, I could make myself understood in a few days. Medhy was so impressed and asked how I managed without having studied Spanish. I merely told him that it comes so naturally to me that small mistakes don't make me stop talking.

With all those changes, I had an intuition that I wanted to do something for myself. So, I started looking for a new job. I agreed to work with Medhy until I found a job. The language barriers didn't make me stop my job search, and I simply targeted international companies. I got an email back from a business owner who said that my profile interested him and invited me for a job interview.

A couple of days later, we met, and he explained to me what my role would be if I joined the company. I expressed my conditions, too, and we firmly shooked our hands. He said, "You are hired." I signed the contract.

November 21, 2017. I started my new job as a Business Manager. I met many interesting people, including Viktoria, who became a dear friend. However, I must mention Peter. He was the tyrannical boss who bullied me. I worked in so many fields and in so many places, but he was something else altogether. A couple of months passed, but he remained the same incorrigible person who didn't act in the right spirit.

A week later, I told him that I wanted to resign. He was shocked! I couldn't believe he still didn't get it. Then, we went into a meeting room where I spoke my mind honestly and told him about his unpleasant behavior, in a manner no employee would have done. Two hours later, I was promoted as the manager with a salary hike. Apart from this, Peter changed his attitude toward us radically. I knew it wouldn't last long, so I decided to leave after a few weeks.

Then, I went through a period of no new job at all. But, I still worked with my husband, developed new projects, and traveled for work. However, I started feeling exhausted from everything. Soon, I took a few days off. My intuition kept telling me that I had to do something for myself.

July 15, 2018. I was in a creative mood. I put on some music and started writing on a piece of paper. Something slowly emerged. Without knowing it at that time, I had already envisioned the name of my company: **My Infinite Ways.**

But within a month, I had a burnout. Stress, all-consuming doubt about my skills, and worrying about my domestic duties had gotten to me. I let weakness consume me. I was forlorn and let sadness surround me.

"Every time you are tempted to react in the same old way, ask if you want to be a prisoner of the past or a pioneer of the future"

Deepak Chopra

I was able to get back on my feet through the support of a psychologist. Talking to someone else helped me a lot. It taught me to value my true self, my power, and believe myself sufficient. After four sessions with him, I regained my strength that I thought I had lost.

October, 2018. I applied for a job. The following month, I started working as a Marketing Manager.

I worked for an LGBT magazine that promoted tourism. I could work from home and manage my hours. Three weeks later, they sent me to attend an event in Malta, where I would meet important leaders. It was there that I met Philip, who was among the speakers, and he took me under his wing, introduced me to the important heads, and explained what it was all about. He worked for an international hotel chain in Germany. On the last night of the event, they organized a farewell dinner.

Philip looked at me and said, "I have spent two days watching you and I can tell you that you are going to quit your job!" I said, "Yes, I agree with you, I don't really belong in this job." I have nothing against the LGBTQ community, but I didn't see myself evolving professionally. Then, Philip suggested that I look at the field of life coaching. He said it was something that I would identify with, and I could clearly see why. From that moment on, everything changed in a positive way. I spent days learning about what life coaching is, how to become a coach, and how to get certified.

January 2019. I enrolled in my coaching course and purchased a website.

Nine months later, I became a certified coach, opened my business coaching company, and started coaching people. But I was still missing a piece of the puzzle.

I met Matt, a Master Coach and Master Practitioner of NLP, through a social platform, and he is now my mentor. It took us more than seven months to learn from each other, and he helped me a lot throughout this period until the day he became the part of the puzzle that I missed as a mentor. He showed me the path to success, highlighted my strengths that I should focus on, and asked me to let go of false beliefs. With his help, I achieved more clarity in the purpose of my life and realized that this is my path. This is exactly where I am meant to be, and it's my destiny. I made mistakes, and there were hurdles, but it was okay. There were difficulties on the way, and that was okay.

I've worked at a number of jobs in my life where I've accumulated the learning and experience needed until I was fulfilled, and then I shifted to another one. I can wear any hat, and you can put me anywhere in the world, I will manage myself. I have developed many skills throughout my years because I never gave up. I built a strong mindset in order for me to thrive. I'm just like a cat—they always land on their feet and then walk forward.

I have always been in transition. Right from my birth until today. I have allowed myself to change and adapt to any situation, like a chameleon. I'm always in a state of change, I learn incredibly fast, and I become the person I want to be.

The challenges are important keys in your life to go beyond your limits, to know who you are, and to recognize your real purpose in life. In the miles I have gathered throughout my life, I have nourished my roots with heritage, integrity, and certainty.

Today, I am an entrepreneur, owner, founder of **My Infinite Ways**, a Leadership and Career Transition Coach, a brilliant speaker, an author, and a philanthropist. I embrace each of my journeys, smile at difficulties, forgive failures, and thrive to succeed because I choose who I want to be. I am passionate, I am grateful, I am fulfilled, I am living in a state of being, I am unstoppable, I am limitless, and I am an Alpha Woman.

"To be, or not to be, that is the question."

William Shakespeare

SONIA SAÏDI

Sonia Saïdi is a coach, a speaker, and an entrepreneur. She has written several articles along with a book about empowerment, career transition, and life transition. She knows all that there is to it. Being in the same challenging vortex for more than a decade sounds effortless for you but for others, it's a never-ending situation, a draining rhythm to keep up with. You're in a life of constant transition. Too many people are in this loop without knowing where to go or how to get out of it.

How do you manage your life when you are in the middle of reinventing yourself at any age? How do you manage a boss bullying you? What do you do when you stop believing in your potential?

How can you look for new opportunities to move faster when you don't know who or where to turn for support? So, instead of accumulating heaps of information that will never be useful to you, come and take concrete action to change your life with Sonia's help.

What makes Sonia Saïdi different is her ability to see through you and unveil all your power, as well as her faculty to overcome internal and external obstacles, and she can help you do the same. Her insight is very profound. By providing a step-by-step strategic plan, Sonia will create an ultimate roadmap with a clear vision for you.

To learn more about Sonia Saïdi, please visit
www.myinfiniteways.com.

Contact Details

Website: www.myinfiniteways.com

LinkedIn: https://www.linkedin.com/in/soniasaidi/

Instagram: https://www.instagram.com/myinfiniteways/

FINDING MY FOCUS IN LIFE

Tanya Focus

This is the story of how it took me two near-death experiences to realize that I needed to change the way I lived my life— a life that was focused on the needs of others before my own. This is the story of how I embarked on a two-year journey to find the answers to break free from the cycle of over-giving—the cycle that was making me ill again and again. This is the story of my realization that the only thing I was really looking for was me.

Perhaps, you are wondering about the journey that brought me here. Let me take you back to the very beginning.

'We' and Never 'Me'

My life has always been about 'we'" and never about 'me.' I was born a twin, and during the pregnancy, my brother got most of the food. Even before I was born, I was probably putting his needs before mine!

Twins are usually considered to be one unit by most people. And in turn, you become used to working toward what is best for the unit, which is 'we' and not 'me.' I had never known a world that was just 'me.'

I was taught it was good to put other people's needs before my own, and that happiness came from doing things for others. I ended up giving too much, physically and mentally, as I didn't know when I was giving too much. The balance was wrong, although I did not know it at the time.

Maybe you can relate to putting the needs of others before your own?

At the tender age of 16, my life changed forever. I found my mum collapsed at home, and she was turning blue. With only me and my brothers in the house, I called 999. I did my best to follow the instructions from the operator, desperately trying to give my mum CPR. It wasn't enough, and later we had to make the heartbreaking decision to turn off her life support.

I did my best to keep it together and to be strong for the family. Back then, you didn't really speak about your feelings, so I just kept myself busy. I had to keep going as I couldn't see any other way around it. I had grown up helping my mum around the house, so I stepped into my mother's shoes after her death. I looked after my brothers and ran the house whilst my dad went out to work. As my brothers grew up, I started a career in the public sector, helping people in their time of need. I enjoyed being part of a team. It could be long hours, but it was fun, and we were making a real difference. In my spare time, I set up a dyslexia support group and coached others to overcome the challenges I had experienced myself. Serving and helping others through their tough times have always been second nature to me.

I am the type of person you would call in an emergency, your go-to woman. Those who know me would say I am driven, resilient, reliable, diligent, and a problem-solver. Where people see problems, I just find a way around them. My go-to method for overcoming any challenges earlier was diligence and effort. It meant I was always busy and on the go. Life was good; I was living my dream.

In 2008, I found myself at a crossroads in life. My boyfriend wanted to move in together and settle down, and the next step for my career was a well-deserved promotion. Deep down, I just wanted to do something for myself—to go explore the world a bit and maybe find myself along the way. I know it sounds like a cliché, but it appealed to me nonetheless. I had to choose between the promotion and settling down or take a leap of faith and work things out along the way. The decision would affect the rest of my life, and it was now or never. I chose to take the leap and went traveling. It was exciting, but then I started to worry about what others might think. I was surprised when both my office and boyfriend supported my decision. Everyone thought it was about time I did something for myself.

Near-death #1

In 2009, I took a career break and embarked on a solo trip around the world. It was the first time I really did something for myself, since my mum's death 11 years ago. Suddenly, I only had myself to look after, and I had no idea how to relax. I just planned every single minute of every single day of the six-month trip. It worked, and I was back to being busy, just how I liked it!

Do you ever keep yourself busy as you have no idea how to relax?

After carrying my entire life on my back for four months, I decided to treat myself to a massage. I had just started on a group tour of South-East Asia, and it was just what I needed. It felt so good, but afterward, I started to get really bad headaches. I took painkillers and thought it would pass with time. But, it didn't.

It only got worse. I didn't want the group to suffer because of me, so I just pushed on. That was until I couldn't anymore. My tour guide took me to see a doctor who dismissed it as a virus. Luckily for me, she called my insurance company since, by that time, I could no longer walk and was having trouble talking.

They sent a Boeing 747 with a doctor onboard to pick me from Laos and fly me to a hospital in Bangkok. I had urgent scans, and they discovered that the headaches were being caused by an aneurysm.

They told me I was going to die, and that they were calling my family.

Imagine being alone on the other side of the world, far away from everyone you love, and being told that you are going to die?

I remember being in complete shock. I just kept thinking it was only a headache. How was I about to die? I was only 28; this couldn't be it. I should have taken better care of myself. There was so much I wanted to do with my life, so much I wanted to achieve. But, at that moment, it seemed that I might never get the chance.

A kind nurse took my hand and said, "In my culture, we believe in positive energy and visualization. If you believe that, you will see your family again, you will. If you don't, you won't."

So that's what I did.

I promised myself that if I ever got out of the hospital, I would never ignore my body again. I would make the most out of my life, which in my world meant doing as much as I could with the time I did have.

The massage had ripped an artery in my neck, which caused the aneurysm and a stroke. I had an operation (whilst awake) to stent the aneurysm, in order to prevent it from bursting. However, it turned out to be too dangerous. I had to just live with a ticking time bomb in my head.

I approached my recovery from the stroke very carefully, and I must say that it was a long process. I put in the hard work and remained focused. Slowly I retrained my body to walk and talk again and built it up to master more complex tasks like typing. It took time, but soon I was back to work full-time. It was a purely physical recovery for me; I never considered that I might need to process what I had gone through. I didn't really do feelings. So, I filed the memory of nearly dying somewhere deep in my brain, hoping it would suffice.

Time flew by, and I slowly forgot what I had gone through. My body was healing, and the aneurysm naturally scared over. Another miracle to add to the list.

I had escaped death, and I was grateful to be alive. Slowly my life got back to normal, and I was back to being busy. I used to hate the words self-care or self-love because, at the time, I had no self to care about. The one time I did do something for myself, I nearly killed myself. So I was more than happy to look after others from now on as that was way more safer in my book!

Whenever I was asked to help someone, I always said yes. After all, I loved helping people. When life and work got even busier, I just started to pay less attention to myself and focused on the task at hand. At the time, I thought it was what I had to do. I took on more and more responsibility, and there was little room left for me.

In 2017, I started to get headaches again. I took painkillers and continued on when I really should have gone to see a doctor. I had responsibilities and didn't want to let anyone down. I was just hoping it would go away on its own (this method rarely works by the way). I should have known better, but sometimes it gets really easy to lie to yourself.

I was forced to go to the doctor after a paramedic friend noticed that I couldn't turn my head, and I was bumping into things. After a quick once-over, he demanded I go see a doctor, or he would take me to a hospital. Wanting to avoid the hospital at all costs, I took his warning and went to see the GP the next day—who sent me straight to the hospital anyway!

I was my normal positive self, reassuring everyone else that everything would be fine. I think I even believed it at that time. That was until my flatmate pointed out that I was in acute care, and the doctors were extremely worried about me. Later that night, I watched helplessly as the person opposite me died.

After that, I wanted to do everything I could to get out of the hospital, as quickly as I could. After a long night and day of tests, I was offered a discharge to go home, with a referral to see my old specialist. I jumped at the chance. I didn't want to stay in the hospital even a minute longer than was necessary. I promised myself I would never end up in a hospital bed again. However, some promises are ones you are never meant to keep.

The headaches continued, and I could hardly function on a day-to-day basis. I did what I could to get better, whilst the doctors continued to investigate the cause. After some time off and rehab for my balance, I returned to work. I just wanted to get my life back and go back to normal.

Near-death #2

In 2018, I ended up back in A&E with even worse stroke symptoms. I had trouble talking and moving my body, and all I could say was my name. I was just so glad I had made it to the hospital.

I recall sitting on a chair in the A&E.

I closed my eyes, and there was a white spiral.

I felt an instant sense of peace and safety, and the further I went down it, the safer I felt.

That was until I found myself on the hospital floor, surrounded by doctors.

I had no control over my body, which was shaking all over.

I felt pure terror, and I was confused and disorientated.

I had no idea who these people were, and what was happening to my body.

I was quickly whisked into a side room and bombarded with questions from the doctor, which my body couldn't answer.

Luckily for me, the same paramedic friend turned up and was able to share my medical history with the increasingly concerned doctors.

A neurologist was called and conducted some tests. My mind was still switched on, and I was desperately trying to get my body to work, but it wouldn't.

Can you imagine not being in control of your body?

After the test, the neurologist looked me straight in the eye. Like he knew I was still in there, and could hear him.

They say the eyes are the portal to the soul and that they never lie. People can control their emotions, but their eyes always portray what is going on. I saw that he was gravely concerned for me. Even recalling it now makes me tearful.

He explained that they thought I had an infection in my brain. I was going to be moved to acute care, and my family was going to be called.

The first time I had been naive and in shock. This time, however, I fully understood the consequences of his words. I had promised myself that I would never find myself in a hospital bed again, and here I was in a much worse condition.

When you are in a hospital bed, it strips away all the obligations and responsibilities of life, and it leaves you alone with just yourself. Perhaps, you too have gone through a moment where everything in your life changed?

I had traveled down a white tunnel and was extremely aware of how close my brush against death might have been. This actually could have been the end of the road for me.

No more chances.

I had gotten so caught up in trying to do it all that I had actually forgotten to live my life. Worst of all, I had failed at the most important thing—looking after myself.

I kept myself busy, and it distracted me from my own life. It was much easier looking after everyone else, as I knew what they wanted and needed. Doing something for me was risky and full of unknowns. I had used being busy as a way of avoiding the things I needed to deal with and didn't know how to.

I started to think about how I wished I had believed in myself more. I had dreamed of coaching professionally, speaking on a stage, writing a book, creating a community of new thinkers, and there was so much more that I wanted to do with my life. But, I never believed 'I' could achieve these things, so I never did anything to make it happen.

I wished I had been closer to the people around me. I had always been the person they came to for help, but who did I go to? Ever since my mum died, I had always just worked it out on my own because I thought I had to. I really needed help now, and I didn't know how to ask. I wished I had been honest and told everyone how I really felt, how grateful I was for them being in my life, and how they had helped me in their own way without knowing.

I had a powerful urge to tell them at that moment as it could have been my last chance.

I could not talk properly, but I had regained some control of my arm and could point a finger. I reached for my phone, and I sent a message to all the people I could. It was a shock to the people who received them. They had no idea I was in the hospital, and it was not like me to be so open about my feelings. The love and support I received in return really helped me to keep going when things got really tough.

In the process of finally telling the people I loved and cared for, how I truly felt, I became free. I was no longer holding anything back, and I had made my peace with death. I was no longer scared to die.

An amazing thing happens when you are no longer scared of death. There is nothing left to be scared of, and you are finally free and there is nothing left but love.

Love was quickly followed by the feeling of joy—the relief and happiness of still being alive. Finally, I was able to appreciate all of the things I had achieved and overcome in my life. It allowed me to move from a feeling of fear to a feeling of gratitude.

I then experienced a deep knowing that it was not my time yet. I was going to make it through this. This was a sign from the universe, a chance to get back on track. I was going to change the focus of my life and look after my well-being and be more intentional with how I lived my life. I finally understood that I had to look after myself first, and then I could continue to help others.

I was going to use my experience to help other people overcome similar challenges. I was going to inspire them to choose life so that they don't find themselves in a hospital bed later on and regret the person they wish they had been, the impact that they could have had, and the lives they could have touched. Like I had twice!

And then people ask why I have transformed my life since I got out of the hospital.

It comes down to the fact that life is not a dress rehearsal – THIS IS IT. My dreams had gotten lost in the business of life. I had been so caught up doing other things that I actually forgot to live my life.

I am living my life now and with no regrets.

The turning point for me was a doctor telling me that the only way I would recover and get better was if I learned how to put my needs first and accept help from others. It was going to be tough, but I was going to give it everything I had.

I want to use my story and my experiences as an example to inspire others so that they can focus on themselves and live in the present. I want to make sure that each one of us lives a full life, and when our time comes, we can say that we have no regrets. There wasn't a thing we could have done differently. A life lived with no regrets.

I am also building a legacy to help people when I am no longer here. Writing this chapter is part of that plan. While our lives end, words live on. If only one person gets inspired to change their life after reading my story, I would feel that my mission is complete.

Change begins with a single person. Change begins in a single moment. You have to make a conscious decision to start living your life now, with you being the center of it. It is like a pebble in the pond – the ripples will continue to positively impact others.

The Bit in Between

I skipped over my life between near-death experience #1 and #2. But, I think now would be a good place to start. They say you can only join the dots going backward, and I think it is true in my case.

Getting seriously ill brought my solo trip around the world to a grinding halt. And, it turned my world upside down. I had gone from being free and doing as I pleased, to being dependent on others, even for the most basic tasks. I only gained some independence after intense rehabilitation. My boyfriend at the time was my rock; together, with my family and friends, they all did their best to help me (when I would let them). I am now deeply grateful for the support and love they all showed me. At times I made it harder on myself than it needed to be.

Traveling and nearly dying fundamentally changed me as a person, but I didn't know it at the time. Looking back, I now realize that I never gave my body and mind the time it needed to heal or grieve — heal from the trauma and grieve the life and future I had lost. I had never learned how to feel my emotions, so I just kept myself busy as a coping mechanism. During my travels, I had started to slowly get to know myself outside of anyone else's expectations or rules (including my own). That all stopped when I got ill.

As I regained use of my body, everyone started treating me like nothing had ever happened. The damage to my body and mind was invisible. I looked ok, and I seemed ok, so I must be ok. Even I started to believe that myself. I picked up my life where I had left off before the trip. I pushed myself to get better quickly, and I slotted right back into the plans that had been made before my travels. I settled down and got promoted.

I thought this would make me happy. I had overcome the odds, and I had achieved everything I previously thought I wanted. I had a perfect life; I had the boyfriend, the flat, and the amazing job. I had it all. It was everything I thought everyone else wanted me to be, but I was just so unhappy. I couldn't understand it. When I stopped and thought about it, the last time I could remember being happy was when I had been traveling. I had been trying to fit a new Tanya in an old Tanya-shaped hole. That is when I realized there was something missing from my life, and that thing was me.

Why did it take me nearly dying a second time to make me realize what I really wanted and needed in my life?

Choosing Life

I like to joke that I was reborn in the hospital. I restarted my life again, but with 'me' rather than 'we.' I feel like I have only just woken up in my life and started living it to the core.

I had ended up in the hospital more than twice, so I really needed to do something different this time around. Otherwise, I would end up there again.

"Insanity is doing the same thing again and again and expecting different results"

Albert Einstein

According to the genius of Albert Einstein, I was officially insane. I started to question why was I doing this to myself? Clearly, the way I thought about things was having a negative impact on me. I needed to find a new way to think and live my life. There have been two new ways of thinking—The Three Principles and The Art of Fulfillment—that have helped me see the world and my experience differently.

I started to search online for some training and came across The Ultimate Coach Programme, run by David Key. It promised to transform my understanding of how the mind really worked and deepen my understanding of something called the Three Principles. The more I read, I knew it was just what I was looking for. I jumped straight in and immersed myself into learning more about the mind.

The Three Principles

The Three Principles are Mind, Consciousness, and Thought. Mind is the wisdom and energy behind all things, Consciousness is our ability to be aware of our experiences, and Thought is our ability to create ideas that, in turn, create our experiences.

I had always thought it was the outside world that created the life I lived. The training allowed me to see that it was my thinking about the outside world that created the life I lived. I could choose to think differently. The outside world stays the same, but the way I experience it changes.

I am the director of my own movie. It was my thinking that created the style of the movie I was living in. I ended up asking myself, "If I was the director of my own movie, then why was I always casting myself as a supporting character?" I decided that I was no longer going to do that. I was giving myself permission to step into the lead role.

What role are you playing in the movie of your life?

It also helped me see that a lot of my thinking was just that – thinking. I was wasting a lot of mental and physical energy on things that had never happened and never would. Everything was happening the way it was supposed to. I could go with it and accept and appreciate life as it is or waste my time and energy fighting against it. I chose life.

Always remember that life is happening for you and not to you.

I found that when I wasn't caught up in my thinking, my brain was no longer so busy. I was able to start being creative.

If I was the director, I could design the life I lived in rather than letting it pass me by. My life had always been about the needs of those close to me and my work. I now had an opportunity to do what I wanted, but I didn't have a clue as to what it was! I needed to work out what I wanted my life to be.

"When the student is ready, the teacher will appear."

Buddha

The first-ever self-development event I went to was *Release the Real You* by Ben Ivey – the Fulfillment Artist. You can guess why the name appealed to me! I was blown away by what I learned and started to think more about who the real me really was.

Six months before I ended up in the hospital, Ben had actually sent me an article about burnout. I was so busy that I didn't have the time to read it! He was able to see the path I was heading down, and I was completely oblivious.

Has someone ever tried to tell you something, but you completely ignored them?

Learning the Art of Fulfillment

Ben reached out to me again a while after I got out of the hospital. He offered me an opportunity to work with him one-on-one and become the United Kingdom's first fully trained Fulfillment artist.

The first time I saw him talk, I knew deep down I wanted to do what he did. However, at that time, I dismissed it as a silly idea. Now, I was ready to take on the challenge. It was an opportunity I couldn't miss.

Fulfillment Artist training would give me the skills and tools to help others to achieve fulfillment in the quickest and most sustainable way possible. But first, I had to go through the process myself, so I could guide others on the same journey.

Discovering Values and Beliefs

I started by uncovering the values and beliefs that had been shaping my view of the world.

Imagine you print out a document, and there is an error on the page. You rub out the error and reprint the page. But, the error is still there. You would be confused as you already erased the error out. Why is the error still there?

The error is still there because you are attempting to change it in the external world, as opposed to the internal world.

You need to go in and change the error in the original document on the computer first. Then print the page again, and the error will be gone.

It is the same way in our lives. We often try to change the external world when what we really need to change is our internal world.

A lot of what I believed in had been picked up in my childhood; I had never really questioned it.

Have you ever questioned your own values and beliefs?

I grew up surrounded by the following messages:

- Help others.
- Put others before you.
- Don't be selfish.
- Share.
- Be strong for others.

There were good intentions behind these messages, but it meant I believed that others were worth more than me, so I put their needs before my own. Also, I thought it was selfish to look after myself.

It is crazy that society can consider you selfish if you look after yourself first. If you do not do it, then who will? If anything, I needed to be more selfish and not feel guilty about it. If I did that but still considered the needs of others, it wouldn't even be considered selfish! Even on an airplane, they tell you to put on your oxygen mask first as you can help others better that way. In life, I had been going without oxygen because I was scared about what other people might think. I had been slowly dying inside in the process.

I had to learn to put my opinion and needs first and above what I thought others would think of me. I had to learn to love and value myself, just as much as other people. If I didn't value myself, how did I expect others to? I had a radical idea, "What if I looked after myself the way I look after others!"

Working on my values was instrumental in my transformation. I was printing a new document with new information.

Shining a Light

I started to explore deeper who I was; I started to uncover the parts of me I had disowned and locked away long ago. I learned that no matter what part of you is dark, it is no longer dark if you shine light there. You go there, and it's not as scary as you thought it would be. If anything, it is freeing as you let go and accept what has been and who you are with no judgments. You start to become whole again as you are no longer hiding parts of yourself away from yourself or the world. I slowly started to learn to embrace my feelings, all of them. I learned to experience the bad, so I could also experience the good. It is a bit like a pendulum. If I attempted to try to stop either extreme,

I would cut myself off from feeling anything at all.

I had blind spots in my life, and Ben was able to help me see things from a different perspective—to identify the stories I was telling myself that had been sabotaging my attempts to become the person I really wanted to be.

Overcoming My Story

I believed that I was still ill, and I was always knackered, so I did not want to make myself worse. So, I didn't push myself to do too much. I was upset that I could not live the life I had before, the one where I was always busy and on the go. I saw that as the goal to reach. But it was not until I really looked at my life before objectively that I saw that it had been my lifestyle and decisions I was making before that had been making me ill, but I just didn't know it. The truth is that I am actually healthier now. I eat well, I no longer drink, I sleep better, and I am more self-aware and less stressed than I have ever been. My lifestyle and habits are so much healthier than before.

Once I accepted that my previous lifestyle and decisions had such an impact on my physical and mental health, I was able to change the story and make real progress in my life and work. Perhaps you are running a story that is stopping you from getting where you need to be?

I had also always thought I had no one to turn to for help. There had been people trying to help me, but I did not recognize it at the time. Also, I didn't know how to accept help without feeling selfish. I learned that in life, there are times when we can give, and other times when we need to receive. I had the balance all wrong. When I understood that I needed both and it was ok and part of being human, I was able to change my perspective and learn to accept help gracefully. I learned to love to receive just as much as I loved to give.

The thing with the stories you are telling yourself about your life is that you do not know the impact they are having until you take the journey inside and examine it for yourself. If you do this, you can then choose a more empowering one. It is like getting all the dirty washing you piled somewhere in a corner of your brain and giving it a good old clean!

Do you have any dirty washing piled in a corner of your brain that could do with a good clean?

Creating My Vision

I spent time looking at the person I wanted to be and the life I wanted to live. I created a vision for all areas of my life—a vision for my health, finances, work, relationships, and how I could contribute and give back to others. Setting up my coaching business was part of this new vision and focus in my life.

I also looked at how I would bring more fun and creativity into my life. My life had been lacking any fun and creativity as I had always been too busy. My job before had been very analytical and computer-based, mainly using the logical left side of my brain. There was little room for artistic expression.

I love two things: art and being by the sea. I had started to explore this whilst traveling, but it had stopped when I got ill. I had promised myself that when I retired, I was going to learn art by the sea. When I started working with Ben, he asked me why I couldn't do it now? After working through the many excuses I came up with, I realized there was nothing stopping me except for my own mind and the limits I was putting on my own life and happiness.

I have since learned to draw and paint at a lovely little art school, tucked away on the Kent Coast. I have an amazing teacher and community of students, most of whom are retired! They all think I'm an inspiration for learning art now, rather than waiting until I retire. It has helped me in my recovery, using the right side of my brain, which my body and mind find very relaxing. Best of all, I am doing it for myself and for the fun of it.

Daily Power

With Ben's help, I crafted new principles, values, beliefs, identity, and life purpose in order to become the person I wanted to be and live the life I wanted to create. I use this in my 'Daily Power' recording to remind myself every day of my vision.

I use this to focus on my needs first. And, in turn, it has given me the capacity to help others to do the same.

Next up, I needed to find a way to make friends with my body. We were definitely estranged and not on talking terms!

What is your current relationship with your body?

At first, I was angry with my body that it had let me down, and it wouldn't work the way I wanted it to. I felt betrayed and like we were at war with each other. Then I started to learn about the body, and I realized I had been the one in the wrong all along.

I had always treated my mind and body as two different things. The more I learned about the mind-body connection, the more I saw that it was just one thing. I stopped looking at them as separate entities and now treated myself as a whole—we were in this together.

The body had one job, and it was to keep me alive at all costs. It had been trying to talk to me all the time. The language it had been using was pain and illness. It was trying to tell me that something was out of balance. I was just not listening until it made me listen. I had seen it as an attack when actually it had been trying to look after me all along.

The Fulfillment and Exhaustion Cycles

When I looked at what I had been doing to my body, I realized I had been stuck in a cycle of overdoing and giving, until I started to burn out and use up all of my body's resources and eventually became exhausted. I would then be forced to recover, and the cycle would start all over again. I was trying to do too much and never making time to recharge and fill myself up again. I was in a state of emergency all the time. It was also a great way to avoid the deep work I really needed to do.

I needed to balance my overdoing/giving over time in order to come back to a state of balance.

I now think of my body moving between two states: State of Balance and State of Emergency. These are within two cycles: the Fulfillment Cycle and The Exhaustion Cycle. I have created an image to help quickly understand the cycles.

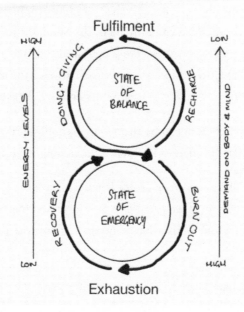

The Fulfillment Cycle

The Fulfillment Cycle represents a fulfilled life where there is time for work, family, friends, hobbies and exercise, and interests. We have time to fill our lives with the things that make us happy, and our energy levels are high with the demand on the body and mind being low. There is lots of time for ourselves, as well as others. If you are forced to switch into the State of Emergency, your body can handle it so long as you make time to Recover & Recharge to fill yourself up again and come to the State of Balance easily.

The Exhaustion Cycle

The Exhaustion Cycle represents a life where all the things that allow your body to recharge and come back to balance disappear. Your life has been stripped bare and down to the basics. The energy levels are low, and demand on the body and mind is high. There is no time for 'you.' If you do stop, it is because you have to, just to recover enough to carry on. You can only be in the State of Emergency for so long before you use up all the body's physical and mental resources and become exhausted. If you never do anything to bring yourself back to the State of Balance, you stay stuck in the Exhaustion Cycle.

The cycle our body is in can be affected by both physical and mental states. It can also be affected by what is happening in your life.

Our body will try to give us feedback and warning signs that something is wrong. If we listen, we can do something to Rest and Recover, to give our body what it needs to return to the State of Balance.

Previously, I had been focused on serving everyone else's needs before my own. That meant if I was busy, the first thing I would cut out of my life was my gym time, hobbies, sleep, etc. to make sure I could get it all done, so I wouldn't let anyone down.

I didn't realize that what I really needed to do was protect these things. The things that gave my body and mind a chance to Recharge and Recover, so I could come back to the State of Balance.

Instead, I just tried to cram more in and look at ways to optimize my time and energy. I wanted to do more with less. I didn't know what I didn't know back then. I was just doing my best with what I knew at the time. I ignored the signals, and I paid the price.

Have you ever ignored the signals your body is sending you and paid the price?

I now recognize that the energy in needs to match the energy out. Otherwise, we end up pushing our bodies over into energy debt. It takes more time to recover than it usually should.

Perhaps you can relate to this?

The Ritual of Me

I needed something I could do every day that would remind me of what was important to me. To allow me to learn and listen to what my body was telling me, and to help me recognize what cycle I was running. I needed something to give me a chance to refocus and get back on track.

I tested out many different techniques and routines and found a mixture that really worked for me. This has become more than just a routine; it is now a daily ritual for me. Maybe you will be inspired to give it a try and see if it helps you start and end your day with yourself as the focus.

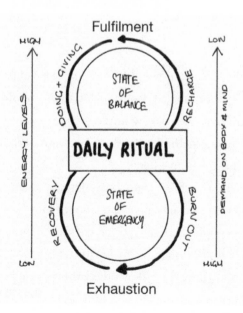

Morning Ritual

- I wake up, and I am grateful for starting another day with full control of my body and mind.
- I drink a 500 ml bottle of water (which I put by my bed the night before).
- I turn on some music that always puts me in a good mood.
- I listen to my 'daily power' recording whilst moving my body – five minutes.
- I stretch my whole body – 10 minutes.
- I then settle down and complete a 10-minute meditation.
- In the end, I ask my power question, "*What is the highest priority action I can do today that will bring me one step closer toward the vision for my life?*"
- I set myself the task of completing that during the day.
- I am then set and ready for my day. 😊

Evening Ritual

- As the sun goes down, I turn on my side lamps.
- An hour before bed, I turn off all my electronic devices.
- I turn on some relaxing music.
- I prepare and drink a night time tea, whilst I read a few pages of an inspirational book.
- I then write three pages in my journal about how the day went and what emotions came up for me.
- In the end, I ask my power question, "*How did I move closer to the vision for my life today?*"
- I end it with writing down three things I am grateful for.
- I am then ready to have a restful sleep. 😴

Every day, I make a decision to make myself a priority in my life. I also get clear on what is important to me, so I can consider it when I start to respond to the needs of others. So I can be more intentional with my time and energy. It also acts as a check and balance to see what cycle I am running.

How do you start and end your day?

You may be wondering why I included some of the above in my daily ritual. I go into more detail and the reasons why in my guide *The Fulfillment & Exhaustion Cycles* and the *Daily Rituals to master them*. You can download it via the link in my bio! It's my free gift to you.

It's not about being perfect every day, but it is about getting back on track when you realize you are off.

Awareness is the first step to change.

There are mornings or evenings where I fall off track. I used to be regimental with my rituals, but I realized over time that I needed to give myself some freedom, as sometimes my body needed a lay in or an early night. The world will not stop if I do not do it, and I end up wasting mental energy, telling myself off for not being perfect. So, now I aim to stay on track 80% of the week and allow myself some freedom to do as I please.

If I have had a few demanding days, the first thing I do is give myself some dedicated time to just do nothing and Recharge and Recover. This can be whatever my mind and body need at the time. It can be a daytime NASA nap using the PZIZ app or just sitting out in the garden drinking a cup of tea whilst watching the clouds go by. I could have never done that before as I couldn't sit still. I have learned to slow down and not feel guilty about it. This acts as a way to bring me back to the State of Balance. This works well for me.

Find what works for you.

What I Learned

It has only been through a slow reconnection with my body and mind that I started to love and look after myself, the way I needed to. Once I started showing myself that much love, care, and attention daily, I naturally started to ask, "What other positive things can I do for myself today?"

I learned that I didn't have to do this all on my own. I just needed to learn how to ask and take help when it is offered. We can actually achieve so much more together. This has included spending money on my own coaching and training. Without this help, I would never have been able to transform my life the way I have. I am so grateful for the new people and experiences that have come into my life as a result. It has given me a completely new focus in my life.

I no longer need to be the one giving all the time. It was ok to be on the receiving end and not feel guilty about it.

I now keep my life as balanced as I can. What I previously considered selfish, I now consider an act of self-love. I can still give, but I balance it with what I need as well. When life throws a problem at me (e.g., serious illness of a family member), I can change my focus to help my family because I now have the physical and mental reserves in place to do that. I then allow myself space to recharge after. Previously I would have just kept giving and going until I couldn't anymore.

A big change for me has been believing in myself, finally. To believe in myself, I had to rediscover 'me.' I know who that person is now. I am building my life around that rather than trying to be the person I think everyone else wants me to be. I am happier now than I have ever been. I accept that it's ok to change my plans for my life. I see it as a good thing. It is a part of growing into who I'm really supposed to be.

There will always be highs and lows in my life, but I now know how to reduce the difference between the highs and lows and use new healthier coping mechanisms. I can stay on track with my vision, no matter what life throws at me. So, it becomes just part of who I am.

The real transformation of self comes from an accumulation of new ways of thinking with new habits and actions. Until one day, it's just who you are. When I started to care for myself better, I had a greater capacity to be there for others, but in a completely different way.

What about "You?"

You may also be thinking, "Well, all that sounds really nice Tanya, but I barely find time to shower every day, never mind spend 30 minutes stretching and meditating. I have got people who need my time and things to do."

If you are struggling with time, then the first step is to look at your day and see how you are spending your time? Are you busy doing things for others? Why are you doing these things? Is it something you really want to do? Or are you doing it because you think you should be doing these things? Start by just finding five minutes for yourself in the morning or evening? Little steps make the biggest changes.

Every time you say yes to someone, you say no to something you could be doing for yourself.

I had a client who was always busy and exhausted. Once we started working together, she started to see she was busy because she didn't want to let others down. It was impacting her health, and she couldn't do it all. Something had to give. The first time she said No, she felt guilty. We worked through it, and she was able to see how empowering it was. She now says No more than she says Yes!

We looked at her day. We started by scheduling just five minutes a day and built it up. We set specific times and actions to help her drive her business forward. I love her recent update:

"Just about to start day 14 (out of 16), exercise regime! Really enjoying it - feel more alive and more like "me." I missed 2 days and didn't feel bad. I have come a long way already by just stopping – weird! More space in my head and just enjoying faffing and standing still! Enjoying looking at and watching the plants grow and feeding the birds. Not guilty about any of it. I feel I have made a clear space for me to re-start."

She is a completely different woman with a whole new focus, and she is making real progress on her business goals. She is so inspirational that it makes everything I went through to be able to guide her on her own journey worthwhile!

Sometimes, it is the standards we hold ourselves to that can cause our lives to become unbalanced. One client was burning out from working extra in her teaching job because she wanted the material to be perfect for the students. So, she had no life outside of her job. Working together, she was able to change her perspective on how she was spending her time. She was also able to see how unbalanced her thinking and life had become. She started to set cut off times for working at home and also introduced exercise and walking back into her life.

Other times, it can be finding the balance and energy to transition into something new. I helped a woman who really wanted to start her own online business. She was working extra hours in her day job to keep on top of all the work she said yes to. By the time the weekend came around, she was so knackered that all she could bring herself to do was zone out in front of the TV. She would then beat herself up for not having made any progress on her dream. Then the cycle would start again the next week. We got clear on what she really wanted, and she found time to go to the gym before work, which gave her more energy. She started to say no to extra work so she could finish earlier and actively rest during the week, so her weekends were freed up for working toward her dream business.

From 'Me' to 'You'

I am now lucky enough to help other over-givers to change the focus of their life back to themselves. So they can learn to balance what they need and want with the needs of the people in their life so they can live more intentionally. I help them move from exhausted to fulfilled. They get to choose life now; a full life lived with no regrets.

They do not need to be better or fixed. I just guide them to change their perspective so they can start to prioritize what they want in their life and act on that. They learn to love and look after themselves the way they do others.

A powerful exercise you could do once you have finished this chapter is to grab a pen and paper and write two pages freestyle about where you feel you may be overgiving or overdoing in your life? You may also want to cover any specific memories or thoughts that come up for you whilst reading this chapter. Do not censor yourself or judge what you are writing, as this is just for you. If you are an overgiver, you may have become good at suppressing your true thoughts and feelings. This is an opportunity for you to start giving them some room. If you catch yourself censoring your thoughts and feelings, start to explore this by writing why this is happening. You may be surprised by what you learn about yourself by doing this simple act. It helps to bring the unconscious conscious and gives you a wider perspective on a situation. What you may view as a bad thing may turn out to be a blessing in disguise with a simple change in perspective. It may even be the first step on your own journey of self-discovery.

I look back on my two near-death experiences and see them as a blessing as these experiences made me who I am today. It can be these challenging times in our lives that push us to become the person we are supposed to become. It is hard to see it at the time, but my journey to seek the answers allowed me to change the way I think, which in turn has changed the way I live my life and my future. I just had to find myself to believe that I could.

Always remember:

If you think you can't, change the way you think.

Tanya Focus

TANYA FOCUS

Tanya is the UK's first trained Fulfillment Artist. She has learned the skills to help people live a truly fulfilled life in the quickest and most sustainable way possible. Having spent just under two decades serving and coaching others in the public sector, it took Tanya almost dying twice to change the focus of her life back to herself. By doing this, she was not only able to regain control of her health but also create the life and business she had always secretly dreamed of. When she is not helping change lives, Tanya can be found exploring London and escaping the city to walk and paint by the sea.

Tanya helps other overgivers to change the focus of their life back onto what they need and want, transforming the way they think and live their life. Her clients are normally stuck in a cycle of giving to others until they are exhausted. Deep down, they know there has to be more to life than the one they currently find themselves living, one with no time for themselves. She helps them move from being exhausted to fulfilled.

Tanya helps her clients create a vision for all areas of their life whilst helping them redefine their identity, reorder their values, and install empowering beliefs and new behaviors. She restores the alignment between their daily routines and the life they want to live so they can be more intentional with their time and energy whilst working on their dreams. She brings their life back into balance so they choose life now.

Visit www.findyourfocusinlife.com/bookguide to start your journey by downloading *The Fulfillment & Exhaustion Cycles and the Daily Rituals to master them.* You'll also discover the #1 mistake that is keeping you stuck in the exhaustion cycle!

If you need help changing the focus of your life, or you have been inspired by my words, please reach out. I would love to know how it has inspired you to live your life differently.

Contact Details

Website: http://www.findyourfocusinlife.com

Email: info@findyourfocusinlife.com

Instagram: https://www.instagram.com/findyourfocusinlife

Facebook: https://www.facebook.com/findyourfocusinlife

SILENT THOUGHTS

Tim Wolford

Are They My Parents?

My parents are aliens. I am supposed to be asleep above my brother in the bunk bed we have shared for as long I can remember. Being the elder one, I spent my dreaming hours in the top bunk. Actually, the hours I recall in my fort in the sky were spent tracing patterns in the wall paneling, like one of the mazes found in an elementary school workbook. Dead-ends rarely encountered, and I would spend many sleepless nights and bored Sunday afternoons tracing and tracing. Going nowhere.

The four adults outside the closed door, down the hall, and congregating around the kitchen table were in loud conversation about whose turn was next. Two of the adults were supposed to be my parents. It just never made sense to me though. How is it possible that a large, overbearing bully of a woman and an introverted, midwestern, adventure-dreaming farm boy could be my parents?

The theory, an untested hypothesis, this eight-year-old child came up with was 'They have got to be aliens.' Their friends, too. After the children, myself, my six-year-old brother, and farther down the hall, in his own room, my other three-year-old brother fell asleep, the four adults would unzip one another's human suits and continue their drunk card games as the reptilian creatures they really were. I was convinced they were sent here from some far-away planet to complete their parenting assignments.

These are not the mere musings of a bored eight-year-old child. They are not the product of a day (night) dreaming, fantasy imagining child. They are the desperate attempts of a confused, lost little boy trying to make some sort of sense out of his existence.

Good-Bye Family

I recall a night. A very particular night. I was seven years old. I checked out. That is to say, I disconnected. The very first intention I can remember declaring occurred that night, and I believe, it set the trajectory for the next 46 years of my life. There was this ritual that transpired every few months in my home. The prelude was most likely different each time. The finish was always the same with mom, dad, brothers, and Tim adjourning to the parent's bed, one loving and happy family of five. I said night, actually, though it was dark outside, the ritual always took place early in the morning, let's say 2:30 a.m. It begins with tears, usually my mother's, often my youngest brother's. I am awakened by either these tears, more like sobs, or with a loud thud. The thud means there will be a new framed poster in the hall in the morning. The poster will remain until dad gets it together and patches the hole he punched in the wall, thankfully, choosing the wall over his wife. Mom and dad will be finishing whatever inebriated argument they chose to imbibe in. Youngest brother will be crying 'please stop.' Middle brother and I will enter the melee and do our best to negotiate a truce. We all retire to the back bedroom and go to sleep, one happy, healthy family. Except that night, I chose differently. I changed the coda. You see, the play was not working for me. I did not experience joy or love in the back room. I loathed being back there. I clearly remember making a huge decision that night, when I was just seven years old. 'I no longer am a part of this family. From this moment on, I am alone. I will take care of myself. I will watch over my brothers. These people do not know how to take care of me.'

I refused to go to the back room, went into my room, closed the door, climbed into my fort in the sky, and disconnected from my family.

I disconnected from any possibility of feeling loved.

This is a story about the struggles and challenges one man has faced since making that fateful decision. Although most of what I share has wandered around silently in my thoughts for years and years, I have never bothered to write any of it down. The process is painful, and the tears seem endless.

Independence

The year 1969 was huge. A revolution was happening in my homeland. I grew up from age three until 20 in the Silicon Valley, San Jose, California, good ole U.S. of A. Body bags coming home from Vietnam, riots in our nation's learning institutions, Charlie Manson, and Woodstock were all happening around me that fateful year. Two stand-out events took place that year. The first, a three-day backpacking trip. The second, well, that's in the history books of all the nations. July 20, 1969, my seventh birthday. That was the day I could finally go to our local swimming pool without a parent or babysitter. A day I had anticipated for ten long months. The problem was that there was something else allegedly more important happening. Instead of celebrating my new freedom and independence, my father informed me that we would be watching a historic event on TV. Today, I look back on that day and am grateful. I missed our neighborhood pool's noontime opening and, instead, watched Neil Armstrong take the first step on the moon. It's the former event that has an impact on this story though.

I discovered true freedom the first time I put on a backpack filled with a sleeping bag, tent, stove, food, and jacket. Trading city lights and urban sprawl for snow-capped peaks, the smell of sugar pines, and cedar, I felt alive, wide-awake. I fell asleep that first night in the wild, counting stars, hundreds, then thousands of shimmering lights each telling its own story. I felt like I was home.

I mentioned the divorce I created from my family, my disconnect. This first backpack trip allowed me to complete the pact I'd made with myself. On this trip, I realized I had all the skills necessary to shelter and eat. Procure some food somehow, and I did not need anyone. Those were my thoughts, at least. I continue to spend dozens of days each year in the backcountry and am grateful that my father introduced me to this possibility. There is a sore spot, though, from this first foray into the wild, an infectious blister not on my foot but in my mind, my memories. It is my trauma, the secret I kept locked away, buried for more than 40 years. You see, one of the kids that came along on that trip, a well-respected young boy, three years my senior, would several years later become my rapist.

Rapist!

It's dramatic when I think about it sometimes. I did not use that word for the 40-plus years I shamefully ignored my memories of the events that transpired for two years of my life when I was 10. The word came about only recently, halfway through a coaching program I committed to for 'Adult Survivors of Childhood Sexual Abuse'. The coach, Rachel Grant, painfully suggested the word after I shared with her and two other participants, my memories of the first time I was abused. From my workbook:

> " ...I didn't understand why we were sleeping on the dewy grass, away from the dry patio, and with access to the kitchen. Nor did I understand what was happening when he returned outside from the kitchen with a handful of butter... Then he locked my hands above my head with one hand and pushed his penis into my ass..."

And so began the most confusing events I've ever experienced in my 58 years in this life. The price one pays while making a declaration. I am still angry that my parents did not protect me during this period of my life, even though I had disowned them.

Sexual abuse for a child is a complicated scenario. The idiosyncrasies of my experience are not unique and are very, very personal. A story to be told at another time. What I convey to you, reader, is the shame associated with this episode of my life and the disconnect from my family three years earlier. These are the pivotal events that determined the trajectory of my life for the next 42 years. Thank you to the heavens above for the amazing lady that sauntered into my life at this time. My first love and close friend to this day.

First Love

Patti turned 16 on April 26th, 1976. The day before, I had the fortunate opportunity to attend my first concert with her and a group of her friends. My circle of relationships was expanding, and the older girls surrounding me while the music played left me tongue-tied and dreamy. Some miscommunication the night before the concert caused a delay in the onset of our relationship. It would take three more months before our first kiss. A late-night walking beneath giant Sequoias in the foothills of the Sierra. My 14th birthday, I remember the evocative touch of our arms and hands as we strolled through the campground. The grasp of fingers when startled by a bear. I remember the first kiss as if it were last night, not knowing how, nervous I might not get it right and ruin any chance of being with this beautiful angel. Patti and I would spend the next five years in a relationship that I am eternally grateful for.

Innocence Lost

In the summer of '76, my life completely changed. My father went to northern Africa for work, leaving an innocent elder son, only to return four months later and encounter a young man who had begun to taste all the fruits that life had to offer. Rock concerts, a girlfriend, alcohol, weed, sneaking out, and high school; life was starting to get fun, really fun. Up until this time in my life, I was the perfect kid. Perfect grades, perfect manners, perfect room with the bed made, shoes lined up, shirt tucked in, chores complete; I was that kid that every mother loved and wished their son was like. I did everything possible and more to be perfect, to give my mom no reason to be in conflict with me. I equated perfection with not having to deal with parents. I did my job, they left me alone. It all changed in the summer of '76, and by the end of the year, there was no turning back.

I managed to keep my perfect grades intact for the first two years of high school. I played water polo and swam. I had a job working in an art gallery/picture frame shop on the weekends. I tutored kids in math.

At all times in my life, I've managed to retain an exemplary work ethic. You see, in order to maintain my disconnect, I knew that it would require money to fulfill this intention. Not so in the other areas of my life. The drugs, the alcohol, the sneaking out, and the shows were all contributing to the demise of my grades. My relationship with Patti began to get tumultuous for the first time. I hated my parents. I hated school. By the start of my junior year, I would wake up and do bong loads, get high before water polo/swim practice, after practice, at the break, at lunch, after school, before afternoon practice, before dinner, after dinner, then before bed. I was high all the time. On the weekends, I would supplement getting high with getting drunk, most times blackout drunk. Acid and mushrooms became a regular past time as I hit my senior year. Life was one huge party. My grades suffered (not my work though). By the time my graduation was upon me, I had to rely on an unaccounted-for math class I had taken four years previously in order to have enough credits to graduate. Dad had finally left. As I said, I never understood how the two aliens had ever been a couple. I don't believe they had slept in the same bed for a few years.

I moved into my own apartment shortly after graduating, just shy of my 18th birthday. In the last year of high school, I was rarely home anyway, staying with friends or Patti's. Living on my own allowed me to finally be free from the family I divorced a decade earlier. I tried college, twice and kept on working at the frame shop. My relationship with Patti deteriorated, and I will never forget the day when I knew it was over. We both have different versions of the end. In mine, I told her I could not do this anymore, said goodbye, and proceeded to get drunk and cry for two days. Then the party continued.

We did not speak for six months, and I was having the time of my life, working and partying. More concerts, more drugs, more blackouts, a few girls and anger; I remember riding my bike home one night after two or three or four pitchers of beer from Hueys, the local pizza parlor where I could drink underage. My father had an apartment close by, and even though we lived and worked close to one another, I cannot recall having seen him even once during the previous year. He certainly never saw my apartment. I rode my bike and detoured to his place during the three-mile ride. I detoured and stopped on the street in front of his pad at around midnight. I was drunk, and I was angry. Really, really angry. I picked up a hand-sized rock and threw it at his front door, screaming obscenities and hate at him. Nobody came out, and I rode home. We never discussed the incident. Maybe it never happened.

Second Love

It took six months before Patti and I spoke after our breakup. Some mutual friends were visiting her, and she invited me over for a barbeque. For the next couple of days, all I could think about was being able to see her, to sleep with her, to have sex with her. I remember being rather obsessed about it. I went, we slept together, had sex, it was great and... I met the second love of my life. Cheryl was the most stunningly beautiful girl I had ever come in contact with, way out of my league. One night of cards and one day at the beach had me completely in love. I ended a casual relationship with a girl I'd been seeing at the time and spent the next year traveling 150 miles as often as possible to be with this incredible creature. I can still remember the painful goodbyes each time I returned home, the long tearful bus rides dreaming of how I could be with her always. The dreams turned into reality after just one year. We packed up, moved into a van, and steered toward Colorado. I was the happiest guy in the world and beside me was the most beautiful girl who had ever lived. We were moving to the Rocky Mountains, and life was good, really, really good.

Responsibility

Before we left for Colorado, on the weekend of my 21st birthday, I managed to travel up to Cheryl's place in the Sierra foothills for a weekend of fun rafting on the American River. A four-hour Greyhound bus ride and a six-pack of beer were all it took for me to arrive in paradise to celebrate one of our society's inebriant milestones. Although I had been drinking for at least six years by then, I could now do so legally. This weekend I received a gift. A gift that completely altered any thoughts of being a barely responsible adult, living on my terms, no one else's. I did not find out about the gift until many weeks later. My girlfriend picked me up at a convenience store after work during a snowstorm. My greeting was a black and white polaroid picture of my 15- or so week-old daughter who was growing in the womb of my 20-year-old girlfriend. Kids having kids is a comment one of my therapists mentioned after an intense EMDR session many years later. Torey was born on April 18th, 1984. We went into the hospital during a raging spring snowstorm as two and went home the next morning as three, with beautiful blue skies that matched her beautiful blue eyes.

Desperate

Life in a ski town, Vail, Colorado, in the '80s was, for the most part, one huge party. Beer, shots, happy-hour meals and cocaine, a lot of cocaine, and I had as much of it as the next guy. For three years, I skied, I worked, and I partied. There were fights, makeups, infidelities, and Torey. After three years of fun and crazy times, I began to recognize that living in a ski town, 1,000 miles from any family or support, might not be conducive to raising a child. Opportunity knocked, and I desperately opened the door despite huge misgivings from my soon-to-be wife only to be greeted by an adventure that would last the next 10 years of my life. I thought I was creating an opportunity to give college another try. I gave it a try and instead became a federal criminal. California, we are coming home.

Farming

It was my father-in-law who created the opportunity. I believed he was some sort of land developer, and he was offering us a place to stay and help out while I went to school. I was so desperate to leave Colorado that we had already moved when I found out that he was not a land developer. Yes, he had done his fair share of development and made lots of money. The money was gone, the developments were done, and now he was inviting me to join him in the agricultural business. We were going to be farmers, marijuana farmers. For the next three years, we created the largest indoor grow operation law enforcement had ever busted. Three years of trial and error experimentation with growing techniques from all over the world is what I ended up doing. I made it through two semesters of school and even played water polo for a season. And I continued to party. Booze, pot (of course), cocaine, speed, we did it all and I, despite living a life of complete paranoia, was having a pretty good time, until I wasn't. In January of 1989, I told my partners that I wanted out. We agreed to some terms that involved production numbers and dollars. Cheryl and I signed up for a nothing down real-estate workshop in July, and we intended to move to Coeur D'Alene, Idaho. My idea was to buy cheap properties, fix them up, and rent them. My real idea was to buy a home and build a high-tech indoor grow room in the basement. I'd figured out a way to make a very modest income in a very small space that no one would ever know about, no more partners, no more paranoia. In June, while prepping for my annual solo backpack trip, I returned home from some errands, and something seemed a little strange on the farm. Where was my wife? When I left, she was out painting some flower boxes; now the farm seemed eerily quiet until, while parking the truck, a gun appeared at my head. The female officer wielding it told me to leave my hands on the wheel and that I was under arrest. I guess I should have negotiated to leave in May.

Prison Camp

Two years later, I began serving my three-year sentence for conspiracy to manufacture a controlled substance. I was a federal prisoner for a crime that is 100% legal today. Kinda like the Kennedys during prohibition, only I didn't have that kind of money or power. My wife also received a felony conviction for a slightly more minor offense with no jail time, just probation. Federal Prison Camp Boron became my home for two of the next three years. One of my new cellmates, a middle-aged Jamaican man, gave me a gift. Zadock Reid gave me back my love for mathematics. We met the first time before the daily 4:00 pm stand-up count. I'd been working on a couple of math problems from the bi-monthly inmate newsletter, trying not to look scared and minding my own business. Reid noticed my work and commented that I had a few things wrong. I was a little offended until I discovered from my other cellmates that he had a PhD. and two postdocs in mathematics. For the next year, he gave me lessons in math, lessons in the import/export business, and most importantly, lessons in humility. I watched this man teach trigonometry in a classroom filled with, I am talking standing room only, criminals, gang bangers from the notoriously rival gangs the Bloods and the Crips, and scared white dudes (me). Every night for a year, he would give me a problem to work on before he went to bed. The next day, he'd review my work and show me what was possible now that I'd proven some theorem. The reason I completed my degree in math and created a decent living working for myself the last 25 years is because I met you, Reid. Thank you.

Actually, I learned a lot in the prison camp. In the first 18 months, I perfected the ultimate stealth grow room. Thankfully, my sentence was for 36 months. In that time I won a triathlon, learned to play guitar, was in a band, started a yoga practice, got really strong, started meditating, did sweat ceremonies with the native Americans, sang in a choir, taught mathematics, learned some HVAC skills, some microelectronics skills, CPR, and Life Saving certifications. I earned income doing the laundry for the wealthier inmates, writing papers for inmates taking courses, and buffing people's floors. In federal prison, one must have some sort of job. You could work in the kitchen, clean the dorms, the visiting room, work in plumbing,

HVAC or carpentry, or be a landscaper. All maintenance for the compound was done by the inmates. I always tried to get a job that would give me the most amount of time to not work. There was way too much to learn to waste time raking rocks or grilling fat-filled hamburgers. When I got out in 1994, there were a few weeks I struggled with the challenges that I was facing trying to put my life and family back together. I wanted to go back. How crazy is that?

Mathematician

Instead, I enrolled in school. My new home was now in Southern California, Laguna Beach, the OC. Torey and Cheryl had made the move here while I was away. I spent two years at the local junior college and three at the closest state university. I received my degree in mathematics in June of 2000. My intention, what Reid had inspired in me, was to get a PhD. After the first two years, I realized that barely getting by and spending six to 10 hours a day doing school stuff for seven years was not part of any dream I envisioned. The professors at our local junior college seemed to have a pretty good life; maybe I'd just get a master's degree and teach there. It took just one year of commuting to university, three hours a day, for me to realize that it simply was not worth it. I really disliked going to school. During this time, I taught private swim lessons, did handyman type work, moving jobs, and just about anything that would allow me to go to school, and still spend time with my family. During my first year, I discovered a tutoring lab on campus that would give my name out to the community as a tutor if I were to take a two-unit class. This landed me three students and the emergence of a business that has joyfully served me to this day. By the time I graduated, my wife and I were earning enough income to move to the beach and buy a condo that I still live in today. One of those first three students, and now close friend, Dana introduced me to her brother, who remains one of my closest friends today. And the party continued. My new friends were all 10 to 15 years younger than me, just starting out on their own. We drank, smoked, and surfed every day, every weekend. I had my crew, and for the next 10 years, life was fun. I worked a lot, typically seven days a week. I took many camping, surfing, and backpacking trips.

Financial Risks

In the mid-2000s, just before the financial meltdown in this country, my wife and I decided to become real estate moguls. We took $200,000.00 of equity out of our home and bought two million worth of rental and vacation homes. We bought a delivery service business in the closest major ski town and were on our way to becoming real entrepreneurs. Except, we had no idea what we were doing. When the financial crisis struck, everything imploded. I was too ashamed to reach out to the many knowledgeable parents of students I had relationships with and ask for support. For three years, I worked twelve hours a day, seven days a week, and poured all the income right down the drain. It all collapsed, and then, my mom died.

Mom Is Dead

Mom did the best she could. That's the mantra I run through my head whenever I think of her, so sad. She was a big lady, big in stature, big in size, big in opinions, and big in bitterness. And she was the best grandma my daughter ever had. Mom always showed up for Torey. I did not tell my family about Torey until two weeks before her birth. I was ashamed and scared. I've paid enormous prices for disconnecting from my family when I was a kid, and despite that, mom never hesitated when it came to helping out with her first granddaughter. Hereditary genes, terrible lifestyle, and unhappiness led to her passing at the age of 67. I still have not shed a tear. I stayed with and cared for her in the last two months. She did not want to die, and she had no choice. When I returned home, I informed my wife that I would be pursuing all the activities that I had dreamed of since being a little boy, with or without her. Rock climbing became my passion.

Climbing and My Third Love

My marriage was a mess. I had stopped drinking excessively. I was sharing some of my challenges with people I knew and trusted. I was unhappy and alone. I was almost 50, and rock climbing became an obsession. I hired a guide in Joshua Tree, California, a two-hour drive from my home and spent every weekend over the winter learning the craft. I had dreamed of being a climber since the age of 10, when I took my first trip to the Palisades Glacier in the Sierra. I had met a Norwegian workmate of my dad's on that trip who carried an ice axe while backpacking with his wife and two young daughters. His name was Harold Ike, and I remember silently wishing he would take me with him to climb the giant peaks that surrounded the glacier. I had since climbed several of the peaks, but none of them had required ropes, ice axes, and crampons.

The next two years, my life was consumed by climbing and training for climbing. The friends I had spent countless hours with over the past 15 years were all married, raising kids, and our time together diminished. Living the life of a dirtbag climber was like starting a new life for me, meeting new people to climb with, hanging out around campfires, and dreaming of bigger adventures. My work was on autopilot; I'd work with kids, and train during the week and go climbing on the weekends. I'd drag dozens of people out to the desert with me (climbing requires at least 2 participants to assure survival), students, friends, and strangers I'd meet on the various climbing forums I read each night before going to sleep. It did not take long before I left my wife and moved into my car. Having no home responsibilities left me even more time to climb and train. It was during this period that I met the third love of my life, another Cheryl. She had come on a couple of climbing trips that I put together for the Crossfit crew I trained with and was one of the few that showed interest in pursuing the activity more seriously. I was smitten. We climbed, we started going on trips, she became my adventure buddy, we became lovers, and I was happy, really, really happy.

Flashback

During this period, climbing trips were plentiful, and one such adventure landed my partner and I in the majestic Sequoia National Park. After an amazing day of canyoneering and dinner with drinks, we retired to the tent and proceeded to do what lovers do. Perhaps we were going to make love a second time, or maybe we'd just started, all I know is that I was having some performance issues. Then came the anxiety, and while she was patiently fondling me, I experienced a horrendous flashback. Despite having taken way more than my share of hallucinogens in my youth, I had never had a flashback. This one, I was completely unprepared for and choose to never go through it again.

Lying on my back, stroking her hair, her hand gently, patiently caressed me. My mind was relaxed and present to the amazingness of the moment. My body, for some reason, was not. I had already been experiencing some insecurities, self-worth conversations about my relationship with this incredible lady. She was younger and more independent than I was. I often questioned why she would be hanging out with me, living in fear that someone younger, sexier, would whisk her away. It had nothing to do with her demeanor toward me. She never avoided me or acted in any manner that would cause me to question our relationship. I just never felt like I was enough. While we laid there enjoying the moment, I suddenly started to smell the odor of my abuser from 40 years before. Her hand began to feel like his, and my heart began to race. I recall feeling his coarse, reddish pubic hair against my face. It was disgusting, dirty, wrong, and really, really bad. I left the tent and walked off into the night forest, shaken. I don't recall when or how we were sitting together in the moonlight. I just remember telling her that I had had a flashback to something really bad from my childhood. We shared some, and that was it. I never talked about it again, though it was now always on my mind. I started developing full-on anxiety any time we were going to make love. I did my best to hide it and avoid it.

At the moment, I did not realize it, but she was the first person I had ever told about my secret. There had been two other occasions that I came close. The first, during a cocaine-fueled, six-hour marathon sexcapade with my wife back in my pot-growing days and the second, during a therapy session when doing 'Parts' work with Dr. Landis. Except we never discussed it again. Shut down, disconnected, angry, lack of self-worth, alone, and not-trusting pretty much describes my state of my mind and my emotions. These words, these feelings will resonate deeply in the months to come because soon after this event, I received a visit. A visit from a childhood friend that I had remained close to but distant. A friend that knew me, perhaps, better than any other friend.

Transformation

Deron had been coming down to Socal from Spokane, Washington quite often the past year or so. We only got together once and had a super fun time canyoneering in the local mountains and dining out in Venice. I was surprised and pleased one spring afternoon when he showed up on my deck for a planned one-hour visit. I assumed he was here for one of his Tai-Chi workshops he'd been taking for the past few years. I recall him telling a little bit about the leadership training he was currently down for and asking me just two questions. I do not remember the questions. What I do remember is my mind opening upward and to the right with an invitation, a possibility. One might say it was a message from God or a higher power. All I knew at the moment was that I was receiving the message loud and clear. 'This is your last opportunity to handle the shit you have been hiding from your whole life. Commit now, or you will never deal with this in your lifetime.' As I said, I don't remember what he asked, only saying yes, how much, and when. I gave him a $300.00 deposit, and that was that. Three or four months in the future, I was going to a five-day leadership training. I was finally going to deal with this secret that had plagued me for so long. Thank you, Deron. I promptly forgot about it.

Sometime later, in the middle of August 2015, while climbing up in Canada, I got a call from Deron letting me know that the training was starting in a few days, and I had better start driving home, so home I went.

Walking into a room with more than 200 strangers was slightly daunting. Contemplating, 'making up a story' about what it was going to look like sharing my secret was downright terrifying. We were in a large banquet room of a hotel, and I was uncomfortable, extremely uncomfortable. During the next five days, it only got worse. I so wanted to be back in Canada climbing the 1,000-foot granite walls above the sound in Squamish, but here I was, silent, afraid, and alone. The training consisted of roughly 90-minute lectures from a charismatic facilitator, exercises in groups of 10 and dyads, 100 or so groups of two exchanging words from prompts by the facilitator, super weird, very awkward.

Five days and hundreds of hugs later, I was no closer to dealing with my secret than I had been the past thirty years. So I signed up for another, and ten days later, I was back in the room, this time with only 100 students, and none were strangers. This time I was committed to participating. The second training was rumored to be way more intense, with no place to hide. My commitment did not last long, perhaps twenty minutes, and again I just wanted to be back in the wilderness. I managed to seat myself next to a beautiful, vivacious young lady but was deathly afraid of asking her to be my buddy when the choosing time came about. Thankfully she chose me. Michele Silva, surrogate daughter and partner in transformation, is now my intimate friend for eternity. I believe it was the second day of the training when finally, I spoke about my secret, my abuse. Michele and I were in a dyad, the room was dark, and I let go of something that had been eating away my soul for so, so very long. At this very moment, dear reader, I pause, the tears will not stop flowing.

I am sworn to yet more secrecy as to the actual exercises that take place during these LGAT leadership workshops. This is, more than likely, one of the reasons that companies that put on these type of trainings are often considered cults.

For me, I completely honor the code of silence. If participants were aware of the many exercises that take place, the effect, the outcome, and the impact would be greatly reduced. I've spent over 200 hours in therapy with a handful of reputable psychologists, and the results pale in comparison with what I got out of these two workshops.

That's why I enrolled in the third segment of this program. This one was not five days though. The Legacy Program lasted five months, and it completely transformed my life.

I am LP 128, the Wolfpack. I am a loving, trusting, free man. I've spoken these words hundreds of times in the past five years. I am grateful beyond description for what this group of 43 students, eight seniors, and Captain Quincy did for me.

We raised thousands of dollars to fight human trafficking, we fed thousands of homeless, I have repaired all the broken relationships in my life and continue to work on them daily. Work opportunities present themselves weekly; my students' performance in school and thoughts about the impact they can have in life have grown immensely.

If there were one sentence to describe the conversations in my head during the first 50 years of my life, it would be:

"I am not good enough."

That single belief has created every single breakdown in my life. It has gotten in the way of hundreds of opportunities that have crossed my path. It has robbed me of relationships, experiences, and, most of all, love, love for myself, love from others. During leadership training, I learned to identify this belief, this story and many others I had invented over the years. I will never forget the night that I looked in the mirror and, for the first time ever, told the man staring back at me that I loved him. It changed my world, my experience of the world.

I trusted no one. Imagine having doubts about every single person in your life. Imagine judging every person in your life, always having a story about them. How about being right? Imagine never being wrong, or there always being some excuse if someone were able to point out an error in your logic. Right, and alone is how I think about that life. My relationship with feedback did not exist. If anyone ever tried to point something out to me that I did not agree with, well, fuck them.

Right, and alone, that's the invisible scarlet letter I proudly wore on my chest.

Transformation changed all of this. It taught me that every single belief I had was nothing but a story. A story I made up so I could survive when I was incapable of using my mind and my heart. Feedback is my friend, and I request it daily from people who are close to me. Transformation released the emotional sting, the bruised ego, and hurt feelings I experienced whenever someone criticized how I show up. It gave me the capacity to trust and the ability to create boundaries. It quieted my mind and healed my heart. It has given me a new life. I am not just good enough, I am amazing.

Coaching

Two weeks after graduation from LP 128, I started an Academic Life Coaching Certification program. It seemed to be the most effective way to implement my new skills and experiences into the community that I already served. In August, after completing the course, I began enrolling a few of my students into, what I believed to be, the most amazing, life and school performance altering program ever created. I was passionate about the outcomes that kids could expect by simply following along in my workbook and utilizing me to transform the way they thought about education. I spoke with parents, created excitement, and began implementing some of the tools that I had learned over the previous six months. The results were… not a single yes. Even when I offered to give it all away, not a single kid signed up. My conclusion, first, it was the parents, more than the kids, that could use some coaching. Second, I am not interested in working with a client who does not see a need. My coaching career was over, and I got so busy tutoring, that I did not bother to look for a solution. Until I met and partnered with a group that had solutions to the problems I encountered.

Dad Died

Just as I was getting into the important stages of developing a coaching business, identifying my niche, my father's prostate cancer moved into his bones. Dad had been diagnosed more than 20 years ago and went through hormone and radiation treatments at that time. The tumors retreated as desired, however, his backpacking days came to an end. The treatments somehow completely altered his cardio-vascular stamina, particularly at high altitudes. The cancer had moved into his bones in November, he was dead by early March. I have yet to shed tears of grief for his passing. Now, both my parents are gone. During my last visit to see him and say goodbye, I contacted a coach I had found while researching possible niches. Rachel had a program for survivors of child sexual abuse, and I believed she could support me with some challenges I was dealing with. My relationship with my partner Cheryl was in breakdown, I was experiencing anxiety and depression, and although my secret had been revealed, I intuitively thought there were some issues worth exploring in a formal setting with regards to the abuse.

Adult Survivors of Childhood Sexual Abuse

The exact length of Rachel's 'Surviving' program escapes my memory. We, Rachel, myself, and two other gentlemen, began in March, shortly after my father's death, and concluded in late July. Weekly two-hour meetings, where we shared and discussed writing and reading assignments, were the core of the program. The tools Rachel handed us are the foundation, along with what I took away from leadership, for how I deal with the emotional challenges I face. In the exact middle of the program, we were invited into sharing our experience, as I mentioned before. Actually, she asked us to first write it, in as much detail as we can remember, all the smells, all the sounds, the surrounding, the abuse, the feelings, the emotions, everything. Then we were invited to share during the meetup. Finally, when we solidified our inner circles of trust, she invited, perhaps encouraged, us to share with those we hold closest. This last step has proven to be the most powerful manner in which I have created intimacy in a handful of relationships. Scary, vulnerable, and risky is the best way I can describe the exercise, and it has gradually reduced the shame I've carried for so very long. Name the shame and watch its power over you dissipate. The incredible thing about my group is that we each made every meeting and always had our work complete and in excellence. Well, except for me. I missed the very last meeting. I was busy having my sternum sawn open.

Heart Rebuild

Looking back on the experience, I probably began noticing some symptoms a couple of years earlier. A general decline in my endurance that I attributed to getting older. At the time, I was experiencing tightness in my chest whenever I exercised. This had been going on for about three weeks whenever I climbed, surfed, or danced. I was waiting for summer school to end in a week before going in to get a checkup when I had an episode simply from watching an action movie at home. Previously, the episodes were always exercise-induced. I started to get a little scared. My fear only escalated when deep breathing did not subside the pressure. Now I was really scared. I reached out to my daughter to let her know what was happening. At the time, she was an ER technician for Kaiser, my health-care provider. She calmly told me to relax, grab my computer, phone, and be prepared to spend the night in the hospital. This was getting serious. Torey had already called her charge nurse at the ER, and within moments of arriving, I was stripped, shaved, and attached to multiple medical devices. The lab tests came back, and yes, there were some serious problems. Two hospitals and a procedure later, I was being prepped to have my chest ripped open. People were flying into town from all over, and I was scared, really really scared. I ended up having five bypasses. The recovery in the hospital took four days. Six weeks later, I was rock climbing. I had a new heart, one that would be broken nine months later. Broken so badly, I still don't know if it will ever recover.

Depression

While researching a possible niche, I discovered that for most of my life, I had more than half the symptoms of mild depression. Maybe this was just a case of "Second Year Med Student Syndrome," but it got me thinking. I never understood why I had to work so hard to be happy. My wife asked me once during one of our breakdowns, 'What do you want, Tim?' My reply was, 'I just want to be happy.'

I had accepted feeling hopeless and unworthy as part of my life. Perhaps that was why I spent so much time in the wilderness and having adventures, some sort of a dopamine thing. Around ten weeks after my open-heart surgery, I went through four months of suffering that I do not ever intend to experience again.

Imagine wanting to do nothing but sleep all day long, all night long for days and days turning into weeks and weeks. No desire to eat, to work, to play, to talk, to have sex, to love, to hate, no desire to do anything but lay in bed and sleep. That's what I experienced about two months after having my heart repaired. I had already laid the groundwork for my coaching niche. I had all the tools, the exercises, the journal entries, the breathwork, the diet, the support groups, the meditations and music, and dancing, I had it all. None of it mattered because all I wanted to do was sleep. I didn't even want to read or listen to podcasts, both past times I used to eat up time with, when feeling blue. I put on a happy face and went to work. I showed up at the climbing gym because I had a commitment, but all I wanted was to be in bed and sleep. This is what my recovery from the surgery looked like. This went on for four months before I took decisive action to remedy the situation.

The process was simple, I created a vision of being in incredible physical shape by summer to go on a three-month climbing trip. I made a commitment and enrolled someone to hold me accountable to hike at least six miles every day. I emptied my fridge and pantry of everything that had sugar or was not organic. For forty-four days, I ate nothing but raw organic food and pure water. I got back on my yoga mat. I was making plans for the summer, and life was beginning to have meaning again, purpose. My relationship had been in breakdown for close to two years. We remained friends and still went on adventures together, but the intimacy was gone. We took a trip to Big Sur, went to a show and made some plans for summer. I was beginning to think that maybe, just maybe, we could work things out. Then the most emotionally painful thing I have ever experienced occurred. She started seeing someone else.

I choose not to go into all the details of what happened to me during the next 11 months. In truth, I am still dealing with the pain today, 14 months later. I will only say that I now understand the depths to which one can fall when dealing with grief, with heartache. I understand what it feels like to have no desire to live. I wish it on no one.

Closing

I've shared many of the challenges that I've faced. Sometimes I glance back and wonder, how did I get to be so damn lucky?

There's this song from a band I followed for many years, The Black Crowes, called 'Wiser Time'.

The first line goes,

"No time left now for shame, horizons behind me, no more pain."

The beauty of being nearly 60 is, I have wisdom. The gift transformation gave me is, no more shame. Pain is simply part of life, it comes, and it goes. Avoid it, and it will return tenfold.

I believe anything is possible if one has a vision, declares it to the world, carries out an action plan, welcomes feedback and never, ever, gives up.

I have refrained from telling my tale in the language of a coach. Since transformation, nearly five years ago, I have had the pleasure of coaching more than one hundred students through their own transformation. In the matrix, a personality style assessment consisting of controllers, promoters, analyzers, and supporters, I land firmly in the supporter quadrant. I am a giver, always in contribution. The fire that burns in my soul is stoked when I am supporting others. The only time that I could function during my episodes of depression was when someone requested support from me.

There are dozens of tools that a coach can give to a student, and in my personal experience, no one tool suffices for creating breakthroughs. Instead, it's the daily implementation of these tools and, trusting, that over time, shifts in awareness, thoughts, and actions will take place. For me, there is a systematic process for working through any challenge. Create a vision of the outcome one is seeking. Develop precise action steps to attain the outcome. Declare the intention of fulfilling the vision and take the action steps.

Create a feedback loop for the action steps. Celebrate the outcome. That's it, pretty simple.

Except, it was not!

"I am depressed." These were the words I spoke into the mirror three months after my heart surgery. I repeated this mantra for nearly two months before I finally reached out to my inner circle and let them know I was suffering. Then the breakdowns happened. Day after day of promising myself tomorrow would be different only to crawl out of bed and find an excuse not to do anything about it. Then one day, one night actually, very late, I wrote, on a card, the words, "I want my life back." Instead of going back to bed to toss and turn, I put on my running shoes and went on a walkabout. I hiked all night till the sun rose and worked out all the details of my recovery. I, again, reached out to my daughter, my coach, and three friends to outline the steps I would be taking to feel normal again. For the next six weeks, this inner circle checked in with me daily and did whatever it took to keep me on my game plan. After six weeks, I celebrated with a trip to Big Sur.

What did it take from me?

Every tool I've been given. And, an inner circle of people who I could count on to hold me high no matter how much I resisted. I shared my Vision. I created an action plan. I made a declaration. I got feedback. I celebrated.

So, if you are feeling down, or stuck, I invite you to reach out. Let's go on an adventure together. It could be a phone call, a letter, or why not come and spend a week with me in the wild. I promise you, your life will never be the same.

The words you have read are merely a story. My story. It may not be true. It may not be false. It's simply my interpretation of what my life has looked like through my eyes. There is not a single soul that I know of who has ever heard this story. Most who know me will be in complete shock when they read it, and it's uncomfortable knowing they may. And, it's a story that gets to be told.

I love you all,

Tim

TIM WOLFORD

Tim Wolford has spent the last 25 years coaching, mentoring, and teaching high school and college students in math, science, and goal-oriented life skills. An avid outdoor adventurer, he spends much of his time climbing, surfing, skiing, and practicing yoga. Five years ago, he went through his own transformation during a year-long leadership training, where he intended to come to terms with the sexual abuse he endured as a child. His gratitude for a new perspective on how life can be experienced fuels the passion he has for supporting others with their own challenges. Tim is known for his ability to create safe spaces for people to share and explore the thoughts they keep hidden behind a wall of silence, fear, and shame. Having broken free of his lifelong dance with depression, he now coaches women dealing with it. A huge believer in the power of nature, it is not uncommon to spend time with him in the mountains, desert, or seashore. Tim is a vision-oriented coach who relies on a systems approach to creating change in one's life. Life after COVID has allowed him to get a jumpstart on his dream of being nomadic, and he now works and plays while traveling the western United States.

Contact Details

Website: www.timwolford.com

Instagram: https://www.instagram.com/itinerantim/

THE MIDDLE LINE

Todd Kramer

As I sit here in my recently converted attic, now office, during a quiet London lockdown and write, I can appreciate just how much everything about the world we live in has recently, rapidly and drastically transformed. In fact, I and everyone else has also changed dramatically in the process. The shape of the world is always changing in one respect or another, and each day is at once different but the same. A person grows, develops, and is impacted by his environment, circumstances, influences and experiences. Now that we live in the era of the coronavirus, it's more obvious to each of us, at least it should be, that Nature alone determines our condition and direction. So, where does that leave me—the individual? Where does my free choice and capacity for transformation rest?

When I was a little boy of around three or four, I used to sit on a tiny rocking chair in front of my doorway and wave to all the folks who passed by. I did this because I was certain that everyone I encountered was a friend. I knew inherently even then, as many children do, that we are all somehow related. I felt intuitively that we came from the same place and now, we were all here. And I wanted to wave and greet all my friends to say, "Hey, look at me! I'm here too. I made it!"

I naturally felt that everyone in this world was somehow a part of me, like a family. And every time I was ignored or received an odd glance, contrived smile, or condescending wave back, I became ever more aware that, although we are all from the same source and we are all connected, somehow, we had forgotten. My ego had yet to evolve. I was innocent and full of love. A lot of children have this innocence and deep sense of connection in them. In fact, it is this undeterred openness, purity and sincerity that we love most about children. Overall, we try to treasure and protect that in them for as long as we can because we, as adults, know that life is going to eventually kick the ever-loving crap out of them just like it did for the rest of us. Life will come and corrupt them eventually and, in that process, it will destroy what is the most precious of sensibilities and times in a person's life—childhood innocence.

~ For the longest time, I felt robbed of having a childhood. I was upset that I hadn't been nurtured more by my parents and others around me to be the best, brightest and most successful person I could become. I felt this because of the bullying, abuse, and the lack of fairness or justice that was levied on me (which, again, is always huge for children). That and what I perceived to be the total incompetence I endured from those who were meant to be my guides, teachers and caregivers.

I felt that the combination of all of these elements had cheated me out of a future marked by maximum achievement and great affluence. A quality of success that I might have reached had I received more care, love and support. However, I later recognized that this was all an illusion. I had actually been afforded abundant love from the very beginning, and my future success would be explicitly determined by the fact that I had received so many blows (awakenings) in my childhood. However, this brand of love wasn't coming from the likes of family or romantic relationships, and it certainly hadn't come in a form that I wanted or expected. Rather, it came from a hidden, upper source, and it was delivered in an extraordinary, if not inconceivable way.

Having come from divorced parents with nine marriages between the two of them (yes, nine!), my relationship with my mother and father was never "exceptional." My childhood was definitely more interesting than most, worse than some, but not at all as bad as others. I moved around a fair bit, and I experienced relative extremes of poverty and wealth. Along the way, I met many wonderful, interesting, wise and cruel people. My boyhood was rich in experience. Good and great. Bad and miserable. I was exposed to so much diversity growing up. I was a normal kid who grew up in abnormal circumstances. I enjoyed and appreciated that, even then, and I carried that drive for experiential exposure, more than anything else, into adulthood. Life was rarely dull, and that suited me just fine because I knew that the more experiences, sensations and influences (good, bad, or ugly) that one could accumulate, the more prepared one would be later to engage and relate with the world and the people in it. I didn't care about wealth, honor or fame as much as I did about understanding the lives and motivations of others. I would bank each new experience like small change into a savings account.

I suffered through a fair bit of verbal and physical abuse and generally felt emotionally and physically neglected as a boy. I was a latchkey kid from the age of seven. I remember vividly my mother coming into my classroom at school and the murmur of my classmates, "Whose mom is that?" She told me she had gotten a job and that I was to get myself home from school. She handed me a key to the house. The teacher, taking some mercy on me, hung the key around my neck with a bit of yarn so I wouldn't lose it. My mother told me that I should go home, make a sandwich, and that there was a gift waiting for me. I got home, opened the box and the present? It was a keychain. And that was the day that I officially became a latchkey kid. From that moment, I started to grow up.

I remember being disappointed often in my parents and most adults in general. I didn't understand how they could be so corrupt. I saw such great potential in everyone, focusing on their best side and, of course as a child, relying on them to show guidance, wisdom and leadership. I had, my whole life, yearned for a great guide, a teacher, to help me understand the enigma of this life, this world. I would find only the opposite in most, especially my father.

My father was incredibly charming and very funny when he wanted to be, and an absolute tyrant the rest of the time. He was raised hard by hard people in a small Northern Michigan town where you had a choice of working at the limestone quarry, in logging or on the steamships that ran the Great Lakes. He took one of the few escapes available and joined the Marine Corps when he was 17. He has been an alcoholic his whole life, certainly my whole life. The kind who starts his day at 04:30 with a shot of tequila, and *then* pours himself a drink. He was a cop for a few years before he was injured on the job. He never did much else with himself. My father could have been a truly great man, but he never put any effort toward it. Now he lives alone in a dark, smoky house. His only companion is a nurse who steals from him.

~ However, I learned more from my father than I can fully express. I learned about the dark places that fear could take you. He was a man who was always afraid, and he expressed that fear through rage. I witnessed how the ego can ride a person like a beast of burden his or her entire life and how any potential greatness will simply wither and die under such a burden. Imagine an acorn with the potential to become a mighty oak, but never accorded the light it needed to grow above the forest canopy. I witnessed and felt the sadness and the shame of that.

Ultimately, I couldn't abide by my mother either. She was stunningly beautiful. The kind of woman who would get whistled at from across a busy street. She commanded a room and was admired by men and revered by women. An extraordinary combination. However, she didn't know what to do with me. I saw all of her flaws, and I wasn't buying into her eccentricities. She was, by my own diagnosis, a covert narcissist with severe OCD. She compartmentalized everything for her own protection. That I knew this about her, coupled with the fact that I presented a certain amount of competition for the attention that she demanded, made for a very strained relationship between us. We were more like friends by the time I got into my teens. I stopped calling her "mom" pretty early on.

~ Parents are critically important to a person's development, and that's why I am including something about them here. I don't disparage or judge them (anymore) for who they were or are. I see now that the people in your life are all simply players in a kind of theater. One's parents, family, friends, colleagues and neighbors are nothing more than skilled actors in one's own personal spectacle. And in the case of parents especially, one should love and cherish them, not because they raise you (or didn't in my case) or simply because they are your parents but precisely because they lovingly played their necessary role for your development. Now I am able to aim myself back toward that source of love that sent my parents to me on life's path. And because of this realization, I am more dedicated to playing my given part as well. As the Shakespeare quote goes, "*All the world's a stage and the men and women merely players....*"

Only by skewing our vision and changing our perception, by separating our egoistic selves from the circumstances and observing the scene objectively, can we see what is real. Day by day, we are all witnessing a kind of our own personal, ongoing film or theater play. Life presents us with a series of false truths that are interpreted as real simply out of habit and because of the way that our minds process the input. I learned and recognized that I was merely looking at a false reality—a shrouded truth. Like Plato's *Allegory of the Cave*, I was watching the wall of shadows cast by real things and, along with the rest of the world, I regarded what I saw and felt through my five limited senses as authentic. It is not until we turn around and come out into the light that we discover the true world that is casting those shadows.

I had many in my life who guided and shaped me. Often, you can learn the most from people you don't like or who don't like you. Most often, one learns from just observing. I was very keen as a boy to be around the adults. And because of my circumstances, where and how I grew up and what I was exposed to, I met all kinds of people. I would go from engaging with celebrities and the super-rich while riding on private jets to having deep conversations with migrant workers, transvestite prostitutes, the homeless and drug addicted. They were from all walks of life, and I was interested in all of them. I wanted to hear and experience everything that they knew and felt. I become a researcher of the ego. Soon, I began to see that within each person, there are two parts. There is the pure form of them that is perfect, exceptional, full of love and altruistic, while, at the same time, on their back rides this ego-shaped creature that tugs, manipulates and corrupts them into wanting, doing and pursuing absolute bunk. It's phenomenal, really. And the most challenging part of that is, you, the observer, have an ego, too. And you have to try to stay objective (as any good researcher does) while your ego is being attacked by the other and is compelling you to react egoistically. It is very difficult to remain objective in this science.

I moved to Los Angeles, California at the tender age of 18 to attend university, and honestly, I was way too young to go. I looked young, too. I easily looked 14 years old; I was a late bloomer. Some of my dorm-mates spotted my youthful appearance immediately. Before they could ridicule me, I convinced them that I was a fourteen-year-old genius. I had even found an article in the newspaper titled "Fourteen-Year-Old Genius Receives University Scholarship," and I cut it out and taped it to my door. Just the headline of course, not the actual article, which had nothing to do with me obviously. It was enough to support the lie, at least for a few weeks until they figured out that I was actually just some prepubescent, 18-year-old, wise-cracking dope with nothing discernibly interesting or useful about him; aside from having a color TV and a mini-fridge.

My university days were essentially a drug-fueled, ego-driven, and volatile four years of "personal discovery" and jackassery; not in that order. It was not the most ideal place for an emotionally and physically stunted teenager to become a man. However, I did push my university professors pretty hard to make their classes bend to my desire to understand the meaning of life. I remember coercing my *astronomy* professor to teach his class more like *astrology*. "Talk about the big bang as it relates to the eternal soul, not the universe!". I had to take religious study as a requirement in university. I took a lot of Zen Buddhism classes (as opposed to anything soteriological) and it was here that I really activated and developed spiritually.

I also met a lot of interesting people in university. I was, while admittedly under a thick matted covering of self-loathing, anger, doubt and aggression, still burning to discover the meaning of life, and I couldn't understand why nobody else cared. Then, I started meeting people who did and they were as interested in the searching for Truth as I was. This was the early nineties, just be clear, and back then, we were experiencing a sort of mini-resurgence of the sixties. New-ageism had just started to hit, and we, Californians, lapped it up.

New-age bookstores with crystals, incense, dreamcatchers and Peruvian music CDs for sale were popping up everywhere. People were getting into yoga, health and meditation, Buddhism, crystal healing and star signs, and everything had a vibration, an energy, or an aura to it. And I was all in. Bear in mind too that this was all happening just a few years before the internet had launched in earnest. It was the last few years of those innocent times before you could "Google" the answers to universal questions. You had to go down to the Bodhi Tree Bookstore in West Hollywood if you wanted answers!

There was a resurgence of a desire for personal, social and spiritual development. We grew weed in our closets and went to see the Grateful Dead (even though we all hated the Grateful Dead). We had drum circles on the beach and organized poetry slams. We read authors like Carlos Castaneda and books like *Zen and the Art of Motorcycle Maintenance*, *The Way of the Peaceful Warrior*, and

Richard Bach's *Illusions*. We went out to the Southern California deserts and dropped acid under the stars. We took road trips to San Francisco and shared ideas and insights over long, stoney conversations with friends. And everyone was hoping to get a glimpse of Nirvana (both the band and the state of enlightenment).

Actually, I had my first real epiphany while at university. I realized that we are all born selfish. That from the moment of birth, our first impulse is to receive. From the mother's breast we crave and demand nourishment, and we are provided that warmth, comfort and nourishment without any requirement to produce anything in return. The mother receives great pleasure from this however, and not from the giving of the milk (this is inherent and mandated to her by genetic code) but from the fact that the baby takes the milk from her. The mother gains pleasure from giving instead of receiving. I accepted this early on as a truth that is <u>confirmed by Nature,</u> and I learned to start to observe Nature to understand Truth in general. If it is present in Nature, then it is evidence of how humanity should design its own society.

I remember sitting and exploring this new revelation by the fountain in front of our theater building when a girl I'd had a crush on came up and sat next to me. She asked what I was doing sitting there looking so contemplative, and I explained my theory to her. Pretty heavy stuff for a 20-year-old kid. Naturally, the conversation quickly dissolved. She obviously wasn't going to care about my flash of insight, and I obviously wasn't going to be able to parley my emotional intelligence and spiritual fervor into any sort of romantic encounter with her. So, I dropped it.

However, I began to understand two key things in that one combined moment.

- 99.999% of the population isn't going to relate to my spiritual insights, so I should probably keep them to myself for the most part.
- In order to confirm anything as being true spiritually, it must first be confirmed by Nature. If you can see the example within the construct of Nature, you can therefore accept it as also being spiritually accurate.

I had issues with commitment and relationships and trusting people as well as an incapacity to be in or express love. I lacked confidence and social prowess. I didn't care about anybody apart from what I could get from them or what they had to offer me. I literally had the gates to fame, fortune and celebrity opened up to me, but I blew it. I couldn't handle the responsibility; I had too much anxiety and was too lazy to even pretend to care about people most of the time. Despite how influential or powerful they were or how they might have helped me; I only saw them as corrupt, baseless, or fatuous and I judged them. Oh, how I judged people! A constant bellowing in my head of disgust for everything and everyone, and despite being an actor, I couldn't or wouldn't hide my disdain from people.

Still today, the grooves (they're not even wrinkles but grooves) in my face bear witness to my past predisposition, not only to be in contempt of others but to visibly express it. Today, however, that has all changed. People are better, less corrupt, kinder and easier to understand and care for. People are not ignorant or dumb, and they don't deserve to be punished or scorned for what I perceived to be their stupidity. Certainly, I am the least worthy to pass judgement on others. Is it a miracle that people have changed so dramatically over the years? Did everyone finally come around to my way of seeing things? It's no miracle and, in fact, people have actually not changed at all. They are very much the same that they have always been. The only thing that has changed in this entire, universal equation is me. I had learned and began to practice "judgement with mercy" out of a faith in a higher source that was presenting me with everything I needed to see in order to make my own personal corrections. What I felt from the outside was not real but merely a reflection of my inner flaws.

~ There was no book, drug, psychotherapist, lover, mother, brother, religion, or friend that was going to help me change. I certainly could never do it on my own. I wanted to, of course, but only because I didn't like not having the things I wanted. That only made things worse. Not getting what you want is the worst feeling a person has. Blaming others and yourself for not getting those things is what I would call a criminal activity. But you cannot stop "wanting." It is built into us. The solution, however, is simple. Change what you want to that which the system is giving you and you solve your problem. You will always get what you want if you choose to want what you get. Get it?

In the end, I couldn't stand Los Angeles. At least that is what I tell people. Ultimately, LA couldn't stand me. And, I didn't like who I was becoming there. Lost Angels, the land of the "Big Ego," as I called it. What a place for all the uninhabited egoists to thrive. Something about the combination of sun, desert and ocean that gives people license to go nuts. There is no bad weather in LA! There's no walking, and even the homeless live on one of the world's best beaches. In other words, there was very little in Los Angeles to humble a person, but everything to assist in one's pursuit of self-interest, vanity and empty fulfillment. If I wanted to grow, I had to go. So, at the age of 28 (before it was too late in my estimation), I left for Europe and I eventually landed in Prague, Czech Republic. A spirited and mysterious setting in the deep, dark East with few rules and fewer obligations. I loved it.

I have failed at nearly every "project" I have ever started. I have been only mildly successful in my chosen career. I've worked a hundred different jobs and lived in a dozen different cities in several countries. I was never at peace in one place and usually, I start over and over again every few years, burning every bridge behind me as I go. I had every opportunity handed to me but squandered it out of apathy, a sense of entitlement, cowardice, self-pity, doubt, boredom or shame and, more often than I like to admit, a typically American, overcompensating confidence combined with a total lack of actual competence.

~ This isn't some problem that needs to be fixed however, and I carry only a whisper of regret for any past mistakes and indiscretions. How could I possibly be in control of my own destiny? It's not represented anywhere else in Nature that we are in control of our own lives. We didn't choose to be born or when or to whom and we have no control over our death. Why should I assume that I am somehow in charge of my own life? Only because my ego makes me think so.

How is that? Why am I not rougher on myself? Why don't I try harder? Shouldn't I "pull myself up by my bootstraps," reassess, focus, rise to the challenge, awaken, "get 'er done," reshape, reenvision, change, and transform my life? That, of course, is what the common ideation is, and I did try all that. However, what I eventually learned was that <u>it cannot be done</u>. Not that way anyway. It is impossible for a person to change him or herself simply through sheer force of will. And anyone who tells you otherwise is nothing more than a snake-oil salesman operating on your ego in order to sell more of their nostrum for personal profit. In fact, the worse that you are at "change," the more money they put in their pockets. It's carpetbaggery and, from a spiritual perspective, criminal.

The standard convention that is marketed and sold to us hapless, hopeless saps by the self-help gurus of our time is that we have the power somewhere within ourselves to change our lives and all we have to do is reach down deep inside and grab it out. Then we will achieve wealth, fortune, happiness, and whatever else we want. And, if we are not successfully changing our lives, then we are failing to be good at yet another thing in our lives. A vicious Catch-22, and it's all hogwash. Nobody is able to just *will* themselves into being something different from what they are.

Our path has been mapped out in advance by a root and branch system, and there is only one choice that we have available to us within this closed system. Our free will is activated only when we choose to return back to the initiator. It works like this. A person is born with a set of characteristics, qualities and circumstances. Each of us is given an environment, a family and a culture plus our personality, our skills, and a range of other factors to work with throughout our lives. We are not in control of those, and we certainly didn't make our own stipulations before being born into this world. Our purpose is to work with that which we are given — to integrate our qualities with others and compliment them in order to regain a connection with Nature, God, the Universal Truth, whatever you want to call it. We are all part of one whole, and there is nothing wrong or lacking in any of us apart from our inability to feel and act as being whole, like that system that created us as we are. Any desire to succeed or progress beyond that is nothing more than ego. More simply put, I don't play basketball as well as Michael Jordan, but I want to. How many self-help books do I need to read before I can "Be Like Mike"?

I resented so many people for so long, well into my thirties, until the self-indulgence and folly of it got old. I did what most losers do. I blamed my childhood, parents, friends, teachers and whomever I could for most of my mistakes. And I made plenty back then. I grew up afraid, confused and regularly injured, both physically and mentally, by those who should have looked out for me the most. In my teens and twenties, I was angry, unbalanced, aggressive, and I was still afraid. Emotional instability, anxiety, anger, fear, violence, drug use and "mild" criminality were essentially what defined me.

~ There is no one to blame and nothing to regret. There are no mistakes. Everything we do is leading to something greater, and it's all part of the process that we go through in order to seek and ultimately discover life's purpose. It is normal, natural and healthy to have been through so many trials and tribulations. It is precisely for our benefit that it is so.

Because transformation is done outwardly, one can only affect change from inside out. This is called altruism. Everything else is called hostility, ego, or selfishness. In this egoistic space, I take whatever I can from the outside and use it to profit from and create a good feeling inside myself. Success or accomplishment by today's standard definition only equates to: *how successfully have I managed to exploit the weaknesses/suffering/failure of others in order to feel better about myself?*

~ My success paradigm isn't based on my finances, honor, respect, or power but, rather on happiness. *How successful am I at being happy?* And once you can understand that happiness comes from fulfillment and that is only achieved when one comes into adhesion with the integral system that guides and regulates us, then you know what to aim for. Ultimate success is only accomplished from the effort I put toward being the best version of myself that I can be and that "best version of myself" is realized when I include myself and all of my qualities into the integral system and allow others to do the same. This is called "unity."

In short, we must look for ways in which we can transform each other through connection. How do we achieve connection? Through love. How do we achieve love, and what is true love anyway? True love is when we put the other higher than ourselves regardless of what they give or do or provide for us. The closest example we have to this in our world is the love of a mother to her child. Nothing else even comes close. The reason that this is not only *an* example, but the only example of true love we have, is because this is a love where one actively puts effort toward fulfillment of another's desire without regard for their own sake.

There is no concept of true love anywhere but within the purest form of connection. Why? Because true love is a spiritual phenomenon born in us when we make ourselves of service to fulfill the desires of others. In other words, when we try to rise above our egoistic benefit, we become included in a desire that is not our own. It doesn't matter whether this desire is our partner's or a complete stranger's.

We do not judge whether we think the desires, goals and passions of others are good or bad. If we love them, then we try to fulfill them as if they are our own. That is the essence of "love the other as yourself." You might recognize that little gem as being the basic tenet of all religions, and that is because it comes from the highest spiritual root. I will add an additional caveat here: the way to fulfill the desire of the other is by bringing them closer into adhesion with common unity and Nature. Because this is the direction in which all of humanity is heading, whether we want to or not and whether we like it or not.

Our greatest example of Nature enforcing its laws can be seen now, during this current COVID-19 pandemic. A true blessing that is designed by Nature to facilitate a deeper connection amongst us. See how it pushes us to make corrections in our lives that bring us closer to understanding the interconnectedness of all things. That we are all essential parts of one complete body and we are dependent on one another. Humanity, as a whole, had climbed so high up the tree that no one of us could have possibly found our way back down. In fact, we decided just to live in that tree as if it was completely normal. Each one of us on our separate branch. But now, the pandemic has essentially shaken us out of the tree and we are all dropping back down to earth. A wide, open space where we can see the entire world for what it is. And now we witness and regard each other in that world. We are starting to realize just how interdependent and connected we all are.

Sure, for now we are practicing social distancing and self-isolation, but see how much more aware of each other we have become in this process. Even if our awareness is simply coming from the perspective of trepidation. At least we have finally pulled our heads out of our phones, looked up and noticed that indeed there are other people out here. They exist, move and cohabitate all around me, and I am now becoming more "aware" of them. I am even thinking about their well-being. Albeit, mostly because it pertains to my well-being, but it is a start nonetheless. Humanity is starting to recognize just how interreliant we are, and if I want to see real transformation, then I should aim to support that realization within humanity and serve as an example to it myself.

So, I lived in Prague for nearly a decade or, as I like to say, "long enough to learn Czech," which is a long time. Although I had always been on a spiritual path before, things didn't really amp up for me until after I arrived in Prague. There were a few reasons for this. One, my ego took a hard and necessary hit. Years of growing up and living in Southern California turned me into a prodigious egoistic. I was fueled by my own arrogance and overconfidence externally while being driven internally by fear, anger and self-doubt. I had "ugly-American" stamped in my passport.

In Prague, I had arrived to a postcommunist country with an indiscernible language, bitter cold winters, and deeply rich history and culture that had been lacquered over and neglected by 60 years of communism. That was more "reality" than this California cowboy could handle. I lost all sense of personal pride, dignity and confidence, and probably a few other things that I had taken there with me. My ego was shrunk by that cold, foreign, antediluvian and unforgiving city. As Franz Kafka once said, "Prague doesn't let go… This old crone has claws. One must yield or else." The city grabbed me, pulled me in, and I didn't resist. That city was good for me, and I still love Prague.

I enjoyed many years of philandering, drinking and smoking in Prague. There were long, languid summer days and cold, cozy winter nights. It was a golden era of very little responsibility and plenty of leisure. I didn't pursue my spiritual goals, and they didn't pursue me. At least for a period. I filled my vessel to overcapacity and then the bottom started to drop out. I could feel the old yearnings for answers welling up, so I started poking around again. Asking the old questions about the meaning of my life and seeking out answers. And I looked everywhere.

I remember approaching a group of Freemasons who wanted to open a new chapter (or temple?) in my area, and I had a meeting with them. At some point, they asked me what I had hoped to get by being a freemason and by joining them. I assume that they were assuming networking, contacts, or maybe they were expecting to hear "friendship" or "brotherhood." Instead, I took a pause and said, "I'm looking for the Truth. I want to know Truth." At that point, they looked at each other briefly, sort of shrugged, and turned back to me and said, "Uh, well, the dues are 4000 Czech Crowns per month, do you think you can handle that?"

Truth was hard to find and that was by design of course (like all things). I hadn't found it because I didn't want or demand it in the right way. Because there is a force that surrounds and guides us and in order to activate that force, you ultimately need to cry, like a baby to its mother – from a deep place of yearning, a true demand. 13 years ago, I cried like that. I wanted to know Truth so badly that I literally gave my maker an ultimatum. And my cry was answered. In that moment, I was handed everything I needed in order to advance. However, I was surprised to discover that in true spirituality one is not rewarded with enlightenment in a flash of smoke and lightning and then evaporates, leaving nothing but a charred stain on the carpet, thank God.

Spirituality doesn't all just happen in a moment. What I was given was the gift of the opening of a great new path. And accompanying this opening before me, came a teacher, a vast catalog of written guidance and a collection of individuals from all over the world with whom I would study, scrutinize and discover the spiritual science of connection. Without boring you with all the minor details of that experience or where it has led me today, I will say that it is one that requires a lot of dedication and effort but, as it is the only truth in the world, I see it as the only pursuit that has any value. I have been in this method for nearly thirteen years and have dedicated over 20,000 hours to its study and practice. I have learned and I have advanced, along with others, and what we've discovered is that now some version of this wisdom should be shared with the rest of humanity.

From that moment of discovery my existential journey turned inward. The inward journey is the truest and most bold expedition that a person can take. It is where one discovers themselves, how their ego works, and how, by learning to take their egoistic force of reception and turn it toward bestowal, you can turn lead into gold. Essentially, we only need to work on our own ability to go from *reception* to *bestowal*. We must evolve from care and concern for ourselves alone to care and concern for the entire integral system and, through that process, to discover the connection between us. The perpetual connection has been concealed from us, but it has always existed and we need now only to reveal it between us. Most will never study as intensely or learn the intricate, technical, spiritual science that I have, and it is not necessary. We only need to recognize and work with a handful of fundamental concepts.

What to Know:

1. Know that there is a universal force called Truth, love, Nature, Creator, or God that created and controls the whole world and everything in it. Know this and have faith in it.
2. Know what "faith" is.
3. Know that Nature is a loving force of bestowal and cannot do or make harm to you, anyone, or anything in this world.
4. Know that we are in a closed, circular system with no beginning and no end.
5. Know that failure is good and necessary. Use and work with

it.

6. Know that there is no such thing as failure.

7. Know that everything is purposeful.

8. Know that we are all on a spiritual journey to elevate ourselves to be like that force of Nature.

9. Know that you don't have to be a hippy, tree-hugging vegan to use the term "spiritual journey."

10. Know that you do need to be in the right environment in order to succeed. You can *sometimes* <u>change</u> your environment. You can *sometimes* <u>choose</u> your environment. But you can *always* <u>influence</u> your environment.

11. Know that people and situations change based on your influence, attitude and example. Be the example.

12. Know that the entire universe and all of your impressions of it are based on your attitude toward it and your perception of it. Change your attitude and you will change your reality.

13. Know that you need to come out of the shadows. They aren't real.

14. Know that it's very easy to say "change your attitude" but nearly impossible to do it alone.

15. Know that there are those in the world who are wise in this method and prepared to help. Seek them out and change with them.

16. Know that you need to ask.

17. Know that you cannot ask for yourself but only for others.

18. Know that you are built to receive (an egoist). Don't judge yourself or others for it. (See #1)

19. Learn to receive what you need (and even what you want) but do from a place of altruism rather than of egoism.

20. Know that everything is and is going to be okay.

21. Know that the only thing we need to <u>learn</u> is how to

mutually love and care for one another.

22. Know that the only thing we need to <u>do</u> is unite as one.

23. Know that we will succeed.

I have now settled in London, England. I have a life here where I can be dedicated to one sole mission. I no longer have a requirement or desire (or even for now, the possibility) to move about. The restlessness has stopped. I travel internally, and I am settled and satisfied to be wherever I am. Because where I am at every moment, whether in thought, action, feeling or physical location, is exactly where I need to be. I am not plagued by my past regrets, or mistakes because I don't take ownership of them. Everything has always been lining up simply to get me to this moment I am in right now. And it is the same for you, and everyone. There is nothing left for me to personally overcome. Nothing from my past to cry about or wish would be different because, ultimately, I can't influence any of these things anyway. There are only two things happening currently in this world. Two parallel lines that are operating right now. The left line (of reception) and the right line (of bestowal). And the truth lies in the balance of those two forces—on the middle line.

Now is the time when we need to start helping others in a truly altruistic way. However, help doesn't come in any of the forms we are meant to believe. We can't donate our way out of our global, ecological and social catastrophes. We won't volunteer ourselves into a utopia. What shall we protest next? How about politics? Yes, we'll vote our troubles away. After this next election (considering my candidate or party wins of course), this misguided ship that we all live on called planet Earth will turn around and (finally) get back on course again. By the way, were we ever "on course?" Of course not. Fortunately, now it seems that Nature has done most of the hard part for us. We are, as of early 2020, living in a new world with new rules and we have been given a reprieve from ourselves. I believe that the COVID-19 pandemic could not have come at a better time. We could not have been more fortunate or blessed by Nature to have received this type of assistance at this level right now. Nothing short of a third world war was going to shake us out of the tree that we had all climbed up into.

Up until this point, we have lived in an ever-expanding corruption of us and our planet. Although it has been interesting to watch ourselves grow through this pattern of distancing and developing, we have certainly come to the beginning of the end of the program. We have hit the wall of how far our ego can take us. From walking upright and the discovery of fire to the Renaissance and, now the Industrial and technological revolutions, we have advanced entirely by the driving force of our egos. And if we continue along this path of egoism, the world will continue to collapse. Our new engine for advancement will be called altruism.

We, as a society, are preoccupied with placing the blame for our woes on a whole series of entities from governments to corporations, religions, the banks, the elitists, terrorists and various other enemies real and imagined. The list is long, but what are these groups anyway? Who are they made up of? These disembodied groups of "they" are simply disparate collections of "we." There is no evil autonomous body out there operating on a level that is discernibly "inhuman." There is no "*they.*" If you look at "they," who are they anyway? *They* are *we. We* are *they.* There is no "they." On the contrary, "they" are simply groups of *people.* The entire system that was assembled *for* us was done by a collection *of* us. Real human beings with hopes, dreams, fears and worries. People who love their mothers and their children. There is no faceless, heartless, autonomous organization out there that is trying to hold us down. *We* are responsible for each other, and only we, if anyone, can take the responsibility for holding *ourselves* down.

Ultimately there will be no quick-fix solution to our countless global problems. We need to stop looking outward to place blame or seek for help. There is no system that we have yet to build that will solve the dilemma of our disunion and disharmony. In fact, all of the systems that we have built cause and/or support our division. So, who can fix that? Only *we* can. We, together, need to solve the problem of lack of unity and connection in our society and nothing more. Lack of integrality is the cause and a return to integrality is the solution.

For now, Nature has sent us the coronavirus to facilitate this transformation but the undertaking is still with us. This pandemic is teaching us a lesson about our consumerist, materialist ways. It has forced us, the entire world, to take a pause and reflect on how our endless pursuit for personal gain and pleasure was heading us all right over the cliff. The cliff is still there but for now we have stopped short of driving off of it. As a collective, we must seize this opportunity to reassess our social priorities. We have to work with this "new normal", to adjust with it, and bless it. We must endeavor to build education, economic, culture, healthcare, manufacturing, production and social systems that serve to the greatest benefit of all of humanity. Let this be the vaccine that kills all the viruses, both spiritual and material. Let true unity be the remedy for all of our common woes.

Humanity is us, and our greatest benefit will come when we integrate ourselves back into the system of Nature and we take that understanding of our common connection into whatever it is we next want to achieve next. But in balance with Nature. As long as we aim to achieve our goals for the sake of one another, and *with* one another, we can achieve anything. The answer is "we". **We will bring about our own transformation.** If we do that, then we could be innocent again, like children. Free of the burden of our egoistic pursuits and confident that we are *all* part of the same integral system, connected like a family and full of love, concern and care for each other. We can sit in our rocking chairs and wave to each other and we will feel, recognize and treat everyone as shared parts of our one integral system. And we will be as one body — one family.

TODD KRAMER

Todd Kramer is a writer, actor, instructor, coach and consultant with degrees in theater arts and creative writing, and backgrounds in education, media, social science and spirituality. Native of the United States, Todd has been living in Europe for nearly 20 years, and now resides in London, England. He is the creator of *The Middle Line*, a project aimed at developing and disseminating a methodology that will educate humanity and facilitate a new degree of integral unity within society. In order to bring our system back into balance with Nature, we all must integrate with each other by evolving from egoism to altruism. Every intention that Todd applies himself to now is inclusive of the core spiritual principle, *love others as you would love yourself.*

<u>Contact Details</u>

Website: www.toddkramer.com, www.themiddleline.com

Twitter: www.twitter.com/thetoddkramer,
www.twitter.com/_themiddleline_

Instagram: www.instagram.com/thetoddkramer,
www.instagram.com/themiddlelineproject

Facebook: www.facebook.com/thetoddkramer,
www.facebook.com/themiddlelineproject

DISCOVERING BEING: MY JOURNEY TO UNDERSTANDING UNIVERSAL PRINCIPLES

Vijaya Nair, MD, FAMS, MS

Dedication

This chapter is dedicated with profound love and gratitude to Swami, my Teacher, and Spiritual Guide, and my dearest friend. He has been the guiding force and director of my Divine Life's play with all its many challenges that seem to go against all reason and logic. Now, when I look back, those adversities all seem quite perfect and beautifully timed as they helped in the unfolding of spiritual lessons that lay at the bottom of my heart.

I am also grateful to the many teachers in my life, especially my children Ajay, Sonia, and Nikhil, and their respective spouses Niharika, Mathew, and Lauren. I am also deeply appreciative of my ex-husband for his instrumental role in bringing about the transformations in my life.

This chapter is also dedicated to my grandson Neal Krishna who continues to delight us with his irrepressible joie de vivre.

My profound appreciation for my mentors and teachers, especially Sydney Banks, Mamoon Yusaf, Keith Blevens, and Valda Monroe, George and Linda Pransky, who guided me with infinite patience toward the Universal Principles.

My heartfelt appreciation to my beloved Dominique for his love and patient support.

Most of all, my profound appreciation and gratitude to all my clients. In all the years we have known each other, I want to thank them for the invaluable contribution of their growth to the collective wisdom.

Introduction to the Four Zeros of Life: No Health, No Money, No Family Support, and No Reputation

You can see the current global COVID-19 pandemic crisis in two ways: a personal threat and a global threat. In such a case, you live in constant fear and worry of not knowing what will happen next to yourself, your family, your community, and even your future.

Many people in this current time are confronting their three or even four zeroes of life. Some people would have lost their jobs and hence their financial security, whereas some others have lost their health or their family's health, and because of self-isolation, the mind fills in the blanks with fear.

I hope my story will provide you, dear reader, with your choice of facing any number of zeroes in your life.

You can also see this as an opportunity to look beyond personal conditioned thinking and just see the greater invitation that's available to all of us right now and accept this moment without blame.

The story of my life facing all the zeros was such an invitation—that no matter how dire the circumstances looked at that time, I still moved forward. I trusted and relied upon a bigger intelligence to provide me with profound, insightful understanding more than my intellect could! And that is what ultimately got me through all my challenging situations.

And yes, there were times that I forgot all this and got caught with the fear and worry cycle. I used my imagination to worry about myself and my family's future.

I also discovered that worry is just that and it's not giving me accurate information about anything that is going to happen down the road.

Confronting My Deepest Fears

16 years ago, I faced death when I bled severely, incessantly for several months with no relief.

My doctors diagnosed me to have bleeding fibroids, and urgent surgery was strongly recommended. They were also clear with me that these were cancerous growths.

Unfortunately, I knew I was not a candidate for surgery.

My mother and my maternal aunts had similar problems with excessive bleeding and suffered tremendously from post-surgical adhesion colic, a severe and painful lifelong complication of abdominal surgery in susceptible women who were prone to develop scarring afterward.

I was also going through the start of a messy divorce in my 20-year marriage and was in danger of losing the custody of my three kids and home.

For the first time in my life, I had to face my four zeroes all at once. For several months, I had no job, no income, no health, and no physical support from my family. My reputation was in tatters as divorce was not acceptable to my family and community.

Making the Decision to Immigrate to the United States for Good

10 years earlier, from 1994–1995, the kids were with me as I completed my year-long post-graduate studies at Harvard University in Boston. They did well and were happy in their school.

It was a hard transition for them when we returned to Singapore from Boston.

The Singapore school system was so unlike the free and relaxed approach our three kids experienced with their schooling in Boston.

It was a culture shock for the kids. In addition to having long grueling school days for such young kids, there was daily tuition in the various subjects till late at night in order for them to do well.

During the weekend, there were piano and creative acting classes. It was all a matter of keeping up with the Jones!

As a parent, it was an awful experience for me to see the children's teachers every week and be told that they were barely keeping up with their school work.

We were all caught in the fiercely competitive environment in Singapore.

My workload also increased when I returned. My husband, too, had to travel extensively for his work. We had so little time to spend meaningful time with the kids, in the midst of all the work and increased social activities.

Originally, I had really wanted to go to the Harvard School of Medicine to do a post-graduate fellowship in Psychiatry and Epidemiology. I thought the training would help to get many of the chronic mentally ill patients who were locked up in long-term mental institutions in Singapore safely rehabilitated in the community.

It was a real challenge. One that I hoped to solve. And feel fulfilled and happy after doing so.

Temporarily I felt happy, but soon the stress of training staff and working to rehabilitate chronically mentally ill patients took over. Convincing my conservative colleagues to accept the new and progressive standards of care for rehabilitating the chronically mentally ill patients into the community was an uphill task as well.

Two years later, in 1997, my husband received his posting to the IBM head office in New York.

I was happy for the kids to leave the pressure-cooker environment in Singapore and return to a more sane approach toward their education in the States.

I did not have a job initially, but soon after our arrival, I got admission into the Epidemiology program at Columbia University in New York.

It was a challenging period— balancing work, studies, and home life.

My husband encountered a lot of office politics at his new job.

Our kids, however, did well in their respective schools, and we could see that they were thriving.

Initially, we had planned to return back home to Singapore after living in New York for two years. We were still paying the heavy monthly mortgage on our family home in Singapore.

Unfortunately, within less than a year of his posting, my husband decided he was not happy with his job in New York and expressed his dissatisfaction to the Asian head office of IBM. He was immediately given opportunities to live and work in Asian countries.

I had a feeling that this transfer to Asia wasn't a good thing for our kids. They were sensitive and shy and took time to make friends.

I prayed on this and decided that if I could get a job, I would stay back in New York with the kids. My husband reluctantly agreed, provided we could also find a new home as well as a job for me. He left for Singapore back to his former job at IBM. It was very stressful for him to be separated from his beloved kids, and he had to be creative to find ways to travel back to the States to be with us.

In a very short time, while continuing my studies at Columbia University, I also found a job as a research consultant for a company based in Seattle, Washington, which was into manufacturing a natural product that improves the quality of life for individuals diagnosed with cancer.

We found and moved eventually to a beautiful home in Bedford, New York. The children continued with their schooling.

Soon after, I completed my Masters in Epidemiology and was going into my PhD. program when my husband obtained a new position and returned to the IBM office in New York for his work.

Unfortunately, he was not happy with his job in the States. I was not inclined to return to Singapore. Homelife was unpleasant with all the constant fighting.

After two years, in 2003, he left IBM for good.

Shortly after, I left my position at Columbia University.

We were living on our savings for a while as my husband and I had no jobs.

This decision not to return to Singapore and the financial concerns with our dwindling savings caused a huge rift in the marriage.

We had a beautiful home and the prospect of good jobs in Singapore, where all our extended family lived.

It was not a rational decision on my part, at that point, to pursue to stay in the US.

And yet, I strongly felt that our kids were better off to go after their dreams in the United States. Being out of Singapore's strict school systems meant that there was little chance for them to catch up and do well in the major exams they were to face soon.

There was nothing to hold on to except a pipe dream I had. I believed that we'd be all well if the kids were happy.

The situation at home was getting direr and direr. There were many arguments on the best way forward for the family.

We both tried to get other jobs. My husband was successful, but he was deeply unhappy about staying in New York.

Immigration Dilemma Solved

During this period, I also applied for an exceptional scientist visa to stay and work in the US as I knew we could not count on the green card application my husband had filed a few months earlier on our family's behalf to go through.

Over the next few months, I received news that my father was getting progressively ill and diagnosed to have developed fluid in his brain, which required surgical intervention.

My brother, Raj, who was taking care of him, requested I return to Singapore to be with our father during his surgery.

I knew it was going to be a nightmare facing the United States Immigration officer on returning back to the US if I did not receive the necessary visa or green card papers to come back into the country.

I did not know what to do except pray to the Divine for help.

Something unbelievable happened during that challenging time, and the exceptional scientist visa came through in the quickest time possible, thanks to George Akst, the brilliant attorney I was working with in New York.

This particular visa is only given to highly qualified scientists and individuals. I had received so many letters of recommendation from the scientific communities I had worked with in the past such as Harvard, Columbia University, M.D. Anderson, but I had no idea that the visa application was going to be successful.

And coincidentally, I and later the rest of the family were successful at the same time to receive approval for a green card for the family, and eventually, we became naturalized American citizens.

I felt really blessed as I flew to Singapore and helped to nurse my father back to health after his brain surgery. His recovery was rocky initially, but slowly his condition stabilized.

I returned to the States safely with the green card in my hands!

The Appearance of the "Rat"

It was not a bed of roses after my return home, as I started to bleed severely. The disagreements with my husband were growing out of control. We started seeing different counselors and therapists to help us arrive at an amicable solution to our differences.

I remember one day when I laid in bed totally exhausted and bleeding profusely from my uterine fibroids.

I had not eaten or drunk anything for the past several hours. There was no one to turn to for help, even to ask for a glass of water.

I was so enveloped in self-pity and despair.

I was a victim of an unhappy marriage and kept blaming and beating myself up for not knowing how to get out of the situation. That I should know better. I felt that I was sinking deeper and deeper into the hole I was digging for myself.

And then, right in front of me, it happened.

My eyes were half-closed. I was prepared to give in to my total exhaustion and to the ravages of continuous unrelenting bleeding on my body and emotions for months on end.

In other words, I was going to give up.

I could not believe it. Though my eyes were nearly closed, and my mind was drifting off, I could somehow sense a grey streak quickly running across the floor of the small messy room I was living in that was my prison for several weeks.

I felt my indignation and anger rise up within. There was a rat in my room!

This was not right. I refused to accept the situation. What if there were rats in the children's room? God forbid!

I sat up in bed and walked slowly to the restroom to clean myself up and came out of the stinking prison room I had holed myself in for several weeks.

I then placed a call to a pest control company to get rid of the rats in the house.

All along I had thought, without even checking in with the pest company in the first place, that I would not be able to afford their prices.

But when I approached them on the phone that eventful day, they were so affordable! What was I thinking?

I next called my attorney and got a court processor to serve my husband his divorce papers. I was ready to leave my marriage of 20 years.

That was the beginning of me getting angry with my life as well as the situations I had put myself in. I was finally intent on taking personal responsibility, especially at playing the role of a victim and facing up to my fears that I could not manage on my own.

Facing My Divorce and Health Crises

When I decided to file for a divorce, my intention was to free my husband to pursue the life of his dreams. I did not want him to feel tied down to my irrational decision to continue to stay in the US, despite the severe challenges for the whole family.

I also found out my husband had a girlfriend. I blamed myself for not picking up on his unhappiness much earlier. This self-blame was despite both of us attending numerous marriage counseling sessions with no resolution.

Unfortunately, these sessions seemed to make the marital situation much worse.

My mental and physical health were worsening. Self-blame and constant self-judgment contributed to it.

Soon after, at the start of the divorce proceedings, I started to bleed even more heavily. I was totally exhausted and had to be rushed to the Emergency Room in a semi-conscious state because of the severe bleeding. The doctors informed me that I had to have the surgery in order to remove my uterus.

But I refused the surgery. I knew that my impending divorce proceedings were going to worsen my emotional, mental, and physical state.

Also, given the fact that I was prone to scarring as my late mother, and suffered from the same history of uterine bleeding, I did not wish to proceed with the surgery. My mother also experienced severe post-surgical pains due to internal scarring her whole life after she got her uterus removed.

I did not want to go down that same path as my late mother did.

Fortunately for her, my dad was with her day and night as she recovered in the hospital. It was a horrible time for our family as my mother lay very ill after the surgery. My dad's loving care helped her immensely in her recovery.

I, on the other hand, did not have any family support or close friends I could rely on to help me, emotionally or physically.

My husband was quite upset with me for falling ill and filing a divorce.

My brother in Singapore tried to support us but did not know how to help.

All my other relatives had their own personal problems and did not wish to get involved. Moreover, they did not approve of my decision to get a divorce.

The only consistent advice I received at that time from family and friends was to stop the divorce from proceeding. I felt that there was a sense of intense shame and humiliation around my actions.

It was a dilemma to find the help I needed to heal physically, mentally, emotionally, and spiritually.

So, I did the only thing I knew I could under the circumstances. Facing a hopeless situation, I prayed to the Divine for help.

Divine help once again came through at my worst times. I learned to surrender fully to the unknown, giving up all my doubts when rational thinking failed me.

Getting a Job

Despite the poor medical condition I was in, the former company that I had worked in whilst at Columbia University took me in and created a job opening for me. I became the co-director for research in a non-profit foundation, examining the research and the exceptional health benefits of a unique and patented fermented soy product for use in individuals diagnosed to have cancer.

I was very grateful for the job. Unfortunately, the position meant that I had to travel extensively both within the US and internationally. I was organizing the various research projects and presenting at conferences.

Given the severity of my bleeding at that time, I knew the risks of such intensive travels and speaking at different medical conferences on our research findings involved.

But using the fermented soy product I was researching, and in conjunction with doing a non-invasive radiological treatment to block my uterine arteries, I was able to ameliorate the bleeding for several months. I could do my job to oversee the various worldwide research projects that we started.

Eventually, I found Integrative physicians who could help me manage my health and well-being. This relentless search continued for several years and helped me get back on track with the use of personalized dietary supplements, Chinese herbs, acupuncture, advanced meditation, Reiki energy healing, Emotional Freedom Technique, and even Ayurvedic Medicine, among the many natural and alternative therapies I tried in the beginning.

It took a few years until I had the funds to manufacture and market the Jiva supplements, my own unique and patented line of dietary formulations, which came during deep meditation. They helped to eventually heal my bleeding condition tremendously.

One day, an incredible insight came in during a meditation session. I felt I needed to increase the dosage of my proprietary Jiva supplements that I was taking.

Within a month of following that instruction, my fibroids started to shrink significantly, and eventually, the heavy bleeding finally stopped for good!

I am so grateful for all the amazing doctors, healers, and natural therapies I used to restore my health and well-being!

Most of all, I was and am profoundly grateful to the Divine for the wisdom and the inspired actions to follow through. Everything that crossed my path was for my ultimate good, even if I did not see it that way at the time when the challenge and potential solution occurred!

Facing the Dilemma: Where to Live?

So many banks had rejected my initial application for a mortgage.

The family home had to be sold as part of the divorce proceedings.

I just prayed and surrendered myself completely to the Divine Will. I had no idea what to do. It was another impossible situation that had to be dealt with.

Where were we to live?

I was so exhausted those days that I felt I could not manage a move to another home, physically or financially.

I prayed and surrendered to the Divine to show us a way. The answer to my prayers came really fast and in a shocking way!

We were all quite amazed to receive news that soon after I sent in the loan application, I qualified to get a huge loan of 1.5 million dollars approved by the bank. And this despite having such poor, poor finances on my part to start with!

It brought me some time to consider the next steps as I healed and could move forward.

Later on, I found out that the loan mortgage I received was given out quite indiscriminately and without the proper legal and regulatory filters by that particular bank to thousands of unsuspecting individuals like myself who were unqualified to receive the monies in the first place.

This event happened during the period that just preceded the severe housing and economic crisis we were all going to be in within a few years. That is another story!

Divine help came through to navigate that crisis as well!

Connecting to the Divine

I met my spiritual mentor Sathya Sai Baba or Swami, as I call Him, initially in many dreams since 1988, after the birth of Sonia, my daughter. My late uncle Ken Soman and aunt Lalitha had spoken to me since I was a teenager about their Spiritual teacher, Swami, who lived in Prashanti Nilayam in Bangalore, India. They were deeply troubled by my marital challenges and often counseled me.

Initially, for several years, I could not accept Swami as my spiritual teacher. I could not even understand His messages or even read books on Him beyond the first few pages!

What made the difference was that I could relate to His strong message on doing selfless service to the poor.

I was always drawn to service since I was a teenager and especially so when I worked as a psychiatrist in the largest mental health hospital in Singapore.

Except once when he went briefly to Africa, Swami did not physically travel out of India. There are millions of devotees all over the world who have had visitations from Swami in dreams and have met Him in real life when he was alive.

I had met Swami physically in his ashram in India several times.

He also repeatedly came in my dreams and gave me encouragement and advice on solving my life problems and with loving patience answered all my questions. He also showed me my future predictions in my dreams, which always came true!

Swami showed me that when spiritual aspirants desired self-liberation from the cycle of birth and death, they have to pay the price, and their ego has to go.

I realized that my sense of individuality—"me and mine"—had to go. All that Swami was doing was to make me realize the value of devotion, surrender, and faith to recognize the Divine in my life.

I have always been interested in the path to self-liberation. Anything which blocks that path has to be removed, like attachment to wealth, fame, and dependence on the family and community for social approval.

Swami, in his discourses, had talked of the four zeros and of taking away an individual's dependence on wealth, health, family support, and name or reputation. He wanted to help them through facing adversities, develop their true source of support and creativity, and turn toward the Divine, which is inherently present within everyone.

When I had to face the four zeros, nothing prepared me for it! It was tough going until I learned my lesson of turning to the Divine for help instead of being dependent on externals like wealth, education, and family.

All my ivy-league training credentials and training in medicine and psychiatry were of no use in that desperate state I was in.

Life is a game, as Swami used to say, and we must play it. He coaxed us in the same way, to rise above desire and temptation, to realize our incredible Divine inheritance.

Swami came into my life to show me with His guidance that people and circumstances about which I had made some negative judgment were, in fact, the best teachers. This included my parents, my ex-husband, my illness, my financial challenges, and much more.

It was so hard to do so! I had to keep trying because the rewards point to a true and lasting transformation.

Although I went through severe challenges in my life, I also experienced many remarkable acts of Grace.

I felt Divine Presence and guidance when I called out repeatedly to Swami during my toughest times. He was there when there seemed to be no other help to rely on.

The constant image I had in my mind's eye during those challenging times was one where my hands held tightly onto His feet. I was swept in a merry-go-round swirling faster and faster as a representative of the unpredictable and danger-filled life I was experiencing.

New Beginnings

Eventually, the divorce was finalized, and my kids could stay together with me and continue their education whilst their father returned to Singapore.

My ex-husband continued to be very involved with our children's lives and proved to be a remarkable father figure for them. He married his girlfriend, and they are both exceptional in their loving guidance of our kids and their spouses.

We are all friends now and the blessed grandparents to Neal, our first grandchild! His smiles and happy disposition brings a lot of joy into our lives!

Discovering the State of Being

Paradoxically, it was during my severe health challenge when I discovered the depths of my Being. It was a State beyond personal thoughts and physical pain and discomfort.

This state of Innate health and well-being, peace, happiness is where all healing originates from.

It was the strangest experience. I was well versed in different psychological modalities, as well as the spiritual teachings and deep meditation practices taught in major religions and spiritual faiths.

My challenges required a major letting go of my most cherished beliefs and ideas about myself and the world.

I was shocked to find something solid at my core – innate happiness and well-being that existed independent of any circumstance, thought, or physical ill-health and discomfort that I was facing.

The first time I was aware that I was in contact with this state of Being was when I was receiving my first blood transfusion after falling unconscious because of my severe bleeding. I was brought into the Emergency Room.

I remember lying in the hospital bed with the blood transfusion drip running and looking up at the hospital room's ceiling, feeling grateful for the blessings in my life. And then I felt this incredible sense of Peace and Love filling me up from within.

Sure, I had the experiences of physical ill-health: the breathlessness, the insatiable thirst, the abdominal pains, the dizziness, but my mind was clear.

Mentally I had no experience of any fears, worries, anxieties, or any other negative emotions.

I realized I was familiar with this state. This felt like Home. I thought of it as a state of deep meditation. Except I did not do any formal meditation practices that I was taught to do to go within! I did not have to.

I had turned in the direction of gratitude. And then I was there in the field of this exceptional energy of my Being.

Even though I was physically a mess, mentally, I experienced clarity and even joy.

Over the subsequent days and months, this state of deep inner awareness was easily available for me to access. It was truly transformational.

Over the years, I have experienced profound gratitude to the Divine. When turning towards the Divine within, with wisdom and clarity of mind, I could clearly see my desires manifest themselves with ease and grace. These were some of the instances that I could clearly see the Divine intervention.

- Having the funds for affording excellent and the right divorce and immigration attorneys
- Attracting funding to start my practice and website www.gobeyondstress.com. The website provides help for stressed and burnt out business owners and individuals by transforming their stress into freedom, clarity, and inspired results.
- Receiving spontaneous insights and original ideas as well as funding for developing and marketing the Jiva proprietary dietary formulations, to help heal individuals diagnosed to have cancers and other serious health challenges. The Jiva supplements at www.jivasupplements.org have helped me to shrink my tumors and heal my life. They have been and are helping the lives of countless individuals and even pets suffering from serious health challenges to restore their health and well-being!
- Getting both the green card for the whole family and the exceptional scientist visa in the nick of time and in the quickest time possible, and eventually becoming naturalized American citizens.
- Having a mortgage loan approved by the bank despite being rejected by five other banks I had previously applied to.
- Finding the love of my life even when I was not looking for

someone!

And much, much more…

My insights and intuitive abilities, as well as those of my clients', also flourished.

It took around 10 years of deep searching, reading, and attending courses before I found the exact science and research to explain the phenomena of the State of Being!

Discovering the Universal Principles

One night, exhausted and tired after repeated attempts on the internet with trying to find a way to understand and easily get into the state of Being, I chanced upon a video lecture by an enlightened ninth-grade educated Scottish welder named Sydney Banks who said that, "Every human being is sitting in the middle of mental health – they just don't know it."

For some reason, my mind went completely quiet, and I saw the simple truth of that statement in my life. I knew then I had found someone who had experienced an awakening just as I had many years before. Just like me, Sydney Banks also called it *The State of Being.* Unlike me, he was able to talk clearly about it!

I did not understand anything else he said at that time, but I had a strange feeling that I was being pointed in the right direction.

My soul understood what Sydney Banks was saying. But my intellect did not fully comprehend it at first.

It was an odd experience that I later found many, many professionals and ordinary people from all walks of life shared!

I recollected that these instances of "beautiful" feelings coupled together with no comprehension of my intellect happened whenever I listened to discourses by Swami and enlightened beings.

After that day, I began to discover that there was an entirely different understanding of the nature of the Mind than what I had studied in medical schools!

Sydney Banks' discoveries on the Three Principles of Mind: Consciousness, and Power of Thought brought, for the first time in history, a profound shift and understanding of Paradigms or Principles in human psychological experiences. This new Understanding was the bridge uniting the field of psychology and spirituality!

I discovered what wisdom lay within each of us with **The Three Principles:**

1. *The Principle of Thought:* Thought is the gift that human beings possess; it is the ability to create subjective, momentary images and words in their minds. Sydney Banks also discovered that realizing "the fact that we think" promotes human psychological well-being independent of the specific thought (or the specific content of our thinking).

    Prior to this discovery, thought was seen as only one of many inputs into the creation of people's experience rather than the exclusive source. It was believed that the content of people's thinking should be the proper focus of therapeutic intervention. This discovery suggested that the focus should instead be on "the fact" that they are the thinker rather than "what" they might be thinking.

All our feelings derive and become alive, whether negative or positive, from the power of Thought.

Why this discovery matters: When I discovered that my well-being came purely through realizing the simple fact that as a human being, I am already "a thinker," I did not have to identify with the contents of my thoughts or try to unsuccessfully manage my thinking as I was tempted to do in the past. You would be surprised to know that we have between 60,000 and 70,000 thoughts every day.

It's unrealistic and futile to control this energy called Thought in myself or others. Instead, what I had discovered was exactly right: when I faced the direction of Gratitude to the Divine, the negative and judgmental thoughts disappeared; instead, fresh new thinking and insights into problems and situations emerged from within. That was why I had so many creative impulses even when I was going through my hellish periods!

2. *The Principle Consciousness:* Consciousness brings thought to life through the senses. There are many levels of consciousness as our awareness of life changes according to where we are coming from.

I found, through my life experiences, that whenever I was hungry, angry, lonely, or tired, my consciousness was low. I was irritable, angry, or saddened and had low-level thinking and low energy levels! My consciousness state changed when

I took care of myself and developed sensitivity toward the well-being of others, who were in my vicinity. Everyone benefited when I took care of my well-being!

Prior to this discovery, it was believed that our sensory data, our experience of life, came from forces outside of ourselves, such as life, circumstances, and events.

Why this discovery matters: *When I released the nature of consciousness, I was empowered to take even the most compelling experiences in my life, rather than overreact to them. Realizing that all of us go through low levels of consciousness and awareness helped me to be compassionate, naturally and effortlessly. It helped me understand other people's points of view, especially when dealing with my ex and family.*

3. **The Principle of Mind:** Mind is the creative power, the essence, and the intelligence behind all life.

    Prior to this discovery, "the mind" in the field of psychology was often seen as synonymous with the brain, limited to the understanding of the brain's analytical and memory bank capabilities.

    But the Mind is not the brain. Neither is it a thing or a thought. It is a psychic force that acts as a catalyst and turns thought, conscious or unconscious, into the reality you now see.

    Sydney Banks contributed to the field of psychology by

stating that the Mind is spiritual in nature rather than biological. He said that the Mind is the source of all life and the fundamental intelligence behind all life.

Why this discovery matters: This is a huge breakthrough in the field of psychology and psychiatry. For the first time, I understood that the two aspects of the mind: The big Mind or intelligence present in all of life and the personal mind which each one of us possesses with our thoughts and feelings were not two different minds but rather two different ways of experiencing the same Mind. When the personal mind was in harmony with the Universal Mind, human beings experienced Peace, Happiness, and Quiet.

Mind also is the spiritual power that activates the human brain.

I, like so many others, was awakened to the power and potential of Mind as universal intelligence. It gave me the freedom and power that comes with feeling a part of something bigger than myself!

Why the Three Principles Matter

Sydney Banks says, "Mind, consciousness, and thought are the three principles that enable us to acknowledge and respond to existence."

All human psychological functions are born from these three principles.

All human behavior and social structures on earth are formed through Mind, Consciousness, and Thought.

Prior to this discovery, there was no established set of principles in psychology that explained our mental lives, but there was instead an ever-increasing list of contributing factors.

Why this discovery matters: Understanding these three principles allowed me, like all human beings, to be resilient, take my experiences in stride, and trust that I will have the intelligent/responsive thinking to have a deeply fulfilling and productive life of service.

What Has Love Got to Do with It?

Love and joy as manifested in many desirable feelings like gratitude, peace of mind, and humility, are the core, essential feelings in human beings.

Although these feelings might be overridden by peoples' momentary thoughts, they are indeed the default setting, the homeostasis, in the human race.

Prior to this discovery, human feelings and emotions were seen as culturally and/or individually determined. Human beings were thought to have no core, default feelings.

Why this discovery matters: Seeing love and joy as my default setting allowed me to count on those feelings as an effortless way of life in the knowledge that any negativity is by nature short-lived, a temporary "mirage" that will disappear on its own.

During the early stages of my severe bleeding, I wanted to give up on myself and was shutting my eyes in exhaustion, and then the rat flashed across my room. The Divine did not give up on me!

Although I was terrified of rats and rodents in general, I was awakened into life because of my love for my children and fear that their rooms were going to be overrun by rats!

I cleaned myself up and made the calls to the exterminator despite being told by my ex that it was too expensive and we could not afford their services. I was determined to get help and I did!

This single act empowered me so much to take control of my life and stop playing the victim!

I discovered that courage, confidence, resilience, and empowerment all came from within. They came from a state of Love, despite the challenges of facing the four zeroes of life: no health, no finances, no family support, or reputation.

My clients and I have found that the power of a quiet mind makes it a means as well as an end. While receiving the benefits of peace of mind, one is accessing the benefits of insight and perspective.

The capacity for insight, the ability to release stress, the capacity for connectedness/closeness with others, and the capacity for resilience are all leveraged by a quiet mind.

A famous quote from Albert Einstein describes this phenomenon: "No problem can be solved from the same level of consciousness that created it."

I finally realized what Einstein meant! We can always up level our consciousness with a quiet mind.

Rumi's quote also opened the pathway to my healing: "All doubt, despair, and fear become insignificant once the intention of life becomes Love."

Personal Reflections

My marriage of 20 years and raising our three kids had been my principal spiritual discipline. In retrospect, I can say that nothing else has been as valuable as my challenging marriage and standing for my kids' happiness, in terms of personal growth and development.

From a worldly and a spiritual sense, my ex-husband and I were coming from totally opposite world views! He was grounded in materialism and in being practical, and I strongly believed in the spiritual path. I am not practical or street smart!

There was a constant opportunity for friction between us.

We had our three beautiful children as our common bond of love. What a grand opportunity this presented for our self-interest and ego to expose itself and to be seen and set aside! It was a constant challenge. Love for our kids' happiness kept me sane and moving in that direction!

I believe that life is eternal. Life has no meaning outside of truth, outside of oneness, or outside of unity and love. I realized that the purpose of my earthly life is to awaken and to be grateful for the many wonderful gifts and people that life offers.

To live in our bodies and to grow old, get sick, suffer, die is an investment in death, and that has nothing at all to do with life.

Life is when you are free; life is when you are the Light and give that Light of Love to everyone.

Life is when you become an overflowing cup of pure love, a cup that has to be constantly shared. That's life for me.

The "Four Zeros" and Their Real Meaning for Me Now

I believed in the past that the meaning of the "four zeros" was that God could take any material things away from me, such as health, money, reputation, and family support. But He cannot take my faith from me!

During my severe challenges, I felt totally devastated, without roots of any kind. I believed that there was no existence left, but then I discovered something:

There is no way that my faith in God can be taken away from me!

During my adversities, I experienced many remarkable acts of Grace as described above.

I believe that despite being faced with severe challenges, everyone can tune into the direction of their faith to experience God's Grace.

Despite the severe challenges, I also truly believe mental health and mental clarity are present in all of us, all of the time.

Sometimes we experience mental health and clarity and sometimes we don't, just like sometimes we experience the sun, and sometimes we don't.

The sun is always there behind the clouds. Mental clarity and wisdom are always there, behind our thoughts.

Just like the clouds will always part to reveal the sun, thoughts roll in, and thoughts roll out.

Your healthy mind will always return to a state of well-being if you don't interfere.

Chris Hatfield, the Canadian astronaut, says it well, "There is no problem that you cannot make it worse."

I believe that our negative emotions like fears, self-doubts, insecurities, etc. make all our problems worse!

Our physical body also has this auto self-correct mechanism to heal. But it's not always foolproof.

I think when the personal mind and thoughts are quietened, insights, i.e., fresh new thoughts can come up to the surface of the mind and lead you, if you are tuned in, to ways how you can heal and clean up your life. Just like I experienced.

This happens for all humans. There is no use chasing insights into our problems.

How Do You Access the Wisdom and Clarity Within?

Just having a quiet mind by meditating regularly, taking mindful walks, or taking a short nap can clear your troubled thoughts and feelings. You can do any of these if you enjoy them.

But the easiest and surest way is by understanding the Nature of The Three Principles of Mind, Consciousness, and Thought.

The content of thought is not important.

The fact that you can think and that you can have insights is what matters most.

Why?

As all enlightened spiritual teachers have said throughout mankind's history, you are not your thoughts. You are the one observing—the

Eternal Witness to your thoughts. The Real You is the life force energy that is observing the thoughts and being detached from it.

When I aligned myself to my True Self, my human psychology, i.e., my negative thoughts and feelings, did not affect me.

Just understanding that my core spiritual state, my True Self, was not affected by the ups and downs in my life helped me to better navigate the challenges in my life and thrive.

Miracles happened easily. It's as if my deepest desires just came true, without much effort on my part.

Just like the wide-open sky is unaffected by the clouds passing through.

The Real you is always free and always available. Most of us, like myself, just didn't know how to access the State of our Being. It's always been there!

When you do not cling to your thoughts and feelings like anxieties, worries, fears, anything at all, they pass through, and you feel the deep Peace and Happiness that IS your True Self.

Scary thoughts like fears and worries, whether you will lose your job, or be able to pay your mortgage, or have good health, etc. are like nightmares we have during sleep.

When we wake up from a nightmare, our hearts may still be palpitating, and palms may be sweaty.

But in a few moments, we realize it's all a nightmare and it's not real.

When I had this understanding, I realized that my fears and worries were like my nightmares.

But the former occurred during the day time and were no different in causing tension until I "woke" up to them not being real.

The more times I experienced my core spiritual or Divine state, it brought me back easily to the calm and peace-filled state when I had the day time fears and worries.

I just "woke up" and the appropriate situations healed themselves, both inside me and outside in my external world.

My hell states of worries, fears, and beliefs that I was not good enough, and the worrisome situations loosened its grip on me.

Many of the fear-filled thoughts that we as humans experience are not even ours, to begin with.

They come from our fathers, mothers, teachers, trainers, religious leaders, etc. As kids, we just accept our elders' views of the world.

Later we absorb them as our own fears, worries, and anxieties not understanding that these fear-filled thoughts and feelings can indeed make us physically, mentally, and emotionally ill.

What are Some of The Deeper Lessons behind the Societal Realities We Live In?

As Einstein puts it, "God doesn't roll dice."

When we look within ourselves, we realize a deeper intelligence in life, in nature, and in the inner spirit or energy behind all of life. It permeates life.

It doesn't take a doctorate in any of the sciences or arts to have a deep understanding of life.

Such an understanding comes with simply seeing how Mind, Consciousness, and Thought create our reality from inside-out.

Mental illness, hostility, and insecurity exist not because of how we are put together, biochemically or genetically, but from generations of thinking from ingrained fears, attitudes, and beliefs in individuals, cultures, and societies.

Yet these seemingly insurmountable barriers to happiness are built completely from Thought.

People have insights, via their own wisdom, about the connection between forgiveness, love, and their own mental health. They also have insights about the mystery behind life that is the essence of spirituality and the source of wisdom.

What Does This Global COVID-19 Pandemic Mean for Each of Us?

The current COVID-19 global pandemic is an invitation for us to connect beyond the physical so that we can hold humanity in our thoughts.

Ultimately, it is for all of us to slow down, to connect, to collaborate, and to share the love with each other.

It's an opportunity for us to hold each other in our thoughts at the highest level. It's an opportunity for us to slow down to a new level of possibility for ourselves and for humanity.

With all of the challenges facing us right now, many of us are feeling frightened, tired, worried, or overwhelmed.

Yet, even as we struggle to stay centered and sane amidst our own challenges, we are rapidly becoming aware that there are many people in our society—including our friends, coworkers, and family—who urgently need our help.

For many of us, it feels like an impossible conundrum: How can we find the inner reserves to take care of ourselves AND show up to help those who are in greater need than we are?

When people discover the impersonal, deeper wisdom already within them, just as I have done in my story, they see the harm that prejudice and hatred do to the world.

They cannot imagine why those thoughts made sense or seemed meaningful and real to them before.

More and more people all over the world are waking up to this realization.

I hope this chapter has shown you how to make a simple but profound shift in your own consciousness so that you can immediately begin to tap into and express the most powerful force available to us to meet the challenges of our moment.

It's called Love.

When we as humans realize that sharing alone can reduce grief and multiply joy. People are born to share, to serve, to give, and not to grab.

Rather than fearing the unknown, we can be thrilled by the possibilities that can appear by simply opening our minds, our hearts and souls, and relaxing into the quiet within that brings newfound wisdom, grace, and clarity.

Resources

1) YouTube. YouTube, 2019.
   https://www.youtube.com/watch?v=e9G-4gpY0r4.
2) Webinar: 3 Secrets to Enlightened Business, Leadership,
   Wealth & Success on www.gobeyondstress.com.

DR. VIJAYA NAIR

Dr. Vijaya Nair is an Ivy-league trained physician, medical researcher, author, international speaker. She is a trainer of new discoveries in the nature of the human mind and its unlimited awesome potential through her programs at www.Gobeyondstress.com.

She has faced numerous life challenges and is keen to share how you too can be inspired by your insights in the midst of the most severe experiences. Her clients' stories are living proof that paying attention to awakening one's soul, and its desires is the only pathway to living a fulfilled, healthy, creative, and happy life no matter the challenges.

Dr. Vijaya is also the mother of three happily married children and a thrilled grandmother of Neal, her grandson. When she is not with her family or working with her clients, she can be found in deep meditation and enjoys walking with Dom, her life partner, and studying the Vedas, the ancient spiritual literature that describes the eternal knowledge of the Divine.

You can reach out to Dr. Vijaya and sign up for her emails about new releases and practical insightful advice at https://gobeyondstress.com/blog/ and also watch her inspiring FREE Webinar at www.gobeyondstress.com. Discover how she helps her clients overcome and transform the stress and negativity effortlessly in their lives into living fulfilled, happy, and fearless lives in the shortest time possible.

Why not have Dr. Vijaya on your side as you expand your reach both personally and professionally and live your highest potential and best life ever?

Contact Details

Website: www.gobeyondstress.com

BACK FROM THE DEAD

A True Story Based on My Personal Life

Wail Al Hunaidi

It is hard to believe, isn't it?

Fine ...

Just follow my story to make sure and you can judge for yourself.

Introduction

All through my childhood, I had dreamed about the future. I grew up hoping that it will be promising, bright, and beautiful. I was confident that life would quickly move toward this glorious future, and I will get to fulfill my dreams.

I loved people and society in general. I had a lot of friends. My great love for people urged me to become a doctor. I wanted to choose a profession that would help my loved ones or anyone else who needed my services. And that's why, while growing up, I was devoted to achieving this goal of becoming a doctor and helping people around, to the best of my capabilities.

My goal was to help mankind. I was so keen to accomplish this goal that I wanted to be healthy in every way possible. To maintain my physical health and fitness, I joined a football academy close to my residence and won championships there. I wanted to do all of this to be a role model doctor who believed that a "healthy mind resides in a healthy body."

Years passed by, I kept moving toward my goal consistently and confidently. And the time came when I got to the last and most crucial year of school.

Death

For all students worldwide, it is important to get a high score at the end of last year of school in order to get admission in medical college. This is because medical school is expected to be tough, and you need to hold a good academic background to be eligible for further studies. Some communities make it a very big deal, and children are under pressure to score well to save their image. My community happens to be one of them. I never really considered this a problem since I had been preparing for the final year of high school right from the beginning. All my childhood, I worked hard and studied well to get to the highest level in school. I kept myself away from anything harmful such as cigarettes, drugs, alcohol, etc.

The exams were approaching at the end of the year. I was excited to complete school and get to the university to study medicine and achieve the goal of helping people. I would dream of becoming a doctor and enjoying my life by helping people. I was a month away from going into the medical college—just one month.

But then, something happened that shocked me to my core!

I was diagnosed with a tumor in my lower back. It was painful, and it would color my clothes in the blood that came out of it. I could feel a fire burning in my spine. The pain kept increasing, and I suffered. My father took me to the hospital. The treatments continued for days, and there were new suggestions from doctors every day. Finally, they decided to remove the tumor. Since I was in immense pain, they operated.

The good news was that the tumor was not malignant (cancerous). In conclusion, this nightmare was over.

However, as soon as I got well from the surgery, I got into another nightmare. I had missed my exams and wasn't allowed to give my final year exams that year. The period for re-examination had also passed, and I had no other option than to appear in the examination the next year.

As I waited to take the exams next year, I was extremely frustrated about the fact that I had lost an entire year. 365 days had evaporated from my life.

I would see my friends going to college while I had to rest at home. And if I had hoped that the hard times would be over once I wrote my exams, life had other things planned for me. When I was completing my documents, I noticed that the school files stated that I had "failed" the last year. Since I had been considered a failure that year, my school record book had it mentioned. It was a requirement to have a study record without failing the last three years of high school for admission in medical college. Then and there, I could see my childhood dream shattering into a million pieces. I could not become a doctor anymore, which meant I would not be able to help people. I felt as if the eighteen years of my life had gone to waste, just like that.

It seemed like the world was over to me, and there was no reason left for me to live. All of this made me upset and depressed. I had never imagined myself going into the cycle of depression. I did not want to go to any university or study any other major at all, but everyone around me wanted me to get a degree. As social pressure increased, I joined a business school after wasting another year of my life. All my friends graduated from college with the degrees of their choice, and I was still in the second year of a field that I did not even like. I failed that year and dropped out of the university and got admission to another university. I spent years moving from one university to another and from one job to another.

And I got married because I did not want to lose the only woman I loved in my life.

But after that, I stopped caring about myself. I did not maintain my health anymore. I started to gain weight, and my routine was messed up. All I did was eat, sleep, or watch television. My weight reached 200 kgs i.e., 400 lbs. I had put on so much weight that it was nearly impossible for me to move. I would not even go out with my family anymore.

My family was the only beautiful thing in my life all through this time. I loved my family, but I was ashamed to be portrayed as a failed husband and father. I was fat and therefore a useless person. I always felt like I was dependent on my family and a burden on society. So, I decided to isolate myself. My wife would take the kids out, alone. All my attempts to integrate into social gatherings would fail. Every time I went out with my wife, people would make fun of my weight.

I considered it an insult to humanity.

There were two types of people that I was dealing with. The first kind made fun of me, and the rest suggested a lot of weight loss remedies and tips. When I went to restaurants, I felt like everyone was watching me eat and counting the number of my bites or the food items that I was having. They probably thought I was a wild creature who would eat their meat.

While taking flights, I had to reserve two seats and order an extra belt that would fit around my waist. Throughout the flight, I would be focused on the glaring looks that came my way and worried about what people had to say about me. I had to get off a plane once because the only seat available was next to the emergency exit. So, it was dangerous and against the safety precautions. Another time, I had to deboard as more than one passenger refused to exchange their seats with me. It made me feel like it was better to get off the plane than to overload. And if that was not all, I had to hear people insult me because the plane had to wait until I went down and received my luggage. I was the reason for the flight delay. I sat in the waiting room until the next flight. Everyone was told the story, "This fat guy's sitting and waiting for the next flight as he couldn't board the previous one because of his weight." The irony is that throughout the waiting period, I had nothing but food with me. I am sure this made people think that not only is this guy fat, but also stupid. People's words and comments were like knives tearing my body apart.

I was humiliated and fat-shamed all the time. But the most laborious comments were the ones my children endured from their friends and classmates, who used to describe their father as an elephant. I started to gain more and more weight every day. And since my weight increased, I developed high blood pressure and blood sugar levels. I could see the sadness of my children and my wife—how much they wished to play with their father and how badly they wanted to go out as a family.

All of this led to constant arguments with my wife. We would argue about my weight and, of course, my life. I tried a lot of diet control plans for a long time, but it only made me lose a few kilograms of my total weight. I was desperate, and my weight was getting worse. I stopped implementing the diet plan, and my weight increased even more. So, I decided to play sports. I decided to join the gym, which was in the same building as my house. I was all motivated and wanted to go through another round of my weight fight. I decided to take a positive step. But as life would have it, I wasn't allowed to join the club. They thought that I would ruin their expensive exercise equipment with my weight. I argued with the management that it was immoral. However, the people and the staff gathered in the gym, and I was kicked out. The same happened at six other gyms, and I was so frustrated and upset that I decided to eat until death. I did not wish to see people anymore. I just wanted to sleep and not move at all. I wanted to be dead—buried under the fat.

The Decision to Return to Life

Of course, in the shadow of death, I was still alive. One day, while I was asleep, I woke up to my wife screaming. I ran as fast as my body allowed me to and found that my daughter had got something stuck in her throat. I picked her up, and we ran to the pediatrician on the same street near us, just 100 meters away from home. But how fast could I run when I weighed 200 kgs? I could carry her only a few meters, and I fell. I felt like my heart had stopped beating. I could no longer breathe; my daughter was choking in my hands.

My wife saved the situation and ran the remaining distance to the doctor, carrying our daughter. While I was sitting on the road, covered in dirt and trying to catch my breath, the looks of ridicule strapped me from every direction. But this time, I did not care. All I was thinking about was my daughter's well-being. I kept crawling to the doctor's office and finally made it. My daughter was safe. I left the clinic crying because I knew that if I lost my family, my weight would be the reason. My family, the only people who loved me despite my condition. They were the only reason for my being.

I had a feeling of rage. And there was a voice inside me, my inner voice that was controlled by anger. I did not give up. I knew that the real reason for the condition I was in was not my weight. It was my mind. It was my mind that affected my mental and physical condition. And at that moment, I decided to change my life, forever. I decided that I was not going to let anything get in my way of getting fitter, and I would never give up, no matter what.

Never Ever Give Up!

The Change

It was understood that change had to start from my mind and within myself. As I mentioned earlier, the problem was not in my weight, but my mind. So, the solution had to come from my mind as well. The first step was to replace the limiting beliefs that tied me up with other positive ideas that would push me forward. The second step was to set goals and then build an action plan. I adopted two kinds of goals: short-term and long-term.

The long-term goal was to revive my childhood dream of helping people, especially those who suffer from what I had suffered or something similar. And, my short-term goal was to lose weight. I went to the hospital and met a dietitian there. He advised me to meet the doctor who specializes in obesity. I went and met the doctor. He advised me to go through an operation called " sleeve." They took the necessary tests, and I booked the earliest possible date for the operation. The day came. My family could not believe it was true. It seemed like I was going to a wrestling ring. The opponents were the ones who had been defeating me all along. I wanted to get the operation done by myself, and as quickly as possible.

I wanted to beat my weakness and build my strength, all on my own. So, I went to the hospital alone, even though my family wanted to accompany me. I went to the operation theater, and the "sleeve" was carried out. In this operation, a large part of the stomach is cut to a normal size so that the amount of food intake is less after the operation and the recovery process. It took months to recover. There were times when I was only consuming fluids, but I recovered.

This was over, and it was time for the second step, sports. Now, I could go to the gym, but I did not. I could not bring myself to go to the halls of a place that had kicked me out. With all my ambition, I went back to my house to find a way to ensure that I would exercise daily. I wanted an exercise that I could do at my home, the office, or anywhere else. To this day, I am committed to a regular schedule.

Now came the long-term goal, which was to complete my studies. I decided to study psychology. Since all my problems were related to my mind, I decided to study what increased my knowledge about myself, the mind, and the body in general. I studied this subject to be able to help people better understand themselves. I wanted them to know how to solve their problems. That is exactly what I had been dreaming about since I was a kid. I drove to college for hours every day. After I completed my undergraduate studies, I flew abroad to complete my postgraduate degree. I got my PhD in Psychology, and I still thought it was not enough. So, I decided to increase my knowledge about the mind and soul.

I studied Hypnosis, which was an interesting field. I covered many parts of it and became a hypnotherapist, too. I progressed so well in this field that I became the best Mentalist in the Middle East. I was presented with the Merlin International Award, the same award that was given to David Copperfield and Chris Engel, famous names in the field. After I finished my hypnotherapy, I studied Neuro-linguistic programming (NLP) and Behavioral therapy as well. I studied the course related to life coaching, and eventually, I specialized in Positive Psychology. I learned at the hands of the most skilled people, including Martin Seligman, the father of modern Positive Psychology,

This was the time when I realized that I had the knowledge and experience to achieve my goal of helping people.

Reviving the Dream

I started working to help people who suffered from the problems I had in the past, i.e., obesity, stress, anxiety, relationship problems, and other issues.

I came across many other issues that people go through, and all sorts of people, such as:

- People who hate themselves and cannot forgive themselves for the most trivial reasons.
- People who want to be perfect, and when they don't find anything complete and perfect, they are dissatisfied and disappointed in themselves.
- People who find themselves ugly or think that their body is so bad that they lose the desire to improve their shape or take care of their health.
- People who feel that they are worthless and useless.
- People who are sensitive and feel angry or sad when they are subjected to any criticism.
- People who suffer from fear, stress, and anxiety.
- People who control anger and nervousness.
- People who believe that when they do things that satisfy people, they will get love and attention to the point where they may always feel exploited.
- People who constantly feel the guilt of falling short for their children and their home.
- People who find themselves unable to adapt to society.
- People who live under trauma and living under its influence, whether it is emotional trauma or the result of a painful situation such as harassment or bullying.
- People who feel that they have no control over their own lives.
- People who are running behind unrealistic goals.
- People who are making wrong decisions and following upon them.
- People who cannot find themselves being able to control

negative thoughts about people.

- People who experience constant failure in personal and romantic relationships.

That is when I found out the two phenomena—through my experience with the patients/clients.

The first is that many people do not realize that the problem and the solution both are from within themselves, and it all depends on their thoughts.

The second is that even people who understand the fact that the problem is inside them, don't know how to deal with it.

So, I decided to combine both my experience and my knowledge in developing a mental training program that anyone can apply easily and effectively, and I call it **The Self-Shield Program**.

It is divided into three stages.

1. The first stage is personal tests to understand the basis of the problem.
2. The second stage is to figure out the causes of the problem and ways to solve it.
3. The third stage is to practically apply all the above.

The first phase shows where the weakness is. This is done through some globally qualified psychological tests. Knowing the problem is the basis for finding out the solution.

The second stage comes from the first stage in which we know where the problem is, and in the second stage, we start discussing and understanding the reasons for the problem and ways to solve it. Awareness is important for solving the problem and for being able to deal with future issues.

In the third and final stage, it is the time for the practical application of all that was learned through exercises and psychological techniques. After that, the result is confirmed by repeating the tests that were done in the first stage, and the first result is compared with the one in the final stage.

The whole program is based on real, scientific studies and research. It was proven successful after being applied to all the problems mentioned above. This program is one of the most beautiful things I have ever worked on and succeeded.

I fulfilled a dream that I thought I had lost long ago.

The most important advice I would like to give you is that try to solve any problem that starts in your mind and in the process, do not hesitate to ask for help from qualified people.

Never give up, ever!

Thank you,

Dr. Wail Al Hunaidi

WAIL AL HUNAIDI

Dr. Wail Al-Hunaidi (PhD) is a psychologist, researcher, author, and entrepreneur. He obtained his doctorate on the theme of Self-Motivation. Dr. Wail was formerly depressed, and his depression made him gain weight. At one point, he weighed 200 kgs. However, he decided to win the battle and changed his life around. From a depressed person weighing 200 kgs, Dr. Wail transformed his life and now weighs 80 kgs. Since 2012, Positive Psychology is a major focus of his research and teaching. He wishes to inspire other people, and this led him to create **The Self-Shield Program**. The program uses Positive Psychology and has changed the lives of many people.

Made in the USA
Monee, IL
12 December 2020

52365215R00329